The New Deal Lawyers

THE NEW DEAL LAWYERS

By Peter H. Irons

PRINCETON UNIVERSITY PRESS
PRINCETON, N. J.

For
Mary Walton Livingston
and
Leonard Rapport

Table of Contents

CONTENTS

On the scales of American legal history, books about judges and their decisions far outweigh those about lawyers and their litigation. Even more pronounced is the bias toward biographies of members of the United States Supreme Court and accounts of notable Supreme Court decisions. Marshall, Taney, Story, Holmes, Brandeis, Stone, Frankfurter, Warren, and Douglas— these giants and a host of lesser lights on the highest bench have attracted biographers of varying capabilities and degrees of objectivity. Cases such as *Charles River Bridge, Dred Scott*, the *Steel Seizure* case, and *Brown v. Board of Education* have been plumbed in depth. And doctrinal exegesis, increasingly from a critical or neo-Marxist perspective, constitutes a well-established category of historical study. Lawyers, particularly those who combined political or judicial careers with law practice, have hardly suffered historical neglect, as studies of such luminaries of the bar as Daniel Webster, Elihu Root, and John W. Davis illustrate. But the focus on lawyers has been largely biographical, with little attention paid to questions of litigation strategy—how the cases they argued progressed from the filing of a suit to decision by the Supreme Court.

One reason for the imbalance between studies of judges and those of lawyers is evident. The Supreme Court sits at the pinnacle of the American legal system, and both its members and its decisions command notice as the expositors and exposition of the authoritative body of law that binds, at any given time, the decisions of inferior state and federal courts and that shapes, with due consideration of conflicting lines of precedent and unsettled areas of doctrine, the arguments available to lawyers who seek review by the Supreme Court. Other factors influence historians in their choice of topic: the opinions of judges, collected in bound volumes and often written with elegance and force, are easily accessible and reflect, in leading cases, deep-rooted issues of social, economic, and political controversy. In contrast, historians interested in litigation must search for hard-to-locate briefs and law office correspondence, the latter source frequently lost altogether or protected by the lawyer-client privilege. Private law firms rarely open their litigation files to historians, and lawyers rarely donate their law-practice papers to libraries or archives.

The process of litigation that leads to momentous Supreme Court decisions, however, is a topic deserving of historical study. This book is designed as a contribution to a field limited, thus far, to only two comparable studies. Forty years ago, in *Lawyers and the Constitution*, Benjamin R. Twiss examined critically the lawyers who argued, in the decades that spanned the turn of the past century, the cases that offered a receptive judiciary the opportunity to fashion a jurisprudence based on states-rights federalism and laissez-faire economics. Twiss might well have titled his study *The Union League Lawyers*, since most of the men whose work he discussed— leaders of the corporate bar such as William M. Evarts, Joseph H. Choate, James C. Carter, John F. Dillon, and William D. Guthrie—belonged to that bastion of Wall Street orthodoxy and shared the conservative values of the bankers, brokers, and judges with whom they fraternized in its exclusive clubhouse. More recently, in *Simple Justice*, Richard Kluger illuminated in compelling detail the litigation strategies pursued by lawyers who shared the liberal and humane values of racial equality. These men— Robert L. Carter, Thurgood Marshall, William H. Hastie, Charles H. Houston, Spottswood W. Robinson III, and Jack Greenberg among them— worked with the National Association for the Advancement of Colored People in the long legal struggle that began in the 1920s and culminated in 1954 in *Brown v. Board of Education* and its companion cases. Studies of church and state litigation, and of single cases, have added to this field, but the contributions of Twiss and Kluger stand out in richness of detail and in perception of the lawyer's role in constitutional litigation.

What is remarkable is that, in this slim body of work, lawyers employed by the nation's largest law firm—the federal government—have been all but neglected. And certainly, along with their corporate law predecessors and civil rights successors, the New Deal lawyers constitute the most influential group in bringing to the Supreme Court and in arguing the cases that have changed the shape of our legal landscape over the past century. My decision to study their differing litigation strategies was first stimulated in law school by my reading of Twiss's and Kluger's books, and given a concrete focus by questions left unanswered by Jerold S. Auerbach in his critical dissection of the 20th-century bar, *Unequal Justice*. The New Deal, Auerbach wrote, was a "lawyer's deal," a period in which lawyers, "trained to govern" in the "modern liberal activist state" spawned by the Depression, "enjoyed direct access to its newest and most critical levers of power and monopolized the instruments of governance." However, Auerbach emphasized that his book was not "about how lawyers practice law, nor is it an exegesis of legal doctrine."

Since I have taken up the implicit challenge of filling these gaps in Auerbach's social history, and of producing a study comparable in approach to those of Twiss and Kluger, I feel some need to explain the sources of my ambivalence toward the New Deal lawyers, an attitude that differs from Twiss's hostility to his corporate lawyers and Kluger's admiration of his civil rights lawyers. Part of the reason stems, I think, from my long-standing antipathy toward (or at least suspicion of) the exertion of federal power over both the community and the individual. Raised in a family setting that combined Republican economic orthodoxy with social tolerance and concern for civil liberties, I became active in college (at Antioch in the late 1950s and early 1960s) in the sit-in and anti-draft movements. Experience as a criminal defendant, first in a sit-in case in Maryland and then as a draft resister in federal court, left a residue of resentment toward the government lawyers who proclaimed to be "only doing our jobs" in prosecuting me and others for what we felt were legitimate protests against illegitimate government policies. Twenty-six months in federal prisons, following my draft conviction, offered a chance to read widely in constitutional law and American political history.

Four years of graduate study in political science after my release from prison led to a dissertation on the last years of Roosevelt's New Deal (and the first years of Truman's Fair Deal), in which I explored the domestic political roots of the Cold War period. With the exception of my dissertation research, I found the study of political science sterile and apolitical. But two experiences during this period and the three years of teaching political science and sociology that followed graduate school led me increasingly to an interest in law and legal history. My familiarity with State Department records in the National Archives and the national security records classification system led to my employment in 1971 by the Pentagon Papers Defense Fund, with the task of compiling a list of former government officials who had taken with them on leaving office, or used in subsequent writings, classified documents. Working with Charles Nesson of Harvard Law School and Leonard Boudin, the lawyers defending Daniel Ellsberg, gave me an appreciation of the tactical and strategic issues raised by a highly political case. Second, my interest in the Alger Hiss case, as an offshoot of my dissertation research, grew into a continuing investigation of the tangled roots of the Hiss case and a friendship with Hiss that included fascinating discussions of his role as a New Deal lawyer.

Spurred by these growing interests, I abandoned teaching in 1975 to enter Harvard Law School, with the intention of concentrating in legal history and constitutional law and returning to teaching in law. At the time, I had only an academic interest in litigation, but short stints while in law school as a criminal defense lawyer and in a state anti-discrimination agency whetted this interest, as did a seminar on government lawyers. Thus, when I faced the task of choosing a topic for the required third-year writing project, my knowledge of the New Deal period, my fascination with the litigation process, my historical interest in the background of crucial constitutional cases, and my awareness of the resources of the National Archives combined to make almost inevitable my choice of the topic from which this study evolved. These varied experiences help to explain (if explanation is needed) the mixture of admiration and skepticism that leads me to acknowledge the skill and idealism of the New Deal lawyers, and the worth of their work in establishing a foundation for basic economic protection and federally protected civil rights, and yet to admit the inherent limitations of the government lawyer's role as a servant of bureaucratic rigidity and political repression in those periods (under both Democratic and Republican administrations) when dissent poses a threat to power. As a lawyer, I understand these limitations; as a historian, I explore its sources and consequences with as much objectivity as I can muster; and as a political activist, I admit my profound ambivalence toward the New Deal period, with its accomplishments in social welfare and its legacy of bureaucratic ossification, and toward those lawyers who shaped, administered, and defended the New Deal's conflicting policies.

SINCE readers will soon notice them, I hasten to point out and justify two significant omissions in this book. With a focus on only three of the many New Deal agencies, I have neglected the work of such influential New Deal lawyers as Dean Acheson, David E. Lilienthal, James M. Landis, and William O. Douglas. Two reasons justify this omission: first, these men served during this period primarily as administrators and not as litigators; and, second, the detailed case studies of litigation strategy that follow necessarily have imposed limitations of space and topic. Further studies of the agencies left out of this study (such as the Tennessee Valley Authority and the Securities and Exchange Commission) will, I hope, shed additional (and perhaps corrective) light on the federal litigation process, as will studies of government lawyers in prior and later administrations. The second omission relates to that handful of New Deal lawyers (most in the AAA, and a few in the NLRB) alleged to be Communist Party members or fellow-travelers. Of the lawyers who appear in this book, Alger Hiss, John Abt, Nathan Witt, and Lee Pressman were later accused of membership in a party cell in Washington. Pressman, in the early 1950s, admitted his party membership and named both Abt and Witt (but not Hiss) as fellow members. Abt and Witt declined to acknowledge party membership before congressional committees, and Hiss has consistently and vehemently denied such charges. Some or all of these New Deal lawyers (and others as well) may have been party members during the period covered by this book. But a diligent examination of the available records, with this fact in mind, discloses no evidence that Communist Party membership or sympathy affected in any way their work as lawyers, or that they acted differently from their colleagues who were Democrats or even conservatives. As far as this book is concerned, my conclusion is that the communist issue is a non-issue. I would, of course, welcome and consider any evidence to the contrary.

PREFACE

By far the most gratifying task in completing a book is that of acknowledging the support and assistance of those who have helped along the way. The dedication of this book to Mary Walton Livingston and Leonard Rapport is intended to acknowledge, in the place where it really belongs, my debt to two people who have worked in the National Archives for decades and who have helped me immeasurably over the past decade, first in my dissertation research, then in my work on this book, and presently in my current study of the early years of the FBI. On every visit to the Archives, Mary Walton and Leonard have listened patiently as I listed my research needs, suggested where to look and whom to talk to, and helped me find the next needle for which I was searching in the haystack of federal records. Others on the National Archives staff, particularly Donald Mossholder, Meyer Fishbein, Charles Stovall, and Joseph Howerton, deserve mention for their help in this study. Erika Chadbourne of the Harvard Law School Library has been especially helpful, on this and other projects. In addition, the staffs of the Oral History Collection of Columbia University, the Franklin D. Roosevelt Library in Hyde Park, the Manuscript Division of the Library of Congress, the Yale University Library, and the library of the Cornell University School of Industrial and Labor Relations have all been remarkably cooperative and eager to suggest overlooked sources.

I am grateful as well to those New Deal lawyers whom I interviewed about their experiences, especially to those who responded, often at considerable length, to the draft chapters I sent them: those who contributed reactions (and corrected numerous errors of fact and interpretation in the process) are Eugene F. Bogan, Thomas I. Emerson, the late Charles Fahy, Abe Fortas, Milton Handler, Alger Hiss, Leon Keyserling, David L. Kreeger, Walter L. Rice, Blackwell Smith, and Robert L. Stern. Some of these lawyers took exception to my analysis, but all took seriously my request to criticize and correct the manuscript. Three of those I asked for interviews declined on various grounds; I have tried to treat them in my writing as fairly as I have those with whom I talked.

Morton J. Horwitz of the Harvard Law School faculty not only taught me much legal history but also supervised this study in its first stages and provided a critical reading of the first draft of the NRA section. Robert J. Glennon of Wayne State University Law School contributed his knowledge of Jerome Frank to an exceedingly useful editing of the AAA section, and the opportunity to comment on his paper about Frank at a meeting of the Association of American Law Schools provided the spark, as I listened to his presentation, that led to the models of litigation style around which this book is constructed. David Conrad of Southern Illinois University also commented helpfully on the AAA section. Thomas I. Emerson of Yale

Law School gave me an incisive critique of the NLRB section; and Thomas E. Vadney of the University of Manitoba sent me overlooked documents from the Donald Richberg papers. Jerold S. Auerbach of Wellesley College, whose book *Unequal Justice* helped to stimulate this one, and Harry N. Hirsch of Harvard University, whose psychobiography of Felix Frankfurter aided my understanding of that complex and contradictory figure, both read the entire manuscript and provided suggestions for revisions and refinements. I am glad to acknowledge, as well, the modest but essential grant from the Mark deWolfe Howe Fund of Harvard Law School that made possible my initial research, and the help of Stephen Arons of the University of Massachusetts at Amherst in securing funds for typing. None of those listed above, of course, bears any responsibility for errors of fact or deficiencies of analysis in what follows.

Gail Filion of Princeton University Press has been unfailingly supportive in guiding this book to press, and R. Miriam Brokaw of the Princeton editorial staff contributed a meticulous and sensitive copyediting to the manuscript. Diane Truax, Terry St. Helaire, and Peter Pruhaska expertly typed early drafts, and Susan Munro typed the final draft in a close race with motherhood, retaining her skill as she grew farther from the typewriter (the book barely beat the baby). Howard Zinn played no direct role in this book, but in sending me books while I was in prison, arranging my admission to graduate school during that time, serving as a mentor and model of the committed historian, and remaining as a friend along with Roz Zinn over the past decade, deserves an expression of indebtedness. Stephen Jay Gould, whose lucid and witty writings in science gave me an incomparable model to emulate in my field, has long been a devoted friend and perceptive critic; this book is better for our bowling-alley discussions.

And, finally, there is Priscilla Long, with whom I have shared my life for fifteen years. Her contribution has been that combination of love and living space that has kept us both together and apart, in the best sense of that shared life. To end this preface without expressing my love for Priscilla would leave this book incomplete.

P.H.I.

The New Deal Lawyers

A plague of young lawyers settled on Washington. They all claimed to be friends of somebody or other, and mostly of Jerome Frank and Felix Frankfurter. They floated airily into offices, took desks, asked for papers, and found no end of things to be busy about. I never found out why they came, what they did, or why they left.—*George Peek*

BOYS WITH THEIR HAIR ABLAZE

Bitter conflict between New Dealers and their Old Guard opponents marked the first four years of Franklin D. Roosevelt's presidency. Swept into office with a mandate to repair the ravages of the Depression, the New Deal Congress that began its "Hundred Days" session in March 1933 enacted an innovative package of legislation designed to revive a moribund economy. Debate on the programs of industrial and agricultural reconstruction that formed the core of the New Deal centered around the construction of broadly worded constitutional provisions and the allocation of power between the states and the federal government. The arena in which these issues were most heatedly contested was not, as one might expect, the chambers of Congress. Popular rejection of the charity-basket policies of the Republicans in the 1932 elections had reduced the once-grand old party to a vocal but ineffectual remnant in both wings of the Capitol. Commanding majorities of almost three-to-one in the House of Representatives and two-to-one in the Senate, the Democratic leadership in Congress easily deflected the rhetorical barbs of the GOP minority as it shepherded Roosevelt's legislative program to passage.

The real confrontation between New Dealers and their foes took place, rather, in federal courtrooms dominated by Republican judges wedded to the states-rights and laissez-faire ideologies repudiated overwhelmingly by the voters in three successive elections between 1932 and 1936. The constitutional limitations of ballot-box democracy gave the electorate the power to reshape only two of the three coordinate branches of the federal government. Armed with the judge-made weapon of judicial review and shielded from the arrows of change by the doctrine of *stare decisis*, life-tenured judges at all three levels of the federal judiciary wielded a potent veto over New Deal programs in the name of constitutional fundamentalism. When Roosevelt took office after twelve years of GOP control of the White House, the federal bench reflected a mirror image of Congress. The 140 judges appointed by Roosevelt's three Republican predecessors made up three-fourths of the district court bench and two-thirds of the appellate bench. It was this group, partisan in background and conservative in judicial philosophy, that constituted the most formidable barrier to the New Deal.

Given this balance of political forces, the task of defending the New Deal fell, not to experienced congressional leaders, but to the untested young lawyers who staffed the legal offices of the emergency agencies created by Congress. Between 1933 and 1937, New Deal lawyers matched their skills and idealism against the twin obstacles of equally skilled corporate lawyers and hostile federal judges in hundreds of courtroom battles over New Deal statutes. Their efforts were largely unavailing until the dramatic "Constitutional Revolution" of 1937, in which the Supreme Court capitulated to the reality of the 20th century and upheld the power of the federal government to regulate relations between workers and employers. Four years of working-class eruption, electoral vindication of the Roosevelt program, and growing frustration over the obduracy of the courts lay between the first assaults by New Deal lawyers on the fortress of laissez-faire jurisprudence and the final breaching of its massive walls.

The drama of this conflict and its denouement in itself justifies a re-creation of the litigation skirmishes that ended in three decisive battles in the Supreme Court chambers: first, the invalidation of the National Industrial Recovery Act in May 1935 in *Schechter Poultry Corp. v. United States*; second, the rejection of the Agricultural Adjustment Act in January 1936 in *United States v. Butler*; and, finally, the upholding of the National Labor Relations Act in April 1937 in *NLRB v. Jones & Laughlin*.[1] These were the New Deal cases that tested the federal government's regulatory powers over the central components of the national economy: industry, agriculture, and labor. My concern, however, is less with the chronicle of conflict than with its dynamics. The three case studies that follow explore in detail the litigation process that begins with legislative drafting and ends with Supreme Court decisions in constitutional test cases. Although these two points mark the formal boundaries of the litigation process, the intermediate stage between drafting and decision constitutes the heart of these case studies, since what happens along the route from Congress to the Supreme Court is largely the province of the lawyers on whose work this book is focused.

Two related questions animate this study: first, how do constitutional test cases emerge from the crowded litigation dockets of federal regulatory agencies; and, second, can differences be discerned in the litigation strategies adopted by different agencies in the selection of test cases? The complex process of planting and weeding a litigation docket of hundreds or even of thousands of cases, in search of the sturdiest test case, is subject to several factors over which government lawyers have little control. The assignment of judges, the arguments of lawyers on the other side, the rulings of judges on points of fact and law during trial, and the timing of judicial decisions are vagaries that may suddenly uproot a promising test case. In addition, the discretionary jurisdiction of the Supreme Court provides no guarantee that a case will be accepted for review at a propitious time or even at all. There is, nonetheless, considerable room for maneuver in framing a litigation strategy designed to bring a particular test case to the Supreme Court within a particular term. Agency dockets generally contain cases with similar facts and issues, and the intermediate appellate courts regularly decide cases ripe for final review by the Supreme Court. But, as this study shows in its comparative aspect, lawyers in different agencies vary greatly in the litigation strategies they pursue. At one extreme, an agency's lawyers may seek to avoid a Supreme Court test altogether, or to defer one as long as possible; at the other, the strategy might be to push for the earliest possible test. The factors that influence these choices of strategy are manifold and often obscure. Two factors, however, almost invariably affect the ultimate shape of an agency's litigation strategy. One is that of politics, the forces brought to bear on government lawyers by an agency's administrators, by its constituency, by the White House and Congress, and by the intangible but often powerful pressure of public opinion. The other is that of personality, represented most directly through an agency's general counsel, the official most directly responsible for litigation decisions.

The joint impact of politics and personality, a conjunction of influences often impossible to separate, can most fruitfully be explored in the context of federal litigation through the concept of "style" formulated by James David Barber in his studies of the American presidency.[2] Barber's explorations of the components of presidential leadership—the distinctive handling of words, work, and people, and the balance between them—provide models of political style that have obvious corollaries in the political environment in which government lawyers operate. My conclusion that each of the New Deal general counsel I have studied—Donald Richberg of the National Recovery Administration, Jerome Frank of the Agricultural Adjustment Administration, and Charles Fahy of the National Labor Relations Board—personified a distinctive legal style that shaped his agency's approach to litigation and influenced agency lawyers in their handling of cases, emerged not from any preconceived model of the litigation process but rather from my examination of the decisions made by lawyers in each agency in hundreds of cases. As the dockets were winnowed from hundreds of cases filed in federal courts (chosen in turn from thousands of complaints brought to the agencies of violations of statutes and regulations), to some sixty cases decided on constitutional grounds by lower federal courts between 1933 and 1937, and finally to the handful of test cases decided by the Supreme Court, distinctive patterns of case-handling emerged. It became clear that lawyers in each agency followed the general contours of the legal style of the general counsel under whom they worked.

The labels I apply to the three groups of New Deal Lawyers—Legal

Politicians in the NRA, Legal Reformers in the AAA, and Legal Craftsmen
in the NLRB—are meant to be suggestive rather than definitive. Lawyers
in each agency displayed traits of each approach to litigation. Given the
ferment of the New Deal and the nature of legal training, it is hardly
surprising that New Deal lawyers would exhibit political sensitivity, reformist sentiment, and legal craftsmanship in their handling of cases.
Particularly at the level at which decisions on test case strategy were made,
however, differences in approach between the agencies are evident. The
fact that each general counsel tended to recruit lawyers whose backgrounds
matched his adds force, I think, to the utility of these models of legal
style.

The meshing of politics and personality gives this book a biographical
focus in conjunction with that on the litigation process. Although the three
general counsel stand in the foreground of this group portrait of New Deal
lawyers, a composite picture will help to identify the biographical snapshots
that follow. The 95 lawyers whose work is discussed in this book are those
directly involved in the litigation that led to each agency's test cases. This
sample is biased toward litigators and those at the middle and upper levels
of the agencies, but includes as well a fair cross-section of the 500-odd
lawyers employed in them and in the Justice Department during this period.[3] One shared characteristic defines them: with few exceptions they
were products of the 20th century. Well over half were born in the decade
between 1900 and 1910 and completed law school between 1925 and 1935.
They were disproportionately urban in upbringing, Jewish and Catholic in
heritage, and liberal in politics. In these respects, they differed significantly
from the bar as a whole and from the judges before whom they argued.
They were, additionally, products of elite law schools. Fully 60 percent
attended law school at Harvard, Yale, or Columbia; 4 out of 10, in fact,
were Harvard graduates. The proportions varied considerably between
agencies, however; only 2 of 16 NRA litigators attended Harvard, while
15 of 26 in the AAA were Harvard graduates. But only in the NRA did
fewer than half (43 percent) of the litigators come from one of these three
elite schools.[4]

That these elite law schools channeled lawyers into New Deal offices
is less remarkable, given the prestige of their diplomas, than the unorthodox
and often heretical approaches to legal education of their faculties. Centered
in these three schools, a loosely connected segment of the law school
professoriate revolted during the 1920s and 1930s against the sterile formalism and conceptualism of 19th-century jurisprudence and the case-
study straightjacket imposed on legal education in the 1870s by Harvard's
dean, Christopher Columbus Langdell. The Langdellian notion of law as
a rigidly deductive and mechanistic "science," and its study through the

lens of appellate court opinions, drew the fire of those who championed "sociological jurisprudence" and its offspring, "legal realism."[5] Young legal academics fashioned a new jurisprudence from the intellectual currents sweeping other disciplines; relativism in philosophy, behavioralism in psychology, and indeterminacy in science undermined the certitude of jurisprudential formalism. Law, the insurgents argued, was a social institution rooted in the reality of conflicting interests and shaped by individual predilection; judges did not "find" the law as oracles but "made" it as mortals subject to the biases of their backgrounds.

Columbia and Yale in particular exposed young lawyers to legal realists who put judges on the psychoanalyst's couch and litigation under sociological scrutiny. Karl Llewellyn headed a group of realists at Columbia that included Underhill Moore, Herman Oliphant, Edwin W. Patterson, R. L. Hale, and Hessel Yntema. Their behavioral analysis of the judicial function, which owed less to Freud than to John Watson's stimulus-response psychology, was complemented by the work and teaching of Adolf A. Berle, Jr., Gardiner Means, and Milton Handler, who stressed the positive role of government regulation as a counterweight to corporate power. Courses at Columbia such as Llewellyn's in Law and Society, Handler's in Trade Regulation, and Berle's in Corporation Finance prepared budding New Deal lawyers to look on judges as manipulators of law and on regulation as a modern necessity.[6]

Even more than Columbia, Yale Law School during these decades was the intellectual seedbed of the realists. Under the deanship first of Robert M. Hutchins and then of Charles E. Clark, the Yale faculty abounded with social science-oriented scholars. Thurman Arnold, William O. Douglas, Walton H. Hamilton, Walter Nelles, and Wesley A. Sturges (joined in the 1930s by Underhill Moore from Columbia) viewed law less as a profession than as one of the social sciences. In 1928 the law school joined the medical school and the social science departments to establish the Yale Institute of Human Relations, and added Eugen Kahn, a psychiatrist, and Edward S. Robinson, a psychologist, to the law faculty. Jerome Frank, whose book *Law and the Modern Mind* became the most widely read (and widely denounced) realist work, taught at Yale in 1932-1933; when he left for Washington he took with him Abe Fortas, editor-in-chief of the *Yale Law Journal*.[7]

In contrast to Columbia and Yale, Harvard harbored no realists on its faculty. What it provided, through Felix Frankfurter and his colleagues James Landis and Calvert Magruder (both former students under Frankfurter), was an emphasis on lawyers as members of the emerging mandarinate of the regulatory state. In Frankfurter's courses on Administrative Law, Jurisdiction and Procedure in Federal Courts, and Public Utilities, he preached the ideals of administrative expertise and "disinterested public service." Magruder's and Landis's courses on Labor Law and Legislation reinforced Frankfurter's vision of the lawyer as an indispensable adjunct to the legislative and administrative process. Thomas Reed Powell, who taught constitutional law, disclaimed membership in the realist club but similarly challenged the notion that judges "found" the law in the constitutional bullrushes. Powell propounded his view that judicial decisions depended on "what the judge had for breakfast" with a biting Vermont wit and polemical sharpness in his lectures and writings.[8]

Among these men of divergent but collectively unorthodox views, Frankfurter most directly put his stamp on the New Deal lawyers and, in their subsequent litigation debates, pressed his opinions on them and their superiors. Not only did his former students far outnumber those from other schools and occupy the most influential New Deal legal positions, but Frankfurter's long-standing and intimate relationship with Franklin D. Roosevelt gave him easy access to the White House and a voice in the internal debates over litigation strategy and legislative policy. Eternally combative, Frankfurter epitomized the inherent duality of the New Deal lawyers; preaching to his students the ideal of the lawyer as servant to policymakers, he irrepressibly intruded himself into the whole gamut of policy debates within the New Deal. Given this role as mentor of the "Happy Hot Dogs" whom he stuffed into New Deal agencies, an examination of the fundamentally contradictory values Frankfurter inculcated in his protégés illuminates the conflicts between politics and practice that pervade this book.[9]

With the exception perhaps of the aging Clarence Darrow, no other lawyer of his time shared Frankfurter's undeserved reputation as a dangerous radical. New Deal critics singled him out for attack because of his involvement in two notorious episodes in recent history: first, his defense of aliens threatened with deportation in the wake of the 1919-1920 "Red Raids" initiated by Attorney General A. Mitchell Palmer and led by J. Edgar Hoover, and his subsequent sponsorship of a critical report on the "Illegal Activities of the Department of Justice"; and, second, his passionate advocacy in 1927 of a new trial for Sacco and Vanzetti.[10] Frankfurter's role in these controversies was that of a civil libertarian who disavowed sympathy for the radical views of those he defended, but the legal establishment recoiled in horror. And following Roosevelt's election, it was predictable that Frankfurter's well-publicized role as presidential confidant would make him a target of conservatives. Frankfurter and Roosevelt were a curiously matched pair. Both born in 1882 but totally dissimilar in background—one an immigrant from Vienna to the Jewish ghetto in New York City at the age of twelve, the other the scion of Hudson Valley landowners descended from pre-Revolutionary Dutch patroons—the two men first met in 1917, when Roosevelt sat as the Navy Department representative on the War Labor Policies Board that Frankfurter chaired while on leave from Harvard, whose law faculty he joined in 1914 after stints in Wall Street practice and with the U.S. Attorney in New York.[11]

Bound by reformist sympathies, the two men met frequently over the following two decades and carried on a voluminous correspondence marked on Frankfurter's side by sycophantic flattery mixed with policy prescriptions; Max Freedman, who edited this correspondence, perceptively labeled Frankfurter an "artist in adulation. . . ."[12] Frankfurter reveled in Roosevelt's receptiveness, and during Roosevelt's two terms as governor of New York peppered him with suggestions aimed at making the state a legislative laboratory for reforms in unemployment compensation, utility regulation, and other schemes later incorporated in the New Deal program. Four days after his presidential inauguration, Roosevelt expressed his esteem by offering Frankfurter the post of Solicitor General. Happy in his Harvard position and reluctant to abandon his more influential role as freelance advisor for the striped pants and cutaway of a "technical lawyer," Frankfurter declined with the response that "I can do much more to be of use to you in Cambridge than by becoming Solicitor General."[13] For the next six years, until his belated appointment to the Supreme Court, Frankfurter made himself of use through regular trips to Washington on the Federal Express and by placing, through his protégé, Tommy Corcoran, scores of former students in New Deal legal posts.

In his teaching, however, Frankfurter displayed few of his extracurricular enthusiasms. His students absorbed a view of the lawyer's function as essentially apolitical; a thoroughgoing Anglophile who revered the model of the British civil service, Frankfurter in 1930 expressed his belief that the lawyer's role was that of "putting at the disposal of government that ascertainable body of knowledge on which the choice of policies must be based."[14] Before and even during the New Deal, he urged on his students the advantages of corporate practice as a skill-sharpening experience and recommended more lawyers to Wall Street friends such as Emory Buckner and Henry L. Stimson than he did to the New Deal. And in all his courses and contacts with former students, Frankfurter drummed home his cautionary advice that litigation should never be sought but accepted only as a "last resort" to compromise and conciliation.

Exposure to the realists and technocrats biased young lawyers toward reform and regulation. They ingested as well, however, a powerful antidote in their basic courses in property, contracts, and procedure. The Harvard-trained New Dealers, for example, parsed cases with such orthodox dispensers of the received doctrine as Joseph Warren, Joseph H. Beale, and

Samuel Williston. Most New Deal lawyers, then, emerged from law school with a veneer of progressive liberalism over a foundation of doctrinal orthodoxy and apolitical professionalism. They could hardly escape, in the contentious atmosphere of the early New Deal, the conflicting tugs of politics and practice.

This book observes the New Deal lawyers at work primarily in their litigating function, but also in the related roles unique to government lawyers: drafting legislation, writing regulations, participating in enforcement proceedings, advising policy-makers, and negotiating with a wide range of persons affected by their agency's operations. In each of these roles, government lawyers are enmeshed in a political system that imposes constraints on them and engenders recurrent conflict. Each of the sections that follow examines in detail the effect of these political factors; it is useful, however, to sketch here the four major sources of political conflict, both internal and external, with which New Deal lawyers contended in performing their roles.[15]

The first source of conflict lay within the agencies themselves. In principle, the general counsel of a federal agency is subordinate to its chief administrator, and in most instances an agency head chooses (or approves before presidential appointment) a general counsel on the basis of mutual compatibility in both personality and policies. Perhaps more than any other president, however, Franklin Roosevelt showed no compunction in staffing New Deal agencies with officials whose personalities or policies (or both) clashed. Ego and ambition rather than policy divided Hugh Johnson and Donald Richberg in the NRA; the agency was simply not big enough for both disputatious men. Jerome Frank in the AAA had opposed its first administrator, George Peek, in a bankruptcy battle before either came to the New Deal and their policy disputes exacerbated this personal feud until Peek was forced out; Frank's differences with Peek's successor, Chester Davis, were less personal but equally intractable. Only the NLRB exhibited harmony between its chairman, Warren Madden, and its general counsel, but even in this instance Charles Fahy rarely consulted Madden's fellow Board members and made litigation decisions on his own.

Animosity at the top often colors the attitudes of administrators toward those in lower ranks. Peek in particular had nothing but scorn for the young lawyers on Frank's staff. "Boys with their hair ablaze," he called them, attributing to their machinations a "socialist" plot to collectivize agriculture.[16] Peek's subordinates equally detested the AAA lawyers, finding them insufficiently solicitous of the interests of large landowners and processors. General Hugh Johnson had a similarly bilious view of the "boys" whom Felix Frankfurter had "insinuated" into "obscure but key positions in every vital department" of the New Deal.[17] Richberg's lawyers, in fact, generally sympathized with the interests of the big businessmen who dominated NRA policy, but suspicions of political heresy on occasion prompted Johnson to request FBI investigations of liberal lawyers, and at least one was fired for possession of "subversive" literature. Charles Fahy insulated his staff from Board interference, but conservative Board members and staff who considered some NLRB lawyers excessively pro-labor collaborated with red-hunting congressional investigators who launched a demoralizing probe of the Board's case-handling and decisions in 1940.[18] Internal politics and the resultant power struggles in each New Deal agency complicated the work of the lawyers, often spilling over into debates over individual cases and general litigation strategy.

The relentless bureacratic imperialism of the Justice Department created a second source of conflict. Every federal agency and cabinet department shares litigation responsibility with the Justice Department, if not in the lower courts, then at the levels of appellate and Supreme Court litigation subject to supervision by the Solicitor General. Early in the New Deal, through an Executive Order issued in June 1933, the Department wrested litigation control from all existing agencies; Roosevelt's order, however, did not cover those agencies subsequently created by Congress such as the NRA, AAA, and NLRB. Newly created agencies and the Department generally negotiate complex and delicate agreements ratifying their divisions of labor; in his study of Department-agency relations, Donald L. Horowitz noted that such agreements "have some of the attributes of treaties among sovereign states."[19] But, during the New Deal, the Department fought to impose control over the agencies as if they were subjugated colonies.

Pure and simple expansionism, a feature of the Justice Department since its establishment in 1870, explains much of this conflict. Personality and politics, however, affected litigation differences as well. New Deal lawyers generally considered the Justice Department a haven for political hacks whose sympathy for their programs was suspect, and the Department's composition lent some substance to these charges. Attorney General Homer Cummings (a last-minute choice after Roosevelt's designate, Montana Senator Thomas Walsh, died unexpectedly two days before the inauguration) came from a background as a Democratic party wheelhorse who helped swing the 1932 convention to Roosevelt. A 62-year-old Yale Law School graduate and a politician by temperment, Cummings had little interest in litigation but a ferocious appetite for bureaucratic power. His staffing of the Department with deserving Democrats led two Supreme Court Justices, Louis Brandeis and Harlan Fiske Stone (the latter a former Attorney General), to convey concern over the Department's competence to Roosevelt shortly after Cummings assumed office.[20]

Cummings infrequently intruded himself into litigation debates, and when he did so he generally advocated caution and avoidance. His two chief subordinates with litigation responsibility, however, were constantly embroiled in dispute with agency lawyers. After Frankfurter declined Roosevelt's offer of the Solicitor Generalship, the President inexplicably picked an amiable nonentity for the post. J. Crawford Biggs, a 60-year-old North Carolina judge and politician (widely assumed to owe his job to the influence of Senator Josiah Bailey), lasted two years before his lackadaisical performance led Roosevelt, at Frankfurter's urging, to replace him with Stanley F. Reed. A 51-year-old Kentuckian who served as a state legislator after attending Columbia Law School, Reed had served under President Hoover as general counsel of the Federal Farm Board and then of the Reconstruction Finance Corporation, where his right-hand man was Frankfurter's recruiting officer, Tommy Corcoran. Reed's major distinction (which later won him nomination to the Supreme Court) was an unwavering loyalty to Roosevelt; his ties to Frankfurter created discord with lawyers in the NRA, and Reed harbored deep misgivings about the constitutionality of the New Deal program.

The Justice Department official directly responsible for New Deal litigation was Harold M. Stephens, Assistant Attorney General in the Antitrust Division. A 1913 Harvard Law School graduate who practiced and served as a judge in Utah before joining a Los Angeles law firm, Stephens pursued an ill-concealed campaign for a federal judicial appointment, which he finally achieved in 1935 when Roosevelt placed him on the U.S. Court of Appeals in Washington. Stephens clashed repeatedly with agency lawyers. His innate antipathy toward litigation constituted one reason, but a more important factor was that the Antitrust Division he headed had virtually no antitrust litigation to handle (only five minor cases in 1934) since Congress had exempted both business and agriculture from the antitrust laws in 1933. Quite naturally, Stephens and his staff approached agency litigation with a notable lack of enthusiasm. Stephens' successor, John Dickinson, assumed office after the demise of the NRA and the debacle of the AAA litigation campaign, but his litigation perspective was equally cautious. Dickinson's appointment illustrates the limitations of Frankfurter's influence. A former Harvard economics instructor and University of Pennsylvania law professor, Dickinson earned a Princeton doctorate in 1919 and a Harvard law degree in 1921, and moved to the Justice Department from a post as Undersecretary of Commerce. An economic and legal conservative with a pompous demeanor (Frankfurter's followers called him "the Pope"), Dickinson had earlier opposed the government as counsel for the American Sugar Institute in a major antitrust suit and later became general counsel of the Pennsylvania Railroad. Frankfurter vigorously, but to no avail, opposed Dickinson's appointment for lack of antitrust enthusiasm. Under Stephens in particular, Justice Department lawyers and their agency counterparts sparred over dozens of cases, against a background of ideological dispute and institutional infighting.

The group with which New Deal lawyers most directly clashed was, of course, the federal judiciary. As mentioned above, in the period before 1937 (and for another decade, in fact) the federal bench was dominated by conservative Republicans. Particularly at the trial level, the 140 judges in the federal district courts generally exhibited an innate hostility toward the New Deal. Given the traditions of judicial appointment, such attitudes were hardly surprising. Drawn largely from small-town practice, with judicial nomination most often a reward for faithful party service, these judges shared—in contrast to the New Deal lawyers who argued before them—a 19th-century outlook on law and economics. In 1933, the typical lower-court judge was 60 years old and had completed law school during the McKinley administration; his legal bible was Thomas Cooley's aptly titled *Constitutional Limitations*.[21] Judges at the intermediate level of the Courts of Appeals were somewhat more cosmopolitan in outlook and urban in background, but were even older than their district court colleagues and almost as partisan in composition.

The ultimate barrier to the New Deal, of course, was the raised bench behind which sat the nine justices of the Supreme Court. During the four years covered by this study, the Court's membership remained stable. Seven of its members owed their appointments to Republican presidents, although only three had been active in partisan politics before joining the Court. With notable exceptions, the justices shared with their lower-court brethren an equal commitment to the precepts of constitutional fundamentalism and a similar 19th-century perspective; five of the justices were over seventy in 1933 and the youngest was born in 1875. However, the Court headed by Chief Justice Charles Evans Hughes—like Roosevelt a former New York governor and unlike him an unsuccessful presidential candidate—was not an ideological monolith. Past voting patterns divided the Supreme Court into three blocs. On the far right were the "Four Horsemen of Reaction"—Willis Van Devanter, James C. McReynolds, George Sutherland, and Pierce Butler. Occasionally liberal on issues of criminal law and race (consistent with their anti-government animus), this bloc rarely divided on issues of federalism and economic regulation; states and businessmen could count on four solid votes in every case. An opposing group of three comprised the Court's liberal wing—Louis D. Brandeis, Benjamin Cardozo, and Harlan Fiske Stone. In the center, representing the swing votes necessary for any majority, were Hughes and Owen Roberts.[22]

To place such emphasis on the partisan composition of the federal judiciary may appear to give undue weight to only one judicial characteristic, and to denigrate the image of the judge as impartial constitutional arbiter. Partisan background, however, has long influenced the nomination process at all levels of the federal judiciary, and presidents rarely deviate in appointing to the bench members of their own party. The fact that judicial nominations have historically been subject to senatorial approval adds an additional partisan factor to the equation. Occasional exceptions to this rule (McReynolds, the most abrasive of the Supreme Court reactionaries, was a nominal Democrat appointed by Woodrow Wilson, while Herbert Hoover placed the liberal Cardozo on the Court) only point up its general applicability. Partisanship is not always, of course, a determinant of judicial philosophy, as McReynolds and Stone illustrate. But, within the confines of judicial discretion and precedent, the two factors are closely related. The analysis of constitutional decisions by district judges in cases involving the NRA and AAA, presented in the following sections, clearly demonstrates a partisan split between Republican and Democratic judges. That partisanship gave way to acceptance of the New Deal, in the "Constitutional Revolution" of 1937, only illustrates that the forces of political and social change cannot be indefinitely blocked.

The fourth political factor that affected New Deal litigation was external. Federal litigation at every stage of the process comes under political scrutiny. In Congress, in the press, and in the interest groups over which agencies exercise regulatory control, litigation decisions often become political issues; the imbroglio in 1981 over Supreme Court test cases involving the Occupational Safety and Health Act provides a recent example. During the New Deal period, small businessmen and congressional antitrusters pressured the NRA to shift its enforcement emphasis from gas-station operators to corporate giants; cotton plantation owners and their congressional allies brought down the AAA lawyers; and NLRB lawyers squirmed uncomfortably in the midst of battles between AFL conservatives and CIO militants.

In periods of fundamental social conflict, of which the New Deal is a classic example, government lawyers cannot escape the pressures of politics. How the New Deal lawyers dealt with these pressures, both internal and external, is the subject of this book.

SECTION ONE
THE LEGAL POLITICIANS OF THE
NATIONAL RECOVERY
ADMINISTRATION

Chapter One

CORPORATISM AND CARTELS: THE NATIONAL INDUSTRIAL RECOVERY ACT

I. THE IDEOLOGY OF RECOVERY

During the four-month interregnum between the election of Franklin D. Roosevelt and his inauguration, members of the quasi-official Brains Trust worked furiously to draft a legislative program to deal with the economic wreckage that was the legacy of the failed laissez-faire philosophy of the Hoover administration. The collapse of the paper prosperity of the 1920s left a toll of human suffering only partly measured by dry statistics: since the Crash of 1929, thirteen million workers lost their jobs, industrial wages fell from $17 billion to $6.8 billion, the price index declined by 37 percent, and the output of goods dropped almost by half.[1] A month before the first New Deal Congress convened, Edmund Wilson described the impact of the Great Depression in more graphic terms: "There is not a garbage-dump in Chicago which is not diligently haunted by the hungry. Last summer in hot weather when the smell was sickening and the flies were thick, there were a hundred people a day coming to one of the dumps, falling on the heap of refuse as soon as the truck had pulled out and digging in it with sticks and hands."[2]

Against this backdrop of privation, the task of reviving a moribund economy and renewing the flow of industrial goods from factories to stores to homes was far from simple. Roosevelt's reluctance during the campaign to articulate the specifics of a recovery plan, as well as his commitment to the Democratic platform promise of a balanced budget, complicated the work of the Brains Trusters. The Keynesian solution of massive deficit spending as a stimulus to production and consumption was then an idea in embryo. Several of Roosevelt's advisors, among whom Harry Hopkins was the most influential, advocated a program of large-scale public works construction as a means of putting the unemployed to work, but even the most ambitious plan of this type would have scarcely made a dent in the jobless ranks. The only recovery plan on the legislative agenda at the time was the thirty-hour bill proposed by Senator Hugo Black of Alabama, a populist share-the-work scheme that Roosevelt and his advisors opposed.

17

They considered the Black bill inadequate to meet the structural crisis of the economy, and additionally feared that the Supreme Court would not hesitate to strike it down as unconstitutional.[3]

The process from which the National Industrial Recovery Act emerged as the legislative cornerstone of the New Deal economic program illustrates in classic form the workings of "political capitalism." As Gabriel Kolko has put it, "the cycle of interplay between business constituencies and the state" since the late 19th century has featured "an alternation between primary dependence on voluntary efforts" to deal with the vicissitudes of the business cycle and acceptance of "political regulation and compulsions" on the part of the federal government.[4] This pattern of alternation between self-regulation and federal intervention had two major effects in the half-century that preceded the New Deal. First, it led to passage of a body of federal antitrust law in the Sherman Act in 1890 and the Clayton Act and Federal Trade Commission Act in 1914. Prompted by anti-monopoly sentiment among farmers and small businessmen, these antitrust laws were designed to outlaw "combinations in restraint of trade" and to protect small businesses against "unfair trade practices" and oppression by their larger competitors.[5]

The second effect of the antitrust laws was that they drove a wedge between the small businessmen who were historically allied with the Republican party and the industrialists who sought, through mergers and combinations, to exercise control over prices and production. This latter group chafed under enforcement of the antitrust laws, even after the relaxed "rule of reason" enunciated by the Supreme Court in the *Standard Oil* case in 1911.[6] Basically opportunistic and more than willing to abandon partisan attachment in the pursuit of its interests, the industrial elite was unpleasantly surprised by the vigorous antitrust policies of the Department of Justice during the Hoover administration, and sought relief from the New Deal Democrats.[7]

Led by Henry I. Harriman, the railroad magnate who headed the United States Chamber of Commerce, and Gerard Swope, the president of General Electric, corporate leaders who urged a respite from antitrust enforcement as a stimulus to recovery had a natural ally in President-elect Roosevelt. The model for recovery legislation proposed to the Brains Trust by Harriman and Swope was based on the War Industries Board established during World War I to coordinate industrial production and government procurement of essential wartime goods. The administrative structure of the WIB rested on collaboration between federal officials concerned with procurement and industrial trade associations to which power over production was delegated by presidential proclamation.[8] Not only had Roosevelt been

18

involved in the WIB as Assistant Secretary of the Navy during the war, but he had also served between 1922 and 1928 as president of one of the leading trade associations, the American Construction Council. It was these experiences in government-industry cooperation that prompted Roosevelt's statement during his 1932 presidential campaign that the Depression called "for the building of plans that rest upon . . . the indispensable units of economic power, for plans like those of 1917. . . ."[9]

The ideology of recovery embodied in Roosevelt's campaign speeches and presented to the Brains Trust by Harriman and Swope represented a plan for government by trade association. At its heart was the conviction that the Depression proved that the laissez-faire ideology of unbridled competition was anachronistic and unworkable. In its place, the industrial leaders who supported Roosevelt proposed a plan of political-economic corporatism based on relaxation of the antitrust laws and a system of business-government collaboration in the regulation of production and prices. The basic article of faith in the catechism of the corporatists was that "cut-throat competition" posed the greatest danger to industrial recovery. To combat this sin—essentially that of below-cost price-cutting—corporatists were willing to accept government regulation and agreed, as Ellis Hawley put it, that "the real solution was to forget about competition and concentrate upon national controls, upon establishing a government that could . . . engage in purposeful planning, supervise the big corporations, and insure that the benefits of modern industrialism were more evenly distributed."[10] Benjamin Javits, a lawyer-economist and a prolific advocate of the corporatist approach to recovery, stated this position forcefully in 1932. The "evils of unrestrained competition," Javits wrote in an influential book, could be met only through the trade associations that formed "the basic structure of an industrial order that gives promise of the economic salvation in America."[11]

The catchword of the corporatists who were lobbying the Brains Trust in early 1933 was "industrial self-government." What they meant by this appealing phrase was what Robert Himmelberg has labeled "governmentally approved cartelism" based on industry-formulated codes permitting price-fixing and production controls.[12] The ultimate goal of the corporatists was suspension of the antitrust laws. Although occasionally bested during the 1920s by Justice Department attacks on blatant anti-competitive schemes, the trade associations won Supreme Court approval of some of their less obvious trade practices. Most notably, in the *Maple Flooring Association* case in 1925, the Court sanctioned the industry's open-pricing arrangement: "Competition does not become less free merely because the conduct of commercial operations becomes more intelligent through the free distribution of knowledge of all the essential factors entering into the commercial transaction."[13] This partial victory only whetted the corporatists' appetite for the abeyance of antitrust enforcement by the Roosevelt administration.

Represented in the Brains Trust by Raymond Moley, a Columbia University government professor, the corporatists were an amorphous group united only by a shared vision of a recovery plan rooted in some form of business-government collaboration.[14] The *éminence grise* whose influence welded these disparate elements into a potent factor in the circle of Roosevelt's advisors was Bernard Baruch, the "park bench" financier and Democratic Party angel. Notwithstanding his recent role in the stop-Roosevelt movement, Baruch's stature and contributions to party coffers won him a welcome to Hyde Park after the wounds of the convention healed. A veteran of the War Industries Board, Baruch had long advocated relaxation of the antitrust laws, which he dismissed as outmoded efforts to force business to conform to "the simpler principles sufficient for the conditions of a bygone day."[15]

Although the corporatist approach to recovery prevailed among the Brains Trusters as they drafted a legislative program, it was not without opposition. With varying degrees of intensity, the antitrust flame still burned among those who deplored the increasing growth of monopoly and industrial concentration. The elder statesman of this group was Louis D. Brandeis, whose bitterly contested nomination to the Supreme Court in 1916 reflected his national role as the "people's lawyer" and the scourge of the malefactors of industry.[16] Like their corporatist adversaries, the disciples who shared with Brandeis an economic vision of a competitive system kept in check by vigorous antitrust enforcement differed widely in their prescriptions for the Depression. Brandeis himself, whose cloistered position on the Supreme Court did not curb his intense interest in public issues, would add to the antitrust medicine a stiff dose of confiscatory taxation and public works spending.[17] Moley's counterpart among the Brandeisians was Felix Frankfurter, who acted as a conduit for the Justice's brief but frequent messages to Roosevelt.

In his pre-Court writings, most notably in a book titled *The Curse of Bigness*, Brandeis had argued the case for the competitive ideal.[18] But his most powerful and incisive exposition of the dangers of unchecked monopoly was expressed in an impassioned judicial dissent. The Supreme Court in 1932 struck down a Florida statute imposing a higher tax on chain stores than on small retailers. Brandeis poured out his fears for the future in a rebuke worthy of an Old Testament prophet (showing why Roosevelt and Frankfurter privately and affectionately called him "Isaiah"). In his opinion, Brandeis flayed corporate monopoly as "the negation of industrial democracy" and as "an institution which has brought such concentration of economic power that so-called private corporations are sometimes able to dominate the State." Had monopoly control, he asked, created in fact a "corporate system" of government which was actually a "feudal system" committed to "the rule of a plutocracy"? In taxing chain stores to protect smaller retailers, Florida "may have done so merely in order to preserve competition. But their purpose may have been a broader and deeper one. They may have believed that the chain store, by furthering the concentration of wealth and power and by promoting absentee ownership, is thwarting American ideals. . . ." That Brandeis would take pains to write such a lengthy and pointed dissent in an otherwise obscure case reflected his deep concern that corporate monopoly "is converting independent tradesmen into clerks" and consequently "sapping the resources, the vigor and the hope of smaller cities and towns."[19]

This evocation of the values of an earlier and largely mythic era exposed Brandeis to ridicule from the corporatists. Moley wrote to Roosevelt soon after Brandeis issued this opinion that the need for "controls to stimulate and stabilize economic activity" necessitated "the rejection of the traditional Wilson-Brandeis philosophy that if America could once more become a nation of small proprietors, of corner groceries and smithies under spreading chestnut trees, we could have solved the problems of American life."[20] Unfair as Moley's hyperbole was, as the primary architect of the recovery program he had isolated the central weakness of the Brandeisian ideology as the basis for a legislative agenda: it had no programmatic content other than antitrust enforcement, which held little short-run prospect for increasing production and employment.

The significance of the ideological dispute between the corporatists and the Brandeisians did not lie in their relative influence within the ranks of New Deal advisors and policy-makers. Corporatism was clearly an idea whose time, however brief, had come. And its advocates outmatched their opponents both in numbers and in the specificity of their program for recovery. The conflict was significant at a different level of the political process, the level at which legislative and administrative policy enters the province of lawyers and judges and is tested through litigation. There were no Brandeisians among the Brains Trusters, but the disciples of Brandeis and Frankfurter were clustered in key positions in the New Deal agencies and the Justice Department. Despite their reputation as liberals or even dangerous radicals, the Brandeisians were essentially conservative in their attachment to regulated competition, and their influence in the legal system was magnified by their ability to forge a marriage of convenience with the adherents of laissez-faire economics and jurisprudence who dominated the federal bench. In this position, the Brandeisians and their temporary allies were capable of throwing up barricades against the corporatist juggernaut.

21

II. The Politics of Recovery

The real challenge to Moley and his colleagues in the Brains Trust was posed not by the disciples of Brandeis but by the calendar. As the original small and cohesive group of planners expanded to include self-invited and sometime unwelcome interlopers, the legislative drafting process became unwieldy and time-consuming. The New Deal Congress began its historic "Hundred Days" session early in March 1933; a month passed without a word from the White House on the structure of Roosevelt's economic recovery program. An impatient Congress finally responded to its own sense of urgency and pressure from organized labor; on April 6, the Senate passed the thirty-hour bill sponsored by Hugo Black. The Black bill, which would have barred from interstate commerce goods produced by any business in which employees worked more than six hours a day and five days a week, was frankly considered unconstitutional by many of those who voted for it. However, these reservations disappeared in the face of the threat made by William Green of the American Federation of Labor of a general strike if the Black bill was defeated.[21]

Jolted by this untimely stimulus, Roosevelt intervened to force a consensus among his increasingly factious advisors, who were split into three drafting groups with little coordination. Roosevelt held off consideration of the thirty-hour bill in the more pliable House of Representatives while he watched with mounting frustration as the three groups shuttled legislative drafts back and forth. Public criticism of his inaction took its toll on Roosevelt's tolerance for internal debate and deliberation. On May 10 he summoned the leaders of each group to the White House, listened to presentations of the various proposals, and then directed representatives of each group to "lock themselves in a room until an agreement could be reached."[22]

This presidential shock treatment had its intended effect. The conferees emerged a few hours later with a draft bill whose principal author was General Hugh Johnson, a Baruch lieutenant who held no government post. Far shorter than most previous drafts, the Johnson bill contained four important provisions. The most significant provided for federal regulation of trade practices and wage and hour standards through "codes of fair competition" proposed by trade associations and other industry groups. Definitions of what practices would or would not be considered "fair competition" were left to the code drafters, subject to administrative review and presidential approval. The only restriction imposed on trade associations was that they be "truly representative" of the trade or industry. Equally important, the proposed bill suspended enforcement of the antitrust laws against industries covered by codes, although undefined "monopolistic" practices were prohibited and codes were required not to "oppress small enterprises" or discriminate against them, and the Federal Trade Commission was assigned jurisdiction over practices that violated code standards. Between them, these two key provisions formed the basis for government by trade association, the goal sought by the corporatists for the past two decades.

Two remaining provisions of the Johnson draft satisfied the demands of other important interests represented among the drafting group. Organized labor, for whom Senator Robert F. Wagner spoke, demanded the inclusion of a guarantee that workers could organize into unions and bargain collectively with employers. The requirement that each code contain this provision, which became Section 7(a) of the National Industrial Recovery Act, represented the bargain struck with labor for its abandonment of the thirty-hour bill.* Finally, the draft bill provided in a separate section for a substantial public works program, a victory for Harry Hopkins and a harbinger of the Keynesian future to come. The barest skeleton of a recovery program, the draft bill left the design of its administrative structure to presidential discretion. The drafters also armed Roosevelt with wide powers to force recalcitrant industries into line; one provision authorized him to impose a code on an industry if its representatives could not reach agreement on one, and another empowered him to enforce compliance through a federal licensing system.[23]

Hugh Johnson and his fellow drafters emerged from their locked conference room with an untitled bill scrawled on two pages of foolscap. After polishing by legislative aides over the following week, Roosevelt sent it to Congress on May 17 as the National Industrial Recovery Act. It was, as Raymond Moley later wrote, "a thorough hodge-podge" of recovery plans designed to "lay the groundwork for permanent business-government partnership and planning."[24] Under pressure from an impatient Roosevelt and an equally impatient Congress, the NIRA drafters gave little thought to the constitutional questions raised by their far-reaching proposal; the urgency of the situation did not encourage speculation about the reaction of the courts to the corporatist recovery plan. The only person involved in the drafting process who raised troubling questions about the constitutional soundness of the NIRA was Charles Wyzanski, the young Labor Department Solicitor who represented Secretary Frances Perkins at the drafting sessions.

A protégé of Felix Frankfurter and a 1930 graduate of Harvard Law School, Wyzanski was an anomalous New Dealer, a social liberal and

---

* Because enforcement of Section 7(a) was soon delegated to a separate labor board and later incorporated into the National Labor Relations Board, its enforcement and litigation are dealt with in Chapters 10 to 13.

constitutional conservative who had voted for Hoover in 1932. As a Brandeisian, Wyzanski was disturbed by the anticompetitive features of the NIRA, but he feared even more that the sweep of its regulation to cover small as well as large business crossed the line drawn by the Supreme Court separating interstate from intrastate commerce. Shortly after the bill reached Congress, Wyzanski urged Frankfurter to intervene with congressional and administration leaders. In view of Supreme Court decisions holding that manufacturing was not part of the commerce subject to federal regulation, Wyzanski wrote, "is it enough for the new statute to say in vague terms that it operates on businesses engaged in or affecting interstate commerce? I believe that the bill ought to spell out the belief of Congress that the instability of manufacturing and production have so affected commerce among the states that the federal government for the protection of that commerce finds it necessary to suppress unfair methods of competition and not only in commerce but in manufacture and production."[25]

A few days later, Wyzanski noted a second constitutional concern. The code-making powers delegated to the President, he wrote Frankfurter, "are entirely too broad," adding that the bill as drafted "seemed to me to go so far beyond the bounds of constitutionality that it would be useless" to expose it to judicial scrutiny.[26] On his part, Frankfurter was troubled less by these potential constitutional problems than he was by the corporatist features of the bill. In a memorandum to Wagner, Perkins, and other drafters, Frankfurter argued that suspension of the antitrust laws would only invite big business to form cartels. "There may be some force in the argument that the cartel system in Europe has proved more disastrous than the Sherman Law in America," he cautioned. In place of the code-regulation system, Frankfurter endorsed Wyzanski's alternative proposals that Congress directly set wage and hour standards, that industrial prices be fixed at 1929 levels, and that production be restricted to 55 percent of the 1929 output.[27] In this way, the delegation and commerce clause questions would be finessed and the courts confronted simply with regulatory standards fashioned by Congress.

These warning flags of constitutional roadblocks failed to slow down the bill's supporters in their drive for quick passage of the NIRA. With New Dealers firmly in control, Congress was eager to complete its work on Roosevelt's package of recovery legislation and adjourn before the summer heat struck Washington. Since its busy session had begun early in March, Congress had passed more than a dozen innovative statutes that invested the federal government with unprecedented regulatory powers. The New Deal alphabet soup now included the AAA, CCC, TVA, and FERA. The constitutional quibbles raised by the outnumbered coalition of right-wing Republicans and states-rights Democrats were swept aside in the rush to recovery. Armed with a gag rule, House Speaker Henry T. Rainey had no trouble keeping his troops in line; within a week the NIRA emerged from the House with a favorable vote of 323 to 76. As an "emergency" measure, the act was to expire at the end of two years.

In the Senate, however, the opposition stiffened as populist defenders of the antitrust tradition joined conservative Republicans in taking advantage of the rules that provided for extended debate. Senator Robert Wagner, assigned to defend the NIRA on the Senate floor, found his considerable patience and willingness to compromise tested as he parried the objections of those who feared the NIRA would turn the government over to the "tender mercies" of big business, as Huey Long of Louisiana charged.[28] The most substantive attack on the bill was led by William Borah of Idaho, an unreconstructed antitruster. Charging that trade associations were already anticipating price-fixing under the NIRA, Borah claimed that after suspension of the antitrust laws "we will have the steel industry, the drug industry, and the different industries of the United States meeting and combining for the purpose of formulating a code, the great objective of which will be to fix prices." Wagner offered the weak rejoinder that the NIRA would actually "return to the objectives of the antitrust laws," which he said were "to make competition constructive rather than ruinous, and to permit cooperation whenever a wise policy so dictates."[29]

Wagner's lengthy speech defending the constitutionality of the NIRA was aimed more at judges who would search the *Congressional Record* for evidence of the intent of the bill's sponsors than it was designed to sway the votes of wavering senators. In its outline, the speech served as a model for later briefs by government lawyers in cases challenging the Act. The argument was based on an expansive view of congressional power in three areas: regulation of interstate commerce, application of the "emergency" doctrine, and delegation of legislative power to the executive branch. On each of its major points, Wagner's speech anticipated almost precisely the arguments that would be made before the Supreme Court two years later in the critical NIRA test case. And on each point, the claim for sweeping regulatory powers was grounded in the exigencies of the Depression.

Wagner first argued that the constitutional power of Congress to regulate "commerce among the several states" should extend both to the manufacturing process and to commercial transactions within the states whose impact on the economy "burdened" interstate commerce. "Most goods," he noted, "even when manufactured by an intrastate business and destined for intrastate use, are compounded of ingredients which flow in from other states. Thus unfair or chaotic conditions which put such a business in difficulty clearly affect the flow of interstate commerce."[30] Wagner's re-

25

sponse to the axiom of laissez-faire jurisprudence that wage and hour regulation encroached on the "liberty" and "property" interests protected by the due process clause was to tie the police powers of government to the "emergency" created by the Depression. Since the Depression was "forcing millions to live on a bare subsistence level, and turning thousands to immorality and crime, any comprehensive scheme for restoring wage payments is related to the health, safety, and morals of the people." The emergency doctrine fashioned by the Supreme Court during World War I, Wagner argued, "is absolutely applicable to the present situation, where the economic emergency . . . enlarges the category of businesses which are affected with a public interest."[31]

Significantly, Wagner dismissed the delegation argument in a brief paragraph. "It is true that legislative powers cannot be delegated. But in order that the wheels of government may continue to turn, the Court has always sanctioned the use of administrative agencies to fill gaps in those statutes which set up reasonable guides to action." In the Declaration of Policy that formed the first section of the NIRA, Wagner claimed, Congress had established "careful" standards sufficient to guide the President and his administrative subordinates.[32]

Both the commerce clause and due process positions advanced by Wagner could be, and were, countered by those whose view of the congressional grants of power was narrow and restrictive. Only on the delegation issue did Wagner's argument rest on solid precedential ground. The Supreme Court, as he noted, had never rejected a federal statute as an unconstitutional delegation of legislative power. This fact undoubtedly prompted his almost casual dismissal of the issue. Ironically, it would prove to be the constitutional Achilles' heel of the NIRA. Despite the importance of these issues, however, his hot and weary colleagues paid little attention to Wagner's meticulously prepared speech. In their rush to adjourn, New Deal loyalists rejected the protests of the Senate populists angered by the last-minute scuttling of Borah's antimonopoly amendment, which Wagner abandoned in the House-Senate conference. The surprisingly close vote of 46 to 39 by which the National Industrial Recovery Act was adopted on June 12 became a prophetic forecast of the divisions between the New Deal lawyers charged with its administration and enforcement.

III. THE ADMINISTRATION OF RECOVERY

The national experiment with government by trade association began without the barest semblance of an administrative structure through which to draft and implement the "codes of fair competition" contemplated by the NIRA. The statute simply provided that the President was "authorized to

26

establish such agencies . . . as he may find necessary" and to "delegate any of his functions and powers" to officials appointed by him.[33] When Roosevelt signed the NIRA on June 16, he gave the responsibility for filling in this administrative blank check to General Hugh Johnson, whose appointment as Administrator of the National Recovery Administration became effective the same day.

Roosevelt's choice of Johnson placed a unique stamp on the NRA. With his gruff, profane, bombastic manner, Johnson fit none of the conventional stereotypes of the government bureaucrat, and the agency he headed became indelibly identified with his free-wheeling and rough-hewn personality and administrative style. Born in Kansas in 1882 and raised in the frontier atmosphere of the Oklahoma Territory, Johnson graduated from West Point in 1903 and spent ten years as a cavalry officer in the peacetime army. Bored with outpost duty, he eagerly accepted the army's offer to attend law school after a taste of experience in defending soldiers before courts-martial. Johnson received a law degree from the University of California in 1916 and entered the Office of the Judge Advocate in Washington after a brief interlude of excitement, pursuing Pancho Villa with the Pershing Expedition in Mexico.[34]

His subsequent career in the army was entirely administrative, and brought him into contact with the nation's leading industrialists. Johnson's first assignment after the United States entered World War I was to organize the machinery of the Selective Service System. He then became the army's representative on the War Industries Board headed by Bernard Baruch. This experience in regimenting industry as if it were an infantry platoon profoundly shaped both his corporatist views and his approach to administration. It also led him to a later flirtation with the corporate state theories that underlay Italian fascism, reflected in Johnson's invocation of the "shining name" of Mussolini in his farewell speech in leaving the NRA. After his resignation from the army in 1919 as a brigadier general, Johnson spent "seven years of unrelieved hell and disappointment" as general counsel of the ailing Moline Plow Company in Illinois, directed by his WIB associate George Peek. He left in 1927 to assist Baruch by coordinating studies of industrial technology and organization on projects in which Baruch had a financial interest.[35]

Johnson's role as Baruch's subaltern led to his appointment to the NRA. But an agency created from scratch and invested with regulatory control over some three million large and small businesses could not run on bluster and blarney. Baruch had recommended Johnson, but he harbored misgivings about him, which he relayed to Roosevelt through Frances Perkins: "I think he's a good number-three man, maybe a number-two man, but he's not a number-one man. He's dangerous and unstable. He gets nervous and sometimes goes away for days without notice. I'm fond of him, but do tell the President to be careful."[36] During his ill-fated year with the NRA, Johnson's behavior demonstrated the accuracy of this warning. Johnson had trouble dealing with subordinates, disappeared for days during his sporadic drinking binges, and his poorly concealed romance with his ambitious secretary, "Robbie" Robinson, created a minor scandal. He surrounded himself with aides recruited from his contacts in the army and the WIB, men who shared his shirt-sleeves practicality and disdain for procedural niceties. If the WIB represented corporatism in khaki, the NRA under Johnson functioned largely as the WIB in mufti.

Confronted with the massive task of drafting and negotiating hundreds of industrial codes, Johnson recognized that his choice of NRA general counsel required a tough-minded and politically astute lawyer. Since the codes would deal not only with regulation of business practices but with wage and hour and labor standards as well, Johnson looked for a lawyer who would complement his industrial background. Johnson's decision to reach outside his circle of cronies and to appoint Donald R. Richberg was one that brought to the NRA the distinctive style of the Legal Politician. Unacquainted before drafting of the NIRA began, the two men met after Johnson asked Raymond Moley to recommend an experienced labor lawyer. Johnson later wrote that Moley described Richberg to him as "a subtle and astute lawyer reputed to be a progressive on the radical side. . . ."[37]

Moley's thumbnail sketch of Richberg was accurate in all but one respect. A seasoned labor lawyer and a veteran of the progressive movement, Richberg was far from radical. He was, in fact, a convinced corporatist both in his politics and legal philosophy. Descended from German Lutheran immigrants, and the son of a prominent Chicago lawyer, Richberg was born in 1881 (a year before Johnson) and graduated from the University of Chicago before he entered Harvard Law School. After graduation from Harvard in 1904 he returned to Chicago and practiced law with his father in a firm later joined by Harold Ickes, who joined the New Deal as Roosevelt's Secretary of the Interior. Like Jerome Frank, his AAA counterpart, Richberg dabbled in the Chicago literary scene and was active in reform politics. Beginning in 1912 he devoted himself to the Bull Moose movement which followed Theodore Roosevelt into the Progressive Party after the Republicans forced out their moderate wing. Richberg became dedicated to Senator Robert LaFollette, who assumed leadership of the Progressive Party after Roosevelt's death in 1919, and chaired the resolutions committee at the Party's 1924 convention.

Richberg became widely known as a labor lawyer during the 1920s. In 1922, he challenged a federal anti-strike injunction on behalf of the railway unions, and for the next decade his practice centered on railway labor law.

28

He was the chief author of the Railway Labor Act of 1926, credited with maintaining peace between management and labor in a traditionally strike-ridden industry, and between 1926 and 1933 Richberg served as general counsel of the Railway Labor Executives Association. Richberg also successfully defended the Railway Labor Act before the Supreme Court in 1930 in the *Texas & New Orleans Railroad* case and helped draft the Norris-LaGuardia anti-injunction bill passed by Congress in 1932.[38]

This background led conservatives to label Richberg a dangerous radical, but the railway unions he represented were among the aristocracy of craft workers and Richberg had little sympathy for militant industrial unionists and unorganized workers. During the Depression he advocated the "social discipline" of labor as necessary to recovery and as an antidote to radical union leadership, and after his NRA experience he argued that "strikes ought to be outlawed" when labor strife threatened economic stability.[39] Richberg believed in the inevitability and necessity of "a government of business—that is, an intentional, orderly control of industrial processes" through a structure jointly controlled by government and industry. He linked corporatism to constitutional doctrine through the notion that property rights in corporate society implied "a servitude to the nation" and that "constitutional guarantees of liberty can only be made good by laws imposing restraints upon the anarchy of unregulated individual action."[40] A corollary of the need for centralized industrial control was a recognition that "bigness" was beneficial not only for business but for government and labor as well. Richberg criticized those Brandeisians who sought "political restriction of the advantages of bigness" through antitrust enforcement, and considered "the vigorous assertion of a centralized executive authority" essential to industrial regulation.[41]

Richberg's role in the NRA as a Legal Politician reflected the amalgam of his personal style and ambitions and his approach to the political setting within which the agency operated. He relished the access to the White House afforded by his position, and parlayed his relationship with Roosevelt into an unofficial post as "Assistant President" by assuming a succession of wide-ranging administrative responsibilities. Richberg basked in the press attention lavished on him, which included stories describing him as "the second most important man in Washington" and catapulted him in 1934 onto the cover of *Time*.[42] His skills as a political lawyer enabled him to mix conciliation and coercion in the difficult task of mediating conflicts between antagonistic industrial groups seeking advantages in the NRA codes. But politics is a precarious profession, and Richberg's intense ambition threw him into a cauldron with equally ambitious contenders for influence. Within the NRA, Richberg found the traditionally subordinate role as general counsel constraining and clashed with Johnson for control of the agency. The two men agreed on most policy issues, but Richberg's challenge to Johnson's authority created friction between the two strong-willed and stubborn men. Johnson's increasing suspicions that Richberg was masterminding a plot to undermine his authority eventually became a self-fulfilling prophecy; as Johnson's paranoia mounted, his attention to the day-to-day problems of the NRA declined. Deprived of effective leadership, the NRA became an administrative shambles and Johnson was finally forced in the fall of 1934 to resign in favor of a stopgap regency. At the same time, however, jealous members of Roosevelt's staff resented Richberg's White House influence and the putative "Assistant President" found himself increasingly excluded from the Oval Office.[43]

At the inception of the NRA, the personal and administrative problems that would later cripple the agency's effectiveness were secondary to the task of drafting codes of fair competition for hundreds of industries employing more than twenty-two million workers. This job required lawyers in quantity, to preside at code hearings and to check the lengthy and detailed draft codes for compliance with the purposes of the statute. Concerned more with basic policy questions and absorbed in his White House duties, Richberg had little interest in the minutiae of code drafting and willingly delegated this "nightmare" to Blackwell Smith. Twenty-nine years old when Richberg "turned over to him with a great sigh of relief all the oppressing details" of administering the NRA Legal Division, "Blacky" Smith was a New Mexico native and 1929 graduate of Columbia Law School who came to Washington after four years with a leading Wall Street law firm. Richberg considered Smith "an exceptionally able young lawyer with a great talent for the organization and management of a large law office," and under Smith's direction as assistant general counsel the number of NRA lawyers grew from an initial complement of forty to an ultimate total of more than four hundred.[44]

Despite his comparative youth and Ivy League legal training, Smith leaned toward older, experienced lawyers for responsible NRA posts. In contrast to their younger, Ivy League, and liberal counterparts in the AAA and NLRB, the NRA lawyers whom Smith recruited more often had prior business and political experience. Those who headed sections in the Legal Division came from such states as Oregon, Kansas, and Minnesota, and attended such law schools as Stetson, Denver, and Northwestern. Jack Levin, a Northwestern graduate who headed the Legal Research section, owned an engineering company before joining the NRA; Alexander McKnight, Director of Litigation, was a 55-year-old former bank director and city alderman from Duluth, Minnesota; and Jack Scott, Smith's chief assistant, had represented transportation employers in Denver. Only one section chief was an Ivy League law school graduate, and only one was under thirty years old. Lawyers with such backgrounds were compatible in outlook and experience with the businessmen with whom they dealt in code drafting and enforcement.

The initial problem that faced Johnson and the NRA staff was that of defining priorities. With some four thousand trade associations representing industries ranging in size from iron and steel to powder puffs, and with each trade group entitled to apply for a code, the impossibility of proceeding on a first-come-first-served basis was manifest. Johnson decided "to get the ten big industries—those comprising the bulk of employment—in first."[45] This strategy had the obvious advantage of working out pace-setting agreements with the industrial giants that would serve as models for smaller groups. It held the potential disadvantage, however, of throwing the overworked and inexperienced NRA lawyers up against the cream of the corporate bar, determined to write into the codes every anticompetitive trade practice previously denied them by antitrust law. As a political strategy, this approach carried considerable risks. But Johnson's confidence in his negotiating skills and business acumen was immense.

Hoping to set an atmosphere of activism at the outset, Johnson began code negotiations with the cotton textile industry even before the NRA was formally established, on the initiative of the industry. His eagerness was prompted by the size of the industry (which employed more than a quarter-million workers), the intense competition that led to serious overproduction and depressed wages, and the child labor practices which liberals had denounced and fought unsuccessfully for decades to outlaw. The almost feudal conditions in the textile industry made it a convenient target for reform through the code-drafting process. Johnson's zeal proved dangerous, however, as the industry (after a stage-managed show of reluctance) willingly traded abolition of child labor for code provisions permitting direct restriction of production and price-setting features that favored large producers.[46] After negotiations conducted in the spotlight of press attention, Johnson proudly announced the textile code as "a high mark in the economic history of our country." When he signed the code at a White House ceremony on July 9, Roosevelt stressed the abolition of the "ancient atrocity" of child labor and commended the NRA for allowing "employers to do by agreement that which none of them could do separately and live in competition."[47] But the NRA paid a high price for the largely symbolic victory in ending child labor, by opening the door for anticompetitive practices and setting a precedent for code domination by industrial leaders.

Johnson's determination to follow this initial agreement by concluding code negotiations with the other members of the "Big Six" industries— coal, petroleum, iron and steel, automobiles, and lumber—encountered formidable resistance, particularly over industry intransigence toward union recognition and the labor provisions mandated by Section 7(a) of the NIRA. Henry Ford doggedly refused to sign the automobile code, and auto industry objection to Section 7(a) finally forced Roosevelt to back down from the clear language of the NIRA and to approve a "merit clause" in the auto code that exposed union activists to dismissal on trumped-up charges of inefficiency or absenteeism. Roosevelt was also forced to intervene in negotiations over the bituminous coal code, after bloody strikes broke out in the Appalachian coal fields when employers balked at union recognition. It took another locked-door session in the White House before the coal industry agreed to the last of the "Big Six" codes on September 18, at the cost of explicit price-fixing provisions. It had been a hard three months for the overworked NRA staff: one man dropped dead during the coal negotiations and others collapsed during hearings.[48]

As code negotiations with the "Big Six" industries dragged out over more than three months, accompanied by a wave of strikes called by unorganized workers frustrated by the delay in setting wage and hour standards, the burden on the hastily recruited NRA lawyers and economists became almost intolerable. During July and August 1933, more than 600 draft codes deluged the NRA offices scattered through the massive Commerce Department building in Washington. The elaborate negotiations that preceded the textile code were rapidly replaced by perfunctory sessions as codes were approved in assembly-line haste. Milton Katz, then a 26-year-old Harvard Law School graduate, recalled that he arrived to begin work in Washington straight from his honeymoon. Before he could unpack and report to his office, Richberg called Katz late at night and told him to proceed directly to the White House. When Katz arrived, Richberg informed him that Roosevelt intended to announce the signing of a petroleum industry code at 10 the next morning, and that a code must be produced by 8 a.m. Richberg ignored the protest that Katz knew nothing about the oil industry, and unceremoniously ushered him into a conference room to face a score of industry lawyers.[49] Not surprisingly, the petroleum code that Roosevelt signed reflected the industry's views, as did most of the 1003 codes eventually approved.

The problem created by the sheer number of codes to be processed was compounded by the complexity of the business practices subject to regulation. A Brookings Institution study of the NRA in 1935 noted that "a conservative estimate of the number and variety of trade actions which were brought under some kind of regulation by the NRA would place the number at a thousand."[50] They fell under such general headings as price regulation, production limitation, advertising, bidding, discounts, and credit terms, but no two industries presented identical problems. With industries as disparate as Railway Car Building and Ice Cream Cones seeking code coverage, each negotiation dealt with a unique set of trade practices; regional differences, conflict between large and small competitors, and product definitions and standards additionally complicated the process. Industry lawyers, as the Brookings study acknowledged, "were practically invited to find out what they could secure with the trust laws held in abeyance."[51] In most cases, the match between trade association lawyers and their NRA counterparts produced an unequal contest.

Business domination of the code-drafting process led to numerous anticompetitive code provisions that favored large over smaller producers. Only a few codes, including those for the lumber, cleaning and dyeing, and coal industries, permitted direct price-fixing, but almost four hundred codes prohibited "sales below cost," an elusive concept designed to achieve the same price-setting end. Another anticompetitive device, adopted in 444 codes, was the "open-price" system intended to stabilize prices and inhibit competition. Over one hundred codes permitted limitation of machine or plant operating time or, as in the textile industry, outright limits on productive capacity.[52] In accepting such code provisions, NRA lawyers unwittingly sowed the seeds for a future crop of legal problems, which they reaped in thousands of formal complaints and hundreds of lawsuits. Smaller businesses, squeezed by these provisions, were forced in the struggle for survival to risk prosecution for price-cutting violations or to file suit against NRA enforcement.

The strike wave that erupted during the summer of 1933 added pressure on NRA lawyers whose energies were devoted to negotiation of the "Big Six" industrial codes. Workers in smaller industries and the distribution and retail trades in particular were frustrated by the delay in providing them with the wage and hour standards mandated by the NIRA. They had little interest in the trade practices with which their employers were concerned, but were adamant in demanding the higher wages and shorter hours provided by the widely publicized code agreements in the major industries. Sensitive to the political implications of the strike wave and the growing public impatience with the slow pace of the NRA code negotiations, Johnson eagerly accepted Bernard Baruch's suggestion that employers sign a short form accepting general standards of wages and hours. "In certainly a majority of trades," Baruch said, "the same rule for wages and hours is applicable. The quickest method is to bring the uniform cases to swift action by a blanket rule and then to deal with the exceptions."[53]

The resulting program, which perfectly fit Johnson's penchant for ballyhoo and banners, was based on the twin symbols of the President's Reemployment Agreement and the Blue Eagle emblem. Envisioned as a "voluntary" contract between employers and the President, the PRA functioned as a "blanket code" providing only for temporary wage and hour standards. Roosevelt quickly endorsed the plan. In a nationwide Fireside Chat on July 24, he appealed to employers to agree to "a universal limitation of hours of work per week for any individual by common consent, and a universal payment of wages above a minimum, also by common consent."[54] Employers were asked to pledge that until December 31, 1933, or the prior adoption of a code covering their industry, they would abide by the following conditions: a maximum ·work week of 35 hours for industrial workers or 40 hours for clerical and other white-collar workers; minimum wages of 40 cents per hour for industrial workers, and wages ranging from $12 to $15 per week for white-collar workers, depending on town and city size (with the highest level in cities over 500,000); and prohibition of employment of children under sixteen.[55]

Employer acceptance of the PRA was symbolized by the ubiquitous poster displayed in store windows that carried the Blue Eagle emblem over the legend "We Do Our Part."Johnson deliberately drummed up a wartime psychology behind the Blue Eagle as he embarked on a national tour complete with motorcades and brass bands. He urged housewives in St. Louis to "go over the top to as great a victory as the Argonne," and the Blue Eagle campaign culminated in a massive ticker-tape parade down New York's Fifth Avenue in September that drew a crowd of close to two million.[56] The PRA was not only a popular but an economic success, at least as a stop-gap measure. More than two million employers signed the blanket code, and the NRA claimed that it covered 96 percent of all workers and that it increased employment by almost three million and purchasing power by $3 billion.[57]

However, the initial flush of enthusiasm for the PRA faded well before the end of 1933. It succeeded in blunting the summertime strike wave, but the economic expansion stimulated by the PRA soon evaporated. Blackwell Smith considered the PRA counterproductive in the long run: "The pressure was on for every employer in the country to beat the code by getting out as much goods as he could under the PRA before he got under an enforceable code."[58] An equally serious problem, from the perspective of NRA lawyers, was that the PRA was legally unenforceable. It had been adopted without public hearings, and the only sanction behind it was the force of public opinion. Many consumers did heed Johnson's call to boycott stores and businesses that did not display the Blue Eagle poster, but cynical employers often carried the poster while they violated the PRA agreements. Unable to seek judicial enforcement of the PRA, Smith and his NRA lawyers were helpless to stem the growing tide of violations. Only after they completed the grueling and drawn-out process of extending code coverage to each industry could the NRA lawyers replace public opinion with the more potent weapon of litigation.

Chapter Two

THE BLUE EAGLE IN COURT

I. The "Machiavellian" Approach to Enforcement

Blackwell Smith and the NRA lawyers who worked under his day-to-day supervision in the Legal Division took their cues about code enforcement from Hugh Johnson and Donald Richberg. Neither the Administrator nor the General Counsel had any enthusiasm for litigation as an enforcement policy, preferring instead jaw-boning with recalcitrant businessmen and the application of political pressure through the press and through appeals to patriotism. Despite his legal training (and perhaps because of his disastrous experience with the Moline Plow Company), Johnson had a deep-seated contempt for lawyers and litigation. At one point during an NIRA drafting session, when the lawyers seemed to him to be raising quibbling points about legal procedure, Johnson burst out in frustration that "this law stuff doesn't matter."[1]

Johnson's aversion to litigation was reflected during the early months of the NRA by an emphasis on direct negotiation with businessmen charged with code violations. During the agency's first three months of operation, between June and September 1933, NRA lawyers were largely occupied with the arduous task of code drafting. Given the small number of formal codes approved during these months, the volume of complaints of code violation was correspondingly small. Promulgation of the President's Reemployment Agreement in July was quickly followed by a spate of complaints of wage and hour violations, but NRA lawyers were reluctant to test the legality of this "voluntary" contract in court. Johnson made a point at this early stage of his non-litigious approach to enforcement. "We have tried not to take any action that could be brought into court," he boasted at a September meeting of the cabinet-level committee charged with NRA oversight. In return, he was praised by Assistant Attorney General Harold Stephens, who headed the Justice Department's Antitrust Division that handled most of the government's civil litigation, for having been "exceedingly successful in keeping out of court."[2] During the same week, a leading legal periodical observed that "there appears to be some hesitancy" by the NRA "to invoke any legal remedies in furthering the recovery program," but added that "the force of public opinion will continue to be the most effective method of code enforcement" and called removal of the Blue Eagle "a most effective extra-legal weapon" against violators.[3]

Only a month later, however, the same journal reported an increasing breakdown of code enforcement and suggested "the need of a strong enforcement agency to police codes."[4] The volume of code violation complaints had swelled dramatically in that short time, especially in charges brought by trade associations of retail and service trade price-cutting. The NRA responded in October 1933 by establishing a Compliance Division, which was separate from the Legal Division and was staffed in the NRA regional and state offices. Voluntary compliance became less and less effective as the months passed, and removal of the Blue Eagle increasingly failed to deter code violators. By the end of 1933, in fact, the Compliance Division was swamped by a backlog of some ten thousand code violation complaints.

Richberg and Smith gave literally no thought to the prospect of litigation during the NRA's first six months. They were finally stung into action in December 1933 by an unexpected decision in a case in which the NRA was a bystander and of which it was totally unaware. A national Cleaning and Dyeing Industry code became effective in late October of 1933. The highly competitive and marginal industry proved to be rife with price-cutting, and code violators proceeded with impunity. Competitors of one flagrant offender in St. Petersburg, Florida, brought suit in November in federal district court, seeking a restraining injunction against Samuel Bazemore and alleging that he provided dry-cleaning below code prices and required his employees to work 60 hours per week rather than the code maximum of 48 hours. The case was heard by Judge Alexander Akerman, who denied the motion to enjoin Bazemore, correctly holding that his competitors lacked standing under the NIRA to bring suit and that only the Justice Department could do so. Unfortunately for the NRA, however, Judge Akerman had no sympathy for the New Deal. In addition to dismissing the suit because the plaintiffs lacked standing, Akerman added a gratuitous denunciation of the NIRA as an unconstitutional encroachment on the powers of the states. Citing the concession that Bazemore was engaged solely in intrastate commerce, he wrote that "it would require a stretch of the imagination beyond the power of this court to conceive that a local industry engaged in the pressing, cleaning, and dyeing of clothes was engaged in interstate commerce."[5]

Although NRA lawyers had no forewarning of the *Bazemore* case, they reacted defensively to widespread press reports that the NIRA had been declared unconstitutional and to criticism that they were ignoring the growing wave of code violations. Richberg issued a press release calling Judge Akerman's ruling "*dictum*" which "carries with it no judicial authority," adding that the constitutionality of the NIRA "will not be decided in the newspapers, and it will not be determined by the incidental decisions of the inferior federal courts, or by the casual opinions of judges who have the primary duty of enforcing, and not of nullifying laws."[6] Blackwell Smith echoed Richberg, in a speech delivered in Florida a week after the decision, criticizing Judge Akerman's comments on constitutionality "as a mere statement of what the lawyers love to call *obiter dictum*."[7]

The decision in the first NRA case to reach the courts was more embarrassing than legally damaging, since Richberg and Smith were on solid ground in labeling Judge Akerman's fulminations as dictum that carried no precedential weight. But this was a lawyer's answer, and missed the central point that the public and press suspected that the NRA lacked enthusiasm for vigorous code enforcement. Smith agreed that "we were getting out of control" in dealing with the backlog of code violation complaints.[8] He and Richberg quickly initiated two steps designed to make the enforcement problem more manageable. The first was to eliminate the source of the bulk of complaints by cutting back the scope of NRA code coverage. At the suggestion of his assistant, Milton Katz, Smith met with Felix Frankfurter at Harvard Law School to seek advice. When Smith told him there were over ten thousand compliance cases pending, Frankfurter recommended that the NRA lift code coverage from small employers, arguing that code enforcement across the board would be too costly and would produce endless litigation.[9] It took several months before Frankfurter's advice was heeded. In May 1934, President Roosevelt issued an Executive Order freeing service industries not operating in interstate commerce from all code provisions except those regulating wages and hours and the labor guarantees in Section 7(a).[10] Three months later, the NRA exempted all retail and service businesses in towns with populations under 2,500 from the wage and hour and pricing provisions of the codes.[11] By this time, however, the damage was done and the NRA lawyers were buried in unwelcome litigation.

The second enforcement step undertaken by Richberg and Smith responded to the intense pressure from within and outside the NRA to adopt an aggressive litigation policy. In late March 1934, Richberg established a Litigation Division headed first by Jack Scott, an experienced trial lawyer from Colorado, and later by A. G. McKnight. Two weeks later, on April 9, Smith assumed a new title as Director of Enforcement, with general responsibility over both compliance and litigation. The NRA lawyers assigned to the job of taking code violators to court began their task buoyed with optimism. Their encouragement came from an unlikely source, the United States Supreme Court. The legal community and the press had speculated for almost a year after Roosevelt's inauguration as to which way the Court would swing on New Deal cases. The first hints of its sentiments came early in 1934 in two cases that involved state legislation modeled on New Deal statutes.

NRA lawyers were first encouraged to believe that the Supreme Court would look on their statute with sympathy in a case decided in January 1934. In *Home Building and Loan Association v. Blaisdell*, the Court upheld a Minnesota statute extending the time during which home and farm owners could redeem their mortgages, and which was similar in intent to the federal Emergency Farm Mortgage Act. In affirming the "emergency" doctrine fashioned during World War I, the Court used language applicable to the "national emergency" proclaimed in the NIRA's Declaration of Policy. "While emergency does not create power, emergency may furnish the occasion for the exercise of power," the Court wrote in upholding the statute against a challenge based on the property interest protected by the due process clause of the Fourteenth Amendment.[12] NRA lawyers were even more heartened by the Supreme Court's decision in early March in *Nebbia v. New York*, broadly upholding against due process challenge the power of states to set retail prices.[13] Although the case dealt with a state and not a federal law, the fact that the New York milk pricing statute was explicitly based on the NIRA example seemed significant. One legal periodical hailed *Nebbia* as a boon for the NRA, writing that it "practically forecloses any question" of the NIRA's validity "in so far as any question of due process, interference with liberty of contract, or deprivation of private property is concerned."[14] NRA lawyers were predictably pleased; Jack Levin of the Legal Research section concluded that the Supreme Court had made "the legislative will supreme" and that consequently "the problem of remedial legislation rests wholly with the legislatures."[15] In the general euphoria, the fact that the due process clause did not control the commerce clause was overlooked.

These indications that the Supreme Court recognized the exigencies of the Depression prompted the NRA lawyers to map an aggressive litigation campaign. The first priority was to select appropriate targets for enforcement from a crowded complaint docket. Although Blackwell Smith was empowered by his position as Director of Enforcement to make litigation decisions, he was constrained by both internal and external political considerations. On one hand, lawyers on his staff stressed the need to avoid a scatter-shot attack on the small businesses whose price-cutting and wage and hour violations were simple to prove but largely a reaction to the inequities of the codes. "It seems unfortunate," A. G. McKnight of the Litigation Division wrote to Smith in April 1934, "that we are getting after small cleaner and dyer violators and failing to go after the big fellows."[16] Adding to this pressure was the publicity given in May to the

155-page report of the National Recovery Review Board, a five-member body whose establishment Hugh Johnson welcomed as an alternative to a full-dress Senate investigation of complaints that the NRA had ignored its statutory mandate that codes not "oppress small enterprises." Johnson had not counted on the populist sentiments of Clarence Darrow, whose appointment to chair the Board Johnson had approved on Richberg's recommendation. Darrow's report to Roosevelt that small businesses were "cruelly oppressed" under the NRA codes rankled Johnson, as did the unwelcome front-page publicity given to the report.[17]

The other problem that Smith faced was that the top positions in the NRA, both administrative and advisory, were dominated by big businessmen such as Gerard Swope of General Electric, Walter Teagle of Standard Oil, and Alfred Sloan of General Motors. Not only did these men and their business allies control the NRA, but the codes covering the giant industries had been drafted to their prescriptions and, consequently, violations were more prevalent among their smaller and hard-pressed competitors. As a result, with the exception of Section 7(a) violations whose enforcement had been delegated to a separate National Labor Board, big business was underrepresented among the potential litigation targets.

The litigation strategy that Smith adopted took into account these conflicting pressures, opting for a combination of small targets and maximum publicity designed to deter by example. Smith outlined his strategy in a bluntly worded but revealing memorandum circulated to his staff in April 1934: "Objective: Results; Methods in General: Machiavellian—the end justifies the means (almost)." The means Smith proposed to implement his enforcement plan, he wrote, were based on a combination of "threat and persuasion" and "tricks" designed to "bring to swift justice locally well known chisellers. . . ."[18] In choosing cases to fit into his strategy, Smith sought advice from an experienced political tactician, Franklin D. Roosevelt. During the critical period of late 1934, Smith met weekly with Roosevelt in the White House to review NRA cases. The President looked at each case in detail: "Now how about this case in South Carolina? That seems pretty serious to me; what should we do about them? Should we impose a code on them, or shall we take them to court, or what should we do?"[19]

The Machiavellian strategy chosen by the Legal Politicians in the NRA demanded, to be successful, a coherent and well-plotted battle plan. They moved, instead, from one skirmish to another, hampered by internal conflict with the Justice Department and by determined resistance from a largely hostile federal judiciary. In the end, they ignored the advice of their master strategist, Machiavelli: "Skirmishing can achieve good results as well as bad ones . . . [I]f you fail to gain the upper hand in these skirmishes, however, your troops may be afraid to face the enemy. If a commander is forced to skirmish, he must do so only when he has such an advantage that he is not likely to be defeated."[20]

II. LEGAL IMPERIALISM V. LEGAL BALKANIZATION

The first skirmish fought by the NRA Litigation Division began the same day Blackwell Smith was appointed Director of Enforcement and circulated his strategy memorandum. The enemy, however, was on his own side of the lines. Congress had provided in the NIRA that code violators brought to court would be prosecuted by federal district attorneys "under the direction of the Attorney General." In the handful of NRA cases that arose before April 1934, this provision had been loosely interpreted, and local U.S. attorneys, generally unfamiliar with the statute and the details of NRA codes, had been willing to permit NRA lawyers to handle both preparation and courtroom arguments. But NRA lawyers had barely begun sifting through the complaint docket when the Justice Department abruptly moved to strip them of authority to appear in court. In a letter to Hugh Johnson on April 9, 1934, Attorney General Homer Cummings directed that Justice Department lawyers would "assume full responsibility for the institution and prosecution of litigation." Cummings simultaneously withdrew the permission to appear in court previously granted to NRA lawyers deputized as Special Assistants to the Attorney General. The edict was tactfully phrased, but Cummings made clear that NRA lawyers could only "assemble the facts and law" in cases selected for prosecution, although he added that such preparation "will be welcomed by this department and its district attorneys." The reason advanced was simply that "divided responsibility" between the two agencies "is not advisable for either of the departments concerned."[21]

Although the directive came as a shock to Smith and his staff, the Justice Department move was not directed solely at the NRA, for lawyers in the Agricultural Adjustment Administration were served with an identical order. The timing of the letters reflected the fact that both agencies, faced with a breakdown of compliance, had abandoned non-coercive enforcement methods and had established litigation sections at almost the same time. Confronted with the imminent prospect of substantial litigation, the Justice Department decided to impose on the emergency agencies the litigation control that it had won from the cabinet departments in June 1933. Cummings had made no secret of his designs; he had warned Johnson that same month that he would "reserve the right at any time to say that if the legal staff of the Administrator went too far they would get in trouble" with the Department.[22]

Despite the fact that they had handled relatively few cases up to that point, NRA lawyers (and those in the AAA as well) had in fact gone too far to suit the cautious litigation outlook of the Justice Department. Assistant Attorney General Harold Stephens explained later in 1934 to a congressional committee that NRA and AAA lawyers "had an enthusiasm and a zeal for their statutes which sometimes went beyond the bounds of the Department of Justice attitude toward law enforcement."[23] Since zeal and enthusiasm are qualities generally sought in litigators, there was a somewhat disingenuous note to Stephens' remark. His unexpressed concern, which became explicit as the first NRA test case neared the Supreme Court, was rooted in the profound antagonism of the Antitrust Division lawyers toward the basic conception of the NRA. Both from ideological conviction and from resentment that suspension of the antitrust laws had dried up their case load, Justice Department lawyers were eager to reclaim their prerogatives. Stephens had solicited comments from Antitrust Division lawyers on the NIRA shortly after its passage, and most had responded with reservations about its constitutionality, not so much because of its antitrust features (which they recognized were within the power of Congress to suspend) but because the NIRA stretched the reach of the commerce clause far beyond the limits set by the Supreme Court.[24]

A more basic motivation, however, lay behind the assertion of Justice Department litigation control. Since its establishment in 1870, the Department had fought a back-and-forth battle with the cabinet departments and independent agencies for control of federal litigation.[25] In essence, the argument revolved around the respective merits of centralization and expertise; the Justice Department would claim that the government must speak in court with one voice and with the Attorney General as the official best suited to screen out discordance, while the agencies countered that their lawyers best understood the statutes and the details of their cases. Translating these terms into the political idiom, the conflict represented the fears on either side of legal imperialism as opposed to legal Balkanization. And in a practical sense, the fact that Blackwell Smith's Litigation Division contained over one hundred lawyers while Stephens' Antritrust Division had only fifteen helps to explain the Department's move.

Like many edicts from headquarters, the policy announced by Cummings had less effect in the scattered federal districts than it did in Washington. Local U.S. attorneys, who most often had an independent political base and a tenuous institutional loyalty to the Justice Department, continued to permit NRA lawyers to appear in court and argue cases. So many of them ignored the order, in fact, that in December 1934 G. Stanleigh Arnold of the Attorney General's staff requested that Harold Stephens "ask Blackwell Smith to send a letter to his Division, calling attention to the fact that there is considerable bootlegging into the presentation of NRA cases . . . and insisting that the rule requiring'' the personal approval of the Attorney General for all NRA involvement in litigation "be strictly observed."[26] Stephens sent an admonitory letter to Smith, and added in a memorandum to Cummings that "in the large I have not had confidence in the type of lawyers connected with the Litigation Division of the N.R.A. and should not want them indiscriminately sent out assisting our District Attorneys."[27] In the legal trenches, however, where they faced a common foe in lawyers for alleged code violators, the policy against fraternization seemed illogical and wasteful to NRA and Justice Department lawyers, and orders from Washington were viewed with the same skepticism that privates show to generals.

In several cases considered important by NRA lawyers, heavy-handed intervention at the local level by Justice Department lawyers sent from Washington to displace them created acrimony. Justice Department handling of these cases was bitterly denounced by NRA lawyers, who considered it bungling at best and sabotage at worst. The most divisive of these cases was *Hart Coal Corp. v. Sparks*, which involved a challenge to the Bituminous Coal Code.[28] This code was negotiated against the backdrop of bloody struggle between the coal operators and the United Mine Workers of America. The industry was highly fragmented and prone to disastrous price-cutting wars, and to promote stability the code provided for direct price-fixing, which was anathema to the Justice Department. Several smaller producers in western Kentucky contested the wage and hour provisions of the code by bringing suit against the U.S. attorney in Kentucky, seeking a temporary injunction against its enforcement. Federal district Judge Charles I. Dawson, who would shortly resign his post to represent coal operators, granted the injunction in May 1934 and issued an opinion holding the NIRA unconstitutional on the ground that Congress had no power under the commerce clause to regulate manufacturing, and consequently no power to regulate wages and hours in such businesses.

Conflict between the NRA and Justice Department first arose during oral argument of the case. T. J. Sparks, the U. S. attorney and defendant in the case, asked the Justice Department for permission to allow an NRA lawyer to participate in the argument, but Harold Stephens rejected his request and sent Dwight L. Savage of his staff to argue on Sparks's behalf.[29] A. G. McKnight, who observed the argument for the NRA, reported that Savage, a career lawyer in the Department, "did not know even the most elementary things about the record and he actually stuttered when asked about the law. He had no fundamental grasp of the issues in a matter of this kind. Outside his notes he simply floundered." McKnight was suspicious of the Department's intentions in the case: "Feeling as bitterly as we do right now, it would look as though the Department has deliberately torpedoed the case. . . ."[30] This complaint, greatly expurgated, was conveyed to Stephens, who blandly replied that while "incidents of this sort are regrettable" they "will not disturb the pleasant relations" between the two agencies.[31]

Bad feelings continued during the next phase of the case, as the NRA pressed for a quick appeal of Judge Dawson's order granting the injunction against code enforcement. Irving J. Levy, the NRA supervising attorney responsible for the coal code, felt that the Justice Department was dragging its heels on the case and urged a prompt application for a stay of the order pending appeal. Levy informed the Litigation Division that coal operators who supported the code feared that "Judge Dawson's order will enable [non-complying] operators to again resume their intensive price-cutting," which would foster "chaotic conditions" in the industry. Others with a stake in the case shared Levy's concern; Philip Murray of the United Mine Workers appealed to Attorney General Cummings in June, a month after the injunction halted code enforcement. The Department's delay, he wrote, had led to widespread wage reductions and price slashing and had "a demoralizing effect upon the coal industry. . . ."[32]

Levy convinced Donald Richberg to take the NRA's case to the Attorney General. After a month passed with no action on the appeal, Richberg wrote Cummings that the NRA considered the *Hart Coal* case "exceptionally important" and said the decision that "coal mining does not affect interstate commerce cannot be allowed to stand unchallenged." The NRA had consistently urged that an appeal be taken, but "now we are informed that there is some doubt in your department as to whether any appeal should be taken." Richberg suggested that Cummings deputize "one of our experienced men with authority to proceed in accordance with our views." Otherwise, he warned, if "our views of law and procedure and those of the Department are so seriously in conflict" that code enforcement could not proceed, "I think you and I ought to have a clear understanding of this so that I can at least save the expense of maintaining a helpless division of litigation."[33]

Stung by the charges of procrastination from Murray and Richberg, the Justice Department hastened to prepare an appeal. Harold Stephens requested an opinion from Solicitor General J. Crawford Biggs, telling him that 11,000 miners stood to lose their jobs, that evidence in the record as to interstate commerce "is uncontroverted," and that an appeal would foster cooperation between the NRA and the Department.[34] Informed that both sides anticipated an eventual test case before the Supreme Court, Biggs quickly agreed that an appeal was warranted. Stephens, however, in apprising the Attorney General of the situation, complained that the

NRA "did not seem to appreciate the necessity for careful study" of a case which might reach the Supreme Court. He added that the Department "has been rather unduly pressed" by the NRA Litigation Division and said Richberg's charge that the Department had been dilatory was not based on "first-hand knowledge of the situation. . . ."[35] In notifying Richberg that an appeal had been authorized, Cummings took pains to remind him of his April order. Although the Department "in no way presumes to intrude upon the administrative conduct of matters prior to the inception of litigation," he wrote, the Department retained complete control once a case was filed, including decisions as to appeals.[36]

The NRA lawyers continued their criticism after the Department bowed to pressure and filed an appeal with the Sixth Circuit Court of Appeals, beginning with disparagement of the Department's first effort in drafting an appeal brief. Philip Buck of the Litigation Division wrote Stephens that "we do not regard that the brief adequately presents the arguments necessary to secure the granting" of the government's petition seeking vacation of the injunction preventing enforcement of the coal code. Buck's complaint was that the Justice Department brief "fails to discuss the factual situation presented by the record," and he suggested that Stephens substitute the "carefully prepared" NRA brief, which exhaustively detailed the impact of wage-cutting by local coal producers on national price levels and on the interstate coal market.[37] In the end, the two sides agreed on a brief limited to the questions of law raised by the injunction, supplemented by a voluminous NRA affidavit on the economics of the coal industry, asserting the need for uniform wage levels as a deterrent to price wars. Dwight Savage had more success in his second argument of the case, and the Court of Appeals in December 1934 vacated the injunction on the ground stressed by the Justice Department, that since the NRA had not moved to penalize any of the coal operators no "justiciable issue" was presented by the suit.[38]

Relations between NRA and Justice Department lawyers had been strained since the beginning of the litigation campaign in April 1934, largely as a result of the Cummings edict that shut NRA lawyers out of the courtroom. The progressive deterioration of inter-agency comity caused by differences over the *Hart Coal* case reached a critical point in mid-1934, as acrimony spilled over into disputes on other cases. William H. Griffin, the NRA lawyer in charge of litigating cases under the southern lumber code, repeatedly denounced Justice Department lawyers for raising "flimsy pretexts" in objecting to his aggressive code enforcement. Griffin particularly resented the Department's foot-dragging in a case in which he had promised a federal judge, in return for a prompt ruling in his favor, that he would expedite appeals from unfavorable rulings in two other districts. Embarrassed by the delays, Griffin finally vented his frustration by wiring the Litigation Division that "I specifically do not need any interference or dictation by any bungling young assistant from the Justice Department."[39] Other NRA lawyers encountered a growing resistance from U.S. attorneys after Harold Stephens reminded them of the Cummings order not to permit NRA lawyers to appear in court. A. G. McKnight of the Litigation Division complained to Richberg that the U.S. attorney in St. Louis refused "to enter any NRA cases for prosecution for the simple reason that he believes 'the G-- d--- law is unconstitutional anyway.' "[40]

Although the breakdown in cooperation came to affect every category of NRA litigation, the basic problem stemmed from Justice Department reluctance to file suits that involved NRA codes providing for outright price-fixing, as did both the bituminous coal and lumber codes. Anticipating further problems in the wake of the *Hart Coal* case, Blackwell Smith arranged a meeting with Cummings and several members of the Department's Antitrust Division early in July 1934, hoping to persuade the Attorney General that the NRA should be allowed to test its code provisions through litigation, regardless of antitrust objections. Congress had decided, Smith pointed out, to suspend the antitrust laws in NRA codes, and he appealed to Cummings to let the courts rule on their legality without Justice Department hindrance. Mastin White, the Department's leading antitrust specialist, reminded Smith that the NIRA prohibited "monopolistic" practices and cautioned that "the Attorney General might find himself in an embarrassing position if he sought to enforce clauses which under previous [Supreme Court] decisions would amount to an 'old fashioned monopoly.' " Cummings told Smith that he would go no farther than to promise that a case testing the constitutionality of price-fixing or production control provisions would be pressed "after our first successful appeal to the Supreme Court on issues of a less difficult nature."[41]

Smith's problem was that he had become so absorbed in his internal skirmishes with the Justice Department that he had given little thought to an overall battle plan. He had no coherent litigation strategy, had not thought ahead to the Supreme Court, had not begun to prepare any favorable test cases, and had simply floundered from one crisis to the next. Part of Smith's dilemma, of course, was self-made, the consequence of a political approach to litigation that sacrificed strategy to an unfocused attack on small-time "chisellers." The distracting and divisive conflict with the Justice Department compounded the dilemma. But an equally disruptive factor was the dismal record of NRA litigation in the lower federal courts, a record that left Smith with little choice in the selection of well-prepared and attractive constitutional test cases to bring to the Supreme Court.

III. Partisanship and Precedent

The momentous test cases in which the Supreme Court enunciates constitutional doctrines of enduring importance do not emerge newborn on the steps of the Court, contrary to the impression left by many constitutional historians. With few exceptions, lower federal courts must first decide the cases that become available to government lawyers (or to the lawyers who oppose them) for submission to the Supreme Court. The preliminary rulings of the district courts and courts of appeals significantly shape the process of choice. Which side wins in the lower courts, what issues are stressed in the opinions, what cases are cited as precedent, and the timing of the opinions are all factors that introduce elements of uncertainty and risk into the litigation process and affect the choice of Supreme Court test cases.

These factors are affected in turn by the related influences of partisanship and precedent, particularly in cases that involve statutes conferring on federal officials sweeping and untested regulatory powers, as did the NIRA. If the vast majority of the federal judiciary, the one branch of government most insulated from the shifting currents of political change, is antagonistic by virtue of its partisan and ideological cast to the social and economic policies of the administration in power, the government is more than likely to wind up as the losing party in potential test cases. When they later face the Supreme Court, government lawyers become saddled with lower-court opinions bristling with hostility and studded with citations to unfavorable precedent. In long-established areas of law, the principle of *stare decisis* (that if applicable precedent exists it should govern the outcome of analogous cases) can furnish lawyers with a secure precedential anchor. But in cases that require construction of broadly phrased constitutional provisions or the application of judge-made doctrine, precedent becomes a judicial tool, subject to discriminating citation and quotation. Judges presented with conflicting strands of precedent often display considerable dexterity in sifting through cases for those which best support their ideological predilections. Both precedent and partisanship help to explain why NRA lawyers emerged from the gauntlet of the lower courts with a limited and unenviable choice of Supreme Court test cases. With Republican judges in the majority in nine of eleven judicial circuits, both at the district court and appellate level, partisanship played an obvious role.[42] With these factors in mind, this section will examine the nineteen NIRA cases in which district court judges wrote opinions that addressed the constitutional issues raised by the statute.[43]

The most central of these issues, and the one on which each case turned, involved the provision of Article I of the Constitution, authorizing Congress to regulate ''commerce among the several states.'' In interpreting the reach of that clause, judges were faced with NRA codes that dealt in bewildering complexity with the varying trade practices of a thousand different industries. Available as precedent were cases divided into two separate strands of commerce clause doctrine, each susceptible of application to the NIRA cases. The expansive line of commerce clause cases began with the magisterial opinion of Chief Justice John Marshall in *Gibbons v. Ogden* in 1824, in which the power of Congress to regulate the coastal shipping trade was upheld against competing state claims. Marshall's depiction of the clause as comprehending "that commerce which concerns more states than one" excepted from its scope only those transactions "which are completely within a particular state, which do not affect other states, and with which it is not necessary to interfere, for the purpose of executing some of the general powers of the government."[44]

At the time Marshall laid the groundwork for the economic nationalism demanded by his Federalist ideology and later embraced by his New Deal descendants, only the most rudimentary outlines could be discerned of the transportation network and corporate structure on which an integrated national economy would be constructed. But within the next half-century, state boundaries became mere cartographic artifacts to the industrialists whose raw materials flowed from one state to another in the manufacturing process, and whose finished goods flowed back across those lines.

Close to a century of economic rapacity and big-business domination of the Supreme Court separated the premise first stated in *Gibbons v. Ogden* that those intrastate transactions which "affected" interstate commerce were subject to congressional regulation from the quartet of twentieth-century cases that offered a modern precedential basis for this argument. Each of these cases involved Progressive legislation designed to curb the power of monopolies. In *Swift v. United States*, decided in 1905, the Supreme Court enunciated the doctrine that transactions that formed part of a "current of commerce" among the states could be regulated by Congress if their effect "upon commerce among the states is not accidental, secondary, remote or merely probable."[45] The *Shreveport* case, decided in 1913, added the doctrine that if differences between state and federal regulation of the same industry operated "to the injury of interstate commerce" then " it is Congress, and not the State, that is entitled to prescribe the final and dominant rule. . . ."[46] The Court took a further step in 1922 in *Stafford v. Wallace* when it applied a "stream of commerce" theory to an industry—meat-packing in this case—whose processing of a product extended across state lines from production through consumption.[47] Finally, the Court held the next year in *Chicago Board of Trade v. Olsen* that Congress could regulate those practices which it found would create a "burden or obstruction" to interstate commerce, even if the business affected—the trading in grain futures in this case—did not deal directly with a commodity.[48]

New Deal lawyers naturally seized the expansive line of commerce clause cases as the foundation for their briefs and arguments in NIRA cases. The intellectual spark for this argument was ignited by Robert L. Stern, a 1932 Harvard Law School graduate who began his New Deal career with the Petroleum Administrative Board and who soon moved to the Solicitor General's office in the Justice Department. In a 1934 article in the *Harvard Law Review* entitled "That Commerce Which Concerns More States than One," which was widely circulated among NRA and Justice Department lawyers, Stern argued that it was "tremendously important" that courts move from a mechanical conception of commerce as the mere movement of goods to a dynamic conception that stressed the *effect* of localized practices and transactions on a nationally integrated economic system. "Congress has been obliged," Stern wrote, "in an effort to relieve the nation from the business depression, to exert its power over practices the effect of which upon the movement or potential movement of goods may be slight, although the detrimental effect of a practice in one state upon business in other states may be considerable."[49]

In a parallel line of Supreme Court decisions, however, the Marshallian concept of a seamless national economy had been significantly limited in a restrictive line of cases that drew a sharp line between commerce and manufacture. The two components of the economic process were first distinguished by Justice Lucius Lamar in 1888 in *Kidd v. Pearson*: "No distinction is more popular to the common mind or more clearly expressed in economic and political literature than that between manufactures and commerce. Manufacture is transformation—the fashioning of raw materials into a change of form for use." Commerce, according to Lamar, constituted simply the "buying and selling and the transportation" of goods that followed and were distinct from manufacture, and only that commerce which crossed state lines was subject to federal regulation.[50]

Seven years later, in his opinion in *United States v. E. C. Knight Co.*, Chief Justice Melville Fuller drew a second limiting distinction, when he distinguished the "direct" and "indirect" effects on interstate commerce of business transactions that involved both a manufacturing and distribution process. "Commerce succeeds to manufacture, and is not a part of it," Fuller wrote, extending Lamar's distinction to hold that federal regulation solely of the production component of the commercial process was unconstitutional.[51] Two additional cases in the restrictive line of Supreme Court precedent erected twin hurdles in the path of New Deal lawyers. In *Lochner v. New York*, the Court reached the apogee of the doctrine of substantive due process in holding in 1905 that a state statute limiting the hours of work of bakers to 60 per week interfered with the "liberty of contract" of the bakers and their employers.[52] Although *Lochner* did not raise any commerce clause question, it clearly pointed corporate lawyers to the due process clause of the Fifth Amendment as a weapon against the wage and hour regulations in the NRA codes. Finally, in *Hammer v. Dagenhart* the Court in 1918 struck down a federal child labor law, ending the brief judicial marriage of the commerce clause and the federal police power. Barring the products of low-paid child labor, Justice William Day wrote, was an unconstitutional extension of federal commerce clause powers. Congress could not "require the States to exercise their police powers so as to prevent unfair competition," Day stated.[53]

An almost insoluble conundrum faced the New Deal lawyers whose corporate opponents urged federal judges to embrace the restrictive line of precedent. In the first place, the business practices regulated by the NRA codes dealt most often with those aspects of the commercial process which could be defined as manufacturing. Additionally, those code provisions which regulated wages and hours fell between the stools of *Lochner* and *Hammer*. In joining the *Lochner* doctrine that the Fourteenth Amendment's due process clause barred state regulation of relations between workers and employers with the *Hammer* limitation of the police powers of the federal government, the restrictive line of cases created a "twilight zone" in which both the states and federal government were powerless to act. Edward S. Corwin stated the dilemma precisely in his 1934 book, *The Twilight of the Supreme Court*: " 'Dual Federalism' thus becomes *triple* federalism—inserted between the realm of the National Government and that of the states is one of no-government—a governmental vacuum, a political 'no-man's land.' "[54]

The use of these conflicting lines of precedent was graphically illustrated in a pair of NRA cases that involved essentially the same set of facts. Robert L. Stern, who represented the Petroleum Administrative Board, acted as a government lawyer in both of these cases. In *Victor v. Ickes*, a group of service station operators in Michigan sought to enjoin the Secretary of the Interior, who administered the NRA Petroleum Industry Code, from prosecuting them for giving out free jigsaw puzzles to promote the sale of gasoline. Judge Jesse Adkins, a progressive Republican member of the District of Columbia federal bench, noted from affidavits that the giving of premiums, which violated the code, was connected with price wars that were "so severe that sixteen distributors in Detroit were driven into bankruptcy" since adoption of the code. Rejecting the claim that the businesses were purely intrastate, Judge Adkins ruled that the giving of premiums "imposes a direct burden upon interstate commerce in petroleum products and substantially and unduly obstructs the free flow of such commerce between Michigan and other states. . . ." In support of this ruling, he cited all four of the expansive commerce clause cases discussed above. *Hammer v. Dagenhart*, the only restrictive case that Judge Adkins cited, was distinguished with the observation that the Supreme Court had not suggested that the manufacture of goods by child labor burdened or obstructed the free flow of interstate commerce.[55]

In the *United States v. Mills* case decided several months later, the only difference was that the premiums offered by the gas station operator were drinking glasses and dishes rather than puzzles. Judge William Chesnut, a Republican appointee of Herbert Hoover, rejected the arguments in Stern's brief after discussing them at length. The suggestion "that 'commerce among the states' properly understood" is not limited in concept to mere interstate movement of persons and things from one state into or through another, but "includes such activities within a state as 'affect' the commerce of other states," Judge Chesnut noted, was "a contention for a broader conception of the commerce clause than is generally understood." Conceding the power of Congress to regulate those commodities which moved, unchanged in form, in an uninterrupted "stream of commerce" from producer to consumer, Judge Chesnut looked at the "movement" of petroleum products and found that the gasoline had come to rest in Maryland between its purchase from the refiner and sale to the consumer. Few businesses could be found "more clearly involving only intrastate commerce than the business of local sales of gasoline from filling stations," he concluded. Having exhaustively examined Stern's argument, Judge Chesnut rejected the expansive line of precedent and rested on *Hammer* and *Kidd* for authority. Unlike his more dogmatic colleagues, Judge Chesnut expressed admiration for the NIRA as a "stimulating and encouraging appeal to the business interest of the country . . . to rescue themselves from the economic depression." But his duty was clear. Since the sale of gasoline did not directly burden interstate commerce, he was required by precedent to apply the "fundamental law of the land" and hold the Petroleum Code unconstitutional.[56]

Few of the district judges, on either side of the question, canvassed as thoughtfully as did Judges Adkins and Chesnut the conflicting conceptions of the commerce clause issue. For most it was a simple question, and their opinions were heavily rhetorical. As one judge in Missouri asked, how could "the sale of a bunch of shingles" at a lumberyard affect a national economy in which millions of such discrete transactions occurred daily? Under the expansive view proposed by government lawyers, he answered, "almost every sale made by any merchant in every city, town, and hamlet in the United States is a transaction in interstate commerce. The theory is supported neither by reason nor precedent."[57] But the ideological framework in which the question was posed generally determined the precedent chosen to support its answer. To illustrate, although seven of the eleven NIRA opinions which ruled against the government cited either *E. C. Knight* or *Kidd*, or both, none of the eight which favored the government cited either case. Troublesome precedent can be distinguished, but it can just as easily be ignored.

The commerce clause question occupied the center stage in the NRA litigation, and in each of the nineteen district court opinions the ruling on this issue decided the case. But in view of the later importance of the delegation of powers issue when the NRA codes reached the Supreme Court in the *Schechter* case, it seems puzzling in retrospect that only one of the eleven district judges who addressed the issue made a conclusive ruling on the issue against the government. Two expressed doubt that the NIRA met the test of the doctrine, and eight upheld the statute against a delegation doctrine challenge; eight judges bypassed the issue completely. Since most of these same judges showed little compunction in holding the NIRA unconstitutional on commerce clause grounds, their reluctance to throw a second punch at it seems odd. The answer lies in the total lack of Supreme Court precedent for such a negative ruling.

Delegation doctrine implicates the separation of powers at the heart of the constitutional structure, and applies generally to every statute in which legislative powers are delegated in varying measure to the President and executive officers who execute congressional policy. The question in the NIRA cases was whether Congress had laid down in the statute a sufficiently precise standard to guide the executive branch in formulating the NRA codes. Cases dealing with delegation were few in number, and government lawyers had precedent on their side in each of the four leading cases. In *Field v. Clark* in 1892, the Supreme Court upheld the power of the President to set import duties under the Tariff Act, which authorized him to prohibit the importation of foreign goods on a finding that American goods were discriminated against. In making such a finding, the Court wrote, the President "was the mere agent of the law-making department to ascertain and declare the event upon which its expressed will was to take effect."[58]

Buttfield v. Stranahan in 1904 upheld the delegation in the Tea Inspection Act to the Secretary of the Treasury of power to establish standards of tea purity.[59] *United States v. Grimaud*, decided in 1911, dealt with the power of the Secretary of Agriculture to make forestry conservation rules, and laid down as a criterion for delegation the notion that Congress may establish a general statutory standard and delegate to the executive the power to "fill up the details" by regulation.[60] And finally, in *Hampton v. United States*, the Court in 1928 upheld another tariff statute, establishing this basic standard: "If Congress shall lay down by legislative act an intelligible

51

principle to which the person or body authorized to fix such rates is directed to conform, such legislative action is not a forbidden delegation of legislative power."[61]

Given this array of precedent, it is easy to see why NRA lawyers were cocky in their confidence that delegation doctrine challenges would fail. A. G. McKnight predicted early in 1934 that "it would seem as though there would not be much danger of this particular point of attack being sustained."[62] But it takes little imagination to discriminate between statutes permitting officials to set tariff rates and standards of tea purity and one delegating to the President, as did the NIRA, virtually unlimited powers to set national levels of wages and hours and to regulate the trade practices of more than a thousand industries. All the NIRA required was a finding by the President, through a process left to his devising, that industrial codes "will tend to effectuate the policy" set out in the Declaration of Policy, itself phrased in the most general terms. It is a testimony to the pull of unanimous precedent on a conservative judiciary that judges almost uniformly resisted the temptation to drive a second nail into the coffin of the NIRA. As Judge John P. Barnes, who invoked the commerce clause to hold the NIRA unconstitutional in the *Suburban Motor Service* case, admitted grudgingly, "decisions which have held acts of Congress invalid because of violation of the principle are difficult or impossible to find."[63] He left little doubt that only one prior case would have satisfied his search for authority.

Only one district court opinion exposed the essential vulnerability of the NIRA to the attack later made in the *Schechter* case. In *Acme v. Besson*, Judge Guy L. Fake perceptively noted that the code-drafting process was initiated by industry members and savored of "special privilege." The NIRA, he wrote, "provides that industrial groups made up of individuals, holding no official position under the government and under no oath of office, may assemble and initiate legislation having binding effect upon" even non-assenting members of an industry. Such a system "furnished us at once with two separate and distinct governments . . . one under the authorized constitutional or civic system, and the other through the economic code and code authority system. . . ." Implicit in Judge Fake's opinion was his suspicion that the President did not in fact make independent "findings" when he approved the codes proposed by industry groups.[64]

The delegation doctrine was raised by lawyers challenging the NRA. Government lawyers, in contrast, seized upon the emergency doctrine as a powerful supplement to their more basic argument that Depression conditions required an expansive reading of the commerce clause. As the Justice Department instructed lawyers who handled NRA cases, the "so-called emergency argument really constitutes an integral part of the commerce point, and not a separate proposition. Its basis is that transactions which might not ordinarily substantially affect interstate commerce may do so when, in an economic emergency, factual conditions are changed so as to make the nation a closer and more interdependent economic unit."[65] NRA lawyers were even more certain that the emergency doctrine furnished them with a persuasive argument. "In the present emergency," A. G. McKnight told the Litigation Division staff, "the courts will hardly hesitate to sustain the action of Congress. The rule of self-preservation justifies every step thus far taken to save the nation from the doom that was so clearly impending prior to the adoption of the National Industrial Recovery Act."[66]

Not surprisingly, the emergency doctrine emerged from the shadowy interstices of the Constitution during periods of war. In the World War I case of *Wilson v. New*, the Supreme Court stated the doctrine broadly: "Although an emergency may not call into life a power which has never lived, nevertheless emergency may afford a reason for the assertion of a living power already enjoyed."[67] The reach of the doctrine to regulation of economic conditions was extended in *Block v. Hirsh*, another World War I case in which the Court upheld the constitutionality of rent control legislation.[68] The case which most encouraged NRA lawyers to believe that the Supreme Court would look with sympathy on their statute was *Home Building and Loan Association v. Blaisdell*, decided in January 1934. "While emergency does not create power, emergency may furnish the occasion for the exercise of power," the Court wrote in a reaffirmation of the doctrine.[69]

As an adjunct to the commerce clause argument, the emergency doctrine had limited success. Judge E. Marvin Underwood, a Georgia Democrat appointed by Hoover, quoted extensively in his opinion in *Richmond Hosiery Mills v. Camp* from affidavits showing that over-production threatened "general disaster" to the highly competitive hosiery industry and that workers were earning as little as six dollars per week for more than sixty hours of work. He bolstered this evidence with citation to *Blaisdell* in concluding that the national emergency declared by Congress "may also have the effect of rendering a transaction which in normal times would have only an indirect, incidental, and insignificant effect on interstate commerce, a matter of great moment and of powerful effect in times of great emergency."[70] And in *United States v. Canfield Lumber Co.*, Judge James A. Donohoe, a Democrat and recent Roosevelt appointee, rejected a due process challenge to the NIRA as "without merit because of the national emergency," which required that industry "must submit to reasonable regulations and control in the public interest," notwithstanding the intrastate nature of the business.[71]

However, NRA lawyers added nothing to their arsenal with the emergency doctrine argument. Slightly more than half of the district court judges, ten of the nineteen whose opinions were based on constitutional grounds, discussed the doctrine; the three who accepted it needed no urging to adopt the underlying commerce clause argument. Those judges who ruled against the government noted that NRA lawyers who quoted *Blaisdell* in their briefs did so out of context, ignoring the Supreme Court's admonition that emergency "does not create power . . . or remove or diminish the restrictions imposed upon power granted or reserved."[72] As one of the hostile judges wrote, the emergency doctrine "may not speak into life that which is dead or never was."[73] Another passionately anti-New Deal judge declared: "I cannot conceive of any emergency, especially in time of peace, which would authorize the Congress to ignore the Constitution and enact measures tending to regulate purely local business within the several states."[74] Several of the judges who rejected the emergency argument reached back to the emphatic words of the Supreme Court in 1866: "No doctrine, involving more pernicious consequences, was ever invented by the wit of man than that any [constitutional provision] can be suspended during any of the great exigencies of government. Such a doctrine leads directly to anarchy or despotism. . . ."[75] In the minds of these judges, quite plainly, the NIRA threatened a despotism as severe as that produced by the suspension of *habeas corpus* during the Civil War; economic devastation did not move them as justification for a doctrine that analogized the Depression to a wartime battlefield.

IV. SMALL-TOWN JUDGES AND SMALL-TOWN CASES

On paper, the NRA compiled an impressive enforcement record during its brief two years of operations. The 1,003 codes that covered industries both large and small generated some 43,641 formal complaints of trade practices violations, and additional thousands of complaints were filed alleging infractions of the PRA "blanket code" and the wage and hour standards of the industrial codes.[76] Only one percent of this flood of complaints ever reached the litigation stage of enforcement. Many turned out on investigation to be unsubstantiated, others were settled informally by the Compliance Division staff, and a smaller number produced a formal settlement by consent decree or through referral to the Federal Trade Commission. A huge number, in fact, simply dropped through the cracks of the bureaucratic process and were never resolved at all.

The record of the NRA Litigation Division looked equally impressive on paper. Within two months of its establishment in April 1934, its docket included 201 cases filed in 35 states, a figure that swelled to more than 600 cases in the following year. The majority of these cases died along with the agency when the Supreme Court imposed the death sentence on the NIRA in its *Schechter* decision in May 1935, but in those cases concluded before that time the NRA prevailed in 90 percent, most often through the pre-trial negotiation of a consent agreement with alleged code violators. Even in those cases decided by district court judges, largely on the government's application for a restraining injunction, more than two-thirds (42 of 60, according to an NRA tabulation prepared in March 1935) resulted in an NRA victory.[77]

But this paper record was deceptive. A more realistic assessment of the NRA's overall success in enforcement must take into account three related factors. The first stemmed from the disastrous impact on the NRA of Hugh Johnson's blustering style and personal instability, which by mid-1934 had created an administrative shambles. Donald Richberg, tiring of his bureaucratic struggles with Johnson and preoccupied with his duties as "Assistant President," left the NRA in June to become director of the cabinet-level National Emergency Council and was replaced as acting general counsel by Blackwell Smith. Congressional and press criticism finally forced Roosevelt to ease Johnson out of the NRA in September, replacing him first with an interim regency of Smith and NRA administrator George Lynch and then with a five-member National Industrial Recovery Board chaired by tobacco executive Clay Williams.[78] Essentially leaderless for most of its last year, the NRA resembled a beached whale and businessmen responded by ignoring the codes and engaging in wholesale violations that Smith's beleaguered legal staff was powerless to stem.

The second factor reflected Smith's slap-dash and political approach to litigation. With few exceptions, the NRA cases in which district judges ruled on the constitutionality of the NIRA involved attempts to impose on small businessmen regulation of practices historically left to the business proprietor: the setting of prices, levels of production, and wages and hours for employees. Only 2 of the 19 NRA cases decided on constitutional issues involved even medium-sized concerns; all but 5 dealt with gas stations, car dealerships, laundries and dry cleaners, and lumber yards. Most of the district judges who heard these cases were, before their appointment to the federal bench, lawyers in private practice whose clients operated the same kinds of businesses now regulated by codes imposed from Washington. A federal bench dominated by middle-aged, small-town, conservative Republicans was more than likely to sympathize with small businessmen who claimed that NRA regulation under codes dictated by their larger competitors forced them to choose between violation and bankruptcy. As Judge William H. Atwell put it, the defendant before him "was conducting a little filling station in Dallas, selling gasoline to be burned in Texas, and made out of oil found and refined in Texas." It was hardly surprising that a judge appointed to the bench directly from a small-business practice in a Texas town would conclude that such a business "is wholly beyond the fingers of the national government."[79]

In this context, the outcome of the nineteen NRA cases decided by district judges on constitutional grounds reflects the twin influences of partisan and local attachment. Ten of the fourteen Republican judges ruled against the government, while four of the five Democratic judges upheld the NIRA against constitutional challenges. Significantly, all four of the Republicans who supported the government were from the progressive, Bull Moose wing of the party, and the only Democratic judge who ruled against the NIRA was a states-rights southerner. With these predictable exceptions, party affiliation corresponded precisely with result in the NRA cases. The absolute numbers are small, to be sure, but it would be a statistician's quibble to argue that the difference (especially if the comparable AAA cases are added) was insignificant. With seventy-one percent of the Republican judges holding the NIRA unconstitutional and eighty percent of the Democrats differing, partisanship clearly colored constitutionalism at the district court level.

It is hard to resist comment on the lesson learned from this record by the NRA lawyers whose stake in the NIRA and its corporatist approach led them to the optimistic belief, as Blackwell Smith expressed it during the flush days of 1933, that "its constitutionality is unassailable."[80] Robert L. Stern, whose 1934 law review article expressed confidence that federal judges would follow the example of Chief Justice Marshall in recognizing the validity, a century later, of an economic nationalism based on an expansive conception of the commerce clause, was another NRA lawyer chagrined to learn that the Legal Realists of the 1930s had more perceptively plumbed the judicial mind. A decade later, again in the pages of the *Harvard Law Review*, Stern ruefully assessed the outcome of his attempt to confront judicial conservatism with economic reality, in a review of the early NRA cases. "The judicial scale," he was forced to acknowledge, "is not objective, but subjective. The result depends as much on who does the balancing as upon the weights themselves."[81]

The NRA was created in June 1933. A year later, as critics began to charge that NRA lawyers were deliberately avoiding a Supreme Court test of their constitutional powers, only one case had advanced beyond the federal district courts. And as political pressure for a definitive test case mounted, the Legal Politicians of the NRA found themselves with only three available cases, each of which involved small businesses subject to NRA regulation of the most minute details of their operations: small oil drillers in Texas, an Alabama soft-pine lumber business, and a kosher poultry distributor in Brooklyn. The fate of the entire New Deal recovery program rode on the outcome of these three cases.

Chapter Three

"HOT OIL" AND HOT TEMPERS:
THE NIRA REACHES THE
SUPREME COURT

I. OIL AND TROUBLE

New Deal lawyers seemingly could not have picked a more likely candidate for an initial Supreme Court test of the constitutionality of the NIRA than the petroleum industry. The third largest in the national economy, it was indisputably interstate in operation, encompassing a network of production and distribution from oil wells in half the states through a system of refineries and pipelines to gas stations and oil dealers in every city and town. And of the many industries whose prices and production were disrupted by the Depression, none was in a more chaotic condition when Roosevelt assumed office. The market for petroleum products grew rapidly as America became increasingly dependent on the automobile for transportation during the 1920s, and the discovery of vast oil pools in the midwest and southwestern states drew thousands of enterprising producers into the business of extraction, refining, and distribution.

In the decade before the New Deal, the petroleum industry was regulated solely by the states. However, particularly after the opening of the rich East Texas oil field in 1930, the industry was plagued with overcapacity and overproduction, and demands for federal regulation rose as oil prices plummeted below the cost of production; from a high of $2.31 per barrel in 1926, prices dropped as low as ten cents per barrel in the East Texas fields by the end of 1930.[1] The first attempts to deal with the problems of overproduction were made by the oil-producing states; in 1927 Oklahoma enacted a compulsory proration law (dividing production quotas among producers), and other oil states followed suit.[2] But it proved difficult to police such laws, since oil produced in excess of quotas—called "hot oil"—could easily be diverted in the extensive piping systems, and the states lacked the ability to keep track of illegally produced oil and to prosecute violations. Despite declarations of martial law by the governors of Texas and Oklahoma in 1931, "hot oil" continued to seep into interstate commerce.

Roosevelt moved to deal with the oil problem within days of his inauguration. In March 1933 he convened a meeting of representatives from the oil-producing states to draft a regulatory program. Although only one governor, Alf Landon of Kansas, attended the meeting in person, most of the states were represented and a consensus emerged that the federal government must assume responsibility for enforcing the state quota systems. As Landon put it, "even the iron hand of a national dictator is preferable to paralytic stroke."[3] It became clear following this meeting, however, that the industry was divided on the issues of production and pricing: producers favored restrictions on output which would guarantee higher prices, while refiners advocated higher levels of production which would allow them to pay lower prices for crude oil.

Caught between these conflicting pressures, Roosevelt vacillated for more than two months, unwilling to antagonize either segment of the politically potent industry. Finally, Congress took the lead. Rejecting proposals to deal with the oil industry through separate legislation, Congress appended a provision to the NIRA which dealt with the most pressing problem, that of "hot oil" production and transportation. In Section 9(c) of the NIRA, the President was authorized "to prohibit the transportation in interstate or foreign commerce of petroleum and the products thereof produced or withdrawn from storage in excess of the amount permitted to be produced or withdrawn from storage by any state law or valid regulation or order" of a state regulatory body.[4] In addition to this separate "hot oil" provision, Section 3 of the NIRA also authorized regulation of the production levels and marketing practices of the industry through the regular code procedure. Congress presented the executive branch in Section 9(c) with an easily administered task: regulation of an interstate industry on the basis of state-defined standards of production.

Roosevelt quickly implemented his powers to enforce Section 9(c) through a series of executive orders. On July 11, 1933, he issued an order prohibiting the interstate transportation of oil produced in excess of quotas established by state law.[5] Three days later, he authorized the Secretary of the Interior "to exercise all the powers" vested in the President, including authority to set up and staff an enforcement agency and to establish "such rules and regulations as he may deem necessary."[6] In designating the Interior Secretary rather than the Administrator of the National Recovery Administration to oversee regulation of the oil industry, Roosevelt not only carved out a separate enclave of regulatory power under the NIRA but also created an additional source of conflict between contending groups of New Deal lawyers. Three sets of lawyers now shared enforcement power: those in the Petroleum Administrative Board located in the Interior Department; those in the NRA, charged with Petroleum Code enforcement; and those in the Justice Department, with overall responsibility for NIRA litigation.

This tripartite division of responsibility soon engendered the legal infighting it seemed almost designed to produce.

Roosevelt's choice of Harold Ickes for the dual roles of Interior Secretary and Petroleum Administrator guaranteed that this potential for divisiveness would flower. A self-styled "curmudgeon" who was arrogant and prickly, Ickes had the background of a political chameleon. Born in 1874 and raised in Pennsylvania and Illinois, he graduated from the University of Chicago in 1897 and worked as a political reporter for Chicago newspapers before entering the University of Chicago law school at the age of thirty. After his graduation, Ickes plunged into reform politics, moving from the Republican Party to the Bull Moose campaigns of Theodore Roosevelt, back to the Republican presidential candidacy of Charles Evans Hughes, and finally to support of Franklin Roosevelt, as the leader of midwest Republicans who supported the Democratic ticket in 1932. Wherever he went, Ickes raised political hackles, and he made no secret of his dislikes, which included NRA general counsel Donald Richberg. The former law partners had both sought the Interior post, and Richberg's ill-concealed disappointment in losing out to Ickes colored relations between the two men as joint responsibility for Petroleum Code litigation forced them into an uneasy resumption of their partnership.[7]

On the recommendation of Felix Frankfurter, Ickes selected Nathan Margold, a 34-year-old Harvard Law School graduate, to serve as Solicitor of the Interior Department. After creation of the Petroleum Administrative Board, Margold was designated to chair that agency as well. Born in Romania, Margold came with his parents to New York City at the age of one. He entered Harvard after graduation from the City College of New York, and became a Frankfurter protégé, following Frankfurter's career path by serving as an assistant U.S. attorney in New York City before returning to Harvard in 1927-1928 as instructor of law. A reformer and civil libertarian in the Frankfurter-Ickes mold, Margold spent three years as special counsel to the National Association for the Advancement of Colored People before he joined the Interior Department. Given his urban and liberal background, Margold was initially uncomfortable as a Jew in an agency whose staff and clientele were overwhelmingly non-Jewish, and he anxiously informed Frankfurter that he was "somewhat troubled by the question of race and religion" in recruiting lawyers for his staff. He wondered whether "it is wise for me to lay myself open to the charge which is almost certain to be laid against me, if I choose too many Jewish men."[8] As did Jerome Frank, his counterpart in the Agricultural Adjustment Administration, Margold rejected most of the Jewish lawyers recommended to him by Frankfurter; he and Frank both bowed to fears of anti-Semitism among the conservative businessmen with whom their agencies dealt by practicing it themselves.

Always the battler, Ickes was eager from the beginning to exert the full range of his powers to stamp out the shipment of "hot oil." The zealous and sometimes heavy-handed enforcement of the Section 9(c) regulations (which provoked accusations that PAB agents illegally seized records and physically abused oil company employees) led to charges by smaller producers that the PAB displayed partiality toward the larger companies. Ickes and Margold were, in fact, firmly committed to a policy of accommodation to the interests of the industry's leaders. Smaller producers also resented Ickes' determination to enforce strictly the production quotas set under the Petroleum Code, and claimed that the quotas imposed on them favored their larger competitors. These aggressive enforcement policies led to the first confrontation between Ickes and Richberg, who sat as one of the three administration representatives on the interdepartmental Oil Committee established by Roosevelt to coordinate and oversee oil policy. In questioning the PAB's enforcement moves, Richberg cautioned Ickes not to precipitate premature litigation. Ickes misinterpreted this warning, which reflected Richberg's general antipathy to litigation, as a concession that the NRA believed the "hot oil" provisions of the NIRA were unconstitutional.[9]

After an Oil Committee meeting at which the two men heatedly argued over PAB policy, Ickes sought Roosevelt's backing. In his diary, Ickes reported that Roosevelt ". . . authorized me to go ahead and institute prosecutions for violation of regulations issued in relation to the production of hot oil. I told him frankly that I thought it was a tactical mistake for General Johnson and Don Richberg to give such a clear impression that they were apprehensive of the constitutionality of the National Recovery Act. I told him that instead of waiting for the fight to come to us, we ought to select our own issue in our own forum and make them take us on."[10]

Richberg was actually less concerned about the constitutionality of the "hot oil" provisions than he was about reports that Ickes planned drastic revisions of the foreign import restrictions contained in the Petroleum Code. Early in September 1933, less than two weeks after the code became effective, Richberg wrote to Ickes that he was "profoundly disturbed" about these reports. He considered Ickes' authority to make these changes "most doubtful" and argued that Ickes had no power to revise the code unilaterally and without hearings. Ickes proposed, Richberg wrote, to "exercise an authority not even conferred upon the President" and warned that code revision would provoke suits against the government by affected oil producers. "Litigation over the Oil Code, particularly a losing battle, would imperil the whole recovery program," Richberg predicted.[11]

Criticism came as well from Justice Department lawyers, whose concern was the delegation of legislative power to the Administrator in the Petro-leum Code. A week after Richberg's warning to Ickes, W. B. Watson Snyder, a career lawyer in the Justice Department since 1919 and the Special Assistant to the Attorney General in charge of petroleum policy, cautioned Assistant Attorney General Harold Stephens that, although Ickes had sufficient constitutional power to administer the code, the code pro-vision that allowed him to limit petroleum imports raised problems under the delegation doctrine. The code did not condition this power on any specific findings that imports needed to be curtailed to protect domestic producers, whereas the domestic production control provisions were based on findings made legislatively. "There is doubt in my mind," Snyder wrote, "if [the President] can delegate his authority to limit imports."[12] Ickes, however, professed no doubt about his powers and authorized the code revisions in the face of Justice Department and NRA warnings.

The consequences of this headstrong attitude on the part of Ickes and Margold became evident in the six months between October 1933 and March 1934. As the PAB pressed ahead with its policies, an undercurrent of suspicion and resentment on the part of Justice Department lawyers broke out into open hostility and mutual recriminations. At the root of these strained relations was the conviction of Department lawyers that the PAB shied away from code enforcement against the industry giants who dominated oil refining and distribution. Exacerbating this conflict was a jurisdictional squabble even more serious than those which complicated relations between the Justice Department and lawyers in the NRA and AAA. Two days after Roosevelt signed the Petroleum Code in August 1933, Attorney General Cummings agreed to a request from Ickes that a PAB lawyer be appointed as Special Assistant to the Attorney General, with authority to investigate and prosecute "hot oil" cases in Texas. J. Howard Marshall, a 1931 Yale Law School graduate who came to the PAB after two years as assistant dean and instructor at Yale, was appointed with authority to prosecute "flagrant violations" of Section 9(c).[13]

In the six months that followed Marshall's initial appointment, fifteen more PAB lawyers were designated as Special Assistants to the Attorney General. Invested with dual responsibility and thrust upon an unreceptive Justice Department staff, the two groups of lawyers mixed as poorly as oil and water. At first, Cummings diplomatically smoothed over conflicts between the two agencies and overruled his staff in making concessions to PAB lawyers. When the PAB instituted a campaign of prosecution against gas station operators in October 1933 for violations of Petroleum Code minimum-price regulations, Cummings informed Ickes that he did not believe that retail gasoline sales affected interstate commerce, but "since Interior had committed itself to immediately prosecute retailers" he "did not desire to stand in the way" and would instruct Justice Department lawyers and local U. S. attorneys to cooperate.[14] However, over the next several months Justice Department lawyers became increasingly incensed at what they considered to be favoritism toward industry giants and a pattern of non-cooperation by PAB lawyers.

The deterioration in relations finally boiled over; in May 1934 Watson Snyder assembled a brief against the PAB. After combing case files, he sent Harold Stephens a 4,500-word memorandum in which the entire history of conflict was detailed in indictment form. Snyder summarized his charges in these words: "[The PAB lawyers designated as Special Assistants] have been operating under their authority from the Attorney General, but have consistently ignored the Attorney General, his Department, and the United States Attorneys. It appears that the more active Special Assistants of the group believed that they had complete control and supervision of the prosecution of the cases and that they were acting under the authority of the Secretary of the Interior rather than the authority of the Attorney General. In some instances they completely ignored the United States Attorney and in other instances they proceeded to give him instructions."[15]

Snyder proceeded to set out "the most flagrant instances" in which PAB lawyers had overstepped their authority and worked at cross-purposes with the Justice Department, and presented seven case studies. The most serious involved a federal grand jury investigation of the petroleum industry in California; in January 1934 United States attorney Pierson Hall in San Francisco convened a grand jury to seek indictments of California oil refiners and distributors for widespread violations of the Petroleum Code pricing regulations. J. Howard Marshall of the PAB was authorized, at Ickes' request, to participate in grand jury proceedings. According to Snyder, once the grand jury voted indictments against ten independent oil operators, Marshall attempted to block further indictments against the four major oil companies who dominated the California industry, despite Hall's insistence that they were equally in violation of the code.

At the same time that the grand jury was considering evidence, Marshall was involved in negotiations with the major companies, including the Standard Oil Company of California, which sought Interior Department approval of a proposed Pacific Coast cartel permitting the very price-fixing and production control practices under investigation by the grand jury. Informed by Marshall (who later became counsel to Standard Oil of California) of the cartel negotiations, Hall responded that the major companies were bound by a 1930 consent decree issued by federal judge Adolphus St. Sure under which they were prohibited from engaging in the monopolistic practices they now sought to legalize through the cartel. Hall told

Marshall that approval of the cartel would result in "legalizing a fraud upon the public," and urged him not to proceed until the Justice Department had reviewed the situation. During these discussions, Hall reported, Marshall "expressed himself as being in accord with the views and opinions of counsel for the Standard Oil Company of California." However, on February 13, 1934, the day before Hall arrived in Washington to register his objections, Ickes approved the cartel. Three days later, Standard Oil and the other companies subject to the antitrust consent decree moved in federal court to modify its provisions to permit operation of the cartel.[16] Harold Stephens, with whom Hall belatedly lodged his complaints, quickly moved to bring the matter before the President after failing to sway Margold on the propriety of the cartel. Stephens feared, he wrote to his former law partner, "the likelihood of serious attack on the Administration if the Antitrust laws were completely suspended."[17]

Ickes won the first round of the battle over the cartel. After he and Cummings presented their cases to Roosevelt at a White House meeting on March 8, Cummings conceded defeat. He was persuaded, he told the press, that under the consent decree the California oil industry "had been so damaged by price wars and excessive competition that the cartel was . . . the only visible [sic] basis for rehabilitation of that industry."[18] The Justice Department, however, struck back. Two weeks later, Standard Oil and the three other major companies, as well as forty-one individuals, were indicted by the California grand jury for engaging in "the most vicious price-cutting war in oil history," in the words of the indictment.[19] Ickes, in turn, publicly blasted the Justice Department. Praising the cartel agreement, he asserted that the indictments "have had the effect of once more throwing the oil industry on the Pacific Coast into a state of chaos."[20] Lost amidst the public acrimony over the issue was the charge made by Watson Snyder that Marshall's role in the incident, in which he simultaneously urged approval of the cartel and appeared as a prosecutor before a grand jury considering indictment of the companies involved, smacked at least of partisanship and at most of a serious conflict of interest. (Marshall, incidentally, went on after leaving the PAB to become president and director of several Texas oil companies.)

The remaining cases that Snyder cited in his bill of complaint to Stephens involved less serious charges; their common denominator was the allegation that PAB lawyers ignored Justice Department advice and bypassed local United States attorneys. Charles Fahy, who acted as Margold's chief assistant (and later became general counsel of the National Labor Relations Board), particularly aroused Snyder's wrath. In one case involving the Standard Oil Company of New Jersey, Snyder asserted, Margold and Fahy agreed to a dismissal of the case without consulting the United States attorney. In another, after a federal judge in Maryland instructed U.S. attorney Simon Sobeloff that he would not decide the case solely on the affidavits filed by PAB lawyers, Sobeloff "conveyed the advice in a friendly way to Mr. Fahy and urged that witnesses be called in lieu of affidavits. Fahy refused to accept Sobeloff's suggestion and requested [the Justice] Department to remove Sobeloff from the case. On numerous occasions," Snyder concluded, "Mr. Fahy has indicated that he did not feel that either this Department or the United States Attorney should ever question the facts or the construction of the Code as submitted by the Interior Department. Mr. Fahy has always been very sensitive regarding the public accusation that the Interior Department insists upon prosecution of the small independent oil men and will not ask for prosecution of the major oil companies." Snyder ended his report with the recommendation that "the Attorney General cancel all of the appointments of Special Assistants in the Petroleum Administration" and require the PAB to seek formal Justice Department authorization for prosecution of code violations.[21]

Well aware that Justice Department lawyers, and especially U.S. attorneys, were dependent on PAB lawyers for assistance in unraveling the complexities of the Petroleum Code, Stephens rejected Snyder's advice. He did, however, fully share his attitude toward them. "They are very young and inexperienced and exceedingly brash and difficult to work with," he wrote L. H. Martineau, his former law partner in Los Angeles. "They have, to my mind, a somewhat sophistical and opportunistic viewpoint with respect to the law and the courts, and I myself have found it very difficult to maintain my patience with them."[22] On their parts, Ickes and the PAB lawyers reciprocated with criticism of excessive caution by the Justice Department. "I would not have any confidence in decisions from the Department of Justice," Ickes wrote in his diary. "That Department is simply loaded with political appointees and hardly anyone has any respect for the standing and ability of the lawyers over there."[23] Fahy, during the litigation over the "hot oil" regulations, wrote Stephens that the "failure of the Government to carry through every possible legal remedy open to it cannot in my opinion be justified."[24]

II. "Too Good a Test Case"

The fallout of these strained relations can be detected in the course of PAB litigation, which began in October 1933. Two small independent producers, the Panama Refining Company and the Amazon Petroleum Corporation, challenged both the "hot oil" regulations under Section 9(c) of the NIRA and the production control provisions of the Petroleum Code in civil suits filed in the Eastern District of Texas.[25] Their complaint, shared by most small producers, was that the state and federal production quotas were inequitable. The Petroleum Board, represented by J. Howard Marshall, won an early victory when federal judge Randolph Bryant denied, three days after the suits were filed, the oil companies' motions for a preliminary injunction; Ickes promptly claimed a "sweeping victory" for the oil program.[26] Marshall realized, however, from the tenor of Judge Bryant's comments at the hearing, that he was ill-disposed toward the government, and PAB lawyers were apprehensive about the outcome of the subsequent full-scale hearing on the merits of the cases. Robert L. Stern, then a lawyer for the PAB, subsequently wrote that Board lawyers were surprised to learn "that neither the Department of Justice nor the Recovery Administration had undertaken any preparations to defend the constitutionality" of Section 9(c) or the code.[27]

The *Panama* and *Amazon* cases were procedurally complicated by the fact that each involved two sets of defendants, state and federal officials. After Judge Bryant, as Marshall expected, issued the injunction sought by the companies in January 1934, the government appealed to a three-judge district court panel, under a federal statute permitting such an appeal when the constitutionality of the orders of a state body was questioned. The cases were then bifurcated. The three-judge panel (which included Judge Bryant) decided that it would hear the cases as they affected the Texas Railroad Commission, the state body charged with allocation of the oil production quotas, while the portion of the suits against the federal officials was returned to Judge Bryant for decision. These muddied waters were further roiled by the two decisions issued on February 12, 1934. Judge Bryant, relying on restrictive commerce clause decisions of the Supreme Court which, he said, "show that the making or manufacturing of goods are not commerce," peremptorily rejected the government's arguments and sustained the injunction he had earlier granted against the federal officials.[28] At the same time, the three-judge panel which heard the appeal of the state officials overturned the January injunction and dismissed the suit against them. This decision, from which Judge Bryant predictably dissented, largely ignored the constitutional issues in the cases. Citing "the spirit of the times making for collectivism against individualism" and the consequent "march of the statute law, which stands with us for public opinion and within constitutional limits determines the public policy of the state," the two-judge majority canvassed the "voluminous" evidence presented by the government supporting the necessity for production limitation, and agreed that it would be "greatly disastrous" to grant an injunction in the face of such evidence.[29]

Marshall had been busy in Texas during the month in which decisions in the *Panama* and *Amazon* cases were pending. Operating on the well-founded assumption that Judge Bryant's final ruling in these cases would go against the government, Marshall decided to take the offensive by seeking criminal indictments against other code violators for conspiracy to violate the code. Ickes had made it clear, on the basis of his go-ahead from Roosevelt, that he welcomed an early Supreme Court test of his powers, and Marshall reasoned that Judge Bryant would most likely sustain a defendant's demurrer to a criminal indictment. Existing rules permitted a direct and expeditious appeal to the Supreme Court of such a holding, if the demurrer was sustained on the ground of the statute's unconstitutionality. Assuming a favorable Supreme Court ruling, such a move promised to shut off the massive flow of "hot oil" from the East Texas fields which would otherwise be unimpeded during the year or more that it would take to process an appeal in the civil cases through the Court of Appeals to the Supreme Court.

Marshall pursued this end-run strategy in a blaze of publicity, hoping to deter "hot oil" violators with threats of criminal prosecution. Assisted by Charles I. Francis, an experienced petroleum lawyer then on retainer to the PAB (and later a partner in the leading oil company law firm in Houston), Marshall concluded his campaign by filing indictments against J. W. Smith and several other independent oil producers on February 13, the day after the *Panama* and *Amazon* decisions were issued. As the PAB lawyers anticipated, the defendants immediately filed demurrers to the indictments and Judge Bryant, to whom the cases were assigned, quickly granted the demurrers on the dual grounds that Section 9(c) unconstitutionally delegated legislative power to the President and that Smith (to whose case the others were joined) was not engaged in interstate commerce.[30] Secretary Ickes promptly asked Attorney General Cummings to expedite an appeal to the Supreme Court, to which Cummings reluctantly agreed on the condition that the PAB lawyers clear their briefs with Assistant Attorney General Stephens and the Solicitor General. With this agreement, the *Smith* case was appealed to the Supreme Court on March 20, 1934, the first NIRA case to reach the Court's docket.

The PAB lawyers had succeeded in their strategy, but at the cost of Justice Department resentment of the tactics they employed in the process. Watson Snyder, in his report to Stephens, complained that Marshall ". . . brought about an undue amount of publicity, advertising himself as a Special Assistant and not as an attorney for the Petroleum Administrator. He and several members of the Administrator's staff flew to Texas in a number of Army aeroplanes and the newspapers of Eastern Texas carried great headlines describing the activities of the Attorney General in curbing the flow of 'hot oil' and quoting Marshall as authority for their news items. After Marshall arrived there, it appears that he went before the United

States Commissioners, swore to forty or more complaints, and had the defendants arrested and never consulted the United States Attorney. . . . [T]here is no doubt that the high-handed manner in which Marshall conducted himself was responsible to some degree for the injunctions handed down by Judge Bryant. . . .''[31]

It was unlikely, as Snyder charged, that Judge Bryant's rulings on the *Panama* and *Amazon* injunctions (or on the *Smith* case demurrer as well) were affected by Marshall's ploys, since the judge's hostility to the NIRA was undisguised. The episode did have other consequences, however. Ickes had urged, at the time he requested a Supreme Court appeal, that Cummings permit PAB lawyers to prepare and argue the appeal because of their ''special and exhaustive study of the questions raised and their general familiarity with the problems involved'' in the administration of the oil program.[32] In granting this request, Cummings emphasized that the Justice Department ''must retain control of all Government causes in the Supreme Court'' and warned Ickes that his approval ''is not to be taken as a precedent in the event such a request is made in the future.''[33] The strained relations between the two agencies bore heavily on Cummings' abrupt move, only two weeks later, stripping lawyers in all the emergency agencies of power to argue New Deal cases in court without special permission. And on Harold Stephens' recommendation, the designation of PAB lawyers as Special Assistants to the Attorney General was soon rescinded.

Another complicating factor in the oil litigation was that, over the next month, Cummings changed his mind about the *Smith* appeal. Lawyers in other New Deal agencies had just begun litigation campaigns and urged that any Supreme Court test case be deferred while they tested the waters in the lower courts. Cummings was also advised, he reported to Roosevelt, that the *Smith* case record was ''sadly defective, and that it would be an exceedingly bad case'' in which to risk a negative decision. Ickes and Cummings thrashed the issue out at a White House cabinet meeting on April 20. Over Ickes' protest, Cummings expressed doubt as to the wisdom of the appeal and argued to Roosevelt that ''it was highly desirable to proceed with caution and to present cases that were most attractive,'' adding that ''an attempt to secure at one jump a strong decision on a weak case was poor judgment.''[34]

At Roosevelt's suggestion, Cummings and Harold Stephens met three days later with Solicitor General Crawford Biggs, Donald Richberg and Blackwell Smith of the NRA, and four lawyers from the PAB, including Nathan Margold and Charles Fahy. Over dissent from Margold and Fahy, it was decided that the appeal should be withdrawn; with the Supreme Court term drawing to a close and with work on the brief barely begun, the Justice Department lawyers reasoned, little would be lost with a postponement of the argument.[35] The next week the Court granted the Solicitor General's motion that the *Smith* case be taken off the calendar and re-scheduled for argument during the following October term. Liberal critics of the Justice Department, flushed with optimism after the recent Supreme Court decisions in the Minnesota mortgage moratorium and New York milk pricing cases, reacted scornfully to what they considered an over-cautious evasion of a follow-up New Deal test case. The *New Republic* editorialized that it was "an open secret in Washington that the legal defenses of the New Deal are in a bad way" and that the work of the Petroleum Board "may be completely undone by an uninformed decision of the Department of Justice."[36]

The frustrated PAB lawyers soon gained a second chance at a test case when the Fifth Circuit Court of Appeals, in an opinion issued in late May 1934, decided the *Panama* and *Amazon* appeals in the government's favor. The initiative had now shifted to the hands of the losing oil companies, and early in its fall term the Supreme Court granted their petition for certiorari without opposition from the Justice Department, with argument set for December. In this round of litigation, lawyers in the PAB and the Solicitor General's office worked on their brief-drafting tasks in relative harmony, lulled into a false sense of security by the sweepingly favorable holdings of the Court of Appeals on the central constitutional issues.

The Court of Appeals opinion displayed considerable dexterity in meeting the commerce clause challenge raised by the oil company lawyers, who had argued that oil production was not commerce as interpreted by Supreme Court precedent. Such production, the court acknowledged, was not "ordinarily within the power of Congress to regulate within a state," if the restrictive line of cases was read literally. Having conceded that much to constitutional conservatism, the court responded that "peculiar circumstances" existed "in the relation of oil production in Texas to commerce in oil with and among the other states," creating a burden on interstate commerce that justified federal regulation. Since the state agency that allocated production quotas had undisputed powers to do so, the court reasoned, "the federal regulation is actually only of interstate and foreign commerce, adjusted to aid and not to thwart the state action. Such co-operation between state and central government is not constitutionally wrong, but right and desirable." Considering the unanimous support given the federal oil program by the oil-producing states, considerable logic supported this conclusion.

In its casual treatment of the delegation issue, the Court of Appeals encouraged the government lawyers to dismiss it as insignificant. The congressional delegation of power to the President to prohibit the shipment of "hot oil" was not "seriously attacked" by the oil companies, the court stated, although in fact the point had been strenuously argued. Whether the congressional intent expressed in the Declaration of Policy of the NIRA provided "an intelligible legislative plan sufficient to be filled out and executed" by an executive agency, the court cavalierly asserted, was "a question we need not broadly answer." The policy established by Section 9(c), it concluded, "is entirely clear."[37] The complacent attitude of the government lawyers toward the delegation issue was reflected in the minimal attention they gave it in the Supreme Court brief; only three pages in the 195-page brief addressed the delegation issue.

The Solicitor General's staff took primary responsibility for the constitutional arguments in the brief, while the PAB lawyers added a 200-page appendix documenting the tangled economics of the petroleum industry. This material was designed to buttress the claim that unrestricted production, which the states individually could not control, had depressed oil prices and led to disastrous competitive wars. NRA lawyers played only a marginal role in the brief-drafting process. Although the Petroleum Code was at issue in the cases, it was almost overlooked in the focus on the "hot oil" provisions of Section 9(c). Blackwell Smith of the NRA viewed the oil cases as an easily surmounted hurdle beyond which lay the more difficult challenge of the industrial codes promulgated under Section 3. Stanley Surrey expressed this confidence when he advised Smith that *Panama* "is a good test case, since it involves a business clearly interstate and one which may be classed perhaps as a public utility." The ease of sustaining the commerce clause issue, Surrey added, might make it "too good a test case so that even if the statute is upheld in this case we may still be left in doubt as regards cases arising under other Codes."[38]

As the December argument before the Supreme Court approached, government lawyers were shaken from their complacency by the discovery of an embarrassing oversight. M. S. Huberman, a Justice Department lawyer assigned to the "hot oil" briefing, had gone back to the abandoned *Smith* case materials in search for records. To his horror, Huberman discovered that when the Petroleum Code had been amended by Executive Order in September 1933, the section that provided criminal penalties for interstate shipments of "hot oil" had been inadvertently deleted. Had the *Smith* case actually been argued before the Supreme Court, the government's case would have been fatally flawed, since the criminal prosecution which it threatened would be without penalties. The error had slipped by the PAB lawyers, who had dropped their brief-drafting efforts when the case was withdrawn from the Supreme Court docket. "Had such a brief been submitted to us for our approval," Huberman reported to his superior, "the mistake would undoubtedly have been discovered then."[39] The missing provision did not directly affect the *Panama* and *Amazon* cases, which were civil injunctive suits, but Huberman's belated discovery forced the PAB to withdraw all its pending criminal prosecutions and to inform oilmen of the facts.

Although Ickes quickly restored the criminal penalty provision to the oil regulations, the issue revived the ill feelings between Justice Department and PAB lawyers, who defensively took the position that the provision had never actually been repealed. "No one interpreted the modifications as repealing [the penalties] until the Department of Justice did so," Charles Fahy later asserted somewhat misleadingly.[40] Without notice of the provision, however, the oil producers who received the revised regulations could only have guessed at its whereabouts, which was actually a Washington desk drawer.

The "hot oil" cases were argued before the Supreme Court on December 10 and 11, 1934. The lawyers for the oil companies who led off predictably stressed the restrictive line of commerce clause cases and noted their distinction between manufacturing and commerce. This was the weaker side of their argument, since they admitted the validity of state regulation and could only suggest that Congress lacked power "to aid the State in the enforcement of its conservation laws." This concession eroded the support of precedent such as *Hammer v. Dagenhart*, where federal regulation was forced on unwilling states. Sliding over this issue, they hammered away at the delegation issue, arguing that in Section 9(c) Congress had "laid down no rule or criterion to guide or limit the President in the orders that he may promulgate under it."[41]

Harold Stephens had earlier implored the oil company lawyers not to raise the issue of the missing criminal provision in the oil regulations, and thought he had secured their agreement. But PAB lawyers had once threatened both the Panama and Amazon companies with criminal prosecution, and the threat still remained should the companies lose before the Supreme Court. Consequently, one of Stephens' adversaries could not resist noting in his argument that "Smith was arrested, indicted, and held in jail for several days for violating a law that did not exist."[42] Stephens had hardly begun his argument when his composure was shaken by intensive questioning about the issue. The staid *New York Herald Tribune* reported that "smiles appeared on the usually solemn faces of the Justices and the crowd of lawyers that filled the room when Mr. Stephens admitted that the trial court had sustained a demurrer to the indictment on the ground that the nonexistent section of the code was unconstitutional and that the Justice Department had appealed this decision to the Supreme Court."[43]

When Stephens recovered, he gamely launched an attack on the weakest link of his opponents' argument. He exhaustively detailed the structure and economics of the petroleum industry and stressed the "fruitless efforts"

71

of the states to control unrestricted production. Pressed for time, Stephens was forced to cut short his delegation argument, essentially reciting the prior cases in which the Court had upheld congressional delegation. Lawyers generally discount the importance of oral argument as a decisive factor in the outcome of cases, but Stephens had clearly been bested in the first New Deal cases to reach the Supreme Court. "It makes me sick when I think of the way [Stephens] handled our oil cases before the Supreme Court," Ickes uncharitably noted in his diary.[44]

It took the Supreme Court less than a month to decide the oil cases. Over the solitary dissent of Justice Cardozo, the Court held on January 7, 1935 that Section 9(c) represented an unconstitutional delegation of legislative authority. The commerce clause issue was sidestepped and left undecided, since the majority had no doubt on the delegation question. The opinion written by Chief Justice Hughes began by discarding the Declaration of Policy in Section 1 of the NIRA as the source of any "intelligible principle" for the exercise of the powers granted by Section 9(c): "This general outline of policy contains nothing as to the circumstances or conditions in which transportation of petroleum or petroleum products should be prohibited," Hughes wrote. Cast adrift from its moorings, Section 9(c) was left to founder:

"It establishes no criterion to govern the President's course. It does not require any finding by the President as a condition of his action. The Congress in Section 9(c) thus declares no policy as to the transportation of excess production. So far as this section is concerned, it gives to the President an unlimited authority to determine the policy and to lay down the prohibition, or not to lay it down, as he may see fit. And disobedience to his order is made a crime punishable by fine and imprisonment."

An additional vice of Section 9(c), Hughes wrote, was that, unlike the NRA codes authorized under Section 3, no findings by the President were required before the issuance of regulations and orders. Such findings were essential to meet due process considerations if violations were to be punished. Hughes concluded that if the "hot oil" regulations were held valid "it would be idle to pretend that anything would be left of limitations upon the power of the Congress to delegate its law-making function."[45]

Cardozo, in dissent, took the majority to task for its facile separation of the Declaration of Policy in Section 1 from the intent of Congress manifested in Section 9(c). It was simply not the case that Section 1 provided no intelligible standards for executive action. Looking to "the whole structure of the statute," Cardozo found in Section 1 ample standards to guide the President. First, Congress had established a policy of eliminating "unfair competition," and the transportation of "hot oil" was "[b]eyond question an unfair competitive practice" because "law abiding

72

dealers must compete with lawbreakers." Second, the policy established to "conserve natural resources" provided another standard as sanction for production restriction; Cardozo thought that "prevailing conditions in the oil industry have brought about the need for temporary restriction" because overproduction had the effect of "demoralizing prices and thus increasing unemployment." What Congress had said to the President, Cardozo continued, was this:

"You are to consider whether the transportation of oil in excess of the statutory quotas is offensive to one or more of the policies enumerated in Section 1, whether the effect of such conduct is to promote unfair competition or to waste the natural resources or to demoralize prices or to increase unemployment or to reduce the purchasing power of the workers of the nation. If these standards or some of them have been flouted with the result of a substantial obstruction to industrial recovery, you may then by a prohibitory order eradicate the mischief."

As a matter of statutory construction, Cardozo had the best of the argument. The intent of Congress to halt the shipment of "hot oil" was manifest from the legislative history of Section 9(c)—which the majority simply ignored—and from the plain wording of the statute. Congress could not, as Cardozo noted, foresee changing conditions in the petroleum industry, or predict "how many of the states would adopt valid quota laws, or how generally the laws would be observed when adopted. . . . Much would depend upon conditions as they shaped themselves thereafter." The President was given a "narrow delegation" and the scope of his discretion was "closely and clearly circumscribed both as to subject matter and occasion."[46]

Reaction among the New Deal lawyers to their first defeat in the Supreme Court varied from agency to agency. Justice Department lawyers took an I-told-you-so attitude in the exchange of recriminations that followed the "hot oil" decision; they had taken pains to restrain the enthusiasm of lawyers in the New Deal agencies for an early Supreme Court test, and additionally shared the Court's ill-concealed displeasure at the bungling of the *Smith* case. NRA lawyers in turn felt no real loyalty to the PAB, since Congress had tacked on Section 9(c) to the NIRA without giving much thought to its administrative consequences. The personal feud between Richberg and Ickes also poisoned relations at the lower levels of their respective agencies.

The taste of defeat was nonetheless hard to swallow, particularly since political pressure for a second Supreme Court test of the NIRA continued to mount at the worst possible time. The "hot oil" decision came against a background that included the breakdown of code enforcement, a flood of injunction suits challenging federal regulation, and a growing number of lower court decisions holding New Deal statutes unconstitutional. In shaping their litigation strategy, the bickering New Deal lawyers had naturally sought to present the Supreme Court first with cases that involved narrowly defined issues and undisputed regulatory power over an interstate industry, hoping that an initial victory in a carefully circumscribed case would ease the way for a subsequent test of the NRA codes at the heart of the recovery program, those which extended regulation to the broader areas of trade practices and wages and hours.

Now they confronted even greater danger. Just three days before the "hot oil" cases were decided, the Justice Department had reluctantly acceded to NRA insistence and filed on the Supreme Court docket another expedited criminal appeal, a case involving the Southern Lumber Code. Conflict among the New Deal lawyers continued in this atmosphere of defeat, pitting the apostles of caution against the advocates of confrontation.

Chapter Four

THE FELLING OF *BELCHER* AND THE
SEARCH FOR A SUCCESSOR

I. The *Belcher* Case and the Politics of Indecision

The respective fates of the *Belcher* and *Schechter* cases offer a classic illustration of the vicissitudes of constitutional history. All that remains of *United States v. Belcher* is a terse notation in the end-pages of *U. S. Reports*: "April 1, 1935. Motion of appellant to dismiss the appeal . . . granted."[1] Two weeks later, again on motion of the Solicitor General, the Supreme Court agreed to hear the appeals in *Schechter Poultry Corp. v. United States*. At the end of the next month, the National Industrial Recovery Act lay in ruins, and with it ended the corporatist ideology of the First New Deal.[2]

With its primary focus on constitutional doctrine as expressed in the authoritative pronouncements of the Supreme Court, legal history largely ignores the lacunae created by cases in which the legal process falters. It is unlikely that the outcome in *Belcher* would have differed from that in *Schechter*, given the unanimity of the Court's opinion. Yet the issues raised in the two cases, as well as their factual settings, were sufficiently divergent to raise at least a doubt that the Court's total rejection of the NIRA would have been phrased so uncompromisingly had *Belcher* served its intended role as the first real test of the NIRA's regulatory scheme. The possible outcome of *Belcher* is less important, however, than its role in the continuing struggle between contending groups of New Deal lawyers. Viewed in these terms, the case becomes more than a forgotten footnote. It becomes, rather, a key to the political machinations that accompany the emergence of constitutional test cases.

The lumber industry, out of which *Belcher* grew, is one of the ten largest in the national economy, with a yearly production in the 1930s of more than $1.5 billion. It has long been a fragmented industry, with "widely scattered producing areas, a large number of firms running from very large to very small . . . and severe competition within each branch of the industry, between the several branches, and between the industry and other industries."[3] It was particularly prone, in short, to the type of "cut-throat competition" the NIRA was established to control. Profit margins depended largely on wage rates, which varied widely between regions of the country;

low wages and long working hours gave an advantage to sawmill operators who could force their employees to accept such terms. Between the late 1920s and the depth of the Depression in 1933, wages in the southern pine region fell from 21 cents per hour to 11 cents, and in some areas were as low as 4 or 5 cents, and hours ranged from 60 to 66 per week.[4]

With lumber singled out as one of the crucial "Big Ten" industries, lawyers in the National Recovery Administration began efforts to draft a Code of Fair Competition for the industry soon after passage of the NIRA. The industry had established during the 1920s a number of regional trade associations designed to hold in check the "separatist tendencies of the various regional and product groups" and which hammered out agreements on trade practices such as the grading of products, discounts, and shipping methods.[5] Bernice Lotwin, then a young lawyer in the lumber section of the NRA Legal Division, later recalled that code-drafting sessions were dominated by the industry giants, who were adamant in arguing that stability in the industry depended not only on official sanction of these trade practices but also on explicit price and production controls written into the code. Without such controls, they claimed, the industry would be at the mercy of cost-cutting operators who could force others into selling below cost and eventually into bankruptcy.[6] The NRA lawyers—inexperienced, unfamiliar with the bewildering complexity of the industry's practices, and eager to meet the deadline set for approval of the "Big Ten" codes— acquiesced in these demands. The Lumber and Timber Code, signed by the President on August 19, 1933, provided not only for price and production controls but also established a minimum wage of 24 cents per hour and a maximum work week of 40 hours.[7]

Within two months, William Belcher made known his unwillingness to abide by the code's wage and hour provisions. Belcher and his family owned several sawmills in the soft-pine region of central Alabama. In October 1933 Belcher complained to the Southern Pine Lumber Code Authority that compliance would force him to dismiss from 300 to 500 of his workers. He paid his common laborers from $1.00 to $1.50 per day, he explained, "and at these prices the men seem to be well satisfied."[8] Reports to the NRA, however, indicated that his workers were hardly as satisfied as Belcher claimed. In December an executive of the Southern Pine Association, the regional trade association, wrote the Lumber Code Authority with this story: thirteen of Belcher's employees, with Louis Smith as their spokesman, went to see him to complain that they were not receiving code wages and were being forced to work beyond the code maximum. The group "went to the Commissary and Mill office where Mr. Belcher asked them what they wanted. When Louis Smith tried to tell him he immediately discharged every man and ordered them all to never set foot on his property again and to immediately vacate any house of his in which they were living."[9]

Belcher's recalcitrance disturbed the NRA legal staff, which had received additional reports of maltreatment from Alabama ministers who had attempted to investigate the conditions in which his employees worked and lived; although several ministers were ordered off his property, they had talked with enough workers to conclude that their charges were true. Less than a week after receiving the report that Belcher had fired the workers in the delegation headed by Louis Smith, the NRA made clear its concern by issuing a press release reporting that the Justice Department had been asked to authorize Belcher's prosecution for violations of the wage and hour provisions of the code.[10] The unusual move of publicizing a prosecutive request underscored the seriousness with which the NRA viewed the charges.

No sooner did the NRA request that Belcher be prosecuted than a first period of indecision began. NRA lawyers had discovered that the federal district judge in the area, 73-year-old William Grubb, who had been appointed to the federal bench by President Taft in 1909, was avowedly hostile to the NRA. Several days after the press release was issued, Stanley Surrey of the NRA legal staff informed the Justice Department that Blackwell Smith, who directed NRA litigation policy, wished to defer legal action against Belcher "for several months at least." Surrey explained that the NRA "desires at this time merely to make a show of force, and does not wish to run the risk of an acquittal or of an adverse decision on the constitutionality of the National Industrial Recovery Act."[11] This abrupt reversal reflected the shock of the NRA's first defeat in court, in which an equally hostile federal judge in Florida had declared the NIRA unconstitutional early in December, in a case involving the citrus code. Rather than risk a second embarrassing defeat at a time when code enforcement was beginning to crumble, NRA lawyers adopted a policy of caution.

This switch in tactics annoyed Justice Department lawyers, not the least because after the NRA made its unusual public call for prosecution, the United States attorney in the district, Jim Smith, had begun preparations for grand jury proceedings against Belcher. "It is quite likely," Assistant Attorney General Harold Stephens had written to Smith in January 1934, "that this case will assume important proportions in the National Recovery campaign."[12] Stephens was, however, willing to defer to Surrey's request that prosecution be deferred; Jim Smith also had cautioned the Department that Judge Grubb "had expressed grave doubts of the constitutionality" of the NIRA.[13] And in February the NRA informed Stephens that it could settle with Belcher on terms of full code compliance. Stephens thus instructed Smith to hold the grand jury proceedings in abeyance.[14] But he did display his pique at the NRA's sudden shift from prosecution to settlement by advising the agency's liaison officer with the Department, William Griffin, that to "avoid the possibility of working at cross purposes," the NRA should consult his staff "before adjusting code violations which have been referred to the Department of Justice for legal action."[15]

The NRA soon learned that Belcher had continued his code violations, and for a second time asked the Justice Department to initiate prosecution. Jim Smith accordingly reopened grand jury proceedings in May 1934, and NRA lawyers prepared for him a criminal indictment charging Belcher with numerous wage and hour violations. The case soon assumed the importance in the overall NRA litigation strategy that Stephens had earlier predicted. After several months of indecision, NRA lawyers had settled on the case as the vehicle for an early Supreme Court test of the NIRA, although its place in the timetable was as yet undetermined; the "hot oil" cases under the petroleum code were also candidates for the first test.

Once the decision to proceed became firm, NRA and Justice Department lawyers worked cooperatively. Their strategy was based on anticipation of a negative ruling by Judge Grubb, and use of the Criminal Appeals Act of 1907, which permitted direct appeal to the Supreme Court of a district court order sustaining a demurrer to a criminal indictment on a finding of unconstitutionality of the statute involved.[16] Since no trial would be held, assuming the expected ruling, the lawyers drew up a lengthy indictment; in contrast to the ordinary criminal indictment it was more than 6,000 words long and contained a mass of economic data on the structure of the lumber industry and the deleterious impact of wage and hour violations on competition within the industry and on interstate commerce. Its basic thrust was that Belcher's code violations permitted him to undersell his competitors, and by depressing their sales increased unemployment in the industry as a whole.[17]

Although the grand jury handed down the indictment in August, government lawyers were still hesitant about how quickly to press for a Supreme Court test, and secured the cooperation of Belcher's lawyer in deferring his motion to dismiss the indictment, the procedure that would permit an expedited constitutional test. Earlier in 1934, the *Smith* case had been placed on the Supreme Court docket under the same procedure. When it was decided in late September to withdraw the *Smith* case and to seek review of *Panama* and *Amazon*, the "hot oil" cases, under the regular certiorari procedure, NRA and Justice Department lawyers agreed as part of the same plan to proceed with *Belcher* as a follow-up, on the assumption that it would reach the Supreme Court shortly after the first cases were decided. William Griffin, the NRA lawyer in charge of lumber code litigation, reported to Blackwell Smith on September 22 that Jim Smith in

Alabama was ready "to pursue our plan of more than six months past to utilize an indictment in this case for a test suit."[18] Judge Grubb, whose position was known to both sides, was a participant in this cooperative strategy as well. Belcher's lawyers filed a demurrer to the indictment on October 31, alleging that the NIRA and the lumber code were unconstitutional on three grounds: that the NIRA involved an unlawful delegation of legislative authority; that the wage and hour violations (which were not contested) did not affect interstate commerce; and that Belcher had been denied due process by imposing on him a code he had not signed.[19] The same day, Judge Grubb issued a previously written order sustaining the demurrer and dismissing the indictment, declaring that the NIRA was unconstitutional on all three grounds raised by Belcher.[20]

The stage was thus set for an expedited appeal to the Supreme Court. Judge Grubb signed an order allowing the appeal in late November, and it was formally filed in the Court on January 4, 1935, three days before the "hot oil" cases were decided. That decision derailed the carefully timed strategy, and shattered the shaky truce between the NRA and Justice Department lawyers.

The belated decision to risk a Supreme Court test of the codes drafted under Section 3 of the NIRA was hailed by those who had complained that code enforcement was breaking down because of uncertainty as to their constitutionality. *U. S. Law Week* applauded government lawyers for having found a case "which they seem not only willing but anxious to have considered by the Supreme Court of the United States. It appears that this case is destined to be *the* NIRA case."[21] And the *New York Times*, noting the recent spate of lower court decisions holding the act unconstitutional, editorialized that the *Belcher* appeal was "gratifying" since there had been "more than a suspicion" that the NRA "was deliberately evading any clear-cut court test of its powers."[22] Ironically, the *Times*'s suspicion of foot-dragging was correct but the wrong culprit was identified. Harold Stephens had told the press that since the NIRA was scheduled to expire in June 1935, "its constitutionality should be decided upon soon in order that Congress can determine whether it should make any changes."[23] However, his public support for a test case was disingenuous; in spite of their previous cooperation in preparing the case, Justice Department lawyers were skeptical about *Belcher* and had agreed to its appeal with reluctance.

Fissures began to appear in the apparent solidity of the government coalition within days of filing the case with the Supreme Court. The Supreme Court decision in the "hot oil" cases obviously forced a reassessment of the decision to follow them with a second case. This was only one issue in the debate, however. The long-standing dispute between NRA and Justice Department lawyers over differing conceptions of the antitrust laws was particularly acute in the case of the lumber code. Bernice Lotwin recalled that the Justice Department had consistently criticized NRA code provisions which provided for explicit price and production controls; her impression was that the Department feared that these provisions could not withstand a court test.[24]

The *Belcher* case was scheduled for argument before the Supreme Court on April 8, 1935, but pressure began to mount for its abandonment shortly after the appeal was filed in January. At the urging of Justice Department lawyers, Attorney General Cummings raised the issue at a cabinet meeting on February 8. Cummings reported in his diary that he went "at some considerable length, into the matter of the Lumber Code and the Belcher case, and the general conduct of that class of litigation in connection with Supreme Court matters." One of his concerns was "the difficulties which confronted us in view of the state of the records" in cases such as *Belcher* which were appealed directly from the district courts under the Criminal Appeals Act, since such cases necessarily lacked a full trial record.[25] Although the *Belcher* indictment had been carefully drawn to include substantial data on the lumber industry and the supposedly harmful effects of wage and hour violations, Cummings feared that the Supreme Court would be less receptive than had a full record been available.

Cummings did not ask Roosevelt to intervene in the case at this cabinet meeting, but the NRA lawyers learned of his remarks and quickly moved to counter them. Blackwell Smith informed the National Industrial Recovery Board, the five-man group that administered the agency after the departure of Hugh Johnson, that if the *Belcher* case "is not reached this term, we run the risk that at the first of next term a decision will be handed down completely upsetting the NRA, with the legislature not in session and with no possibility of doing anything about it." In a reference to the *Schechter* case, then pending before the Second Circuit Court of Appeals and the only NRA case to have reached the appellate level, Smith wrote that a "rather bad case is now in the offing and not entirely subject to our control." He requested that the Board send a message to the President asking "that no action be taken to prevent the Belcher case from being heard by the Supreme Court in due course, and request that if the President takes any step to postpone the case, he permit the Board to discuss the matter with him."[26] The Board promptly sent a message drafted by Smith to Roosevelt, which the White House staff then communicated to the Attorney General.[27] Smith, in fact, considered *Belcher* to be "one of the worst possible cases," but recalled that "at that time we considered ourselves in a very bad box for not having suitable cases to get to the Supreme Court ahead of the Liberty League group, so we were grasping at straws to try to find a good case to push successfully." What concerned Smith was that the American Liberty League, the anti-New Deal coalition of industrial leaders and lawyers organized the previous year and bankrolled by the duPonts, had pledged legal support to businessmen challenging the NRA; Smith was apprehensive at the prospect of facing high-powered Wall Street lawyers before the Supreme Court.[28]

During the two months before the case was scheduled for Supreme Court argument, a vigorous but unpublicized debate raged within the government, against the backdrop of uncertainty about the future of the NIRA. As Justice Department and NRA lawyers fought over *Belcher*, the balance of power was altered by the intervention of Felix Frankfurter. Initially a supporter of the NIRA despite his Brandeisian views, Frankfurter doubted its constitutionality and additionally had come to believe that it was ineffective and anticompetitive in practice. As early as September 1934, Frankfurter had confided in Secretary Ickes his suspicion that Donald Richberg's role in the NRA had become that of an apologist for big business. "Frankfurter thinks that Richberg now represents exactly the opposite point of view from that which was supposed to be the one of this Administration," Ickes wrote in his diary.[29] Having soured on the NIRA, Frankfurter felt that it should be allowed to expire and be replaced with a legislative program designed to restore competition to the economy. Frankfurter first exerted his influence in the debate over the NIRA shortly after the government's defeat in the "hot oil" cases, by engineering the removal of Solicitor General Biggs and his replacement by Stanley Reed, a Frankfurter ally then serving as general counsel of the Reconstruction Finance Corporation.

Frankfurter and Reed would have faced no problem in persuading Roosevelt to order dismissal of the *Belcher* appeal had Richberg not shifted his position. Richberg's "first impression was that it was an undesirable test case" because he agreed with the Justice Department that the price-fixing and production control provisions of the Lumber Code "were of doubtful legality and questionable economic wisdom."[30] But pressure from NRA lawyers who feared a complete collapse of code enforcement convinced Richberg to face the risks of a Supreme Court test. When Frankfurter learned that Attorney General Cummings was wavering under importuning from Richberg, he quickly went over Cummings' head, arguing to Roosevelt on March 13 that the NRA position "was a suicidal policy from any point of view." The Attorney General traditionally deferred to the Solicitor General in Supreme Court matters, and with this in mind Frankfurter urged Roosevelt to reassure Reed that "if he were convinced, as he is, of the wisdom of dismissing the appeal he would have your support."[31]

On March 25, two weeks before the scheduled argument, the Justice

Department surprised both the public and the NRA lawyers by issuing a press release announcing that it would ask the Supreme Court to dismiss the *Belcher* appeal. The Department cited two reasons: first, that while "sound in general substance and purpose, [the Lumber] Code contains administrative provisions peculiar to itself with respect to the extension of discretionary powers to non-governmental agencies"—a reference to the price-fixing and production control powers exercised by the industry; second, the release stressed that a "further unsatisfactory feature of this case is that, due to the nature of the action, no findings could be made by the lower court. The Department feels that the fundamental questions involved in the National Industrial Recovery Act should be presented to the Supreme Court in a case in which full evidence of the facts has been given."[32] A week later the Court granted Reed's motion to dismiss the appeal. In this round of the fight over *Belcher*, the apostles of caution had scored a clear victory.

II. THE *Schechter* CASE AND THE POLITICS OF CONFUSION

Frankfurter and his allies had no time to savor their victory. The first chorus of disapproval came from the political right, which had eagerly expected that the Supreme Court would strike down the NIRA and cripple the New Deal. On April 1, hours after the Court granted the dismissal motion, Senator Champ Clark of Missouri, a Democrat but also a fierce New Deal opponent, introduced a resolution urging the Attorney General to reinstate the appeal. Majority Leader Joseph Robinson, a Roosevelt loyalist, only narrowly blocked Clark's move.[33] Business groups such as the American Liberty League and the National Association of Manufacturers predictably deplored the Justice Department's action, and the *New York Times* editorially chided the Department for the "unconvincing reasons" advanced in its press release, adding that the Roosevelt administration "is now in the indefensible position of urging Congress to extend with slight modifications an act the constitutionality of which it is deliberately refusing to test."[34] Reaction from the industry whose code was at stake in *Belcher* was equally negative. The industry periodical *Southern Lumberman*, which had become increasingly critical of the NRA for failure to enforce the Lumber Code, was distressed by the dismissal: "There would be no better way to obtain compliance than to go into the Supreme Court . . . with a self-confessed violator of the Code and vigorously seek his conviction; but the Administration, finally confronted with the necessity for thus getting down to brass tacks, has cravenly run up the white flag and declined to meet the issue."[35]

The sudden prospect of enforcement anarchy also created consternation among NRA lawyers in the field, who flooded Washington with protests. "The effect of the withdrawal of the Belcher case has been devastating in this Region, and it is impossible to expect compliance with the Lumber Code here," one wrote from the southern pine region.[36] Another regional attorney wrote that "the riotous retreat on the threshold of the Supreme Court in the Belcher case, the studied campaign of big business interests to decry regimentation and to stampede the halls of Congress, have caused us many a fear and heartache."[37]

Notwithstanding the intensity of this reaction, Richberg would hardly have resumed the fight with Frankfurter and the Justice Department had he not received help from an unexpected quarter. In a development that was as fortuitous as it was promising, on the same day that the *Belcher* case was dropped from the Supreme Court docket another NIRA case was decided by the Second Circuit Court of Appeals in New York. In *United States v. Schechter Poultry Corp.*, a case that involved the New York City Live Poultry Code, the appeals court upheld the government on seventeen of the nineteen criminal counts on which the company and the four Schechter brothers who owned it had been convicted in federal district court. The case had been pending on appeal since the previous November, and neither Justice Department nor NRA lawyers had anticipated the decision. In fact, the day before the case was decided, the *New York Times* had confidently asserted that there was no NIRA case "pending in the lower courts in which an appeal could be filed with the Supreme Court in time to enable that court to render a decision at its present term," which was nearing an end.[38]

This sudden development threw the situation into confusion, which was compounded by two facts. First, since both the government and the Schechter company had prevailed on separate issues decided by the court of appeals, both parties were entitled by Supreme Court rules to seek review. This placed lawyers in the Solicitor General's office in a tactical bind; if the company alone petitioned for Supreme Court review, the government would lose the advantage of framing the issues on the remaining counts in its terms. Second, President Roosevelt was then on a Caribbean vacation cruise, which meant that communication with him was possible only through Navy Department radiogram.

After a quick reading of the court of appeals decision, Richberg fired the first shot in the rapid-fire battle of radiograms. On April 3 he presented the NRA position to Roosevelt:

"Public opinion on dismissal of Belcher case very unfavorable throughout the U.S. Result enforcement of codes generally impossible and hostility of Congress to new legislation . . . seriously weakened. This week federal Circuit Court of Appeals in New York has sustained indictment under another code and defendant asking Department of Justice to cooperate in bringing this immediately to Supreme Court. Prompt action will reverse general retreat and strengthen entire situation. Apparently Department acting on supposed policy not to expedite cases unless otherwise directed by the President. If you telegraph Department your desire to have earliest possible presentation of a good case to Supreme Court result will be in my opinion of extraordinary help in sustaining NRA and advancing legislation. Otherwise present discouragement will gradually destroy industrial recovery program. . . .''[39]

The President's reaction to this appeal opened the door to Supreme Court review of the *Schechter* decision. Roosevelt scrawled a note to his staff on the Richberg radiogram: "Tell Richberg talk with Cummings about expediting NRA case.''[40]

Frankfurter, however, had eyes and ears in the White House in the person of Tommy Corcoran, who quickly learned of the Richberg message and Roosevelt's response to it. Corcoran immediately called Frankfurter in Cambridge and then wired his countering argument to the President on April 4:

"F. F. called. Has learned very confidentially Cummings under urging of Richberg to silence criticism of Belcher dismissal and pursuant to wire from you intends announcing to press this afternoon that government will immediately expedite to Supreme Court a new N.R.A. case from Second Circuit in New York involving poultry code. F. F. suggests most impolitic and dangerous to yield to press clamor now because fundamental situation on court not changed. Further suggests you wire Cummings not to take hasty action and hold whole situation on N.R.A. appeals in abeyance until you return. Suggests at that time thorough discussion in presence of all concerned.''[41]

To Frankfurter's chagrin, the one-day advantage Richberg had gained in this long-distance lobbying campaign effectively decided the issue. Corcoran's message from Frankfurter was accompanied by one from White House press secretary Steve Early, who controlled radio communication with Roosevelt, informing the President that the Justice Department "in press release late today announced intention to present this case and hopes you will not alter action.''[42] Attorney General Cummings, who authorized the Department's press release, may have interpreted the message conveyed from Roosevelt by Richberg as an order rather than the suggestion it was intended to be. Cummings was an astute politician, however, and certainly realized that the political storm that had been raging since the *Belcher* dismissal had harmed the administration. Roosevelt may have intended to keep the issue open, since he responded to Corcoran's message with one addressed to both Corcoran and Cummings, saying that he would "be

84

back early in week and suggest we talk about NRA appeal cases first unless appeal date interferes."[43]

The final appeal date for the government was actually April 11, which came after Roosevelt's return to Washington. But Roosevelt and the Justice Department could hardly back down a second time from a public pledge to submit an NIRA test case to the Supreme Court. Solicitor General Reed, himself an experienced politician, reluctantly bowed to the inevitable, although up to the last minute he tried to alert Roosevelt to the deficiences in the *Schechter* case. The morning of April 11, Reed sent a final appeal to the White House: the case, he wrote, involved "wages and hours of slaughter house employees after poultry has been received in New York, and not hours and wages involved in interstate transportation. This is the most difficult type of labor provision to maintain."[44] His appeal was rejected, and Reed dutifully filed the hastily prepared certiorari petition; the company's petition had been filed three days earlier, on April 8. The Supreme Court granted both petitions on April 15 and set the case for argument on May 2.

The NRA's Legal Politicians had never formulated a coherent litigation strategy pointed toward a strong and well-prepared constitutional test case. Blackwell Smith later assessed the consequences of his decision to focus on skirmishes over small-business cases: "We were handicapped very badly in choosing any good case to put forward by the fact that the cases that had advanced far enough to be on the next calender of the Supreme Court were very few and not particularly impressive. If we had started much earlier, possibly as early as 1933, we might have had a wider choice. But we didn't *have* a good choice. There were very few cases that we would have thought worthwhile to push."[45]

With Richberg in command, Smith and his staff won their last skirmish with the Justice Department, aided by outside forces and by Frankfurter's miscalculations. But this tactical victory saddled them in *Schechter* with what Smith acknowledged was "the weakest possible case." The former foes now had only sixteen days in which to patch up their differences and prepare briefs and arguments.

Chapter Five

THE *SCHECHTER* CASE AND THE "HORSE-AND-BUGGY" COURT

I. CHICKEN COOPS AND THE COMMERCE CLAUSE

The final battle to rescue the National Industrial Recovery Act from the ignominy of Supreme Court rejection began in an unpromising atmosphere. Stung by their almost-unanimous defeat in the "hot oil" cases in January 1935, New Deal lawyers had fought among themselves during the following three months, and the close-quarters infighting that led to the abandonment of the *Belcher* case and its hasty replacement by *Schechter* left wounds that would be hard to heal. Nonetheless, the young lawyers who faced a May 1 deadline in the task of preparing a brief for the *Schechter* appeal worked together in relative harmony during their enforced collaboration.

Several factors contributed to the spirit of cooperation that marked relations between lawyers in the National Recovery Administration and their counterparts in the Solicitor General's office. First, although the Justice Department had prevailed in the debate that preceded the *Belcher* dismissal, the political pressures which forced its replacement on the Supreme Court calendar eroded the Department's determination to insist on ideological purity. Since Department lawyers from the Attorney General on down were pessimistic about the chances for success in *Schechter*, they had little objection to letting the NRA lawyers frame the constitutional issues in corporatist terms. Second, *Schechter* did not involve the price-fixing and production control features to which the Department had particularly objected in *Belcher*. Third, the drawback in *Belcher* of a case brought to the Supreme Court on an appeal from a district court demurrer was not present in *Schechter*, which had been fully tried with a more-than-adequate record. Finally, not only was the case accompanied by largely favorable district court and appellate opinions but the Supreme Court had recently ruled favorably on a central constitutional issue in a case that involved the same industry, the New York City poultry business.

The *Schechter* case itself involved an industry whose complex structure and trade practices became tangled in the factual and constitutional issues with which the New Deal brief-drafters wrestled. New York City was the largest market for poultry in the country, and the "graft-ridden, racket-ridden'' kosher poultry business that catered to the city's large Jewish population was a $90 million industry which employed some 1,600 workers in over 500 small shops.[1] It was an industry with a strong claim to interstate involvement, as all but four percent of the poultry consumed in New York City was raised and shipped in from other states. Wholesale slaughterers such as the four Schechter brothers—Joseph, Martin, Aaron, and Alex, who operated the A.L.A. Schechter Poultry Corp. in Brooklyn—normally bought their live poultry daily in "coops" of about one hundred chickens from dealers known as "commission men" in Manhattan, although occasionally market conditions or a lack of poultry would send them to Newark or even to Philadelphia. Retail poultry merchants or butchers would visit the "market men," as the slaughterers were known, every day or two and pick out coops or half-coops, and the birds would then be killed and dressed under rabbinical supervision by men called "shochtim." Customers were normally permitted no choice of individual birds from the coops; this rule, designed to prevent charges of favoritism, was known as "straight killing."[2] These practices, and their exotic terminology, would later provoke lengthy questioning and unintended mirth during Supreme Court argument.

Attempts to draft an NRA code for the New York live poultry industry began in May 1933, even before the agency was formally established, but it took almost a year to produce a code acceptable to the competing segments of the industry. The commission men, who bought and shipped in poultry from producers, were at odds with the market men over many code proposals. The Live Poultry Code, finally signed by President Roosevelt on April 13, 1934, established a minimum wage of 50 cents per hour and a maximum work week of 40 hours. It also provided for strict government health and sanitary inspection, required the practice of straight killing, prohibited the sale of diseased fowl, and required that all businesses covered by the code maintain accurate records of sales, prices, wages, and hours worked.[3]

"It didn't take Joe Schechter and his brothers long to see the advantages of breaking the code," Drew Pearson and Robert Allen wrote. "And it didn't take enforcement officers long to catch them." Their willingness to sell diseased and uninspected poultry at cut-rate prices "caused Brooklyn to become the dumping ground of sick chickens for the whole United States."[4] Government inspection agents compiled a massive file on code violations by the Schechters, and in July 1934 all four brothers and their corporation were indicted on sixty criminal charges. Among them were allegations that the Schechters had violated the wage and hour provisions of the code, sold unfit and uninspected poultry, permitted customers to violate the "straight killing" provision, maintained false records, and threatened acts of violence against government agents and inspectors. One typical count in the indictment read: "On or about June 24, 1934 . . . the A.L.A. Schechter Poultry Corporation, knowingly, wilfully and unlawfully sold for human consumption an unfit chicken to Harry Stauber. . . ."[5] It was this aspect of the case which gave it the lasting label of the "sick chicken" case.

Walter L. Rice was the Justice Department lawyer assigned to prosecute the Schechters in the federal district court in Brooklyn. A 1928 Harvard Law School graduate, Rice had gained considerable trial experience during his six years in the Department and was intimately familiar with the New York poultry industry, whose corrupt practices had been under federal investigation since the 1920s. FBI reports had identified "Tootsie" Herbert and Joe Weiner as the leaders of the strong-arm men and extortionists who controlled the Teamsters Union local that represented the industry's kosher slaughterers. Herbert and Weiner were convicted in 1932 for contempt of court for having violated a federal court injunction based on a finding that they and ninety-seven other defendants had conspired to restrain and monopolize trade in the industry, and Rice had represented the government when the injunction decree was appealed to the Supreme Court. In upholding the injunction in 1934 in *Local 167 v. United States*, the Court found that the conspirators, by interfering with "the unloading, the transportation, the sales by market men to retailers, the prices charged and the amount of profits exacted" in the industry, had operated "substantially and directly to restrain and burden the untrammeled shipment and movement of the poultry" in interstate commerce.[6] This finding by the Court that the operations of market men (such as the Schechters) were part of interstate commerce naturally encouraged Rice to approach that issue in the *Schechter* case with confidence.

Although he could not at the time foresee the later significance of the Schechter prosecution, Rice considered it important in cracking down on NRA code violations in a corrupt industry. He took pains during the three-week trial that began in October 1934 to establish through testimony and documents the interstate nature of the poultry industry, and built up a 1,500-page transcript detailing the economics of the industry and the code violations for which the Schechters were indicted. Although relations between NRA and Justice Department lawyers were generally strained at the time, the NRA Director of Litigation, A. G. McKnight, gave Rice high marks for his effective preparation and trial work, calling him "better qualified than any member of this Division. With Mr. Rice's familiarity with the whole background of the Poultry Business of New York, it would have been a mistake to let anybody else handle it," McKnight added.[7] During pre-trial hearings on a demurrer to the indictment, Judge Marcus

Campbell had dismissed all but 33 of the original 60 counts; on November 1, 1934, the jury found the Schechters guilty on 19 of the remaining counts. In addition to imposing substantial fines, Judge Campbell sentenced Joseph Schechter to three months in jail, his brother Alex to two months, and the other two brothers to one month each.

Rice and the NRA lawyers who assisted him were pleased with the jury's findings, but they were equally encouraged by the opinion issued by Judge Campbell on August 28 at the conclusion of the pre-trial hearings. A Republican appointed to the bench in 1923 by President Harding, Judge Campbell broadly upheld the NIRA and the Poultry Code against challenges on delegation and due process grounds. He accepted the government's contention that the code provisions enacted under the NIRA were justified by the congressional declaration that a "national emergency" existed. "The emergency existed," Judge Campbell wrote. "The selection of the remedy and the method of enforcement rested with Congress. . . ." On the question of whether the Schechters were engaged in interstate commerce, Judge Campbell cited the allegations of the indictment that "the defendants themselves trucked the poultry into the state of New York" when they bought poultry in Newark or Philadelphia. He also noted that the Supreme Court had held in the *Local 167* case that the New York poultry industry was one in which all the transactions together "affected" interstate commerce. Finally, he relied on the expansive line of Supreme Court commerce clause decisions for authority. "Under the Commerce Clause," Judge Campbell concluded, "Congress may regulate local transactions burdening or inextricably intermingled with interstate commerce."[8] Rice could hardly have hoped for a more favorable opinion.

The Schechter brothers had been represented at trial by Joseph Heller. Short, stocky, and voluble, Heller was a Brooklyn resident who practiced with his brother Jacob in the warren of law offices that surrounded the federal courthouse in Manhattan. He immediately appealed the convictions to the Second Circuit Court of Appeals in New York, before which he and Rice argued the constitutional issues and Heller's exceptions to Judge Campbell's evidentiary rulings in December. When the Court of Appeals finally issued its decision on April 1, Rice found himself victorious on all but one issue.

In writing for the court, Judge Martin Manton upheld the government on 17 of the 19 counts on which the Schechters had been found guilty. Manton's holding on the commerce clause issue indicated no doubt that regulation of the New York poultry industry fell within the powers of Congress: "Transactions or violations, which amount to more or less constant practice, and which threaten to obstruct or to unduly burden the freedom of interstate commerce, are within the regulatory power of Congress under the Commerce Clause." On the delegation question, Manton distinguished the "hot oil" cases decided by the Supreme Court four months after the district court opinion had been issued. These cases had been based on the absence in Section 9(c) of the NIRA "of any declaration of policy or standard of action and the fact that Congress required no findings to be made by the president in the exercise of the authority given him," Manton wrote. But the Live Poultry Code was based on the Declaration of Policy in Section 1 and the requirement of Section 3 that the President approve codes only after hearings had been held. "Findings by the President were made a condition precedent to action by him, and specific provisions of limitation were declared. Not only were standards set up, but definite restrictions were placed upon the exercise of his delegated power."

On one central issue, however, the Court of Appeals dealt the government a blow by reversing the two convictions based on violation of the wage and hour provisions of the code. "These counts are invalid," Manton wrote, "because they have no direct concern with interstate commerce. They were the wages paid at the slaughterhouse to employees not directly engaged in interstate commerce; the number of hours of labor per week and the wages paid cannot be said to affect interstate commerce. . . ." Manton cited no cases and added no reasoning in support of this bald conclusion.

However, Judge Learned Hand expanded on this issue in a concurring opinion. While the regulations that dealt with the transportation, sale, and inspection of poultry applied to goods "still in transit" in the flow of commerce, Hand wrote, regulation of wages and hours crossed the boundary between interstate and intrastate commerce that was essential to a viable federalism. Hand admitted that the boundary could not be fixed with precision, but said that "where the border shall be fixed is a question of degree, dependent upon the consequences in each case." Regulations affecting the cost of labor, he felt, fell on the far side of this elusive line: ". . . labor done to work up materials begins only after the transit is completed in law as well as in fact, and it is not directed towards the importation of future materials; it is a part of the general domestic activities of the state and is as immune as they from congressional regulation."[9]

Blackwell Smith of the NRA and Solicitor General Reed put together from their respective staffs a team of young lawyers to construct a Supreme Court brief out of the *Schechter* case materials and the mixed bag of constitutional precedent. Philip E. Buck, then the NRA's Director of Litigation, assigned a half-dozen lawyers to the job of preparing the factual component of the brief. Reed selected Robert L. Stern, who had recently come to his office from the Petroleum Administrative Board, to assume primary responsibility for the constitutional arguments. The two facets of the brief required close coordination, since a well-constructed brief is based on a tightly joined match between the facts and the law of the case.

The NRA lawyers who worked under Buck's direction had the advantage of the extensive trial record compiled by Walter Rice. This material, to which they added data combed from the economic reports of the NRA Research and Planning Division and the transcript of the Poultry Industry Code hearings, was distilled into a 100-page supplement to the brief. The argument that poultry purchases by the Schechters were part of interstate commerce seemingly presented little difficulty. Rice had called several agricultural economists to testify at the trial, both to establish the interstate nature of the New York City poultry industry and to show that code violations by the Schechters would "demoralize the local and national price structure, reduce the returns to interstate shippers and in other ways burden and divert interstate commerce," as he reported to the Justice Department during the trial.[10] These points were buttressed by evidence in the trial record, noted also in Judge Campbell's opinion, that the Schechters had frequently made purchases in Newark and Philadelphia when poultry was unavailable in Manhattan.

The Justice Department lawyers, however, were uneasy about the evidentiary underpinnings of the commerce clause argument. They recognized that reliance on the expansive line of Supreme Court precedent required a showing of some "burden" on an uninterrupted "stream of commerce" that extended from producer to consumer. The problem was that the poultry handled by the Schechters "came to rest" (in the language adopted in the restrictive line of cases) at two points: first, at the railway terminals at which market men bought live poultry; and second, at the Schechters' shop, when the "coops" were broken up and individual birds slaughtered and dressed by the shochtim. Stern later admitted that "no amount of economic research to unearth judicially noticeable matter could fortify the meagre record on the crucial point so as to show in a convincing manner that these practices in New York substantially affected the interstate poultry market."[11]

These facts not only complicated the commerce clause argument but also weakened the wage and hour issue on which the government had been reversed by the court of appeals. If the shochtim worked on poultry only after it had come to rest in commerce, then their wages and hours were a part of intrastate commerce and subject only to state regulation. Blackwell Smith, who directed the NRA lawyers, became increasingly concerned that this was the weakest link in the brief and that the Justice Department lawyers needed prodding to strengthen it. After consultation with Stanley Reed in mid-April, Smith informed Donald Richberg that he had assigned a lawyer to work on the argument that "a flow of goods in interstate commerce only terminates with the sale to the customer at retail" and that therefore "all processes incidental to the flow of goods to the retail stores affect interstate commerce so as to be subject to regulation." As a fall-back proposition, since he knew that authority for this argument was minimal, Smith advocated the position that congressional rather than state regulation of wages and hours was necessary "because of the tendency of adjacent states to bid for industry on the basis of lower costs" and because "the payrolls received by the masses of workers and their standard of living" affected the volume of interstate commerce. Smith admitted to Richberg that "these arguments can go too far," but he convinced Reed to bolster the brief on this point.[12]

Smith's concern was heightened when he received the Justice Department draft of the brief less than a week before argument was scheduled. The promised strengthening of the weak link did not satisfy him. "The picture of the flow of commerce in poultry to the counter at which it is sold, being very temporarily arrested in the slaughterhouse, could stand more emphasis," he warned Richberg and Reed. The draft brief had conceded a temporary interruption between purchase from commission men and sale to retail merchants, which distressed Smith. It was essential, he urged, to stress that "the slaughterhouse operation is a vital chain in the flow of interstate commerce stream of chickens to the consumer at the counter" and that "this operation is single and cannot be carried on without the workers' services" being regulated as to wages and hours, "inasmuch as a breakdown in this operation would absolutely stop the flow."[13] As it turned out, Reed deserted Smith on this issue during his oral argument.

The *Schechter* case brief-drafters approached the commerce clause issue gingerly, fully aware of the pitfalls placed in their path by the restrictive line of cases. In their own minds, however, they did not question the reach of congressional power to the New York City poultry industry. Stern, whose 1934 *Harvard Law Review* article had brought up to date the economic nationalism of Chief Justice Marshall's 1824 opinion in *Gibbons v. Ogden*, was convinced that "business in the United States has become a single integrated whole." Since "almost all business substantially affects business in other states"—the only exception he could think of was barbershops—Stern concluded that Congress was empowered to regulate all phases of commerce, including wages and hours.[14] The NRA lawyers had no quarrel with this approach; if anything, they found it somewhat timid. Blackwell Smith, for example, had earlier argued to Richberg that "I think we should not admit for a minute that there is such a thing as intrastate business under the present circumstances, and should lay the best foundation possible for an eventual decision" which would recognize the power of Congress to "control any business, whether local or general in itself, which affects the flow of interstate commerce."[15]

It was impolitic, given the need to search for possibly wavering votes on the Supreme Court, for the final *Schechter* brief to adopt the certitude expressed by Stern and Smith. Nonetheless, their views were unmistakably reflected in its central commerce clause argument:

"The contention is not that Congress may control any form of activity which may conceivably to some degree affect interstate commerce, or that an economic crisis confers such power. The contention rests upon the facts. The depressed state of the national economy made it evident that interstate commerce was demoralized and endangered by acts which under other conditions might not seriously affect it. Because of this effect and this danger, Congress could bring those acts within its regulatory power under the commerce clause."[16]

As it took shape during day-and-night drafting sessions, the *Schechter* brief took on a political coloration that reflected Richberg's approach to the forthcoming Supreme Court argument. Richberg had little to lose, considering the essential weakness of the constitutional basis of the government's case, by casting the brief in a political context. Having deferred to the NRA lawyers in bringing the case, Reed and his staff put up no resistance to the idea that the brief should focus on the crisis of the Depression. Although less evident in the arguably hopeful commerce clause section of the brief, the treatment of two remaining issues was as much political as legal. The first of these was the "emergency" doctrine. Notwithstanding its almost unanimous rejection by lower-court judges in the earlier NIRA cases, Richberg and the NRA lawyers were confident that the Supreme Court would not invalidate a statute, however broadly it conferred extraordinary powers on the executive branch, designed to meet an unprecedented economic crisis. NRA lawyers successfully pressed, therefore, for inclusion in the *Schechter* brief of an extended discussion of the World War I cases from which the doctrine stemmed. In a first attempt to frame this issue, one of the NRA brief-drafters analogized the doctrine to the ancient "Law of Self-Preservation" with this extreme conclusion: "Whatever is necessary to that end is lawful, is constitutional."[17] Although another lawyer responded that "over-confidence should be avoided" in relying on the emergency doctrine, the final brief nevertheless stressed its applicability to the commerce clause argument.[18]

Richberg's political approach influenced the treatment of the delegation question as well. With precedent uniformly on their side, the lawyers who drafted the "hot oil" briefs had casually dismissed the issue in three pages. After the Supreme Court struck down Section 9(c) of the NIRA on delegation grounds, however, the *Schechter* drafters could hardly overlook the importance of the issue. They attempted at considerable length to distinguish the "hot oil" cases on the ground that, as opposed to Section 9(c), the code-making powers conferred upon the President by Section 3 rested on the "intelligible standards" set out in the Act's Declaration of Policy. The final *Schechter* brief summarized the issue in these terms:

"The delegation will be found justified by the unprecedented economic chaos existing in the spring of 1933, which compelled Congress to provide for the regulation of a subject of magnitude requiring great flexibility in dealing with different conditions and diverse elements in the various industries. . . . When Congress convened, the banks were closed, millions were unemployed, and business was stagnant. The nation was at the verge of panic; hope and confidence was based largely upon the belief that Congress would take immediate action. . . . It was believed that the distress of industry was largely due to the excess of competition, to competitive practices which had caused overproduction, lower and lower prices, wage cutting and unemployment. The Recovery Act was an attempt to combat these evils."[19]

The final product of the drafting session was a 175-page brief delivered to the Supreme Court clerk's office on May 1, the day before oral argument was scheduled. Its internal structure reflected the inherent tension between the dual elements of the NIRA's corporatist approach to recovery. On one hand, the brief stressed the economic nationalism of Robert Stern's commerce clause interpretation; on the other, it relegated the administration of this nationalist scheme to the very corporate interests supposedly regulated by it. Corporatist ideology saw no contradiction in this structure. The powers of Congress under the commerce clause were paramount; the mechanism of their implementation was subsidiary.

It was Felix Frankfurter who most acutely noted the deficiencies in the *Schechter* brief, admittedly from a perspective tinged with skepticism toward both the NIRA and the wisdom of the appeal itself. After a quick review of the brief, Frankfurter expressed his sentiments to Stanley Reed in light of the earlier "hot oil" decision: "I shall be surprised if delegation does not prove to be much more of a stumbling block in the Supreme Court. Apart from other considerations, it will enable them to avoid the knotty problems of interstate commerce."[20]

II. "LIBERTY TO STARVE" OR "NATIONAL SOCIALISM"?

Tradition has it that only rarely can a skillful oral advocate—Daniel Webster and John W. Davis are illustrious examples—rescue a shaky case at the Supreme Court bar, and that it is hard to lose an otherwise sound case with a dismal oral performance. But as May 2, 1935 approached, lawyers in both the NRA and Justice Department were apprehensive. Since it was unlikely that the justices would have had time overnight to digest the bulky *Schechter* brief, the arguments by Donald Richberg and Stanley Reed would have more than ordinary impact. Although Richberg had relinquished his title as NRA general counsel to Blackwell Smith, he insisted on joining Reed in presenting the government's argument. Richberg's motivations were both practical and political. Reed had previously argued before the Court, but he had served as Solicitor General for only two months and had little familiarity with the NRA codes; Richberg also suspected him as a Frankfurter ally. As Richberg later explained, he was concerned that Reed "had never participated in the NRA, and I felt he might not be able to represent the real interests and purposes of the Administration with the same accuracy and conviction which I might give."[21]

In preparing for the argument, the two lawyers had been prevented by the press of time from getting together for the "wood-shedding" sessions in which lawyers rehearse their arguments and answer questions thrown out by colleagues posing as hostile judges. They had simply worked out a basic division of labor on the issues, in which Reed assumed responsibility for the commerce clause and delegation arguments and Richberg for the crucial wage and hour issue on which the government had lost in the court of appeals. The division reflected Richberg's desire to rescue those portions of the NRA codes which the Roosevelt administration hoped to salvage in the pending NIRA extension legislation, but it also placed in Reed's hands responsibility for the commerce clause issue about which he had earlier confessed doubt to Roosevelt. Reed's lead-off role additionally gave him the preliminary duty of stating the facts of the case, an often-neglected task that frequently frames the issues addressed by the justices in their questioning. Blackwell Smith, who had helped Richberg prepare for the argument, told an associate shortly before the Supreme Court session that Reed had confessed to him that "he was having his worst trouble with the statement of the facts."[22] Should Reed falter at the beginning, Smith feared, the government's case might not recover.

The arguments in the *Schechter* case began late in the afternoon of May 2. Attired in the Solicitor General's traditional swallow-tail coat, Reed rose to begin his argument before a packed and attentive audience. Despite Smith's misgivings, he made a workmanlike presentation of the facts, outlining the structure of the Live Poultry Code and the nature of the nineteen counts of the indictment under review. However, Reed had barely launched into his commerce clause argument when the weakest link in the government's case threatened to part. His attempt to portray an unbroken "flow of commerce" from the farm to the consumer was quickly interrupted by Justice Sutherland: "Is everything that the defendants do which affects the poultry done after it is passed to them?'' he asked Reed, who reluctantly conceded that it was, "so far as slaughter is concerned.'' The facts presented in the brief, Reed weakly countered, would "convince the Court that the New York market is the dominating power over the markets of the country.'' Sutherland's question, however, had broken the chain of his argument, and Reed was unable to repair it.

After this damaging concession, Reed moved on to the delegation issue; here he damaged his case more seriously. In attempting to distinguish *Schechter* from the "hot oil'' cases, Reed argued that, as opposed to the unfettered delegation given the President under Section 9(c) of the NIRA, the standard of "fair competition'' established by Section 3(a) provided the President with sufficient guidance from Congress for the approval of codes. Once again, Sutherland interjected a question. Since the standard set forth in Section 3(a) was that of "fair competition,'' he asked Reed if he would define that term as "anything which is not unfair competition.'' The question gave Reed an opening to rely on the Federal Trade Commission cases cited liberally in the government's brief, and to argue that "fair competition'' was easily definable as the antithesis of the "unfair competitive practices'' subject to FTC regulation. Reference to such a standard, defined in a long series of decisions by the Commission dealing with trade practices, would have eased the delegation problem by pointing the President to a well-established body of precedent. The *Schechter* brief, in fact, explicitly linked the NIRA to the Federal Trade Commission Act and tied the two terms into a common definitional standard. But Reed was baffled by Sutherland's question and feared a semantic trap. Fair competition, he responded warily, was "that type of competition which was accepted by the great majority of those who were in a particular business'' as "fair and proper.''

Justice McReynolds then sprang the trap Sutherland had set. Under the NIRA, he asked, did the President merely accept as "fair competition'' those practices defined as fair by the businessmen subject to regulation? Yes, Reed replied. If this was so, Justice Stone followed up, "what is the standard which the President has to follow?'' Unable to extricate himself from the trap into which he blundered, Reed could only define the standard as those trade practices accepted by a majority of the regulated industry and approved by the President in "his own discretion.'' Delegation had now slipped dangerously far from its mooring in the FTC cases. Justice Butler untied the final knot: "Where in the statute are the standards fixed?'' Having abandoned the standard of "unfair competitive practices'' established by the FTC, Reed admitted that "there is no primary standard in the statute other than that of fair competition.''[23] But if this was the only standard, the President's discretion was by definition unlimited. Frankfurter's warning to Reed that delegation would prove to be a "stumbling block" was prophetic; the Solicitor General had tripped badly over the issue.

Reed's argument concluded the day's proceedings, and when the Court convened the next morning Richberg was confronted with the unenviable task of contradicting his fellow advocate. Only two pages of the 46-page draft of Richberg's oral argument dealt with the delegation issue, but he extemporaneously addressed it at length. "The question of fair competition," Richberg began, "involves the antithesis of unfair competition." The clear intent of Congress, he contended, was that violations of the NRA codes "shall be deemed an unfair method of competition, within the meaning of the Federal Trade Commission act." It was apparent, he concluded, that Congress anticipated the "complete tie-up" of the two standards into one of equal application to the practices regulated by the two agencies. Under relentless and time-consuming questioning from Justices Stone and Sutherland, however, Richberg retreated to a definition of the standard as "nothing but the application of established customs" adopted by businessmen and accepted by courts "without proof," through the expedient of "taking judicial notice of their common practice." Richberg finally begged off from further discussion of the delegation issue; by the time he dropped it, five justices had indicated through their questioning a highly skeptical attitude on the question.

The bulk of Richberg's argument, when he returned to his original outline, consisted of an impassioned political defense of the NIRA and the New Deal. Likening the economic crisis facing the nation in 1933 to such physical disasters as tornados, floods, and fires, he said that Congress had enacted the NIRA at the insistence of "millions of destitute people" who believed that "individual self-protection must give way to an orderly common effort." Richberg's corporatist approach, although clothed in populist and humanitarian rhetoric, was evident in his claim that the NIRA rested on "the sound theory that thousands of businessmen themselves should know better than any small group of lawmakers" what would best stimulate recovery and what were fair business practices. After sparring with Justices Stone and Sutherland over the question of whether NRA codes permitted price-fixing and thus encroached on the antitrust laws—Richberg argued that such practices were actually "in aid of fair competition" and did not restrain trade—he moved on to his primary assignment, a defense of the wage and hour provisions of the code.

Richberg faced a precedential roadblock on this issue; *Lochner* and its progeny, particularly the *Adkins* case which struck down federal wage regulation, stood squarely in his way. His response was to take a circuitous detour. The code provisions, he insisted, did not prescribe wages and hours but rather prohibited unfair trade practices. Wages and hours were regulated not "for the individual betterment of the employee" or to protect his health and welfare but were designed to "promote the health of trade and industry as a whole" to avoid "a complete breakdown" of the economic system. Skipping over the lengthy discussion in his draft argument of the constitutional standards for such regulation, Richberg appealed to the Court not to render Congress and the federal government "impotent" by permitting code violators to continue "sweatshop operations and the worst evils in trade and industry."

Richberg pulled out the rhetorical stops in his emotional peroration, urging the Court not to apply a "narrow legalistic construction of the Constitution" based on "medieval dialectics" solely to "preserve a theoretical liberty—which, without meaning to be brutal, I may say has been very properly described as a 'liberty to starve.' "[24] When Richberg concluded the government's argument, the conceptual and stylistic gap that separated him from Reed remained wide and unbridged. Reed's deferential, hesitant, and narrowly legalistic approach contrasted sharply with Richberg's aggressive, bombastic, and highly political presentation.

The advocates for the Schechters presented an equal contrast, but it was one of demeanor, not of substance. Joseph Heller had been no match for Walter Rice of the Justice Department either at trial or before the court of appeals, and this was Heller's first argument before the Supreme Court. Blackwell Smith's worst fear was realized, however, when he and Richberg learned two weeks before the argument that Heller would be joined by Frederick H. Wood. A partner in the powerful and prestigious Wall Street firm of Cravath, deGersdorff, Swaine and Wood, he was experienced in Supreme Court argument and had recently opposed the government in the Gold Clause cases. Significantly, Wood was a member of the National Lawyers Committee, the branch of the anti-New Deal American Liberty League made up of fifty-eight leading corporate lawyers. The Schechter brothers could hardly have afforded to pay the stiff legal fees normally charged by the Cravath firm. But the small Brooklyn poultry firm and its owners were actually clients-by-proxy for the Liberty League and the Iron and Steel Institute, the most influential and well-financed of the big-business trade associations that had turned against the NRA. Having regained their financial feet with the aid of the NRA code, the steel corporations represented by Wood and his firm now chafed under its labor provisions and hoped to topple it through the *Schechter* case. Thrown together as abruptly as Richberg and Reed had been by the exigencies of the case, the loquacious and colloquial Heller and his sober Wall Street colleague had the advantage of complete agreement on the issues of the case.

Heller led off his portion of the argument by denouncing the poultry code provisions as disruptive of normal business practices. His earthy exposition of the details of the kosher poultry industry sparked the interest of the justices, and the ensuing badinage sounded much like a vaudeville routine. Asked by Justice McReynolds to explain the code requirement of "straight killing," Heller replied that "you have got to put your hand in the coop and take out whichever chicken comes to you." *United States Law Week* reported the succeeding exchange:

" 'And it was for that your client was convicted?' asked Mr. Justice McReynolds.

" 'Yes, and fined and given a jail sentence,' Mr. Heller replied. 'But if a customer wants half a coop of chickens, he has to take it just like it is,' he further explained.

" 'What if the chickens are all at one end?' enquired Mr. Justice Sutherland. Counsel's answer to that question was lost in the laughter from the bench and the bar which ensued. As to the charge of selling diseased poultry, Mr. Heller explained that it was based upon the sale of one chicken which had passed federal inspection, but which, upon an autopsy, was found to be 'eggbound.' "[25]

Upon a more serious note, Heller then hammered away at the delegation issue, stressing the President's "absolute discretion" and the "complete abdication" by Congress of its legislative responsibilities. He distinguished the prior cases in which the Court had upheld delegation; in each of these cases Congress had provided "a policy, a standard, and a method of procedure." Contrasting the limited, fact-finding function of the Federal Trade Commission to the powers given by the NIRA to "an undefinite, unascertained trade group" to draft a code to regulate itself, Heller concluded that the grant of authority contained no intelligible standard and vested "unrestrained discretion" in the President.[26] In his first appearance before the Court, Heller injected a note of humanity and reality in painting the Schechter brothers as struggling small businessmen abused by an oppressive bureaucracy. It was an effective performance; by shifting the focus to a single "sick chicken," which he explained away, Heller deflected attention from the remaining sixteen convictions, which showed a pattern of disregard for health, safety, and reporting requirements.

Frederick H. Wood, after needling the government for its withdrawal of the *Belcher* case, made as political an argument as had Richberg. Carried to its logical conclusion, he said, the government's extreme interpretation of the commerce clause would lead to a "planned economy" and permit Congress to "nationalize industry" and establish "some form of national socialism—whether Soviet, Fascist, or Nazi. . . ." Wood stressed those cases, such as *Kidd v. Pearson*, in which the Court had drawn a line between commerce and production, arguing that "the slaughter of live animals'' was as much a form of production as were manufacture and mining. Sounding very much as if he were reading from a Liberty League tract, Wood concluded by labeling Richberg's commerce clause argument ''an interpretation which would be destructive of our dual system of government and subversive of our political, social and economic institutions.'' On the wage and hour issue, Wood countered Richberg's claim that their regulation was incident to the protection of the general health of the economy with the comment that ''if the power asserted be supported on this ground, then Congress may regulate the wages and hours of all wage earners in whatever pursuit engaged.'' It was the government's recognition of the potentially limitless scope of this position, Wood concluded, that forced the withdrawal of the *Belcher* case.[27]

When the six hours of argument ended, the New Deal lawyers present could only hope that the barrage of hostile questioning to which Reed and Richberg had been subjected would give way in the Court's conference room to sober second thoughts about the consequences of striking down the heart of the recovery program. In a rueful post-mortem a few days later, Reed confessed his pessimism to Frankfurter:

''Unfortunately, you were quite correct in your anticipation that delegation was the 'hot spot' of the argument. . . . Justices Sutherland, McReynolds and Butler made my life miserable by demanding to have pointed out to them the lines of the Act which laid down the definite standards for Presidential action. . . . The argument did not close in any victorious paean, and one can only hope that the brief and an examination of the Act will persuade the Court that we are within the limits of the possibility of delegated authority.''[28]

One of the spectators who shared Reed's faint hope was Joseph Schechter. It was reported that after listening to Richberg predict the disaster that would befall the country if the NIRA was declared unconstitutional, Schechter whispered to a companion, ''I hope they gives it a conviction, so NRA will stand.''[29]

III. ''This Is Delegation Run Riot''

But when the Court convened on May 27, three weeks later, it was immediately apparent that the day would be a disaster for the New Deal and the Roosevelt administration. After the overflow audience, which included Reed and Richberg and dozens of New Deal lawyers who had been alerted that decisions in three key New Deal cases were imminent, suffered impatiently through the routine preliminaries, ''Black Monday'' was underway. Justice Sutherland began by reading a unanimous opinion that Roosevelt had grossly exceeded his authority over the independent regulatory agencies by removing William E. Humphrey, a recalcitrant Republican, from his post on the Federal Trade Commission. Justice Brandeis then read another unanimous opinion, holding unconstitutional the congressional Frazier-Lemke Act, which attempted to protect farmers from mortgage foreclosure; the similar state law upheld the year before in *Blaisdell*, which had cheered the New Deal lawyers, was distinguished on due process grounds.[30]

Richberg and Reed were understandably apprehensive as Chief Justice Hughes then announced that the decision in *Schechter* was next. Speaking in his stentorian tones, Hughes recapitulated in a few minutes the facts of the case. He then paused for a moment, looked up, and pronounced the next sentence with emphasis: "Defendants do not sell poultry in interstate commerce."[31] Paul Freund recalled that "Richberg literally slumped in his chair; he seemed crushed."[32] Having pronounced the death sentence on the NIRA, Hughes went on to elaborate the Court's reasoning, beginning with a brief dismissal of the emergency doctrine invoked by Richberg on the basis of *Blaisdell*. Alluding to Richberg's argument that the NIRA "must be viewed in the light of the grave national crisis with which Congress was confronted," Hughes returned the doctrine to its earlier, narrow limits. "While emergency does not create power," Hughes had recently written in *Blaisdell*, "emergency may furnish the occasion for the exercise of power." The power exercised in that instance, he now reminded his audience, was the legitimate police power of the state, independent of any federal constitutional provision. No equivalent power capable of linkage to the emergency doctrine was available to Congress in enacting the NIRA: "Extraordinary conditions may call for extraordinary remedies. But the argument necessarily stops short of an attempt to justify action which lies outside the sphere of constitutional authority. Extraordinary conditions do not create or enlarge constitutional power."

Hughes next reached the delegation question. First acknowledging that the Court had "repeatedly recognized the necessity for adapting legislation to complex conditions involving a host of details with which the national legislature cannot deal directly," he then exploited the breach opened between Reed and Richberg at the oral arguments. Posing the question of whether the NIRA standard of "fair competition" could find a reference point in the Federal Trade Commission cases defining "unfair competition," Hughes stated that the latter, "as known to the common law, is a limited concept" dealing essentially with the misappropriation of what belongs to another, a somewhat crabbed reading of the term in light of its elaboration by the FTC. "We cannot regard the 'fair competition' of the codes as antithetical to the 'unfair methods of competition' of the Federal Trade Commission Act," he concluded, notwithstanding the clear congressional intent expressed in Section 3(b) of the NIRA to relate the codes to the FTC definition as a statutory analogue.

The delegation point next addressed by the Court went to the heart of the corporatist position. Congress had delegated code-drafting power not to an executive agency over which it might have exercised control, but rather to non-governmental trade associations. Hughes admitted that Congress had in the past delegated limited law-making power, in such areas as the making of rules relating to mining claims or the height of railroad drawbars. In such areas, Hughes said, the regulated groups possessed specialized knowledge and acted in the public interest. He continued:

"But would it be seriously contended that Congress could delegate its legislative authority to trade or industrial associations or groups so as to empower them to enact the laws they deem to be wise and beneficent for the rehabilitation and expansion of their trade or industries? Could trade . . . groups be constituted legislative bodies for that purpose because such associations of groups are familiar with the problems of their enterprises? . . . The answer is obvious. Such a delegation of legislative power is unknown to our law and is utterly inconsistent with the constitutional prerogatives and duties of Congress."[33]

With this statement, Hughes forged the link between the Court's conservatives and liberals. Only one point united them: a shared conviction that the execution of congressional policy was limited to those ultimately responsible to the electorate. A long succession of prior cases made clear their differences on the substance of the policies Congress might establish. But the liberals led by Brandeis distrusted as much as did the conservative bloc an "unelected government" acting in its own economic interest; it was this affront to the competitive ideal, and the tendency of the NIRA to institutionalize the "curse of bigness," that shifted Brandeis from his earlier opinion that the NIRA was defensible.[34]

The delegation question provided the Court with sufficient grounds to strike down the NIRA. Hughes went on, much like a judge sentencing a murderer to consecutive life terms, to invalidate the NIRA on commerce clause grounds, clearly motivated by a desire to attack wage and hour regulation. The court's reasoning on this issue was curiously truncated and conclusory. At some undefined point the poultry bought, processed, and then sold by the Schechters had come to rest, thereby breaking the "flow" of interstate commerce. The Schechters "held the poultry at their slaughterhouse" before its sale to retailers, Hughes said. But what distinguished this act from the "holding" of cattle in a stockyard before their sale, which had been held not to interrupt the flow of commerce in *Swift v. United States*, was ignored. Hughes seemed to rely on the assumption that the poultry "was not destined for transportation to other States." This was an assumption with no factual basis in the record and, even if true, one which was not crucial to the decisions on which the Court relied. Hughes could hardly concede, however, given his determination to block the NIRA, that the flow of commerce extended in an unbroken chain from the producer to the consumer; such a conception would imply an illimitable reach to the federal commerce power. Forced to sever the chain, Hughes conveniently did so in the Schechters' slaughterhouse.

Since it had been decided that the kosher poultry-slaughtering business was not part of interstate commerce, it was seemingly unnecessary to add that wage and hour regulation was equally unrelated to it. But the Court was somewhat uncomfortably faced with its holding the year before, in the *Local 167* case, that the New York poultry trade *did* involve interstate commerce. Hughes dealt with this problem by reviving the distinction between acts having "direct" and "indirect" effects on commerce. Because it had the effect of restraining trade in the industry as a whole, the conspiracy held unlawful in *Local 167* fell in the first category. Since they involved only a single business, the wage and hour violations of the Schechters affected commerce only indirectly. Walter Rice had presented at trial voluminous economic evidence that low wages and long working hours depressed the national price structure, but Hughes made no reference to this data in concluding that "hours and wages have no direct relation to interstate commerce." Hughes did, however, reveal the broader grounds of his objection: congressional regulation of wages and hours opened the door to regulation of "other elements of cost, also affecting prices, such as the number of employees, rents, advertising, methods of doing business, etc." That the Live Poultry Code attempted none of these was immaterial; the admission that any of the practices of local businesses, measured cumulatively, might affect the national economy would invest Congress, under the aegis of the commerce clause, with a conceptually unlimited power. After more than an hour of reading the opinion, Hughes finally concluded with an echo of Frederick Wood's warning that the NIRA, if upheld, would empower Congress to "nationalize" the economy: "It is not the province of the Court to consider the economic advantages or disadvantages of such a centralized system. It is sufficient to say that the Federal Constitution does not provide for it."[35] The ostensible neutrality of this statement concealed little of its hostility toward economic centralization.

The Court's decision was unanimous. But Justice Cardozo, having dissented from the delegation holding in the "hot oil" cases, felt it necessary to explain why he joined the Court on this issue in *Schechter*. In a concurring opinion joined by Justice Stone, he first pointed to his conclusion in the earlier opinion that Section 9(c) of the NIRA had given "no grant to the Executive of any roving commission to inquire into evils and then, upon discovering them, do anything he pleases.'' Congress had explicitly prescribed the means by which the flow of ''hot oil'' in interstate commerce could be halted. It was a simple matter for the President to ascertain that the regultions had been violated and to act to punish such violations. Similarly, the Federal Trade Commission could define and prohibit ''unfair methods of competition.'' Both were essentially proscriptive means of regulation. Cardozo found a distinction, however, between them and the prescriptive ''planning of improvement'' inherent in the codes of fair competition:

''What is fair, as thus conceived, is not something to be contrasted with what is unfair or fraudulent or tricky. The extension becomes as wide as the field of industrial regulation. If that conception shall prevail, anything that Congress may do within the limits of the commerce clause for the betterment of business may be done by the President upon the recommendation of a trade association by calling it a code. This is delegation run riot.''[36]

It was this last sentence which best captured the disillusionment of the liberals; it was their pained reaction to the touching of a most sensitive nerve. Eighteen months earlier, Donald Richberg had confided to a group of businessmen his satisfaction that ''the administration of the law has been entirely in the hands of industrialists.''[37] As he left the Supreme Court on May 27, Richberg was bitterly disappointed at the rejection of his corporatist ideology. But other New Deal lawyers in the courtroom were quietly pleased.

IV. The ''Horse-and-Buggy'' Court

Before Tommy Corcoran could depart, a Supreme Court page tapped him on the shoulder and said that Justice Brandeis would like to see him in the justices' robing room. Brandeis wanted Corcoran to convey a message to the White House: ''This is the end of this business of centralization, and I want you to go back and tell the President that we're not going to let this government centralize everything. It's come to an end.'' Brandeis had a second message for the New Deal lawyers: ''As for your young men, you call them together and tell them to get out of Washington—tell them to go home, back to the states. That is where they must do their work.'' Corcoran was only too pleased to relay the first message. He knew, however, that the second request was impracticable; the demise of the NIRA meant only that the corporatist approach would be replaced with a less ambitious legislative program. New Deal lawyers, in the coming months and years, would be equally involved in regulatory work, directed now by federal administrators rather than industrialists. "Mr. Brandeis," Corcoran replied, "I've known you for a long time; don't mind if I'm impertinent, but they won't go back. The only chance of using these brains is in the federal government right now."[38]

By the time Corcoran returned to the White House, Roosevelt had begun a week-long marathon of meetings with advisors from inside and outside the administration. The President first conferred with Richberg, Reed, and Attorney General Cummings; Richberg was clearly the odd-man-out and resigned his NRA posts and left the administration within two weeks. Reed and Cummings viewed the Supreme Court decision with relative equanimity. Reed reported on the congressional reaction; Senator Arthur Vandenberg, a moderate Republican from Michigan, had told him that the decision was "a great stroke of luck for the President" which would stop his "ultra-radical advisors" from insisting on passage of Senator Wagner's bill to establish a National Labor Relations Board, a measure Roosevelt opposed.[39] Cummings also saw the *Schechter* decision as a bar to the Wagner bill, which he reported to a cabinet meeting the next month was of "rather doubtful constitutionality," and to the bill introduced by Senator Guffey of Pennsylvania to reenact an NRA-type of code for the troubled coal industry, which Cummings called "clearly unconstitutional." On his part, Cummings considered the decision "a God-send to the Administration."[40] His perspective was more political than legal; rather than risk repeated invalidation of New Deal legislation, the Attorney General favored a direct confrontation with the Court in the political arena, over the issue of the reach of its powers. At this time, Cummings had no specific plan in mind, but he encouraged Roosevelt to begin planning a political response. During the week which followed "Black Monday," Roosevelt also met with Felix Frankfurter, who had immediately been summoned from Cambridge and who differed with Reed and Cummings in urging presidential support for a new legislative package including the Wagner and Guffey bills. Frankfurter, however, agreed with the general consensus "as to the incubus that N.R.A. 'as administered' was becoming for F.D.R., and as to the help that its demise will be to him," as he put it to his friend Charles Burlingham.[41]

During the same week, the cautionary voices of Roosevelt's advisors were drowned out by a chorus of denunciation of the Court from the public. From every state, letters and telegrams flooded the White House, expressing outrage and frustration; many of these messages urged the President to declare war on the Court, either through congressional legislation limiting its appellate powers or a constitutional amendment rewriting the commerce and due process clauses.[42] A substantial number of these communications came from small businessmen who feared an orgy of price and wage cutting by larger competitors. A typical telegram reached Roosevelt from a group of Indiana drugstore owners: "We commend you for what you have done to protect the small businessman from ruthless destructive trade practices. We hope you will continue your sincere efforts to the end that Constitutional legislation be enacted that will save the small businessman from eventual extinction."[43]

The pressure on Roosevelt to make a public statement on the *Schechter* decision was intense. In his first meeting with the press, two days later, he deflected questioning on the issue. Finally, on Friday, May 31, Roosevelt was ready. Two hundred reporters crowded into the White House auditorium in which press conferences were held. On the desk behind which the President sat were a pile of telegrams and letters and a copy of the Supreme Court opinions. In contrast to usual practice, his remarks were on the record. "I have been a good deal impressed," Roosevelt began, with "the rather pathetic appeals that I have had from all around the country to do something." He then read to the reporters more than twenty of the messages from the public, from individual businessmen, trade groups, lawyers, and disgruntled citizens. Picking up a copy of the opinion, Roosevelt then launched into a page-by-page exegesis: "The implications of this decision," he began, "are much more important than almost certainly any decision of my lifetime or yours, more important than any decision probably since the Dred Scott case. . . ."

Roosevelt next explored the history of the national economy, from its agrarian roots at the time the Constitution was framed to the industrial present. During this century and a half, he said, the country had become an integrated economic unit, with state boundaries increasingly an impediment to regulation of conditions affecting the national standard of living. "The big issue," Roosevelt told the press, "is this: Does this decision mean that the United States Government has no control over any national economic problem? That actually is the biggest question that has come before this country outside of time of war and it has got to be decided. . . ." He finally reached, after a virtually uninterrupted declamation of almost ninety minutes, his verdict on the *Schechter* decision: "We have forty-eight nations from now on under a strict interpretation of this decision . . . we have been relegated to the horse-and-buggy definition of interstate commerce."[44]

The White House press corps was delighted to have the "horse-and-buggy" quotation on the record, and it was spread across headlines around the country the next day. The more significant story, however, was left to conjecture and speculation. Roosevelt deftly avoided any comment on plans for a campaign to limit the Supreme Court's powers or to reform its structure. The press was not deterred, and filled in the gaps without prompting. Roosevelt's speech, concluded *Time* magazine, "was obviously a trial balloon to see whether the U.S. would rally to a constitutional amendment giving the Federal Governemnt centralized powers which it has never had."[45] More than eighteen months would pass, however, before this eager prediction of a presidential assault on the Court would come true, and then in a different form. In the meantime the Court held hostage the second key element of the New Deal recovery program, the Agricultural Adjustment Act.

SECTION TWO
THE LEGAL REFORMERS OF THE
AGRICULTURAL ADJUSTMENT
ADMINISTRATION

Chapter Six

THE SEARCH FOR PARITY:
THE AGRICULTURAL
ADJUSTMENT ACT

I. A NEW DEAL FOR FARMERS

"For all of the loose talk in America about red revolution," wrote the New York *World-Telegram* at the outset of the New Deal, "Americans are slow to understand that actual revolution already exists in the farm belt."[1] Industrial workers endured four years of growing unemployment after the Crash of 1929, but the Depression began for farmers almost a decade earlier, as the relative prosperity of the 1920s passed them by. The toll of human misery in rural areas, recorded graphically in the gaunt-faced farm families and weather-beaten shacks photographed by Dorothea Lange, was incalculable. But the financial plight of farmers and their families, who constituted almost one-quarter of the population in 1933, could be measured. The long decline in crop prices since the end of World War I was staggering: gross farm income in 1919, at the end of the war-induced boom, was $17 billion; by 1932 it dropped to $5 billion, with a net income of less than $2 billion.[2]

At the heart of the farm problem was the paradox of rising production and falling prices. Advances in technology in such areas as farm machinery, fertilizers, and plant and animal genetics boosted farm productivity. Crop prices plummeted under the twin burdens of domestic overproduction and the closing of foreign markets, a consequence of Republican high-tariff policies. The dilemma faced by farmers after four years of the Depression was that a huge gap had opened between the prices of the agricultural goods they sold and those of the industrial and consumer goods they needed for their homes and farms. Expressed by economists in the bloodless term "parity" (the ratio between agricultural and industrial prices), the parity index fell from 100 in 1919 to 55 in March 1933.[3] In other words, since the war farmers had lost almost half of their purchasing power.

Behind these statistics stretched a decade of panaceas and protest, the backdrop of frustration against which Roosevelt's Brains Trust met to draft a farm bill that would satisfy the conflicting interests of historically antagonistic segments of the agricultural community. Not only were farmers themselves divided by region and by crop and product, and further split into farm organizations that ranged from the conservative Grange and American Farm Bureau Federation to the radical Farm Holiday movement, but farmers as a group faced a common foe in the agricultural processors. Farmers naturally pressed for relief in the form of higher crop prices, while processors opposed schemes that would raise the prices they paid farmers for their goods. Much as the divisions between small and large businesses, and between retailers and manufacturers, produced in the National Industrial Recovery Act a built-in conflict between corporatist and competitive approaches to recovery, the Agricultural Adjustment Act similarly reflected incompatible approaches to the problems of swollen production and shrunken prices.

The debate within the circle of Roosevelt's farm experts and advisors was complicated by the insistent claims of those who continued to fight the inconclusive battles that raged in the 1920s. On one side were those whose solution to overproduction was a plan to regain parity by "dumping" crop surpluses over tariff walls at below-market prices, with farmers to be compensated for the gap between domestic and foreign prices through an "equalization fee" levied on the domestic processors. This export subsidy scheme, known as the "two-price" approach and embodied in the 1920s in the McNary-Haugen bills twice passed by Congress but twice vetoed by President Coolidge, was the brainchild of George Peek. A veteran of the War Industries Board and later the president of the ailing (and eventually bankrupt) Moline Plow Company, Peek voiced the views of the agricultural processors and farm equipment manufacturers whose markets depended on a high volume of farm ouput. An obvious element of Peek's plan was the assumption that any scheme to restrict farm production would cut back the exportable surplus. Accordingly, legislation designed to curtail production was anathema to Peek, who proclaimed himself "steadfastly against the promotion of planned scarcity."[4] As an antidote to the lower farm prices such a production-stimulating program would foster, Peek advocated a compensating system of "marketing agreements" between producers and processors, which would set prices (in much the same way as the NIRA) at artificially high levels. The resulting price increases in food and other farm goods would be passed on to the hapless consumer.

A contender to Peek's plan emerged during the Depression in the form of a production-limitation program. This alternative plan, first outlined in 1929 by John D. Black, a Harvard professor and the dean of American agricultural economists, became known as the Domestic Allotment Plan. Black's proposal rested on two complementary mechanisms designed simultaneously to restrict production and to raise farmers' income. In essence, it would set for individual producers of the staple crops a production quota at a level that would reduce overall output. Such a plan, if successful, promised to raise farm prices to the parity level as demand more nearly balanced supply. Since Black envisioned voluntary participation in the crop-limitation program to avoid the stigma of coercion, an incentive to farmers to cut back on acreage would be provided through a federal subsidy paid to farmers for the amount of the crop that was *not* grown. The subsidy component of the Domestic Allotment Plan represented the contribution of Black's disciple M. L. Wilson, a former wheat farmer and professor of agricultural economics at Montana State College. Wilson devised the idea of funding the subsidy program through a "processing tax" levied on agricultural processors and returned directly to participating farmers.[5] The only point of convergence between the otherwise divergent plans pressed by Peek and Wilson was that, in the end, consumers would bear the burden of higher food and fiber prices. In every other respect, the competing proposals were fundamentally at odds.

The job of choosing between these antipathetic schemes was dumped on Rexford Tugwell, the only agricultural expert on the Brains Trust. Among the triumvirate of Columbia University professors who coordinated the formulation of the New Deal legislative program during the months between Roosevelt's election and the conclusion of the "Hundred Days" session of the first New Deal Congress, Tugwell was the only advocate of comprehensive economic planning. His compatriots, Raymond Moley and Adolf A. Berle, respectively represented the corporatist and pluralist approaches to economic recovery, and neither man challenged Tugwell, who was raised on an upstate New York farm, on agricultural questions.[6]

Tugwell had long advocated crop restriction as the answer to overproduction, and wrote that section of Roosevelt's 1932 speech accepting the Democratic nomination directed at the farm vote. In his speech, Roosevelt held out the promise of higher prices for farmers in return for "such planning of their production as would reduce the surpluses" and make unnecessary "dumping those surpluses abroad in order to support domestic prices."[7] Roosevelt was careful during the ensuing political campaign, as he was on other controversial topics, to avoid commitments to any particular plan for implementing his vague farm program. Already convinced that "it was essential to control production" on the farms, Tugwell took advantage of his Brains Trust post after the election to urge on Roosevelt "again and again and at length" the necessity of a crop reduction plan, and brought M. L. Wilson to Hyde Park to present the details of the developing legislative program to the President-elect.[8]

To his dismay, the politically naive Tugwell soon learned an unpleasant political lesson. Despite his certainty that Roosevelt "understood the necessity of restriction, however much the farmers might object," Tugwell discovered that George Peek had reached Roosevelt's ear.[9] Like his former

War Industries Board colleague and business partner, Hugh Johnson, Peek was a protégé of Bernard Baruch. And, in Tugwell's choleric view, Baruch had purchased access to Roosevelt, insinuating both Johnson and Peek into the rapidly expanding ranks of junior Brains Trusters. By the time Tugwell learned that Roosevelt had been exposed to Peek's importunings, it was too late to repair the damage to the draft farm bill based solely on crop limitation and processing tax subsidies. Peek's plan to allow processors freedom to fix prices and escape the antitrust laws, analogous to the industrial recovery plan embodied in the NIRA, "made a good deal of sense," Roosevelt told Tugwell.[10]

Tugwell had not been able to complete work on his legislative proposal by the time Roosevelt moved from Hyde Park to Washington for his inauguration in March 1933. The task of fashioning an acceptable farm bill was complicated by a volatile political situation. Congress was in an impatient mood, prodded by farm-belt members who realized that their constituents needed to know the outlines of the administration's farm program before the spring planting season began. Cash-short farmers, particularly in the Midwest, faced a wave of mortgage foreclosures to which they reacted with vigilante outrage; sheriffs' sales were broken up, and in Le Mars, Iowa, a Farm Holiday mob dragged a judge from his courtroom and hung him from a telegraph pole. Only after it became clear that the judge would die before he agreed not to foreclose any more mortgages did the abashed lynch-mob release him.[11]

Against this background of urgency and turmoil, Tugwell and Henry A. Wallace, the new Secretary of Agriculture, accelerated their efforts to reach agreement on a farm bill with the divided factions of the agricultural community. Tugwell and Wallace summoned fifty farm leaders to a Washington meeting on March 10, fully aware that among this unwieldy group were advocates of every possible approach to the farm problem. To their surprise, the meeting went smoothly, marred only by the intransigence of the Farmers' Union leaders, who stubbornly held out for a politically unacceptable program of monetary inflation. It turned out that many of the delegates had agreed, during their train ride from Chicago to Washington, that no single-approach plan could satisfy the advocates of crop reduction and those of production stimulation. In order to avoid the congressional blood-letting that would certainly ensue if they remain divided, the farm leaders presented to Tugwell and Wallace a unique proposal. Rather than forcing the administration and Congress to choose between these plans, the conferees suggested a bill that would authorize *both* programs, with the Secretary of Agriculture granted broad discretionary powers to implement either approach or even both. When a delegation from the group met the next day with Roosevelt, accompanied by Tugwell and Wallace, they discovered that the President was delighted with this eclectic proposal, and was more than willing to give Wallace such power. The White House meeting concluded with agreement that a new agency, the Agricultural Adjustment Administration, would be established within the Department of Agriculture to carry out the new programs.[12]

The details of the farm bill were worked out over the next five days, in drafting sessions attended by Wallace, Tugwell, Peek, Hugh Johnson, Bernard Baruch, and the chairmen of the House and Senate agriculture committees. Two additional drafters were lawyers, each brought in to represent the interests of their sponsors, Peek and Tugwell. Frederic P. Lee, Peek's personal lawyer, was a seasoned Washington operator who had formerly served as counsel to the Senate Agriculture Committee. A spokesman for the processors (and later a partner in a Washington law firm that represented International Harvester, General Mills, and other agribusiness interests), Lee had drafted the original McNary-Haugen bills. Jerome Frank, a corporate lawyer with little knowledge of agriculture, advised Tugwell, whom Wallace had chosen to serve as Assistant Secretary. Uneasy allies in the drafting process, the two lawyers distrusted and disliked each other.[13]

Despite the personal and policy conflicts among the drafters, it was a relatively simple task to draft a bill that provided both sides a chance to pursue their own programs. The Agricultural Adjustment Act began with a congressional "Declaration of Emergency." Citing the "present acute economic emergency" as being "in part the consequence of a severe and increasing disparity between the prices of agricultural and other commodities, which disparity has largely destroyed the purchasing power of farmers for industrial products," it declared that these conditions "have affected transactions in agricultural commodities with a national public interest" and "have burdened and obstructed the normal currents of commerce in such commodities. . . ."

The bill went on to declare a congressional policy that farm production and consumption be balanced so as to establish "prices to farmers at a level that will give agricultural commodities a purchasing power with respect to articles that farmers buy" equivalent to that enjoyed by farmers in the prewar base period of 1909-1914. To effectuate this policy, the Secretary of Agriculture was given power in Section 8 to "provide for reduction in the acreage or reduction in the production for market, or both, of any basic agricultural commodity, through agreements with producers . . . and to provide for rental or benefit payments" in amounts determined by the Secretary to be "fair and reasonable." This was all the bill provided for the crop reduction plan, and was cast in such broad terms as to delegate almost unlimited administrative power. The processing tax provision of

Section 9, for the funding of rental or benefit contracts with farmers reducing acreage or production, provided for taxation "at such rate as equals the difference between the current average farm price for the commodity and the fair exchange value of the commodity," which in turn was defined as the price that would "give the commodity the same purchasing power, with respect to articles farmers buy" as it had during the 1909-1914 base period.

The marketing agreements provision was equally terse, giving the Secretary power to "enter into marketing agreements with processors, associations of processors, and others engaged in the handling, in the current of interstate or foreign commerce of any agricultural commodity or product thereof, after due notice and opportunity for hearing to interested parties." Such agreements would "not be held to be in violation of any of the antitrust laws of the United States" and would be enforced through licenses granted by the Secretary, who would retain final authority to suspend or revoke them after a hearing; any person handling agricultural products without a license would be subject to a $1,000-per-day fine.[14]

Roosevelt sent the hybrid farm bill to the House on March 16, less than a week after the White House meeting at which its outline took shape. The haste with which the bill had been drafted reflected the imminent onset of the spring planting season, but congressional action was slowed down by the delaying tactics of the easy-money advocates and their silver-state allies, and it took two months to wear down the resistance of the gold-standard Democrats who opposed inflationary schemes. Roosevelt finally bowed to the political reality that the inflationists commanded a congressional majority, and secured the release of the hostage farm bill by agreeing to an amendment that authorized him to issue silver-backed currency (a power he never exercised). With this roadblock removed, Congress approved the Agricultural Adjustment Act on May 12. The dominant mood of the Democratic majority was expressed by Rep. Fulmer of South Carolina: "I am willing to give the President absolute power and control over production, the marketing of farm products, and the fixing of minimum prices until we can bring agriculture out of the serious difficulty it is in today." Even a Republican who considered the bill "bad legislation" and a product of "national hysteria" pledged his vote for it, explaining that the people had chosen in the election to reject democracy for "the theory of a benevolent autocracy."[15]

In the rush to complete action on the bill before the planting and farrowing seasons passed the point of no return, Congress paid little attention to Republican lectures on its constitutional infirmities. Unlike its companion in the recovery program, the NIRA, the farm bill did not tread on any precedential mine-field such as the well-established distinction between industrial manufacturing and commerce. The processing tax provision of the AAA was entirely novel, and the crop reduction program rested on basic contract principles. The constitutional fundamentalists in Congress nonetheless put their objections on the record. With House debate limited to six hours by a leadership-imposed "gag rule," the only substantial attack on the bill in that chamber was mounted by James Beck, a Pennsylvania Republican and former Solicitor General. Beck's argument was premised on the "very elementary principle" that "the Constitution never vested in the Congress any power in respect to agriculture as such." Dismissing the claim that the federal commerce power extended to agricultural production, he noted that the "only other theory" providing constitutional justification "is the suggestion of an emergency. I think of all the damnable heresies that have ever been suggested in connection with the Constitution the doctrine of emergency is the worst. It means that when Congress declares an emergency there is no Constitution. It means its death." Evoking the specter of the recent grant of legislative power to Hitler by the German Reichstag, Beck drew a sinister parallel: "Chancellor Hitler is at least frank about it. We pay the Constitution lip service, but the result is the same."[16]

An equally futile challenge was raised in the Senate by Beck's Republican colleague from Pennsylvania, David A. Reed, who enjoyed the privilege of unlimited debate. Reed listed five objections in his lengthy oral brief against the bill. First, he said, Congress had no power to fix prices of goods "that are not of public use." Second, Reed scored the processing tax provision, citing the 19th-century Supreme Court decision in *Savings and Loan Association v. Topeka* for the proposition that Congress could not "tax one citizen in order to give the proceeds to another"—such a use of public funds to aid private enterprises, the Court had held, "is nonetheless a robbery because it is done under the forms of law and is called taxation." Reed's third objection was to the licensing power vested in the Secretary of Agriculture, and he cited the recent case of *New State Ice Co. v. Liebmann*, in which the Supreme Court held in 1932 that "the production or sale of food or clothing cannot be subjected to legislative regulation on the basis of public use." He then attacked the delegation of taxing power to the Secretary, who was given "uncontrolled discretion" to fix the processing tax "anywhere from zero to infinity." Under such power of delegation, the Congress could authorize the President to tax any item at any level for any purpose. Echoing Beck, Reed said that if Congress delegated such an unlimited power "we could adjourn and go home, like the German Reichstag, for the next four years." Finally, Reed argued that the bill "does not even limit its application to interstate commerce" and would thus bring every transaction in agriculture under regulation.

Reed and Beck well knew that they were making constitutional arguments before the wrong tribunal. Sourly assessing the pull of expedience over principle, Reed guessed that "there are not half a dozen Senators in this Chamber who sincerely believe that the bill is constitutional." It was easier for his colleagues, faced with the clamor for farm relief, to "shrug their shoulders and pass the responsibility" to the Supreme Court.[17] Of the bill's sponsors, only Senator John Bankhead of Alabama met Reed's arguments directly. Conceding that in his attack on the processing tax provision Reed had "raised one question which is serious," Bankhead predicted that the Supreme Court would uphold the "broad and plenary" powers exercised by Congress.[18] The burden of justifying this prediction now fell on the AAA lawyers.

II. Dirt Farmers and Legal Reformers

It seemed almost perverse that Roosevelt selected George Peek as Administrator and Jerome Frank as General Counsel of the Agricultural Adjustment Administration. Especially in its first years, an agency granted such sweeping regulatory powers and embodying antipathetic programs would seem to require compatibility between the administrators selected to define and implement policy and the lawyers charged with interpreting its statute and defending it in court. Roosevelt certainly knew that there would likely be personal and policy clashes between the two men. But the President seemed almost to relish the prospect of such conflicts, and displayed no reticence either as Governor of New York or during the New Deal in creating bureaucratic cock-pits. In Peek and Frank, however, Roosevelt could not have picked a more combative pair of antagonists. The two men literally shared nothing but a common Illinois heritage which had, ironically, brought them into earlier conflict and left a residue of personal hostility.

Peek was sixty in 1933, and had been raised on a regimen of early-rising farm work. After one lackluster year at Northwestern University, he left to become an aggressive and successful farm implement salesman.[19] During World War I, Peek joined the War Industries Board, where he met Hugh Johnson and became a protégé of Bernard Baruch. At the war's end Peek was enlisted by his friend John Willys to serve as the $100,000-a-year president of the ailing Moline Plow Company in Illinois. Peek brought Johnson with him as his assistant and general counsel, and the two men struggled for several years to revive the foundering concern. The farm implement industry obviously depended on expanded farm production, and Peek had no objection to the crop surpluses created by expanded acreage and advanced farm technology. He and Johnson planted the seeds of the export-dumping plans that took shape in the unsuccessful McNary-Haugen bills in their 1922 pamphlet, *Equality for Agriculture*.[20]

Roosevelt knew that Peek represented the views and interests of the farm processors and had opposed the crop reduction provisions of the farm relief bill, but Henry Wallace assured him that Peek's administrative skills were needed, and that he could effectively enlist the cooperation of the processors in the delicate job of shaping the marketing agreements. Peek did not yield easily to Roosevelt's entreaties to join the AAA, and skillfully exploited his knowledge that his participation was considered indispensable. He initially demurred and urged the President to appoint Baruch to head the AAA, knowing that Baruch had turned down the job and had recommended him. During a meeting with Roosevelt and Wallace, Peek said that "I could not take the job without a lot of things being understood" and agreed only on the condition that he be given access to the White House to discuss policy matters without going through Wallace.[21] Having opened his office door to dozens of officials without regard to organizational charts, Roosevelt did not object, and Wallace did not immediately apprehend the potential threat to his authority.

In temperament, Peek resembled his friend Hugh Johnson: he was gruff, profane, and unyielding in debate, and preferred the company of "practical" farmers and businessmen like himself. Despite his big-business background, he shared the Midwest dirt farmer's distrust of bankers and lawyers. Peek recruited subordinates for key administrative posts in the AAA from the ranks of old McNary-Haugenites and like-minded supporters of the processors' views. As Co-Administrator he brought in Charles J. Brand, an executive of the American Fruit Growers and the National Fertilizer Association. The AAA organizational plan provided for three divisions dealing with farmers and processors, and Peek headed each with a conservative ally. Chester Davis, a Midwest farm editor who had publicized the McNary-Haugen bills and served as Commissioner of Agriculture in Montana, became head of the Production Division, responsible for the crop-reduction program. General William I. Westervelt, a West Point graduate and for several years an executive of the Sears, Roebuck Company, directed the Processing and Marketing Division, in which marketing agreements with processors were negotiated. The third key official was Oscar Johnston of the Finance Division, which managed the benefit payment programs; Johnston was a Mississippi banker and lawyer who managed the world's largest cotton plantation, sprawling over sixty square miles of Mississippi delta and owned by a combine of British cotton mill companies.[22]

In no New Deal agency did a sharper clash in style and personality exist than that between Peek and Jerome Frank. Of all the New Deal lawyers,

Frank most clearly personified the "experimentalist" strain of legal philosophy which mounted the attack on legal orthodoxy under the banner of Legal Realism. "I am—I make no secret of it—a reformer," Frank proudly admitted.[23] At the same time, Frank emphatically rejected the labels of "radical," "collectivist," and "socialist" pinned on him and his staff by Peek and other critics. Although the distinctions were lost on his opponents, Frank's reformist self-image illustrates the limitations accepted by those New Deal lawyers who sought social reform within the constraints of the capitalist system and the legal framework built around it.

Frank's background exemplifies the tensions facing the reformers who left corporate practice and the law schools to join the legal ranks of the New Deal. The son of a lawyer, Frank was born in New York City in 1889 and grew up in Chicago, where he was a precocious graduate of the University of Chicago in 1909 and the university's law school in 1912. After law school, he practiced in Chicago until 1929 in a firm that specialized in handling corporate reorganizations for large Chicago banks. But there was another side to the successful corporate lawyer. Chicago during the 1920s was the center of a school of poets, novelists, and playwrights who celebrated the city's factories and workers with a vigorous, muscular style. Frank and his wife, Florence Kiper, were both writers and became part of the literary circle which included Sherwood Anderson, Floyd Dell, Max Eastman, and Carl Sandburg.

Frank was also involved in reform politics during the 1920s as a member of the "kitchen cabinet" of William E. Dever, Chicago's progressive Democratic mayor, and assisted Dever in his populist fight against the traction magnate Samuel Insull, over the issue of public management of the city's transportation system. His role in this politically messy struggle illustrates the basic commitment to moderate political reform that Frank would carry into the AAA; the proposal he helped prepare for Dever and the city council, which would have combined public ownership of the traction system with control by a joint public-private board, was attacked both by socialists who favored complete public control and by those who wanted to retain private ownership and control. This unlikely coalition defeated the plan in a public referendum, and Frank's disillusionment with his futile effort solidified both his distaste for electoral politics and his advocacy of administrative expertise to solve economic and social problems.[24] "The preservation of our kind of economy" against the attacks of the communists and laissez-faire capitalists, Frank later wrote, should "be assigned to adequately staffed governmental administrative agencies."[25]

In the areas encompassed by Frank's omnivorous interests—literature, science, and politics—the 1920s was a decade of ferment and clash between intellectual rigidity and experimentalism. Given the broad, if somewhat unfocused, range of his mind, it was not surprising that he became dissatisfied with the "factory system" of corporate law practice. He found himself "restless, wanting to do everything except what I was doing."[26] His outlet for frustration was to immerse himself in the ideas and writings of Sigmund Freud, and during a six-month stay in New York on legal business in 1927 Frank explored his interest in psychoanalysis through twice-daily therapy sessions. His experience on the analyst's couch led to the publication in 1930 of *Law and the Modern Mind*, which applied Freud's insights to the judicial decision-making process and established Frank's position as a seminal contributor to the Legal Realist movement. In this book, Frank argued that the search for certainty through logically deduced and inflexibly applied legal rules represented the desire of the adult, in a world of stress and conflict, to replicate the emotional security of the child's world and to transfer to the judge the patriarchal function of the omniscient father. "The Law—a body of rules apparently devised for infallibly determining what is right and what is wrong and for deciding who should be punished for misdeeds—inevitably becomes a partial substitute for the Father-as-Infallible-Judge."[27]

It was Felix Frankfurter's admiration for *Law and the Modern Mind* that led to Frank's selection as General Counsel of the AAA. Frank had moved to New York in 1928 to join the Wall Street firm of Chadbourne, Stanchfield and Levy, but he was no happier than he had been in Chicago, and greeted Roosevelt's election as an opportunity to escape the confines of corporate law practice. He knew Frankfurter only casually, but they shared a mutual friend in Judge Julian Mack of the U.S. Court of Appeals in New York, who recommended Frank as a New Deal recruit. Early in 1933, Frank wrote Frankfurter: "I know you know Roosevelt very well. I want to get out of this Wall Street racket. More important, this crisis seems to me to be the equivalent of a war, and I'd like to join up for the duration."[28] Knowing that Rex Tugwell wanted to find a Solicitor for the Department of Agriculture who shared his economic views, Frankfurter recommended Frank for the post even before the outlines of the AAA were submitted to Congress.

"For your purposes," Frankfurter wrote Tugwell, "it is extremely important to have a man who knows what law he has to get away from and with, as well as to be aggressively imaginative in devising new forms for achieving your policies. That's why I think it is so important for you to have someone who has had not a little experience in the forum, who is steeped in the ways of courts as well as in the thousand and one problems that the practical exigencies of practice and negotiations teach a man." In an insightful comment reflecting more his admiration for Frank's book than his acquaintance with him, Frankfurter added that "Frank has two sides of him—the playful, dialectic, argumentative side, which is very much the minor part of him; and the penetrating, practical-experience talent for bringing results to pass in the world of affairs. Then you must recall also that he is widely read in the modern literature of economic and social thought, and has simply a fiendish appetite and capacity for work."[29]

Although Tugwell had never heard of Frank, Frankfurter's encomiums satisfied him sight unseen and, after a meeting with Tugwell and Wallace, Frank was offered the position of Solicitor. At this point, Frank experienced the first of what would become an unending series of battles with the patronage-hungry, old-line Democrats to whom Roosevelt owed his nomination. Postmaster General James Farley, for whom patronage and party loyalty were the currency of politics, got wind of Frank's impending appointment and somehow confused him with a former political foe in New York state politics; the Solicitor's post, he convinced Roosevelt, had been promised to a Midwest party stalwart named Seth Thomas. Fortuitously, Tugwell persuaded Frank that the job as General Counsel of the AAA would prove more important and interesting than that of Solicitor, which in fact involved only the most routine legal business of the Department.[30]

Farley's opposition to Frank stemmed from a misunderstanding, but Peek's campaign against his appointment was deliberate and determined. Following his successful dictation to Roosevelt of his terms for accepting the top post in the AAA, Peek returned to the White House to argue that Frank was unqualified for the job as general counsel. "I advanced among other reasons the thought that he had no experience with farm organizations and farmers, that he had been a city lawyer, and that his personality was such as not to inspire the confidence of the farm leaders," Peek later wrote. Peek's "other reasons," however, were at the root of his objections to Frank. In his autobiography, Peek blandly described his prior relations with Frank in these words: "I found that I knew him—I had met him at a time when he was counsel for a group of banks."[31] But Frank had represented, in the 1920s, the Chicago banks which liquidated the Moline Plow Company after Peek struggled for years to rescue it from bankruptcy, and Peek did not forgive or forget this humiliating encounter. Peek understood from his meeting with Roosevelt that the President agreed with him and would tell Henry Wallace to arrange Frank's transfer to the Justice Department. But Wallace resisted and turned the issue into his first confrontation with Peek. "If you force Frank to resign," he told Peek the next day, "I will also have to resign; it will interfere with all our plans."[32] The outcome of this imbroglio ensured that the resulting struggle within the AAA between the administrators and the lawyers would be short and bloody.

Peek did, however, gain a measure of revenge by challenging Frank's authority as general counsel. In an unprecedented move, Peek retained Fred Lee as his private counsel in the agency, a step he characterized as a "precaution" against the "left-wing lawyers" in the General Counsel's office.[33] This highly unusual arrangement, in which Lee was paid from Peek's personal funds, was based on an understanding that "any matter which I may refer to you for advice under this relationship shall be held in complete confidence," and was approved by Wallace, who had disregarded Frank's fierce objections.[34] Frank felt that Lee "wasn't very bright," and continually clashed with him. "Fred Lee would sit in meetings where I would give opinions. Then he would tell Peek not to pay any attention to it."[35] It was clear that Peek regarded Lee as his lawyer and Frank as an unwelcome, radical interloper.

Frank responded to the administrative domination of the AAA by agribusiness interests by staffing his office with lawyers who shared his reformist views and urban, liberal background. In a 1933 speech to law school professors and deans, Frank described the qualities he sought in his lawyers. The ideal AAA lawyer would be first an idealist who shared Roosevelt's goal of giving "the forgotten man a decent life, free of gnawing insecurity," a goal which could be best achieved through "an elaborate series of experiments which . . . will permit the profit system to be tried, for the first time, as a consciously directed means of promoting the general good." Frank's ideal lawyer would also realize that "experimentation is an imperative necessity" in a period of "economic catastrophe." He would ask such a lawyer whether, in interpreting a "highly ambiguous" statute, "a proposed program for the relief of the destitute would be lawful." The answer he sought was simple. "This," the ideal lawyer would respond, "is a desirable result. It is all but essential in the existing crisis. The administration is for it, and justifiably so. It is obviously in line with the general intention of Congress as shown by legislative history. The statute is ambiguous. Let us work out an argument, if possible, so as to construe this statute as to validate this important program."[36]

But the idealism and experimentalism Frank sought in his lawyers were not the starry-eyed and slap-dash kinds. Practical experience in the intricacies of corporate law was also a prerequisite. While the ultimate purpose of the AAA "is to aid the farmer," Frank told Roosevelt, its legal work would "involve for the most part dealings with industrial groups." The AAA lawyers would deal with "some of the largest and wealthiest corporations in the country, such as the packers, the millers, and the tobacco companies. They retain as their counsel the ablest and highest-paid lawyers." To cope with these Wall Street paladins, "our lawyers must have considerable background of commercial and corporate law and a knowledge of industrial and corporate relations" and be "extremely ingenious and alert to detect subterfuges, evasions, and artful devices designed to frustrate the purposes of the Administration."[37]

Most of the lawyers Frank recruited for the AAA matched his ideal profile, and combined the idealism, experimentalism, and corporate background he sought. Two lawyers in particular became Frank's closest associates and exhibited the characteristics of the Legal Reformer in almost pristine form. Lee Pressman and Alger Hiss were classmates at Harvard Law School, and served together on the *Harvard Law Review* in 1928 and 1929. Both became protégés of Felix Frankfurter, from whom they absorbed the ideal of the lawyer as the indispensable civil servant, and of Thomas Reed Powell, who preached in his constitutional law classes, Pressman recalled, that the decisions of judges depended on "the nature of the breakfast they have in the morning."[38] Hiss in particular was transformed by his law review experience. "I was pretty conservative in college. I became a liberal at Harvard Law School. My first taste of liberalism was working on a yellow-dog case for a law review note, which Pressman assigned to me; I'd never heard of a yellow-dog contract. And as I went back in the cases, I could see how unfair the courts had been."[39] Hiss's emergent liberalism was evident in his law review note, in which he praised the "enlightened attitude" of two recent New York decisions refusing to enforce yellow-dog contracts and predicted that, if followed by other courts, they would "go far to cut down the effectiveness of the yellow dog devices in curtailing union growth and collective bargaining."[40]

The two lawyers took slightly different paths to Washington. Pressman returned to New York after graduation from Harvard and worked in the Wall Street firm that Frank joined after his move from Chicago. Hiss, who was closer to Frankfurter, was annointed with a prized clerkship with Oliver Wendell Holmes, and although Holmes was nearing ninety and in failing health, the patrician young liberal and the patrician old skeptic formed a close bond. Following his year as a Supreme Court clerk, Hiss returned to Boston and spent two years in corporate practice before he moved to New York and the Wall Street firm of Cotton and Franklin. During the Hoover years, most of the work that occupied Hiss and Pressman dealt with the complexities of corporate reorganization. Hiss was Frank's first recruit, having been recommended by Frankfurter, and needed no prompting to leave Wall Street. "By the time the New Deal came along we were all raring to be public servants," he recalled.[41] Hiss in turn recruited Pressman, although Frank needed no urging to add him to the nucleus of the AAA legal staff. Frank had been greatly impressed by Pressman during three years of association with him in New York, and considered him "probably the best lawyer that I've ever met" and "the quickest legal mind I've ever encountered."[42]

Along with Tommy Corcoran's brother Howard and Leon Keyserling (who soon moved to Senator Wagner's staff), Hiss and Pressman worked without pay for the month before the AAA was formally organzied. During the next few weeks, Frank added several lawyers to his staff: John Abt, who would become Director of Litigation, had been a junior lawyer in Frank's Chicago firm; Arthur Bachrach, Abt's brother-in-law, was considerably older and an outstanding trial lawyer whom Frank felt would contribute maturity to decisions on litigation problems; and Nathan Witt, a 1932 Harvard Law School graduate and a friend of Pressman, was a working-class product of the Lower East Side of New York who drove a cab to finance his law school education. Frank also enlisted, on a special assignment basis, three members of the Yale Law School faculty; Wesley Sturges and Thurman Arnold were seasoned lawyers and law teachers, and Abe Fortas, who served as editor-in-chief of the *Yale Law Journal* in 1932 and 1933 and who remained at Yale as assistant professor until 1937, had impressed Frank during his part-time stint as a law school lecturer.

Frank's staff eventually grew to include some sixty lawyers, a predominately young, city-bred crew with a heavy Ivy League representation. Imbued with the Frankfurter's civil service ideals, they were confident almost to the point of cockiness that the farm problem would yield to their reformist zeal and technical skills. The fact that only a handful had any farm background did not dissuade Frank from hiring them; since the AAA programs rested on a system of contracts and taxation, Frank sought out lawyers with background in these areas. "While we are seeking to aid the farmer," he explained, "our method of doing so is in large part not through dealing with the farmer but through contracts with large industrial corporations." Therefore, Frank concluded, "a lawyer from the smaller towns will not fill the bill."[43]

Frank's deliberate policy had a predictable consequence. The conservative ruralists who dominated the AAA grumbled that Frank was foisting on the agency a Harvard cabal of lawyers with no sensitivity to farm problems. Peek's patronage assistant, Julian Friant, complained about the composition of Frank's "personal machine." Demanding that Frank hire lawyers with proper political credentials and farm backgrounds, Friant caviled that "Harvard does not specialize in agricultural subjects, and great as it is, the graduates of that college are not entitled to the large percentage of appointments they are securing" in the Legal Division.[44] Friant singled out Hiss, Pressman, and Witt as examples of the Harvard cabal in Frank's office. Frank responded that it was "plain nonsense to say that I am trying to build up any kind of a personal following." It was only natural, he added, "that in selecting reliable men I should pay some attention to those men whom I know fairly well. To do that is not to endeavor to build up a machine."[45] It was a disingenuous debate on both sides, since the heart of the conflict was that both Frank and Peek surrounded themselves with like-minded associates with compatible backgrounds.

What Friant framed as a question of patronage and credentials had deeper roots, which stemmed from Frank's role as a Jew in an agency inhospitable to Jews. In the background was the virulent strain of anti-Semitism which had infected elements of the agrarian movement since the 1890s and which stereotyped Jews as big-city bankers and lawyers. This factor, and Frank's response to it, illustrates the precarious nature of his role in the AAA and the ambiguities of his self-image as a reformer. Jerold Auerbach has written that Frank and the heads of other New Deal legal offices "were troubled by the overabundance of qualified Jewish lawyers and by the political liabilities inherent in placing too many of them on their staffs."[46] Frank was more than troubled. Whether real or imagined, the issue so disturbed him that he adopted a conscious policy of reverse anti-Semitism in his hiring practices.

The harsh realities of the legal job market in the Depression era placed Frank in a dilemma as he recruited lawyers. Both as an expanding source of scarce legal jobs and as an outlet for idealism, the New Deal agencies attracted young Jewish lawyers barred from employment in most prestigious law firms by long-standing exclusionary policies. And Jews were disproportionately represented among the most highly qualified law school graduates. By the early 1930s, for example, close to a third of the *Harvard Law Review* editors were Jewish.[47] Applications from Jewish lawyers, accompanied by glowing recommendations from well-connected law school professors, inundated the offices of the New Deal general counsel. Frank's dilemma was more acute than that facing most of his counterparts, since many of the AAA administrators made no secret of their prejudices. As with most forms of prejudice, class and cultural differences overlay the related ethnic and religious components. Arthur Schlesinger, Jr., in his listing of Peek's objections to the lawyers on Frank's staff, identified an entire constellation: "There were too many Ivy League men, too many intellectuals, too many radicals, too many Jews."[48]

What is surprising, however, is that Frank manifested a sensitivity to the issue of hiring Jewish lawyers before any indication of opposition from AAA administrators. He wrote Felix Frankfurter, even before Congress approved the farm bill, lamenting that "one of my problems, as you can well appreciate, is the possibility of having too many Jews on the legal staff. Unfortunately, most of these capable young fellows from Harvard or Columbia, and even Yale, bear that disability."[49] Within days of his appointment, Frank sent Henry Wallace a list of a dozen lawyers he wanted to hire, including several who volunteered their services during the bill-drafting process. Frank noted that, with one exception, "none of the persons in the foregoing list are Jews. . . ." He was especially eager, he told Wallace, to hire Lee Pressman and Arthur Bachrach. As a junior member of Frank's New York law firm, Pressman impressed him as "an exceptionally able lawyer. . . . However, he is a Jew." Frank had worked closely with Bachrach in Chicago, and called him "unusually skillful in assisting in handling a legal staff. Unfortunately, Bachrach is a Jew." In addition to the dozen lawyers listed in the memorandum, Frank concluded, he had interviewed another ten who "would be excellent additions to the staff; only one of them is a Jew."[50]

Frank did, in fact, hire Pressman and Bachrach, but he made a point of limiting the number of Jews on his staff. In August 1933 he reported to Wallace a comment by Charles Brand that his staff included "an exceptionally large number of appointees, or proposed appointees, who are Jews." This was not the case, he assured Wallace; in addition to himself ". . . there are only two Jews on the staff and I have recommended two others. The total staff will be something over thirty, and I do not think that five Jews out of this total would be a disproportionately large number. Indeed I have taken such care to discourage Jewish applicants that I have gained the reputation among my non-Jewish friends, at Columbia, Yale, and elsewhere, of being anti-Semitic. At least half a dozen very able lawyers have been rejected by me on this ground. . . ."[51]

Frank's self-deprecating comments did not mask his obvious insecurity. More than a year later, after Peek and Brand had resigned and the current Administrator was Chester Davis, against whom no allegations of anti-Semitism were ever raised, Frank wrote to Alger Hiss and two of Hiss's assistants (none of them Jewish) that he had recommended to Davis that the legal staff be expanded. "I was very much embarrassed," he reported telling Davis, "by the fact that a very considerable number of the particularly able lawyers available for such work were Jews. . . ." He had cautioned Davis that appointing more Jews "might cause comment unfavorable both to him and to me." Significantly, Davis instructed Frank to disregard such criticism and to appoint "the ablest lawyers available" regardless of ethnic considerations. But Frank remained sensitive and criticized Hiss and his assistants for his predicament:

". . . I have for some time been disturbed by the fact that there have been recommendations . . . of many lawyers who are Jews. Perhaps the majority of those recommendations have come from you three gentlemen, and as you know I have again and again urged you, if possible not to make such recommendations, and if possible to recommend lawyers who are not Jews."[52]

Can this hypersensitivity be squared with Frank's self-image as a "reformer" and his reputation as a defender of oppressed groups such as sharecroppers? It may be true, as Auerbach argues, that Jewish lawyers created political liabilities for the New Deal agencies. But Charles Fahy, a more conservative lawyer with a Catholic-Jewish heritage, hired many Jewish lawyers for the National Labor Relations Board and defended them vigorously against the political attacks of a congressional committee headed by a blatant anti-Semite. A more plausible explanation than deference to the prejudices of Peek and the AAA administrators is that Frank was constrained by the essential conservatism of his professional identification, psychologically segregated from his reformist approach to policy questions. As an assimilated German Jew, he wanted to avoid the opprobrium of the "Jewish lawyer" stereotype. Two comments are unconsciously revealing of Frank's distancing of himself from the problem. Adlai Stevenson, who joined Frank's staff through patronage and a family connection with Peek, revealed the eagerness of the genteel, upper-class anti-Semite to distinguish assimilated Jews from those displaying the "pushy" traits which offended his WASP sensibilities. "There is a little feeling" in the AAA, Stevenson wrote his wife after a short time on the job, "that the Jews are getting too prominent. . . ." Frank, he added, "has none of the racial characteristics" of the other Jewish lawyers who, although "individually smart and able, are more racial."[53] And Frank himself, after his AAA career, responded to rumors that his hoped-for judicial appointment was delayed because he was Jewish by assuring Harry Hopkins of the White House staff that he was "a good soldier . . . and won't start a rumpus. . . ."[54]

III. THE FIRST TRIPLE-A PURGE

A curious consistency linked Frank's defensiveness in dealing with the ethnic composition of his staff and the aggressiveness with which he pursued his positions on AAA policy. To the extent that he deflected criticism on the first issue, Frank freed himself to battle Peek over substantive policy differences. This perception may have been entirely internal, a psychological ordering of priorities invisible to Frank's adversaries within the agency (as seems true from the evidence of Peek's sentiments and suspicions). Nonetheless, Frank's self-imposed deference on the Jewish issue stands in marked contrast to the assertion of his prerogatives within the policy-making process. The seven-month-long internal struggle that ended with Peek's resignation revolved around this question.

From the outset of his tenure, Frank firmly insisted that his position as

General Counsel made him an equal participant with Peek in framing AAA policy and in ensuring that all crop-reduction contracts and marketing agreements effectuated the purposes of the statute. Frank only took the job, he recalled, on Wallace's assurance that he would be "more than a lawyer."[55] And, as he told Peek, the wide powers invested in the Secretary by the statute made it "impossible to draw a nice line between policy and law" and thus made it equally impossible "for the lawyers to dismiss all questions of policy as none of our business." He was thus obligated to examine each exercise of the Secretary's power "to determine whether, in the light of the declared policy [of the statute], the Secretary is acting within the scope of the powers delegated to him by Congress."[56]

Peek disagreed vehemently with this attitude. He viewed Frank as *his* subordinate (and an unwelcome one at that) and not as Wallace's legal advisor. That position, Peek felt, was held by Seth Thomas, the departmental Solicitor, and the very structure of the AAA as a semi-autonomous agency within the Agriculture Department was simply an administrative convenience. Peek additionally felt that the condition on which he had taken the post as AAA Administrator, of access to Roosevelt without interference by Wallace, implied a free hand in formulating AAA policy subject only to Roosevelt's oversight. The Secretary's second thoughts about this unique arrangement came quickly, but too late to head off the power struggle between Peek and Frank. Within days of Peek's appointment, Wallace complained to Roosevelt about Peek's "insistence on you as an umpire between him and myself" and urged a "clear and final understanding by the three of us that I am definitely Mr. Peek's chief. . . ." Wallace particularly cited Peek's opposition to the choice of Frank as General Counsel. If the Secretary's power to choose his staff could be appealed to the White House, Wallace argued, "my position, and even yours, will become anomalous."[57] But although Wallace prevailed on the selection of Frank, Roosevelt refused to rescind his agreement with Peek. This characteristic hands-off attitude toward personal conflicts within New Deal agencies guaranteed that the fundamental policy differences within the AAA would persist.

Although Peek and Frank clashed on virtually every issue faced by the AAA, their differences flared into open warfare over two significant issues during 1933. Both reflected Frank's concern that agricultural processors were determined to pass on to consumers considerably higher prices than those paid growers under the marketing agreements. Most processors, he felt, could well afford to absorb the cost of higher farm prices. Peek, on his part, did not share Frank's solicitude for the consumer and disparaged attempts to limit consumer price increases as an "anti-profit line" pushed by "collectivists."[58] With his single-minded desire to raise farm prices,

Peek ignored Frank's larger view that failing to limit price pass-ons to the consumer would ultimately hurt farmers in the form of higher prices for the goods they had to buy.

The first policy issue over which Peek and Frank battled involved the cigarette tobacco industry. Prices paid by cigarette manufacturers to planters on the auction market fell precipitously during the summer of 1933 in response to increased supply, and the eight companies that dominated the market resisted proposals by the AAA that they increase their bid prices. Such a voluntary move, in anticipation of a negotiated AAA marketing agreement, would protect smaller planters against a profitless season and the threat of bankruptcy or mortgage foreclosure. When the manufacturers refused, sporadic violence broke out at tobacco auctions and the governors of North and South Carolina ordered markets closed in those states. The impasse was broken when the AAA took the initiative and proposed a marketing agreement raising the price of flue-cured tobacco to 17 cents a pound (from the prevailing low price of 10 to 12 cents) and additionally requiring that manufacturers not raise their consumer prices without the Secretary's approval. The agreement drafted by AAA lawyers also included a provision, designed to permit policing of price levels, that gave the AAA access to the "books and records" of the companies.[59]

Tobacco processors vigorously resisted the proposed "books and records" clause (as did processors in general) on the ground that the resulting inspections might reveal confidential financial data to competitors. Their unstated but obvious fear was that such inspections might uncover evidence of industry-wide price-fixing agreements. Processors additionally feared that Wallace would reject any move to raise consumer prices. In this event, the cigarette manufacturers stood to absorb market price increases paid to planters, which they calculated would cut their profits by some 12 to 15 million dollars. The muscle behind the AAA proposal lay in the Secretary's power to impose the marketing agreement on the industry through the exercise of his statutory licensing provisions.

After an inconclusive internal debate with Frank over the issue, Peek presented the processors' grievances at a White House meeting with Roosevelt in October 1933. Peek attacked the criticisms made by AAA lawyers of the industry's "excessive profits" and their proposal that the AAA "take direct control of the markets by licensing all buyers at once." He urged Roosevelt, in this first test of his authority, to allow him to set the "basic policy" of the AAA, and won the President's approval of the compromise agreement that processors would use "all reasonable effort" to limit consumer price increases; the compromise also limited the Secretary's authority to examine the books and records of the companies. Frank and Wallace lost their first White House confrontation with Peek,

130

whose later assessment of the outcome was accurate: "The show-down on tobacco made the cabal even more determined."[60]

The second showdown was already in motion, and Peek was correct in assuming that Frank was determined not to lose another policy battle. At issue were marketing agreements in the anarchic dairy industry, with more than four million producers and thousands of processors and distributors. A recurring situation of overproduction and wildly fluctuating prices gave the large processors the upper hand in setting prices to both dairy farmers and consumers. The policy difference separating Peek and Frank crystallized in the dispute over the marketing agreement for the Chicago area milkshed. The large processors, organized into the Pure Milk Association, proposed an agreement fixing prices at a level considered too high by the smaller dealers represented by the Chicago Milk Dealers' Association. Consumer groups, who had a sympathetic ally in Dr. Frederick Howe of the Consumer Counsel's office in the AAA, also complained that retail prices under the proposed agreement were too high, and the chain groceries urged that the agreement allow them to charge lower prices than home-delivery companies, based on their lower costs.

Frank and his staff resisted pressures from Peek and the Dairy Section of the AAA to rush through the proposed agreement. The economics of the dairy industry, fragmented into dozens of regional milksheds, were incredibly complex, and Frank and Howe insisted on giving each marketing agreement careful scrutiny. Frank reluctantly approved the Chicago agreement, which went into effect on August 1, 1933 and which incorporated a mandatory licensing provision and a price schedule that the small processors claimed was discriminatory. He realized that the licensing provisions of the milk agreements (which were to generate most of the AAA litigation discussed in the next chapter) operated to the disadvantage of small producers and "raised hair-raising problems legally."[61]

On his side, Peek was inundated with complaints from large processors that Frank's staff was slow to institute license revocation proceedings against their smaller competitors for violating the price levels. A personal dispute between Frank and Clyde King, head of the AAA's Dairy Section, complicated matters. Frank accused King of spreading "the nastiest kind" of insinuations that he "was guilty of venality" through the connections of his former Chicago law firm with milk processors. The slow pace of license revocation proceedings, Frank replied, was due to King's failure to provide adequate evidence of violations which produced "an embarrassing situation where we do not dare to proceed with the enforcement of license provisions which, at your insistence, have been promulgated."[62]

The conflict escalated when King wrote Frank that "your psychoanalysis is rotten" and "smells of the sewer," and complained to Peek of the "nervous strain" brought on by "the sabotage that has handicapped my work and made yours difficult."[63] Under pressure from the large processors and his staff, Peek wrote Wallace on November 15 demanding that Frank be dismissed. "If you do not agree," he asked, "may we not discuss the subject with the President?" Wallace sided with Frank, and responded with a proposal that Peek ask for King's resignation as head of the Dairy Section, which Peek refused to consider. The conflict came to a head on December 6, when Wallace called a press conference and, with Peek standing speechless at his side, declared that the milk marketing agreements were a failure, that the export subsidies for which Peek was pressing were not the solution to the farm problem, and that he was endorsing Frank's proposal for a sweeping books and records inspection provision in the pending marketing agreement with the powerful meat-packing industry.[64]

It was obvious that Peek would not survive what one of the newsmen at the press conference called "the coolest political murder that has been committed since Roosevelt came into office."[65] Later that night, Peek and Wallace spent several hours with Roosevelt, with Peek bitterly denouncing Frank as a meddler in policy and demanding that he be fired. In this crisis, however, Roosevelt sided with Wallace and Frank and, after another day of canvassing his advisors, offered Peek a new post as special assistant to the President for foreign trade policy. Peek held out for a week before he accepted the face-saving offer and left the AAA. His successor, Chester Davis of the Production Division, headed a crop-reduction program that he had earlier opposed as a McNary-Haugenite. But if Peek and Davis were ideological twins, Davis at least had maintained cordial relations with Frank and his staff; to this extent, their policy differences were not complicated by corrosive personality conflicts.

Wallace had engineered the first "purge" in the AAA, unwilling to accept Peek's challenge to his authority. The *New York Times* reported accurately that the "chief bone of contention" that led to Peek's departure was his dispute with Frank, in which Peek had been "consistently in favor of a minimum of regulation, particularly regarding profits, taking the position that processors should be able to make as much as they wish, as long as the farmer gets a fair return."[66] Peek's replacement by Davis eased the atmosphere in the AAA, but the policy divisions within the agency remained, as did the conflicts between farmers and processors over what would be a "fair return" under the marketing agreements, and between farm owners and their tenants over the terms of the acreage-reduction contracts. During the crucial year of 1934, these conflicts tested the AAA's Legal Reformers, the first through unwelcome litigation and the second in a divisive battle with their internal foes.

Chapter Seven

THE TRIPLE A IN COURT

I. LOOKING OUT FOR THE MACARONI GROWER

Jerome Frank came to the AAA with the Wall Street lawyer's attitude toward litigation: it was embarrassing proof that the lawyers on both sides had failed to negotiate and draft agreements satisfying the needs of their clients. Successful corporate lawyers also prided themselves on their ability, when such agreements broke down, to compromise disputes and avoid recourse to the courts in resolving them. Only as a last resort, and then with an eye toward increasing pressure for a settlement, did the corporate lawyer turn the problem over to the firm's litigation section.

Frank initially assumed that the major task of the AAA lawyers would be the technical job of negotiating and drafting benefit contracts and marketing agreements which would accommodate contending interests and be largely self-enforcing. This assumption colored his policy of recruiting lawyers with a corporate background similar to his own. Early in his tenure, Frank met with Harold Stephens of the Justice Department and Felix Frankfurter to lay out procedures for AAA enforcement. The three men agreed, Frankfurter reported to Stephens, that "resort to the courts should be the last and not the first measure." Frankfurter expressed confidence that AAA enforcement would not burden the Justice Department with litigation responsibilities, since "Frank has surrounded himself with an unusually seasoned and well-perspectived lot of lawyers," many of them, of course, Harvard products who had absorbed Frankfurter's strictures on the evils of precipitate litigation.[1]

Frank had no quarrel with this cautious approach. In fact, as originally structured, the General Counsel's office did not include a litigation section. "There will be little in the way of litigation for these men to engage in," Frank predicted in August 1933. "Consequently, men who are highly skilled as trial lawyers might prove to be very mediocre" in the legal work of the AAA, he explained in defending his recruitment bias toward corporate law-office experience.[2] Frank set up his office to parallel the administrative structure of the AAA, with divisions responsible for benefit contracts, processing taxes, marketing agreements, codes and licenses, and an opinion and briefing section. His appointment of Arthur Bachrach as Special Advisor on litigation was designed as a backstop, and Frank viewed

Bachrach's role as that of providing general legal advice and supervising the younger, less-experienced lawyers on the staff.

Just as their NRA counterparts spent their first months wrestling with the negotiation of hundreds of complex industrial codes, the AAA lawyers immediately plunged into the difficult and time-consuming task of negotiating hundreds of agricultural marketing agreements. They normally worked sixteen or eighteen hours a day and often slept on office couches. "For madhouses, I am sure the A.A.A. in its early days has had few equals," Adlai Stevenson recalled. "Although the crop year was far advanced, we were deluged with angry delegations demanding help of some kind, before any adequate administrative machinery had been provided." The sheer number of farm crops complicated the task, since each required a separate marketing agreement, often on a state-wide or regional basis; California alone produced more than 125 farm commodities. In Stevenson's six months with the AAA, "I negotiated with producers, processors or handlers of everything from Atlantic oysters to California oranges, and from Oregon apples to Florida strawberries."[3]

Few of the AAA lawyers had any prior knowledge of the commodities with which they dealt, and their inexperience produced a flock of stories, some undoubtedly apocryphal, poking fun at their naiveté. Lee Pressman is reputed to have demanded at a meeting of macaroni producers that "I want to know what this code will do for the macaroni growers." And Stevenson recounted that his first assignment was to draft "a marketing agreement for the fresh California deciduous tree fruit industry. The delegation from California was only a little upset when I asked what 'deciduous' meant." However humorous, these tales illustrate the point that the AAA lawyers were more often than not forced to ratify agreements, many involving multi-million dollar industries, solely on the basis of data presented by the producers and processors. Although the small staff of Agriculture Department economists, headed by Mordecai Ezekial, offered some assistance, the pressures of time and limited background effectively precluded any critical evaluations of the terms of the agreements, and the lawyers had few illusions about the product of their labors. Stevenson expressed the reality of the situation when he wrote his wife after a few weeks on the job that "in essence we're really creating gigantic trusts in all the food industries."[4]

The AAA lawyers viewed the marketing agreement system with suspicion. In theory, such agreements promised to provide needed stability to agricultural production and marketing. The allocation of production quotas, set by state or regional committees of producers of each commodity on the basis of past levels of output, would eliminate the pressures toward overproduction and the consequent depression of prices. Agreements between producers and processors on long-term price levels would guarantee predictable incomes for farmers. Such agreements on production levels and prices had been common during the previous decade, but had risked prosecution under the antitrust laws. With the advent of the AAA, farmers' and producers' cooperatives could legitimate their formerly illegal pacts in the form of government-sanctioned marketing agreements. It was understood that these agreements would result in higher consumer prices, but it was also assumed that consumers would ultimately benefit; the increased purchasing power of farmers would enable them to buy more farm equipment and household goods, which in turn would generate industrial production and reduce unemployment. The resulting "multiplier effect" would spread throughout the economy like ripples on a pond.

From the perspective of the AAA lawyers, there were two flaws in this Panglossian notion. One was legal and the other political, and both stemmed from the domination of smaller producers and processors by their larger competitors. The legal aspect of this problem particularly bothered Jerome Frank. Section 8(3) of the Agricultural Adjustment Act empowered the Secretary of Agriculture to require the licensing of every producer and processor of commodities "in the current of interstate or foreign commerce," and authorized him to suspend or revoke these licenses "after due notice and opportunity for hearing," with violators subject to potential fines of $1,000 per day. The marketing agreements themselves were voluntary, but the mandatory licensing scheme bound non-signatories to their production allocation and pricing provisions.[5] The National Industrial Recovery Act contained a similar licensing provision, but it was never invoked. In the AAA, however, George Peek and Chester Davis both insisted that licensing be implemented as a means of forcing compliance with the marketing agreements.

Frank was uneasy about the potentially Draconian consequences of the licensing provision. He felt that it was "very badly worded" and had been "crudely handled" by Fred Lee in drafting the act. The enforcement dilemma faced by the AAA lawyers was that the act provided only one sanction against violators: forcing them out of business through revocation of their license. Frank was acutely aware of the due process objections to the mandatory licensing scheme. "That raised hair-raising problems legally," he recalled. "For one thing there was no provision in the statute for giving them notice as to such a license. How could you impose a license constitutionally on people without any preceding hearing?" His stopgap procedure was to publicize the licensing requirement through press releases; presumably, those affected would receive notice of their duty to secure a license through newspapers and radio. "That's all. I was sure that it was no good and scared to death about it."[6]

The second flaw in the marketing agreement scheme was that it was hardly conceivable that the millions of farmers and processors subject to their provisions would unanimously endorse the resulting production allocations and price levels. Many farm industries had a history of conflict between larger and smaller members, with recurrent episodes of price-cutting and other methods of economic warfare. Particularly during periods of overproduction, smaller producers were prone to evade cooperative pricing agreements by selling their output at below-market prices, thus incurring the wrath of those who adhered to these agreements. Under the AAA regime, these acts of price-cutting risked prosecution or license revocation. With their professed sympathy for small farmers, AAA lawyers did not relish the prospect of taking violators to court, or the equally distasteful task of defending the agency against legal challenges to the licensing provisions.

As eager as Frank and his staff were to avoid litigation, the pattern of competition within one major farm industry made it impossible. Milk and milk products such as butter and cheese are necessities for every family, and the dairy industry involves millions of farmers and thousands of distributors. In 1930 more than 4.6 million farms had one or more cows, and some 605,000 dairy farmers derived their primary income from the sale of dairy products; many of the remaining 4 million farmers sold some of their milk production.[7] Perhaps no other product was so universally considered a family staple, and the power of the states to regulate its quality and healthfulness had long been conceded.

Several factors combined to produce conflict over the AAA milk marketing agreements. Dairy farming is a business with high fixed costs but subject to wide price fluctuations largely beyond the control of farmers; although demand for milk and milk products is fairly constant, production levels fluctuate widely. Periods of overproduction generate fierce price-cutting wars which hit hardest the smaller and more marginal producers. Beginning in the 1920s, milk distribution increasingly became dominated by large retail chains such as Borden Milk, whose modern refrigeration and storage facilities enabled them to manipulate prices to both producers and consumers. Through thousands of retail outlets and the growing spread of cash-and-carry markets, the large chains threatened the survival of the smaller home-delivery companies saddled with higher costs and lower profit margins.

The first AAA cases stemmed from the marketing agreement for the Chicago area milkshed, the first of 49 regional agreements ultimately approved by Secretary Wallace. Negotiations leading to this agreement, which became effective on August 1, 1933, took almost three months to conclude, during which time it was rewritten twenty-eight times. One reason for the delay was the lack of experience of the AAA lawyers, few of whom, the nation's leading dairy economist archly commented, "knew enough about past experience with collective bargaining in milk products to have any weighty opinions on the subject."[8] A more important factor was the difficulty in resolving the differences between the cash-and-carry and home-delivery distributors over pricing levels. The eventual decision to impose a uniform pricing schedule on both groups, which fixed a standard retail price of ten cents a quart for milk, precipitated an immediate court challenge by the former group, who argued that the agreement and license requirement was "confiscatory of their business, since consumers would not purchase their milk over the counter when they could get milk plus delivery from other distributors at the same price."[9]

Within days of the effective date of the Chicago milkshed agreement, two cash-and-carry dairies sought an injunction in the federal court in the District of Columbia. Their argument that the government lacked power to regulate milk prices relied on the commerce clause (one dairy bought milk in Wisconsin for distribution in Illinois, and the other conducted solely an intrastate business), the due process clause of the Fifth Amendment, and the contention that Congress had improperly delegated legislative power to the Secretary. In his argument before Judge Daniel O'Donoghue, the lawyer for the dairies contended, on the basis of the decision of the Supreme Court in 1932 in *New State Ice Co. v. Liebmann*,[10] that the milk industry did not fall within the category of businesses "affected with a public interest" and was thus not subject to federal price and rate regulation. The argument that regulatory power extended only to those businesses specifically listed by the Supreme Court did not impress Judge O'Donoghue. "Do you then contend," he asked, "that once a thing has been decided to be not impressed with a public interest that as the years go on it could not change and become impressed with the public interest?" The dairy company lawyer conceded that the "Constitution is an elastic document."[11]

James Lawrence Fly, a 1926 Harvard Law School graduate who joined the Justice Department during the Hoover administration as Special Assistant to the Attorney General, argued the case for the AAA, still without a litigation division at this point. Jerome Frank was more than glad to rely on an experienced litigator from the Justice Department, and Fly worked closely in briefing the cases with Thurman Arnold of Yale Law School, who had volunteered his services to the AAA. Fly fully exploited his opponent's concession. "I need not point out to the court," he told the judge, "that milk is a vital commodity upon which the health and vitality of the race depends." In their brief, Fly and Arnold cited the "foundation" established by Chief Justice Marshall a century earlier in *Gibbons v. Ogden* for the proposition that "with business being done more and more on a national scale, the coverage of the commerce clause has gradually been expanded." As a result, the distinction between intrastate and interstate commerce was becoming progressively attenuated: "That the Congress has power to reach and control intrastate commerce whenever such control is necessary to the effective exercise of its power over interstate commerce is no longer open to debate."[12]

The restrictive line of Supreme Court precedent laid this expansive claim open to considerable debate. But Fly's argument was bolstered by the recent decision of the highest state court in New York in the case of *People v. Nebbia*. New York, in April 1933, had been the second of 21 states between 1933 and 1936 to pass laws regulating milk prices, and on July 11 the New York court upheld the conviction of Leo Nebbia for selling milk below the state-mandated minimum price of nine cents a quart. The court held that milk production was "of such paramount importance as to justify the assertion that the general welfare and prosperity of the state in a very large and real sense depend on it," and distinguished *New State Ice* on the grounds that the New York statute did not create a comparable monopoly, that it was adopted to meet an emergency situation, and that "milk is a greater family necessity than ice."[13] Although *Nebbia* (later upheld by the Supreme Court) did not involve the federal commerce clause and delegation arguments advanced in the AAA cases, Judge O'Donoghue disregarded these issues and issued a sweeping decision only six sentences long, citing *Nebbia* as the only precedent, upholding the constitutionality of the AAA, and denying the injunctions sought by the Chicago dairies:

"The Court finds that a national emergency exists and that the welfare of the people and the very existence of the Government itself are in peril. The day has passed when absolute vested rights in contract or property are to be regarded as sacrosanct or above the law. Neither the necessities of life nor commodities affected with a public interest can any longer be left to ruthless competition or selfish greed for their production or distribution."[14]

The AAA lawyers had not sought these first cases, although the outcome and Judge O'Donoghue's emphatic endorsement of the statute pleased them. Their enforcement powers remained untested, however, since the suits preceded any attempt to revoke the licenses of the two Chicago dairies. Additionally, the decision ignored the troubling questions of due process and federal power to regulate interstate agricultural commerce. A case soon arose, however, that encouraged the AAA lawyers to take the initiative; it involved the California cling peach marketing agreement, and it was seemingly made to order for a favorable decision on the unresolved constitutional questions.

Under the agreement approved by Secretary Wallace on August 17, 1933, the AAA issued a license to the Calistan Packers company of Modesto authorizing a quota of 77,000 cases of canned peaches. After receiving complaints from its competitors the AAA found that the company "had been working day and night and that it had produced more than 150,000 cases."[15] Concerned that the peaches would be sold before the lengthy license-revocation process could be concluded, the AAA urged the Justice Department to seek an injunction prohibiting sales in excess of the quota. Jerome Frank wrote Harold Stephens that the case was "a matter of very great moment" to the AAA and that the violation was "upsetting the whole structure of the quota device which is otherwise operating most effectively."[16]

Although the statute made no specific provision for enforcement by injunction, Stephens was impressed with the urgency of the situation and approved Frank's request. James L. Fly again represented the Justice Department, and Frank sent Thurman Arnold and Abe Fortas to San Francisco to work with Fly and the U.S. attorney. At this point relations between the two agencies were amicable and they had no jurisdictional squabbles over litigation control. The two sets of lawyers, in fact, formed a mutual admiration society; Arnold reported to Frank that he was "completely satisfied" with Justice Department cooperation, and the U.S. attorney in turn praised the "ability, energy and courtesy" of the AAA lawyers.[17] The facts of the case facilitated this cooperation: more than ninety-nine percent of canned peach production was shipped from California and entered the current of interstate commerce; and Calistan Packers was unanimously condemned by its competitors, who supported the quotas provided by the marketing agreement.

The decision in *United States v. Calistan Packers*, issued on October 2, 1933, supported the AAA on every point. Judge Adolphus St. Sure, a progressive Republican, answered both of the constitutional questions avoided by Judge O'Donoghue in the first dairy cases. Congress had "laid down fairly definite standards" under which regulations could be made, Judge St. Sure wrote, adding that in such circumstances delegation "is highly essential to the efficacy of such statutes." He cited Judge O'Donoghue's decision in dismissing the due process argument, taking "judicial notice of the economic distress throughout the nation" and asserting that "overproduction and glutted markets travel hand in hand with ruthless competition." Finally, while he acknowledged that "the statute makes no express provision" for injunctive relief, Judge St. Sure assumed power to "prevent irreparable injury to the country" under the "general equity powers" of the federal courts.[18]

The AAA lawyers were optimistic about the effect of these first decisions on the future of the marketing agreement program. Jerome Frank quickly issued a press release claiming that Judge St. Sure's decision had "established the constitutionality of the licensing provisions" of the AAA and that it "should remove many of the obstacles to the making of satisfactory agreements of this kind."[19] *U.S. Law Week* concluded that the *Calistan Packers* decision "accords to Congress an almost unlimited power over intrastate commerce."[20] And in a form of leap-frog jurisprudence, *Calistan Packers* was cited later the same month by Judge O'Donoghue, who again upheld the AAA against a challenge by a milk distributor. "The production and distribution of milk, a necessity of life, for large congested urban centers, left to selfish, ruthless, uncontrolled competition," he wrote, "have not only failed but are threatening ruin and chaos to producer, distributor and consumer."[21]

The favorable outcome of these cases prompted Frank and his staff to reassess their cautious attitude toward litigation and to begin thinking about the prospects of a Supreme Court test case. At this time, near the end of 1933, the Court had not yet given a hint of its attitude toward the New Deal statutes. Frank realized that the chances of forging the five-member majority necessary to outvote the four convinced conservatives on the Court hinged on Louis Brandeis, whose expertise on regulatory issues carried great weight with his remaining colleagues. Frank was an occasional guest at the Sunday afternoon teas at which Brandeis held court, but the Justice had characteristically deflected Frank's subtle efforts to probe his attitudes toward the AAA programs. Brandeis had, in fact, suspected from the outset that the New Deal farm program would entrench the power of the corporate segment of the industry, and its antitrust exemptions offended his competitive ideology. As early as August 1933, Brandeis had informed Felix Frankfurter that he was "increasingly skeptical" about the AAA.[22]

With this fear in mind, Frank dispatched Lee Pressman and Arthur Bachrach to Cambridge in November with instructions to pump Brandeis' friend Thomas Reed Powell, the Harvard constitutional law professor under whom Pressman had studied, for advice on litigation strategy. This purpose was not simply a pretext, but Frank hoped also that Powell might have some first-hand knowledge of how Brandeis might vote on an AAA case. Powell reported on this meeting to Frankfurter, then on a sabbatical year at Oxford, that "Lee is much concerned about the particular form in which litigation arising out of the A.A.A. will get before the Court. He says that Brandeis is very strongly opposed to much of what is going on because it is making for control of the big fellows and suppression of the little fellows." It would be dangerous, Powell cautioned Pressman and Bachrach, to base their litigation strategy on a guess as to Brandeis' vote or his influence over other members of the Court. He reminded them that

Brandeis' undoubted skepticism about the corporatist features of the New Deal program was balanced by his deference "in favor of legislative experimentation and of judicial respect for the judgment of the legislature. . . ." Powell urged Pressman to warn Frank not to read too much into the Delphic comments that Brandeis may have made over tea. On that note, Powell wrote Frankfurter, "we left the subject of Brandeis with my conclusion that no one could give a safe guess as to his attitude."[23]

Frankfurter was pleased that Powell had reinforced his earlier admonitions to Frank. "I am glad to infer from your account of the talk with Lee Pressman," he replied from his English redoubt, "that the legal boys in Washington are not too cavalier in seeking litigation and court approval." Frankfurter nonetheless harbored a suspicion that his disciples, encouraged by their recent judicial victories, might disregard his "urgent advice" to avoid litigation and had become "cocksure" about their Supreme Court prospects. He also suspected that Frank and his staff were influenced by Supreme Court clerks "who tittle-tattled too much on what comes to them in their confidential relations," and urged Powell to remind the AAA lawyers that "action taken on such advice was apt to miscarry."[24] This last comment reflected Frankfurter's awareness that the Harvard graduates he selected to clerk for Brandeis (who in 1932 and 1933 included Paul Freund and Louis Jaffe, the latter joining Frank's staff in 1934) met frequently with their former classmates in the New Deal agencies and exchanged the behind-the-scenes gossip on which Washington has always thrived.

II. Six Months at Hard Labor

Intimations that the AAA lawyers would disregard the cautionary advice from Powell and Frankfurter became evident early in 1934. The year began on a positive note for Frank and his staff, who had reason to be pleased with their performance over the past six months. Dozens of complicated marketing agreements had been negotiated, and the only two which provoked litigation had been settled in sweeping decisions upholding the constitutionality of the statute. And, at least on the surface, relations between the AAA and the Justice Department were amicable. A particularly favorable augury that the Supreme Court might eventually sustain the New Deal farm program came on March 5, when the Court affirmed the decision of the New York Court of Appeals in the *Nebbia* case. In writing for a narrow five-to-four majority, Justice Owen Roberts upheld the state's milk-pricing scheme against a due process challenge. Roberts echoed Judge O'Donoghue's words in the first AAA decision (and horrified laissez-faire fundamentalists) in holding that "neither property rights nor contract rights are absolute; for government cannot exist if the citizen may at will use his property to the detriment of his fellows, or exercise his freedom of contract to work them harm." Roberts concluded that "upon proper occasion and by appropriate measures the state may regulate a business in any of its aspects, including the prices to be charged for the products or commodities it sells."[25]

Emboldened by this decision, the AAA lawyers abandoned their earlier caution and plunged into an aggressive enforcement campaign. But, in so doing, they ignored the early signs of fissures in the foundation on which their litigation strategy was constructed. Judge Alexander Akerman of the federal district court in Florida, a conservative Republican and avowed foe of the New Deal, opened the first crack in January 1934. A month earlier, Akerman had been the first federal judge to hold the National Industrial Recovery Act unconstitutional, and he quickly seized the chance to swing his judicial sword against the AAA. The case, *Hillsborough Packing Co. v. Wallace*, was brought not by the AAA but by two packing companies who challenged their production allocations under the marketing agreement for the Florida citrus industry.

The case went badly from the beginning. James L. Fly and Abe Fortas, who had worked together smoothly on the California peach case, were again paired by their agencies; Fly was joined by Ashley Sellers, a Texas lawyer who had recently received a legal doctorate from Harvard, and Arthur Bachrach worked with Fortas. The two sets of government lawyers were divided over their approach to the case, which was complicated by a procedural tangle. One troublesome factor was that the packing companies sought to enjoin imposition of the production quotas by both Secretary Wallace and the Florida citrus commission, established by the AAA to set and enforce the quotas. The commission had retained an eminent Florida lawyer, Francis Whitehair, whose goal in the case was to win approval of the marketing system. Fortas, however, knew that Judge Akerman would inevitably rule against the AAA, and consequently advocated a defense based on two procedural points: first, that Wallace, the ostensible defendant, had not properly been served with process by the packing companies; and, second, that the case was arguably moot since the citrus commission had withdrawn its production control orders the day before Judge Akerman heard the injunction arguments.

This tactical plan ran into two problems, which created the first strains between Justice Department and AAA lawyers. One was that Whitehair, on behalf of the citrus commission, feared that dismissal of the case on procedural grounds would undermine the marketing program. Fortas was sensitive to Whitehair's concern. Although "extremely able" as a lawyer, Fortas recalled about Whitehair, he was "fairly emotional about the case, and it involved problems which were somewhat outside of his professional experience. From the point of view of the AAA, a cardinal element was to restrict the damage that would be the foreseeable result of a decision by Judge Akerman, and at the same time to avoid mortal offense to Whitehair and the local Citrus Commission.'' As Sellers later reported to Harold Stephens, in a post mortem of the case, Fortas and Bachrach felt that Akerman's ''admittedly biased predisposition'' against the entire New Deal program made it advisable to limit the argument to the narrow procedural issues, in the hope that ''by pressing the jurisdictional issues in their strongest light'' even Judge Akerman might dismiss the suit and pass up the chance to rule on the validity of the statute.

Fly and Sellers, however, considered the case important ''from a political and economic standpoint,'' and responded that refusing to argue the constitutional issues raised by the packing companies ''would give the Court opportunity to criticize the Administration in general and the Department of Agriculture especially. . . .'' This professed solicitude for the AAA was somewhat suspect, since in most New Deal litigation it was the agency that pressed for argument of constitutional issues and the Justice Department that stressed the narrowest possible issues. But Fortas soon discovered that the Justice Department had bigger plans for the case and was ''primarily motivated by a desire for a constitutional decision to present to the Supreme Court.''[26] Torn between his desire to placate Whitehair and his reluctance to press the case as a potential Supreme Court test, Fortas urged his Justice Department colleagues to rest the argument before Judge Akerman on the narrow procedural issues. With little time to decide, Fly deferred to the tactics suggested by Fortas.

Judge Akerman's decision, announced orally from the bench at the conclusion of the arguments, guaranteed that the initial tactical dispute between the government lawyers would escalate into open warfare at the top levels of the two agencies. As Fortas had requested, the judge dismissed Wallace as a defendant. But he did not dismiss the suit, and simply substituted in Wallace's place the citrus commission chairman, I. A. Yarnell. Akerman additionally ruled that the case was not moot, since reinstatement of the production quotas was likely and the prospect of criminal prosecution of the packing companies remained. And the judge rubbed further salt in the government's wounds by holding in his vitriolic oral opinion that Congress had no power to regulate agricultural production in any form. Akerman went beyond his holding that the AAA was unconstitutional to denounce the New Deal as a ''revolution'' and an ''insidious encroachment'' on the Constitution.[27]

Defeated on both the procedural and constitutional issues, the government lawyers reacted to their first setback in an AAA case by bickering over the risks of a further, and potentially more damaging, loss at the appellate level. The Justice Department, by this time dropping any pretensions that the best interests of the AAA were paramount, gave up on the case as a possible Supreme Court test of the AAA marketing agreements. In arguing that the risk be taken, Jerome Frank antagonized Harold Stephens by leveling personal criticism at James Fly. Disregarding Fly's concession to Fortas and Bachrach on trial tactics, Frank complained that Fly had "been somewhat peremptory in insisting" that they comply with his instructions during the case, although Frank admitted that "it might have been better" had the procedural questions been abandoned and "an argument on the constitutional question had been made" before Judge Akerman. But Frank vehemently denied that any resulting misjudgment "was ascribable to me and members of my staff. . . ."[28]

Stephens did not respond to Frank's fulminations, since at the time (mid-March 1934) he and Attorney General Cummings were in the midst of planning a drastic move designed to cut off such internecine disputes at their roots. Although he had decided not to pursue any Supreme Court test of the AAA programs, Stephens approved Frank's request that Judge Akerman's decision be appealed, as a way of defusing the immediate controversy. This move ultimately allowed both sides within the government to claim victory. Fortas bowed out of the case before the appeal was argued to return to his teaching post at Yale Law School, leaving it in the hands of Fly and Sellers, whose argument before the Fifth Circuit Court of Appeals incorporated both the procedural and constitutional issues. In its ruling in April 1934 the appellate panel, without a nod to Fly's constitutional arguments, held that the packing companies had failed to exhaust their administrative remedies. Since the Secretary had not yet moved to revoke their licenses and since the citrus commission's orders "begin and end in nothing but threats," the court held, the case was not ripe for decision. The constitutional objections to the statute, the court added, were consequently premature and inappropriate for decision.[29] Fly had not argued the exhaustion of remedies issue before the appellate court, but the AAA was nonetheless gratified that its marketing agreement had been rescued from Judge Akerman's constitutional bear-trap.

This belated vindication came too late, however, to save Frank and his staff from the retribution planned by Stephens and Cummings. The background of the decisive break between the two agencies was compounded by the twin ironies of personal goodwill and an initially successful litigation record. Frank began his service in the AAA with approbation from Stephens, whom he had not met before each joined the New Deal. Stephens knew Frank only as the reputedly radical author of *Law and the Modern Mind* and, as a former judge, "feared that I would find him something of a fault-finder towards judges and lawyers generally," he wrote Frankfurter in July 1933. But after meeting Frank, Stephens confessed: "I am compelled quite to reverse this impression. In addition to being alert, keen and discerning professionally, he is a most genial and kindly person, very agreeable to work with, and with a real personal charm."[30] Frank's charm wore thin as his new emphasis on litigation conflicted with the earlier agreement that the AAA would pursue litigation as a last resort.

Once again, the milk industry was the culprit. Frank found himself caught in an almost intolerable conflict of loyalties as the dispute reached the litigation stage. His sympathies lay with the smaller dairies, which complained with considerable force that AAA milk marketing agreements put them at a competitive disadvantage. He was committed by his role as General Counsel, however, to enforce the agreements, and pressure from the agency's Dairy Section gave him little choice but to head off a wave of price-cutting through the initiation of license revocation proceedings. As early as August 1933, Frank sought Stephens' cooperation, warning that "the entire license arrangement will break down if decisive steps are not taken." Stephens was unreceptive to this plea, responding that the Justice Department would not encourage "any decisive steps leading to a revocation inasmuch as this would invoke litigation."[31] In making this reluctant request, Frank had swallowed what he later told Chester Davis were his own "gravest doubts" about the power of the AAA to set production quotas and fix prices through the marketing agreements.[32]

The combination of internal pressure and encouragement from the courts overcame Frank's innate caution about enforcement through litigation. He encountered no opposition from the Justice Department until April 1934, in the wake of Judge Akerman's decision in the Florida citrus case and Frank's second-guessing about trial tactics. Having adopted a policy of punishing violators of the milk marketing agreements with license revocations, Frank discovered that Stephens once again expressed opposition to his enforcement plans. If the AAA did not "take steps to avoid inconsistent positions" with the Justice Department, Stephens warned Frank, "your program of enforcement might be embarrassed."[33] The events of the few weeks that followed this undiplomatic hint of Stephens' forthcoming assault on the AAA not only embarrassed Frank's enforcement program but humiliated him personally.

Stephens and Frank met at the Justice Department in early May in an effort to smooth over the animosities heightened by their contentious exchange of correspondence. The meeting, however, only served to ruffle their already strained relations. Frank understood that Stephens agreed with his proposal that AAA lawyers be permitted to initiate enforcement suits and to work directly with local United States attorneys on these cases without first securing approval from Justice Department lawyers in Washington. A week later, after returning to Washington from a trip, Frank was upset to learn that his understanding was not shared by Golden W. Bell, whom Stephens had designated as his liaison with the AAA. A 1910 Harvard Law School graduate, Bell joined the Justice Department in 1933 after more than twenty years of maritime law practice in California. Frank had recently appointed John Abt as chief of a newly organized Litigation Section with authorization to build up a staff of fifteen lawyers for trial work. In Frank's absence Bell had instructed Abt that the Justice Department "must pass on all our papers and conduct all dealings with the district attorneys," Frank reported to Stephens. "Perhaps I was obtuse," Frank added, "but I had no notion that Mr. Bell would make any substantial modification of the plan on which you and I had agreed. . . ." He was sure, Frank concluded, that Bell had misinterpreted his instructions from Stephens.[34]

It was Frank who had misinterpreted his conversation with Stephens, who shortly completed his campaign to strip lawyers in all the New Deal agencies of control over litigation. Stephens and Cummings conducted their lobbying effort at the White House with such secrecy that Frank had no advance word of the Executive Order that Roosevelt issued on June 10, placing the Justice Department in complete control of federal litigation. Roosevelt's order shocked the AAA lawyers. Bell immediately called Abt and Arthur Bachrach to the Justice Department and repeated his earlier instruction that the role of AAA lawyers would be limited to preparing pleadings, legal briefs, and supporting economic data under his supervision. Bachrach countered with a compromise suggestion that conceded the Department's veto power over the initiation of litigation; he urged Bell, however, that AAA lawyers be permitted to argue cases in court, since the agency now had experienced trial lawyers familiar with "the extremely complicated nature" of the licenses and marketing agreements. These cases, Bachrach and Abt argued, required lawyers "who completely steep themselves in these problems." Pressing the point, they questioned the competency of local U.S. attorneys. But Bell "made it quite clear that this suggestion was rejected and would not fit in with the Attorney General's plan," Bachrach reported to Frank. Returning from this meeting, Bachrach and Abt immediately urged Frank to intercede.[35]

The next day, Frank sent Bell an eight-page letter noting that widespread violations of the milk licenses made litigation essential as an enforcement tool; a recent congressional amdendment giving the AAA authority to seek injunctive relief to restrain violations facilitated enforcement and would "very materially increase the volume of litigation" to enforce the licenses. Frank tactfully acknowledged that "formulation of policy" regarding litigation rested with the Department, but he reiterated his contention that AAA cases "must be handled by men from Washington who are thoroughly familiar with the difficult mixed questions of law and economics involved in our licenses." Pointing out that in anticipation of this litigation he had been "searching the country" for experienced trial lawyers, Frank promised that they would consult with the Department before bringing suits and arguing in court. But, he warned, "inadequate conduct of these cases may be fatal to the agriculture program." Asking for a rehearing of the decision, Frank concluded with an implicit threat: "An incorrect decision now may lead to our being suddenly confronted, in the near future, with a litigation situation with which neither you nor we can cope."[36]

The tone of Frank's letter sufficiently alarmed Bell that he suggested that the Attorney General reply personally, making it clear that the Department's policy was unshakable. Cummings wrote Frank that the Department "in no way presumes to intrude upon the administrative conduct of matters prior to the inception of litigation," but stressed that he would retain control. He rejected Frank's implication that Justice Department lawyers lacked the ability to argue AAA cases and said that if the volume of AAA litigation increased he would assign additional lawyers to handle it.[37] Confronted with the Attorney General's authoritative pronouncement, Frank bowed to reality and gave up his resistance. He was in no position to do otherwise, since he was then embroiled in a dispute with Tommy Corcoran. Frank realized that he had no political capital at the White House and could hardly approach Roosevelt to argue for a reversal of the Department's grab for power. He consoled himself with a report to Chester Davis that the decision "will somewhat slow up our enforcement" because of the need to educate the Justice Department lawyers. "This is unfortunate, but I do not see how we can avoid it."[38]

Frank's rift with Corcoran illustrates the inherent difficulties he faced in trying to reconcile his reformist sympathies with the demands of his constrained legal role. Frank was committed to the enforcement of programs whose approach and constitutionality he questioned, and this commitment not only engendered resistance from the Justice Department but also distressed his erstwhile friends outside the AAA. Frank owed his job to Felix Frankfurter, and had accepted Corcoran's help in recruiting lawyers. But Frankfurter and Corcoran shared an antipathy toward the corporatist approach of the AAA, and its suspension of the antitrust laws particularly grated on their Brandeisian sentiments. As both men became progressively disenchanted with corporate domination of the farm program, Frank's association with it made him an ideological apostate in their eyes.

This political falling-out was accompanied by a growing personal feud between Frank and Corcoran. Their estrangement began early in 1934 with the kind of cocktail party carping that is soon magnified into unrestrained billingsgate. Corcoran heard that Frank was denouncing him for having lost faith in the New Deal, and Frank in return was told that Corcoran "was spreading news around that I was radical, trying to nationalize everything. . . ."[39] What annoyed Frank was that Corcoran refused to acknowledge the "black and blue" marks Frank had suffered in his unpublicized battles with corporate interests in the AAA. It was inevitable that word of this schismatic dispute would reach the public. When it did, at the hands of Raymond Moley, Frank bore the brunt of the resulting criticism. A charter member of the Brains Trust, Moley lasted less than a year as a New Dealer (in a State Department post) before his basic conservatism forced him into a critical role, expressed in the pages of Moley's weekly magazine, *Today*. Moley had little sympathy for Corcoran's Brandeisian views, but even less for Frank's brand of Legal Reformism. In May 1934 Moley printed a thinly veiled attack on Frank and his staff. The AAA lawyers, Moley wrote, "talk too much in public and in private." They could best advance the New Deal, he suggested, "through hard labor at their prosaic duties. They can well leave social theory, patronizing references to 'folkways' and 'experimentalism' to less responsible outsiders."[40]

The accusation that he and his staff were shirking their duties distressed Frank more than the blast at his Legal Realist writings. Frank had no doubt that Corcoran, despite his own ideological differences with Moley, had instigated this assault; he turned for relief to Frankfurter, who was in the midst of his sabbatical year at Oxford. The dispute would get out of hand, Frank wrote, unless Frankfurter took steps to "call off his boys."[41] On his part, Corcoran disclaimed any part in the Moley article and urged Frankfurter to intercede, arguing that "only you have a sufficiently universal esteem to harmonize" the "strained relationships" of the two factions. Corcoran attributed the affair to the "Tugwell crowd" and its program of regimented national planning. This group—including Frank—"has been pushed by its enemies—and its own loose talk—away over to the left," Corcoran advised Frankfurter.[42] Although he was deeply concerned about the situation, Frankfurter declined to engage in long-distance diplomacy. Without a mediator, tempers continued to flare. The break between Frank and Corcoran became irreparable after the two men engaged in a shouting match at an ill-fated reconciliation meeting arranged by their mutual friend, Ben Cohen.

Although this brouhaha resulted in part from the clash of two irrepressible personalities, it also reflected the suspicious attitude of the Brandeisian purists toward those New Dealers forced, however unwillingly, to compromise with corporate interests. Frank was clearly in a bind at the time:

having disregarded Frankfurter's advice to avoid litigation, he was hemmed in by the Justice Department and increasingly frustrated by imputations that he was a leftist of the Tugwell stripe. In fact, Frank rarely consulted with Tugwell, whose position in the Agriculture Department was divorced from the AAA. But Frank could not appeal his case to the ultimate New Deal arbiter, Franklin Roosevelt. Frank's recent defeat in his struggle with the Justice Department made the White House an inhospitable refuge, and Corcoran's closeness to Roosevelt made further argument futile. When Frank was later purged from the AAA, he blamed Corcoran for having underminded his reputation with the President. "Corcoran's propaganda," Frank claimed, eased the way for the purge "because he helped to create the opinion that I was very radical."[43] There was, in reality, some truth to Frank's charge. But his position was undermined as well by other factors, one of which was the dismal record of the AAA lawyers in their litigation campaign, conducted with the hobbles placed on them by the Justice Department.

III. THE CURDLING OF THE BUTTER THEORY

The AAA litigation campaign began on a note of encouragement. Shortly after the Supreme Court decided in the *Nebbia* case that New York's milk-pricing law was constitutional, Secretary Wallace revoked the license of a Chicago dairy owner named Shissler, who had purchased milk from producers at prices under the minimum level set by the regional marketing agreement. When Shissler refused to cease his operations and continued to purchase under-priced milk, the AAA sought an injunction restraining Shissler from continuing in business. The case came before federal judge William Holly in Chicago. A Democrat and one of Roosevelt's first judicial appointees, Holly was not only a New Deal supporter but was also a former law partner of Clarence Darrow and had worked with Frank in Chicago reform politics in the 1920s. To avoid the problems raised by Holly's close ties with lawyers now on the AAA staff, Frank hired two private lawyers to represent the government.

After hearing the argument presented for the AAA by John S. Miller, an eminently conservative corporate lawyer, Holly had no difficulty in deciding the case. He found no interstate commerce problem, since Shissler admitted buying milk from producers in Wisconsin. Shissler's lawyer had argued that these purchases were incidental to the bulk of those made in Illinois, but Holly declared that Congress had power to regulate the intrastate transactions when there was an "interblending" of the two sources of milk. The other claim raised on Shissler's behalf was that the price-fixing regulation violated the due process clause of the Fifth Amendment.

"This court is not required to search for an answer to this question," Holly wrote. "The answer has been given by the Supreme Court" in the *Nebbia* decision.[44]

The victory in *Shissler* proved to be an early spring blossom. Every marketing agreement case that followed it withered under the heat of judicial scrutiny. Three factors combined to uproot the litigation strategy of the AAA lawyers. First, the Justice Department edict of June 1934 relegated Frank's staff to a back-seat role in court. Second, since the production and distribution of milk in all but a few of the 49 regional milk-sheds was largely conducted on an intrastate basis, the "interblending" argument that had convinced Judge Holly could not be made. Finally, every AAA case subsequent to *Shissler* was heard by a Republican judge appointed by a Republican president. The combination of partisanship and predilection that crippled enforcement of the NIRA operated with a vengeance against the AAA. What resulted was a legal disaster for the AAA; it lost every attempt to enforce the licensing provisions of the statute.

The first in this year-long string of defeats came in the last case argued by AAA lawyers, and was decided only three days after Attorney General Cummings ended this privilege. The case, *Edgewater Dairy Co. v. Wallace*, involved a challenge to the Chicago milk marketing agreement and was virtually identical in its facts with the *Shissler* case decided by Judge Holly. John Abt and Lee Pressman, accompanied by Arthur Bachrach, argued the case before Judge John Barnes, a Hoover appointee. Abt recalled that Judge Barnes "was an old boss of mine. He had been a member of the Levinson firm, so I knew him very well and knew he'd rule against us. Bachrach had been one of his partners, and had a conference in chambers with Barnes to try to persuade him to disqualify himself on the ground that Bachrach and I were old friends of his."[45] After this request was rejected, Abt and Pressman repeated the argument made successfully before Judge Holly, that since 40 percent of the milk sold in Chicago was produced in other states the "entire market" was inextricably part of the "current" of interstate commerce. Judge Barnes was almost persuaded by this argument, and commended Abt and Pressman in his opinion for their forcefulness in presenting it. But he found a safe haven in the Tenth Amendment; the powers to fix prices and control production, he concluded, were reserved to the states. Although the opinion cited no cases as precedent, it was clear that *Nebbia* had little lasting impact, and would support only state regulation of the milk industry.[46]

This first defeat sobered the AAA lawyers, since most pending cases involved milk markets in which virtually all production and distribution was intrastate. The "entire market" theory on which the *Shissler* and *Edgewater* cases were based applied only to Chicago and to two or three other large cities. With half a dozen cases scheduled for argument in July and August, the first priority became the task of developing a plausible theory that linked economic reality with jurisprudential doctrine.

The AAA lawyers assigned to this task spent two weeks in frantic research and consultation with the agency's economists. The product of this collaboration was an argument which became known as the "butter theory," expressed by its anonymous author in these words:

"As I see it, the only theory upon which we can support milk licenses in those markets where all of the fluid milk supply is produced within the state is the following: That butter moves extensively in interstate commerce; that unstabilized fluid milk markets have a direct and immediate effect upon the price of butter which moves in interstate commerce and hence that the Federal Government has the power to issue licenses correcting abuses in the fluid milk markets for the purpose of removing conditions which adversely affect the butter market."[47]

There was some force behind this argument, since 1931 statistics showed that 44 percent of fluid milk production was made into butter, more frequently sold in interstate commerce than fluid milk.[48] Supreme Court precedent also supported such a theory. In its 1923 opinion in *Chicago Board of Trade v. Olson*, the Court had upheld the Grain Futures Act even though the transactions themselves were in intrastate commerce, holding that they affected the price of grain moving in interstate commerce and were therefore subject to federal regulation under the commerce clause. The effectiveness of their argument, the AAA lawyers realized, "will depend wholly upon the economic data which the Dairy Section can adduce to show that the regulation of fluid milk prices has a direct, substantial and immediate effect upon the price of butter which moves in interstate commerce."[49]

Armed with the butter theory and voluminous supporting affidavits prepared by Dairy Section economists, AAA lawyers spread out across the country to participate in the growing number of milk cases. But under the terms of the President's order, they were relegated to a supporting role and sat voiceless in the courtrooms, chafing with frustration and increasingly critical of the performance of local U.S. attorneys and the special assistants delegated by the Justice Department. By August 1934, two months after the order was issued, their frustration erupted. John Abt appealed directly to Secretary Wallace to find some way to restore litigation control to the AAA, repeating Frank's earlier criticism of the Justice Department lawyers as incapable of mastering the complex legal and economic aspects of the AAA cases. Abt also scored the Department for objecting to the use of the economic affidavits on which the butter theory cases depended, and for delaying the filing of suits while its lawyers argued their objections. He cited a case involving the Boston milk license as an example.

Not only had the Justice Department held up filing the suit for two months, it had substituted at the last minute a lawyer who had never argued an AAA case and was "wholly unfamiliar" with the facts of the case. It was the opinion of the Legal Division, Abt said, that "no effective program of joint operation can be worked out with the Department of Justice," and he urged that Wallace take action to head off a total collapse of his enforcement program.[50]

The chief of the Dairy Section backed up Abt's complaints, and told the AAA administrator that his office was "besieged" with messages from both producers and distributors "pleading and begging for enforcement." If it was not forthcoming, they would be forced by competition to violate their licenses. Should enforcement cases be lost because of Justice Department incompetence, "we had just as well shut up shop. In some places already our program is considered a joke by people familiar with the milk situation solely because of inadequate enforcement."[51] Frank followed up with a letter to Stephens, quoting extensively from this memorandum. The existing arrangement, he argued, had been proved ineffective; it was "leading to delays and, as a consequence, to severe public criticism" of the AAA. The situation had become "exceedingly serious," Frank said, and he asked for a meeting with Stephens to discuss the problem.[52] John Henry Lewin, who headed the AAA's Administrative Enforcement Section, had urged Frank to revive the flagging enforcement campaign by filing suit against at least one violator in each milk market.[53] Frank endorsed this suggestion to Stephens, and urged the Department to proceed "until stopped by an adverse decision."[54]

Reluctant to face an acrimonious confrontation with Frank, Stephens dodged his request for a meeting, but made his position clear in a letter rejecting the proposal to bring additional suits. It would be futile, he told Frank, to file suits in districts where judges had displayed hostility to the New Deal, and he discouraged suits to enforce milk licenses in markets with little or no interstate commerce.[55] This effectively limited enforcement to the markets in Boston, St. Louis, and Omaha. Assistant AAA administrator Victor Christgau, when Frank informed him of Stephens' negative response, reacted by proposing that the AAA bring pressure on the Justice Department with a public blast at its policy. Since the breakdown in compliance was leading to threats of milk strikes across the country by producers unwilling to sell at below-license prices, "it may be necessary for us at once to withdraw substantially all our milk licenses, giving out a statement to the effect that we are doing so because the Department of Justice is unwilling to enforce them."[56]

The prospect of open warfare in the press, shortly after the attacks he attributed to Tommy Corcoran, did not appeal to Frank. But Stephens' evasion of the request for a meeting did provoke him. In a "Personal and Confidential" letter, Frank wrote Stephens that "what I predicted has come true; namely, that insufficient acquaintance on the part of lawyers in the Department of Justice with the background of our licenses is leading, in some instances, to inadequate presentation of our cases."[57] Stung by this criticism, Stephens immediately called Frank to protest the slurs on the competence of his staff; Frank replied that he meant "no criticism of the *ability* of your men," but was simply concerned that AAA cases be argued by lawyers familiar with the economic and legal issues involved. "I don't care who wins our cases," he wrote somewhat disingenuously. "I have no interest in departmental pride or prestige. All I want is that in each instance a highly capable lawyer who knows his case should handle the suit."[58] Once again, Frank's appeal to Stephens was unavailing. In mid-September he finally conceded defeat and informed his litigation and enforcement staff that they must remain in their subordinate roles.[59]

Hard on the heels of this galling setback came the results of the butter theory cases argued during the preceding two months. One by one, in a series of six decisions over a three-month period from September to November, the AAA lost every one of its milk license cases.[60] Although differing in length and complexity of analysis, the opinions were unanimous on the essential point: Congress had no power under the commerce clause to authorize the licensing of any business in which production and distribution were intrastate in nature. Each opinion rejected the butter theory on the ground that the impact of local milk prices on the interstate market in butter and other milk products was, as one put it, "only indirect, remote, ancillary, secondary, or merely probable" and that "it does not follow that the business conducted by the defendants so affects the price of milk in industrial centers as to be a burden on interstate commerce."[61] Not surprisingly, the opinions reflected the constitutional fundamentalism of the Republican judges and rested heavily on the restrictive line of Supreme Court commerce clause decisions. Five of the six cited the 1918 case of *Hammer v. Dagenhart*, in which the production of goods was distinguished from their transport in interstate commerce (as did nine of the eleven district court opinions holding the National Industrial Recovery Act invalid). Only two judges took time to distinguish *Nebbia*: Judge Vaught of Oklahoma City, conceding that state regulation of prices and production would be valid under *Nebbia*, found it "of no assistance to the government in the case at bar."[62]

Preoccupied with arguing these district court cases, AAA lawyers gave little thought until late October to the question of whether to pursue appeals of the cases they were losing. By that time, after a string of five losses, the only appeal pending was in the *Edgewater* case, decided in June. Its strength as a possible test case was that it rested on the "entire market" theory, since almost half the milk sold in Chicago was produced in other states. Raising the question with John Abt, Arthur Bachrach noted that "the butter theory is the least strong theory we have" and urged that *Edgewater* be selected as a test case "even if it is not the strongest case possible because if we are too choosey we may find ourselves in the Supreme Court on a very weak case whether we like it or not." Bachrach proposed short-circuiting the normal appeals process by filing a petition for certiorari with the Supreme Court before a Court of Appeals decision.[63] Abt, however, was gloomy about the prospect for success, and advised Frank that the AAA abandon any plans to test the marketing agreements and licenses before the Supreme Court; the chance of a reversal in *Edgewater*, he wrote, was "extremely remote."[64]

Frank still felt, at the end of 1934, that there remained a "moderate chance" of winning in the Supreme Court and that even a loss might prove salutary in prodding Congress to enact amendments providing a stronger basis for the marketing agreements and licenses.[65] But three factors intervened to foreclose a Supreme Court test of the licensing power. First, the Justice Department informed the AAA in November that no further suits would be filed except in cases where all the milk involved was purchased in one state and sold in another. This was a meaningless concession, since no cases fell in this category. Meeting with Abt and Bachrach, two of Stephens' assistants strongly hinted that the AAA give up enforcement of the milk licenses. Bowing to the force of this argument, Bachrach gave up his advocacy of a test case and suggested to Frank that the AAA abandon the license scheme entirely "because of the doubtful validity of the butter theory" and the likelihood of further adverse decisions, although he added that "if the government terminates all of these licenses there will be considerable and strong criticism from the industry in those markets."[66] The choice posed was a hard one. Abandoning the licenses would return the milk industry to virtual anarchy and the prospect of price wars and reduced income for producers, and would make it difficult to justify the licensing of other products, where marketing agreements were working. On the other hand, enforcement of the milk licenses would be virtually impossible, given the Justice Department refusal to file enforcement suits.

A second factor was the Supreme Court decision in the "hot oil" cases in the first week of 1935, holding unconstitutional the NIRA provision controlling petroleum production. Frank had gone ahead, against the advice of Abt and Bachrach, to seek Justice Department permission to appeal a second decision by Judge Barnes directly to the Supreme Court, in the *Columbus Milk Producers* case. But Stephens, two days after the "hot oil" decision, informed Frank that he would not authorize an appeal.[67]

The third and most important factor was the February 1935 purge of Frank and his key assistants, the subject of the following chapter. The constitutionality of the AAA did reach the Supreme Court a year later, in a case involving the processing tax provision of the statute. But Frank played no role in that case. In the litigation on which they based their enforcement program, Frank and his staff compiled an unrelieved record of failure once the bloom had faded from *Nebbia*.

The AAA lawyers could, and did, blame their defeats on the inadequacies of the statute itself and on the inexperience of Justice Department lawyers. Their bad luck in having all but one case come before Republican judges undoubtedly created an insuperable hurdle. But Frank himself deserved some share of the blame. His preference for corporate-trained lawyers rather than experienced litigators, and his consequent delay in recruiting an experienced litigation staff, displayed a lack of understanding of the agricultural industry and its long-standing divisions. Frank's distaste for politics also put him at a disadvantage just at the time when crucial decisions on litigation strategy were needed. Whatever support Frank could have mustered from the White House was wiped out in mid-1934 when he was simultaneously bested by the Justice Department and Tommy Corcoran. The confluence of these factors produced an inexorable result: those beyond the control of Frank and his staff combined with those which they handled badly to ensure a record of defeat.

Chapter Eight

KING COTTON AND THE
TRIPLE-A PURGE

I. "Everything Promised to Be Delightful"

Late in 1933, AAA lawyers and administrators sat down to draft the 1934-1935 Cotton Acreage Reduction Contract. There was an urgent need to reduce cotton production and to rescue planters from a disastrous loss of income. With the exception of petroleum, no industry had suffered more during the Depression from the twin effects of overproduction and plummeting prices. Behind the need to curtail production lay the enormous demand for cotton by the United States and its allies during World War I. Cotton prices reached an all-time high in 1918, and postwar prosperity continued to stimulate production. Between 1921 and 1926 cotton acreage expanded from 30 to 46 million acres, but growing surpluses forced down prices. As cotton consumption fell sharply with the onset of the Depression, the unsold surplus swelled between 1929 and 1933 from 5 to 13 million bales, and gross cotton income dropped from $1.47 billion to $431 million.[1]

Another bumper crop was already in the ground when the AAA began in the summer of 1933. The hastily devised program put together to deal with this problem provided for "rental contracts" between planters and the AAA, under which planters willing to plow up from 25 to 50 percent of their acreage would be paid approximately $11 for each acre withdrawn from production. Although more than 10 million acres were plowed up under this crash program and rental payments more than doubled 1932 cotton income, participation was voluntary and enough planters were willing to gamble that increased market prices would more than equal rental payments that the 1933 cotton crop made only a slight dent in the overall surplus.[2] Congress responded by authorizing the AAA to replace the voluntary program with one that was virtually mandatory, requiring planters to reduce acreage in both 1934 and 1935 in return for benefit payments financed from the tax imposed on the "first domestic processing" of cotton by textile manufacturers.

Responsibility for drafting the master cotton contract on which individual contracts with planters would be based fell on three members of the AAA staff. Alger Hiss, the 29-year-old Harvard Law School graduate who headed the Benefit Contract Section of the Legal Division, represented AAA general counsel Jerome Frank. Cully Cobb, who headed the Cotton Section, and Oscar Johnston, Director of Finance and head of the Cotton Pool, spoke for AAA administrator George Peek. Both Cobb and Johnston were natives of Mississippi, the largest cotton-producing state. A former farm journalist, Cobb was labeled by one critic as ''the epitome of the Southern mint-julep drinking, backslapping, guffawing planter,''[3] and Johnston combined his AAA duties with management of the largest cotton plantation in the world. Relations between the liberal lawyer and the two southerners, as they met in the fall of 1933 to hammer out the details of the cotton contract, were colored by political factors and divided sympathies, which came to a head over the divisive issue of tenant labor.

It was inescapable that a massive acreage-reduction program would force some displacement of the tenant farmers and sharecroppers who labored on cotton plantations. Not only did planters have natural allies in Cobb and Johnston, but they wielded immense influence in Congress through such well-placed advocates as Senate majority leader Joe Robinson of Arkansas, Senate Agriculture Committee chairman John Bankhead of Alabama, and Senator ''Cotton Ed'' Smith of South Carolina, a notorious race-baiter. Measured against this political clout, the influence of the million and a half sharecroppers and tenant farmers was miniscule, and no equivalent group suffered more from the privations of the Depression. Between 1929 and 1933, the cash income of tenant families dropped from $735 to $216 per year; in more graphic terms, the average sharecropper or tenant had to support an entire family on less than 60 cents a day when Roosevelt took office.[4]

The tenant problem had roots deep in the dark soil of the Cotton South. Black workers inherited the legacy of racism that survived the Civil War and Emancipation, but white workers, in fact a majority on the plantations at the time of the New Deal, fared little better in treatment. Paternalism and dependency characterized relations between owners and tenants during the decades that followed the end of the slave system. Although tenants were commonly provided with housing, seed and tools, and often a garden plot, owners of large plantations forced them to purchase all necessities in company stores at inflated prices. The landlords kept accounts, and most tenants were perpetually in debt. Work in the fields was supervised by often brutal ''riding bosses.'' Tenants had few legal rights to their jobs and homes, rarely having more than a verbal agreement with the owner on a year-to-year basis, and planter-controlled local courts were hostile to those few tenants with the temerity to challenge the terms of their tenancy.[5]

As the AAA contract-drafting sessions progressed, Hiss had little trouble in applying his Wall Street experience to the questions of production allotments and payment levels. But he found himself caught between his corporate-law training and his sympathy for the dispossessed in drafting the contract provision that dealt with the problem of tenant displacement. Hiss favored an explicit contract provision limiting the right of landlords to displace tenants, while Cobb and Johnston opposed such a provision. Cully Cobb, on his part, manifested an initial willingness to protect the rights of tenants and sharecroppers to retain their homes, even when their jobs were eliminated. Cobb realized that many tenants whose labor would no longer be required in planting and harvesting could weather the Depression, despite their loss of cash income, if they held on to their homes and garden plots. During early negotiations, Cobb agreed with Hiss that it was "reasonable that the landowner be requested to keep the same number of tenants in 1934 as he had in 1933." Cobb reported to Chester Davis, who then headed the Production Control program of which the Cotton Section was a part, that although such an obligation "will impose an extra financial burden on the landowner," he was confident that "for general economic and social reasons, the landowner will realize as fully as anyone else the necessity for this, and will, I believe, be agreeable."[6]

Hiss, however, felt that a contract provision which merely "requested" that planters not displace tenants would be inadequate, and urged that such a policy be made mandatory. Faced with Hiss's intransigence on the issue, Cobb urged Davis to intervene to forge a compromise.

Davis responded by seeking expert advice, and called D. P. Trent, a respected authority on tenant problems and the Agriculture Department's Extension Director for Oklahoma, to Washington. Trent arrived in late September, and over the next several weeks he met with Davis, Cobb, Johnston, and Hiss to thrash out the question. Despite Trent's mediating role, the two sides found it difficult to agree on enforceable contract language. Trent expressed the view that planters would be hard-pressed to replace tenants forced from their farms and plantations into the cities once the Depression ended, and succeeded in convincing both sides that the prospective labor shortage would be eased if planters were required to maintain their "normal" complement of tenants during the two years covered by the contract. The question then became whether planters would be required to retain the *same* tenants during these two years, or be free to replace present tenants with others. Hiss advocated the first position, arguing that no tenant should be involuntarily displaced, while Cobb and Johnston upheld the right of the planter to replace tenants as long as the "normal" number hired in 1933 was maintained over the next two years.

The issue was, at this point, largely academic. Hiss was advocating the rights of individual tenants as a general proposition, while his antagonists were simply siding with the historic prerogatives of the planters. But the debaters faced a rapidly approaching deadline, since tenancy agreements traditionally expired on December 31. Incorporated into the master contract as Section 7, the language drafted by Hiss and endorsed by Cobb and Johnston was approved at a November meeting of the AAA Executive Council chaired by Henry Wallace. Like many compromise contract provisions, Section 7 was studded with qualifying phrases. It began by requiring each grower to "endeavor in good faith to bring about the reduction of acreage contemplated in this contract in such a manner as to cause the least possible amount of labor, economic, and social disturbance" and to agree, "insofar as possible," to "effect the acreage reduction as near ratable as practicable among tenants" on his farms. The requirement that the grower maintain the "normal number of tenants" and permit them to retain their homes, rent free, during 1934 and 1935 constituted the most ambiguous provision of Section 7. Finally, and significantly, the grower was authorized to replace any tenant who "shall so conduct himself as to become a nuisance or a menace to the welfare of the producer. . . ."[7]

From the point of view of an experienced corporate lawyer, Hiss had not conceded a great deal by agreeing to these qualifying phrases. He followed established corporate practice in leaving considerable discretion to the parties, subject to interpretation in light of past practices and customs. Hiss was well aware, as he later wrote Frank, that the provisions of Section 7 "which related to the manner in which the producer shall deal with his tenants were not legally enforceable" and that "there were several vague words which would all be primarily matters of opinion" and would be difficult to resolve in the event of dispute. His lawyer-like solution was a suggestion to Davis that "to avoid litigation, a provision that the Secretary's determination of violations shall be conclusive" should be inserted in the contract. Davis agreed, and a sentence was added to Section 9 that the Secretary's ruling on violations "shall be final and conclusive."[8] Hiss felt confident that this would adequately protect tenants from arbitrary and discriminatory treatment by landlords, notwithstanding the vague language of Section 7.

During the brief period in which the voluntary 1933 "rental contracts" were in force, AAA lawyers had faced few problems involving tenants. The contracts in fact contained no reference to tenants, being phrased only in terms of "lienholders" with an "interest" in the crops. It was initially assumed that planters, to whom rental checks were sent, would distribute the proper shares to tenants and sharecroppers, based on existing practice: a sharecropper furnishing the owner only his own labor would receive half of the payment; a share tenant furnishing mules or horses, and tools and seed in addition to labor, would receive three-fourths; and a cash tenant renting the land from the owner in return for a fixed payment in cash or cotton would receive the entire payment, from which he would pay the rent.[9] The AAA lawyers, unfamiliar with the complexities of tenant status and the traditional economic relations between tenants and planters, were confused by the problems of benefit disbursement. Alger Hiss first took the position that payments should go directly to planters. But complaints, often ungrammatically scrawled in pencil and addressed simply to "AAA, Washington," began to reach Hiss's desk, and convinced him that "in many cases tenants are ignorant of their rights and in some cases reported to us there is evidence of fraud" in the distribution of rental payments.[10] But Hiss also realized the difficulty in proving fraud on the part of landlords, given the informal nature of most tenancy agreements and the advantage landlords held over largely illiterate tenants.

Disturbed by evidence of fraud and the greater potential for mistake and misunderstanding, Hiss decided in early September 1933 that rental checks should be made out jointly to owners and tenants. In responding to an inquiry from AAA Comptroller John B. Payne, Hiss conceded that such a procedure might produce "great inconvenience," given the vast number of checks involved, but he felt it was preferable that "the liens of private individuals should be recognized when cash payments are made."[11] Ten days later, however, Hiss reverted to his original position, informing Payne that further research showed that Congress clearly intended that payments go directly to planters and it "is thus my conclusion that the check in payment . . . may be made payable to the producers without recognition of lien holders."[12]

Hiss later recounted that during the conflict over this issue, Senator "Cotton Ed" Smith burst unannounced into his office. "You're going to send money to my niggers, instead of to me?" he asked the startled young lawyer. "I'll take care of them." Hiss suggested politely that Smith direct his criticism to higher officials, explaining that he was just a lawyer applying policy as he understood it.[13] This unpleasant confrontation sensitized Hiss to the paternalistic attitudes of the planters, but he and other AAA lawyers could provide little help to tenants unable to collect their share of payments. Whatever their sympathies, the lawyers realized that the only legal recourse was for the Secretary to rescind the contract with the plantation owner—not only a drastic remedy but one that would hurt the tenants as well. Secretary Wallace admitted this dilemma in responding to complaints forwarded to him by E. I. McKinley, the Arkansas Commissioner of Labor and one of the few state officials sympathetic to the plight of tenants. "Our Legal Department has taken the position," Wallace replied, "that we have no authority to settle differences between landlord and tenant regarding the division of the rental money for land taken out of cotton production." He could only recommend that aggrieved tenants be advised to sue in the local courts for breach of contract. Wallace assured McKinley that Jerome Frank's office was "giving serious consideration to the problem," although in fact AAA lawyers had concluded that contract recision provided the only remedy.[14]

Although charges of illegally withheld rental payments continued to reach the AAA after the 1934-1935 contracts became effective, the problem of tenant displacement soon became far more serious. Section 7 had been in force little more than a month when Hiss warned Frank, early in January 1934, that landlord-tenant problems "are constantly arising as the contracts are interpreted in the field." The goal of crop reduction, Hiss wrote, "is frequently inconsistent with the aim of improving tenant conditions or securing for tenants a fair share of benefit payments."[15] Hiss was optimistic, however, that AAA lawyers and administrators could resolve these problems, since the recent departure of George Peek as Administrator had eased the acrimonious atmosphere within the agency. Frank initially felt that "everything promised to be delightful" under the regime headed by Peek's successor, Chester Davis.[16] Hiss in particular had worked well with Davis during the cotton contract negotiations and considered him intelligent and reasonable. Even Cully Cobb was conciliatory as the year began. He acknowledged to Frank in February that the "chief problem this year will undoubtedly arise out of the tenant-landlord misunderstandings" and suggested that Frank appoint a member of his staff to investigate tenant complaints.[17]

The reality of the entrenched plantation system, to which was added forceful criticism from within and outside the AAA, almost immediately ruptured the shaky bond between AAA lawyers and administrators. Faced with substantial cutbacks in acreage, planters began to evict tenants by the thousands when tenancy agreements expired at the end of 1933. A widespread pattern of withholding of benefit payments under the year-end settlements between planters and tenants accompanied the wave of evictions. At Davis's direction, D. P. Trent, now on loan from the Extension Service to the AAA, toured the Cotton Belt in February 1934 and returned to Washington alarmed at the extent of tenant victimization. In a memorandum to Davis, he urged that either Davis or Secretary Wallace make a "very frank and positive public statement . . . that there is evidence to indicate that many thousands of share tenants and sharecroppers are being denied their rights and their equitable share of the benefits" of the contracts.[18] Trent's findings were buttressed in a more detailed report to Davis by Calvin B. Hoover, a respected Duke University economist on leave to the AAA economic division, documenting hundreds of cases of payment withholding and concluding that "whether the tenant received anything at all often depended upon the charitableness of the landlord."[19]

Davis had no intention of making a public statement that might antagonize planters or their congressional allies. He was on close terms with Senator Joe Robinson and knew that the Majority Leader's support was essential to continued AAA appropriations. Internal pressure was more easily ignored, however, than the outside campaign directed at Wallace by the press. If any single event changed the course of the AAA and ultimately determined the fate of Jerome Frank and the Legal Reformers, it was the visit made by Socialist Party leader Norman Thomas to the small town of Tyronza, Arkansas, in February 1934. Although his party was small in numbers, in Thomas it had perhaps the most compelling political orator and propagandist of this century. A former Presbyterian minister whose socialist principles were formed during a ministry in the poverty-stricken Hell's Kitchen neighborhood in New York City, the patrician Princeton graduate garnered almost a million votes in the 1932 presidential election.[20]

Thomas had criticized the AAA's plow-up program in 1933, arguing that crop surpluses should be distributed at home and abroad to victims of the Depression. In November 1933 he received an invitation from a Socialist Party organizer in Arkansas, urging him to visit Tyronza and meet with sharecroppers: "Here you will find the true proletariat; here you will find inarticulate men moving irresistibly toward revolution and no less."[21] Ten miles from the Mississippi River and twenty miles north of Memphis, the capital of the Cotton Belt, Tyronza was a town seething with tension. At a mass meeting attended by hundreds of sharecroppers and a hostile contingent of plantation owners, Thomas flayed the Agriculture Department for ignoring the rights of tenants. During his visit, Thomas met H. L. Mitchell, the son of a sharecropper and proprietor of a small dry-cleaning shop in Tyronza, who took Thomas on a tour of cotton plantations in the area and introduced him to tenants who poured out stories of fraud and discrimination in the administration of the AAA cotton contract. Before leaving Tyronza, Thomas promised to begin a national campaign on behalf of the tenants and urged Mitchell to organize a tenant union, pledging the financial and organizational support of the Socialist Party. On this trip, Thomas also met in Memphis with William Amberson, a Party member and professor of physiology at the University of Tennessee, who told Thomas that he was undertaking an investigation of conditions on cotton plantations.[22]

Although he was active in a dozen other campaigns for civil liberties and the poor, Thomas's visit to Tyronza stimulated him to focus special attention on the plight of the sharecroppers. In a national radio speech on February 21, he called them "the Forgotten Men of the New Deal."[23] Thomas knew Henry Wallace and respected him as a man of conscience, and the day after his radio speech he wrote Wallace that under the crop reduction program hundreds of thousands of sharecroppers "are either driven out on the roads without hope of absorption into industry or exist without land to cultivate by grace of the landlord in shacks scarcely fit for pigs." Had the AAA, Thomas asked, "any plans . . . other than pious hopes" or did it intend that the sharecroppers "starve quietly so as not to interrupt our much predicted return to 'prosperity'?"[24] Wallace sent Thomas a temperate reply, arguing apologetically that he was aware of the conditions that Thomas described but that the "extremely low standard of living" of the sharecroppers predated the crop reduction program and could not be blamed on it. "We are determined to avoid injustice," he assured Thomas, "and to correct it to the full extent of our power where it may arise."[25] Although Wallace agreed with Thomas privately, he was embarrassed and incensed at what he considered an unfair attack. He wrote Marvin McIntyre of the White House staff that the Roosevelt administration should redouble its efforts to provide relief for displaced tenants, adding that "Norman Thomas has been attacking us rather bitterly on this score in the south and the communist brethren are looking toward this particular field as a rich one to cultivate."[26]

After more than two months of mounting criticism, Davis finally acted early in May by establishing an Adjustment Committee on Investigation of Landlord-Tenant Complaints, chaired by J. Phil Campbell, formerly director of the Extension Service in Georgia. The Darrow Committee report had recently embarrassed Hugh Johnson and the NRA, and Davis was determined that the AAA not be subjected to a similar denunciation. He expected the Campbell committee to whitewash the tenant problem and to deflect public criticism. In confidential instructions to the Extension Service agents who were to serve as investigators, Davis directed them to work through planters and county agriculture agents "in such a way as not to reflect unfavorably upon the work which has already been done by these local leaders. . . . *Nothing must be done which might cause them to feel that their actions are being questioned.*"[27] For public consumption the AAA issued a press release quoting Davis as saying that the "vast majority" of planters were abiding by their contracts, and that the Adjustment Committee would investigate reports that "a few" were in violation. Davis made it clear that the AAA did not intend "to interfere with the usual and normal relationships and tenure arrangements between landlords and their tenants, as these are governed by established practices and by State laws."[28]

The AAA lawyers had no illusions about the purpose of the Adjustment Committee and its preordained conclusions, and began organizing a counterattack. They planned to compile a record of violations in advance of the committee's report, to provide a legal basis for an eventual appeal to

Secretary Wallace that he revoke the contracts of planters violating their tenants' rights. Hiss began by urging Frank early in June to seek from Davis a policy statement defining precisely the rights of tenants under the contracts and putting teeth into the vague wording of Section 7. Frank passed this request on to Davis, reminding him that the AAA lawyers were chafing under the need to obtain policy directions for their legal work. "I wish a decision could soon be reached," Frank wrote, "because as matters now stand Mr. Hiss' assistants are constantly in danger of getting themselves involved in policy questions which I think it desirable to avoid, as I want them, so far as possible, to confine their activities to a discussion of legal questions."[29]

II. "No Use for Your Services"

In the atmosphere of fear and intimidation in northeastern Arkansas, it took several months for the seeds planted by Norman Thomas to germinate and take root. When they did, the result was the Southern Tenant Farmers Union, a militant group of black and white tenants and sharecroppers whose activities precipitated a wave of retaliatory evictions and a bitter battle within the AAA over the meaning of Section 7. The STFU had its beginning early in July 1934, when some two dozen men met in a rural schoolhouse near Tyronza to discuss their common problems. It was most unusual in the Cotton Belt that both races would meet together, and early in the meeting someone raised a crucial question: "Are we going to have two unions, one for the whites and one for the colored?" After several speakers warned that planters would never recognize a union of black and white tenants, Isaac Shaw rose to speak. Shaw had been a member of a black tenants' union which was wiped out in the bloody Elaine Massacre in 1919. "We colored people can't organize without you," he said, "and you white folks can't organize without us." Shaw continued:

"For a long time now the white folks and the colored folks have been fighting each other and both of us have been getting whipped all the time. We don't have nothing against one another but we got plenty against the landlord. The same chain that holds my people holds your people too. If we're chained together on the outside we ought to stay chained together in the union."[30]

When Shaw sat down, the question had been settled that white tenant farmers, some of them former members of the Ku Klux Klan, would join with blacks to form a union to press for their rights. Before leaving the schoolhouse, the men elected a white chairman and a black vice-chairman of their as-yet-unnamed organization. Several days later, a committee called on H. L. Mitchell and the young man who ran a filling station next door to Mitchell's dry-cleaning shop, Clay East, a recent convert to socialism. Mitchell and East knew how to complete the legal formalities, and on July 26, 1934, the Southern Tenant Farmers Union was incorporated, with East as president and Mitchell as secretary. Within months, helped by advice and modest donations from Norman Thomas, the STFU enrolled several thousand members in the cotton counties of Arkansas.[31]

The rapid growth of the STFU shocked complacent planters, used to dealing with fearful and racially divided tenants, and their response was quick and forceful: STFU members were harassed and often served with summary eviction notices. This development spurred both factions in the AAA to renewed efforts. Frank's thinly veiled warning to Davis in late June that without some guidance the AAA lawyers might be forced to formulate Section 7 policy themselves failed to produce a response, and Hiss and Frank moved in July to form a rump committee of pro-tenant liberals. This group, which included Trent, Hoover, and Comptroller John Payne, began drafting a policy statement for submission to Davis.[32] The prospect of further retaliatory tenant evictions particularly concerned Hiss, who was about to take a leave from the AAA to serve as counsel to a Senate committee investigating the munitions industry (the so-called Nye Committee). Hiss remained on the AAA payroll, however, and for the next several months in effect held two full-time jobs, spending his days on Capitol Hill and returning to his AAA office in the evenings. In late July he asked Robert McConnaughey, the acting chief of the Benefit Contract Section in his absence, to prepare a memorandum interpreting Section 7.

McConnaughey's brief two-page memorandum, completed on August 1, was not sent to Davis, since Hiss did not wish to raise the issue of Section 7 before the Adjustment Committee submitted its long-awaited report. Cully Cobb had promised Hiss that the report, held up by the need to investigate the situation in Arkansas created by conflicts between planters and the STFU, would provide sufficient guidance for a definitive Section 7 policy. But the McConnaughey memorandum made it clear where the AAA lawyers stood on the issue. "In our opinion," he wrote, Section 7 "means that all tenants who were on the farm at the time of signing the contract (and the producer has agreed that he will have the normal number) shall be permitted to stay during the term of the contract." Since contracts extended over the two-year period of 1934 and 1935 and were signed in 1933, "no 1933 tenant who wants to stay for the 1934-1935 crop seasons shall be forced to leave, and no tenant shall have his status changed" during this period.[33] The memorandum did not address, except by implication, the question raised by the provision permitting replacement of tenants who posed a "nuisance or a menace" to the planter. On its face,

Section 7 did not deal with evictions that occurred before termination of the normal yearly tenancy agreement. Under one possible interpretation of McConnaughey's memorandum, such evictions would be barred. But the "nuisance or menace" clause constituted a loophole obvious to any planter's lawyer, as did other grounds available under state law. Over the next month, however, the AAA lawyers held their memorandum in reserve, while they patiently waited for the Adjustment Committee report.

On September 1, 1934, the committee submitted its report to Davis. As expected by the AAA lawyers, the 75-page report found little fire among the smoke of tenant complaints. It began by complimenting the county agents, whose jobs depended on planter approval, for their "very friendly" attitude and noted that the agents "were present in person when the majority of cases were investigated." The committee's investigators checked a total of 1,490 complaints; they found no violation in 1,049, or 70.4 percent, of the cases, and all but a handful of the rest were settled by the county agents and committee investigators. In only 22 cases, 1.5 percent of the total, "was it necessary for the Adjustment Committee to recommend the rejection or cancellation of the contract."

The report emphatically rejected claims of wholesale tenant displacement. "In practically every case where one had been removed, the landlord had some good reason for doing so and has replaced him with another, and in most instances, a better one." What constituted "good reason" was not specified, but the committee implied that STFU membership might suffice: "Most of these complaints came from certain counties where agitators had attempted to stir up trouble."[34] An Arkansas cotton warehouse operator was more blunt; what "made it necessary to move more share-croppers than usual has been due to the propaganda of H. L. Mitchell . . . telling them first that they were mistreated and that they were not getting their proper share of government rent. . . . That, of course, created a situation in which some of those fellows were not desirable tenants."[35]

Since the area around Tyronza was the center of STFU organizing and complaints of tenant displacement, the report made a point of refuting these charges. "In Poinsett County, Arkansas, where considerable publicity had been given to alleged wholesale eviction of tenants and share-croppers, a survey by the relief administration showed that there were 317 more tenants on farms in that county in 1934 than in 1933." Of course, this begged the question of whether evictions had taken place. More complaints came from tenants on the 5,000-acre Tyronza plantation of Hiram Norcross than from any other in the country. E. A. Miller, vice-chairman of the committee and an assistant to Cully Cobb in the AAA Cotton Section, personally investigated these charges. He noted that Norcross was chairman of the county cotton acreage reduction committee and wrote that "Mr.

Norcross, feeling deeply his responsibility to the program . . . requested that the situation as affecting his tenants be completely and thoroughly investigated. We spent a good part of a day on his farm interviewing riders and tenants.'' Miller found no violations on the Norcross plantation and complimented him for allowing itinerant cotton pickers to occupy vacant houses rent-free and to use garden plots without cost.[36]

On October 9, a month after this ringing official endorsement, Norcross notified twenty-two of his tenants, all members of the STFU, that he would have "no use for your services next year." He directed each to vacate his house by December 31, 1934.[37] The tenants reacted by contacting H. L. Mitchell, who in turn enlisted the aid of Professor Amberson in Memphis. In mid-October Amberson traveled to Washington to plead the tenants' case and spoke with a low-ranking AAA lawyer, A. B. Book. After his trip, Amberson reported to Norman Thomas that Book "is very friendly to our cause and is anxious to help in any way possible but states that the cotton section is made up of plantation owners, or those dominated by them, to such a degree that it is impossible to influence them."[38] Apparently, Book neither notified any of his supervisors of Amberson's visit nor followed up the situation, and Amberson wrote dejectedly to Thomas several weeks later that he "had no word from the AAA lawyer and have decided that it is impossible to do anything with either the Cotton Section or their legal staff."[39]

Norcross was adamant in claiming that the evictions were permitted under Section 7. In a letter to Paul Appleby, Wallace's chief aide, he said that E. A. Miller assured him during the summer "investigation" that "the landlord was the sole judge of what tenants he desired" as long as he maintained the same number. Since July, Norcross wrote, "agitators, both local and from the outside, have been holding weekly meetings in and around Tyronza disturbing our labor and advising the share-croppers generally, both black and white, that they could not be removed from the farm in 1935." When labor conditions became "intolerable" Norcross visited the County Agent, R. L. McGill, early in September and told him "the only solution I could see was to evict certain undesirable tenants." McGill assured him that "the only concern the Government would have would be that I have as many tenants in 1935 as I had in 1934."[40]

It is not surprising that McGill provided this assurance. McConnaughey's August memorandum taking the opposite position had not been circulated outside his office, and policy was in such disarray that in mid-September another AAA lawyer replied to a query by an Oklahoma law firm representing a planter that "I do not find any particular ruling on the subject" and continued with a totally opaque and contradictory interpretation of Section 7.[41]

167

In December, with the eviction deadline nearing, the STFU persuaded a lawyer from nearby Marked Tree, C. J. Carpenter, to file suit in the local Chancery Court to enjoin Norcross from carrying out the evictions. The twenty-two tenants drafted a petition on December 12 to County Agent McGill, saying that they had "faithfully performed our duties, planting, cultivating and harvested our crops as directed by the said Hiram Norcross and his over-seers." They added that "we have no place to move" and because it was winter "we, and our families, will suffer great hardships."[42] McGill replied with a letter to Carpenter, forwarding a copy to Victor E. Anderson of Frank's office, repeating the advice he had earlier given Norcross:

"It is my understanding that the Department of Agriculture is not interested in whom Hiram Norcross has as sharecroppers and/or rentors— they are interested only in the number that he maintains on the land controlled by him. . . . If Mr. Norcross sees fit, he might move all of the tenants off his place and the only concern that we might have would be that he replace them with an equal number. If I am wrong in this matter the Department will inform me since I am enclosing a copy of this letter to you to the Department with the petition I am sending."[43]

Meanwhile, E. A. Miller of Cobb's office learned of the suit and advised Cobb that in the opinion of the Cotton Section Norcross "appears to be within his rights to change tenants" on the basis of Section 7.[44] On December 28, three days before the scheduled evictions, Chancellor J. G. Gautney ruled against the tenants and dismissed the case, with leave to appeal to the Arkansas Supreme Court. By this time all but six of the tenants, faced with an action for unlawful detainer filed by Norcross immediately after the ruling, had left their homes on the plantation.[45]

January 1935 became a crucial and hectic month for the AAA lawyers. Carpenter wired Frank directly after Chancellor Gautney's ruling, informing him of the impending appeal and imploring him to seek Wallace's agreement that the AAA enter the case on the tenants' side. Paul A. Porter, the AAA press director, told Frank that newspapers across the country were carrying stories about the evictions that stressed that Norcross was chairman of the local AAA committee that rejected an appeal by the tenants.[46] Frank immediately met with Wallace, who already had been briefed on the Norcross case by Paul Appleby, who was a friend of Professor Amberson and had remonstrated with Cully Cobb that the Cotton Section was "clearly loaded on the side of the landlords" and should be moving to withhold benefit payments from Norcross.[47]

Frank's suggested plan of action, which Wallace endorsed, was twofold: AAA lawyers in the Opinion Section would prepare a detailed legal interpretation of tenants' rights under Section 7, and would also research the question of whether the Department could enter the Norcross case before the Arkansas Supreme Court, as Carpenter urged. On January 4 Frank instructed Francis M. Shea, who headed the Opinion Section while Hiss was on leave, to prepare a formal opinion on Section 7. "Suit has been filed in Arkansas involving an interpretation of that paragraph and the Secretary is anxious to have an opinion at the earliest possible moment," he wrote Shea.[48] Frank also asked John Abt, head of the Litigation Division, to begin research on the intervention question. Finally, he instructed Margaret Bennett, his representative on the AAA Committee on Violations, to secure the committee's opinion that Norcross was in violation of his contract and that payments could be withheld from him.

With his lawyers hard at work on these questions, Frank assumed that any action by Wallace or Chester Davis would be deferred until the recommendations were submitted, and that the matter would be considered within the special province of the Legal Division. What he failed to anticipate was that the pro-landlord faction in the AAA would not accept the segregation of policy and legal questions and would launch a violent counterattack designed to usurp the function of the Legal Division. It began on January 5 with an appeal by Cully Cobb to Davis that the AAA support Norcross rather than the tenants. Cobb argued that landlords should be able to remove "inefficient tenants" and pointed out the overwhelming vote the previous summer to join the cotton program (in Poinsett County there were 2,281 affirmative and only 75 negative votes on the Bankhead Act referendum). This lopsided margin "in those communities where the tenant farmers' union was organized, where there has been the most agitation and disturbance, would indicate a general satisfaction . . . with the operations of our program."[49] This vote, of course, was taken long before the eviction notices were sent.

Frank's first setback came from the Committee on Violations. Margaret Bennett drafted a statement to be sent to Wallace that the forthcoming opinion on Section 7 "will state that a producer is required 'insofar as possible' to permit his 1934 tenants to remain on the farm for the year 1935" unless they were proven to constitute a "nuisance or menace" to the producer. Bennett's draft statement noted that Section 7(a) of the National Industrial Recovery Act protected union membership (although it did not cover farm workers), that "it would appear inadvisable for one department of the Federal Government to take a position directly contrary" to the NRA, and that joining the Norcross suit "would give broad publicity" to the problem and help prevent further evictions.[50] But the Cotton Section controlled the Committee on Violations, and on January 9 Bennett was outvoted. In place of her rejected draft, the Committee sent a statement to Wallace saying "it is not in accordance with public policy for the

169

Secretary to enforce Paragraph 7 of the contract in accordance with its interpretation by the Legal Division but . . . producers and tenants should be left free to enter into rental contracts as to tenure.''[51]

Given the composition of the committee, Frank did not expect to prevail. However, the majority statement was more than a temporary defeat; it directly challenged the authority of the Legal Division. Frank was incensed, and heatedly complained to Victor Christgau, assistant AAA administrator, that Cobb's report on the Norcross case and the committee statement to Wallace were unauthorized legal opinions. Referring to Cobb's support for Norcross, Frank said that "this question has recently been referred to the Office of the General Counsel and *an exactly contrary* opinion is being prepared. . . ." Frank urged that Cobb and his staff "should be warned that there are grave dangers that, if they write letters giving interpretations of contracts, the Secretary may be seriously embarrassed, if it turns out these legal interpretations are erroneous.''[52]

Christgau, Frank's most sympathetic ally among AAA administrators, complied immediately and instructed Cobb that he must "hereafter submit all letters, telegrams, memoranda" and other documents "covering legal questions to the General Counsel for approval and see that this memorandum is called to the attention of all your assistants.''[53] The next day, to counteract the Committee on Violations statement and to ensure that Wallace did not hastily adopt it, Frank wrote the Secretary that Alger Hiss, "after having most carefully considered the points made in the majority report and others, has approved a legal opinion, in the conclusions of which I concur, the effect of which" was that Norcross "is under a legal obligation" to retain his 1934 tenants. Conceding that Norcross might be able to show that the evicted tenants were a "nuisance" or "menace" to his welfare, Frank informed Wallace that he planned to send a lawyer to Arkansas to investigate the situation before recommending further action.[54]

By the middle of January a full-scale state of war existed between the Cotton Section and the Legal Division, with both sides pressuring Wallace for support. It was clear that both the AAA administrators and Wallace knew the conclusion of the forthcoming legal opinion on Section 7. The sympathy of the Legal Reformers for the tenants was as obvious as the pro-landlord bias of the Cotton Section. The only unresolved question was whether Wallace would defer action on both the eviction issue and the Department's intervention in the suit against Norcross until he received the legal opinion being prepared under Hiss's supervision.

An unexpected and dramatic sequence of events hastened the crisis in the AAA. Gardner "Pat" Jackson of the AAA Consumer Counsel's office, a long-time social activist, veteran of the Sacco-Vanzetti fight and consistent thorn in the side of Chester Davis, responded to a plea from the

STFU and arranged, through Paul Appleby, a meeting of union leaders with Henry Wallace. On January 10, H. L. Mitchell and three STFU officers from Tyronza held a polite but noncommittal session with Appleby and Wallace. According to Mitchell, Wallace promised "full consideration" of the STFU appeal that the AAA intervene in the Norcross suit, and then sent the delegation to see Cully Cobb.[55] Predictably, the two-hour meeting with Cobb accomplished nothing. Mitchell presented a list of 550 sharecroppers and tenants who had been served with eviction notices in the Tyronza area; a Cotton Section official at the meeting reported that the group was "assured by Mr. Cobb that an effort was being made to see that every person received what was due him" under the cotton contract.[56]

On their return to Arkansas, the STFU delegates were scheduled to report to a mass meeting of sharecroppers in Marked Tree. But they were delayed on their drive back, and the impatient audience awaiting them was first addressed by Ward Rodgers, a young Methodist minister recently employed by the Federal Emergency Relief Administration to teach reading and writing to illiterate sharecroppers. During an impassioned speech denouncing the growing tide of evictions and the violent attempts of planters and sheriff's deputies to disrupt STFU organizing, Rodgers became carried away. Saying that planters had threatened to lynch him and other union organizers, he continued: "I could lead a lynch mob. I don't want to do that. But, gentlemen, if these people are not fed I will lead that lynch mob and lynch every planter in Poinsett County."[57] Deputy prosecuting attorney Fred Stafford (accompanied by a stenographer to record just such incendiary remarks) considered this a call to insurrection and arrested Rodgers as soon as he left the platform. Within days, Rodgers was tried and convicted in the local court on charges of "anarchy" and "attempting to overthrow and usurp the government of Arkansas" and sentenced to six months in jail. Privately, Professor Amberson considered Rodgers "terribly foolish," but the incident increased tension in Arkansas and attracted national press attention. H. L. Mitchell and Amberson quickly wired the AAA that bloodshed and class war could be avoided only if a government representative was sent to investigate.[58]

Frank had earlier resisted suggestions by his staff that he send a lawyer to investigate tenant conditions and the Norcross case, but after the Rodgers arrest and several desperate appeals from C. T. Carpenter that Norcross and other landlords were proceeding with "wholesale evictions" of STFU members and that without federal intervention "hundreds of helpless people will be thrown out of their homes, without a roof, or even a tent, to protect them and their families," Frank decided to dispatch an AAA lawyer.[59] After securing approval from Wallace and Davis, he chose Mary Conner

Myers, a 36-year-old graduate of George Washington University Law School. Her selection seemed designed to placate Davis and the Cotton Section, since she had a conservative reputation as an administrative law specialist, and had no ties to the Legal Reformers who had tangled with Cully Cobb. To reassure Davis, Frank instructed Myers to make no statements to the press and to submit her report directly to him.[60]

On her arrival in mid-January, Myers rented a small office in Marked Tree and accepted H. L. Mitchell's offer to drive her around the countryside and arrange meetings with tenants. Although many were afraid to talk to her, over the next few days she gathered close to a hundred affidavits from tenants who claimed they had been evicted for union membership and cheated of benefit payments. One former Norcross tenant, Henderson Bentley, wrote: "Mr. H. N. Norcross is an out lower [outlaw] the way he is treated some Family While [sic] and Collard and Dear Secretary we need some help and it don't do no good for us to see the county committee for he tole us if Mr. Norcross says move to move for them was Mr. Norcross Houses."[61]

Perhaps because of her prior lack of exposure to the tenant situation, Myers was shocked by what she learned and wired Frank on January 18: "HAVE HEARD ONE LONG STORY HUMAN GREED . . . SECTION SEVEN ONLY ONE SECTION CONTRACT BEING OPENLY AND GENERALLY VIOLATED . . . CROPPERS MUCH HIGHER CLASS THAN I EXPECTED AND ALL PATHETICALLY PLEASED GOVERNMENT HAS SENT SOME ONE TO LISTEN TO THEM."[62] Despite her instructions, she found it impossible to avoid reporters who had come to cover the Ward Rodgers trial, and reports of her mission with hints of her findings began appearing in the press. The STFU leaders were delighted with her reaction. Amberson wrote Norman Thomas that the conviction of Ward Rodgers made "a rather favorable impression on Mrs. Myers, who calls the arrest a 'frame-up' and has so reported to Washington. She is a great admirer of yours. 'One more speech,' she says, 'and I would have voted the Socialist ticket.' She is extraordinarily sympathetic with the people, and is going into every angle of the situation."[63]

Her final report, entitled "Tenants on Cotton Plantations in Northeastern Arkansas," was not submitted until February 8, three days after the purge, and thus did not directly affect it.[64] But press reports anticipating its findings created apprehension in the Cotton Section and among planters who knew that an interpretation of Section 7 was forthcoming and feared that the AAA would intervene on behalf of the Norcross tenants in the pending appeal. Pressure on Wallace began to mount; on January 15 the American Cotton Cooperative Association, the voice of the planters, wired him that a pro-tenant policy "would cause consternation over South and reverse completely the sentiments of thousands of the friends of crop control measures."[65]

In the meantime, as the end of January neared, AAA lawyers continued to work on the assignments Frank had given them. The first report, from A. M. Wilding-White of the Litigation Division, concluded that it "seems quite clear that the United States cannot" intervene to remove the Norcross case from the state to federal court. Under federal law, such a procedure could be effected only on submission of an affidavit that "prejudice or local influence" would make the plaintiff "unable to obtain justice" in the state court. "There does not seem to be any question of local prejudice," the report concluded.[66] A few days later, the Litigation Division advised Frank that the government's only recourse was to appear as amicus curiae in the Norcross case.[67]

III. "THE HIGHEST RESPECT FOR ALL PARTIES CONCERNED"

Both factions in the AAA realized, even before the formal interpretation of Section 7 was completed, that a showdown was inevitable and that Henry Wallace would be forced to choose between them. Chester Davis learned that Frank had prevailed on Paul Appleby to send a telegram to county agents in Arkansas instructing them to cease advising landlords that they could evict tenants. Davis considered this a direct challenge to his authority, and instructed Oscar Johnston, manager of the Cotton Pool, to prepare a memorandum arguing that those who drafted Section 7 had no such intent in mind, as ammunition in the fight with Frank. Johnston dutifully responded with a report of his recollections of the November 1933 meetings in which Hiss participated. "Never, at any time," he wrote, "insofar as I knew was there any thought or suggestion of arbitrarily requiring the owner of a farm to maintain on that farm, the identical tenants who had occupied the farm in 1933." Such a policy, he added, "would be absolutely fatal to the success of the cotton program and would, in my judgment, be a serious political blunder."[68]

Frank, seeking ammunition for his side, asked Hiss for his recollections. In a memorandum dated January 26 (the same date as Johnston's) Hiss recalled that Davis and George Peek had accepted his draft version of Section 7 with the understanding, subject only to the "nuisance" or "menace" exceptions, that "the landlords must retain the same tenants." Hiss added that "in the Norcross case, it seems from the evidence now before us, that the landlord evicted his tenants simply and solely because they were members of a union; that fact alone would not bring Mr. Norcross within the exceptions."[69]

During the internecine warfare between the AAA factions, Henry Wallace remained noncommittal as long as possible. He respected both Frank and Davis, and had no stomach for a repetition of the blood-letting that preceded George Peek's departure. But the combination of press reports of irreconcilable divisions in the AAA and pressure from cotton planters and their political allies finally forced the issue. On January 30 Assistant Administrator Victor Christgau took it upon himself to warn Wallace that relations between Davis and the Legal Reformers had reached the breaking point. Wallace's diary entries over the next several days provide the best firsthand account of the crisis. After meeting with Christgau, Wallace wrote: "Evidently there is a storm brewing in the AAA. To what extent it can be handled by proper administration, and what is inevitable in the situation, I do not know."[70]

Two days later, on February 1, Wallace and Calvin Hoover met with a delegation from northeast Arkansas led by Congressman William Driver and including the president and eight county representatives of the Arkansas Farm Bureau Federation. "They feared the Department of Agriculture was going to take away from them the right to substitute one tenant for another. They said they were in harmony with the original interpretation of Section 7 but understood that this interpretation was going to be changed. Apparently Paul Appleby had sent a telegram which had caused this fear, and evidently the fear was unwarranted." This last statement indicates that Wallace was uninformed on the state of Section 7 policy, since Appleby's telegram was unambiguous in directing AAA county agents that landlords must retain their 1934 tenants.

Hoover, realizing Appleby's influence on Wallace and that the Secretary might take refuge behind the Legal Division report, now in the last stages of preparation, immediately reported on the situation to Davis, who had just returned from a Midwest speaking trip. The next afternoon, a Saturday, Wallace reported Hoover's message that Davis "wanted to have an hour's uninterrupted talk with me but not in his office or my office." Wallace recounted the meeting in his diary:

"I met Davis in what he calls his hideout and talked with him for more than two hours. He is very much disturbed, feeling that there is a definite intrigue going on against him on the part of Paul Appleby and Jerome Frank and perhaps certain others in the liberal group. . . . He referred to the appearance of the plantation owners of northeastern Arkansas as a result of the telegram which Paul sent with respect to Section 7. It seems that Jerome Frank had recently rendered an opinion to Chester on his legal interpretation of Section 7. Chester interpreted this legal opinion to mean that it was incumbent on the contract signers who have tenants to keep . . . the same tenants on the land unless they were proven mean or vicious. Chester said that this was not in conformity with the publicity which I had given out last summer. He thought that Jerome Frank was definitely endeavoring by means of the slippery legal interpretation to put him on the spot. . . .

"I told Chester that I couldn't believe that Paul and Jerome Frank had connived against him to the extent which he indicated. I do recognize, of course, that Paul and Jerome and Rex Tugwell and others of the extreme liberal group want to see things brought to pass faster than Chester does. I can see how in endeavoring to push things along they might do things that would seem to Chester like double dealing."

Although Davis argued that Frank and the Legal Reformers "are interested in social revolution" and that "definitely some of them are socialist," he did not demand at this meeting on February 2 that Frank or any of his staff be fired. Wallace, on his part, was inclined to take a charitable view and reflected that the conflict was "altogether too much emphasized" and "is a result of Chester's extreme conscientiousness and his nervousness and hard work." Significantly, Wallace assured Davis that he would not discuss the situation with Appleby or Frank until he conferred further with Davis later in the week.[71] On Sunday, February 3, Wallace met with M. L. Wilson, who advised him not to take any precipitous action and suggested that perhaps a month's vacation for Davis would ease things. Wilson agreed to have a "heart to heart talk" with Davis; Wallace's assessment was that all those involved "are so honest and earnest in their approach that I believe their intriguing, on the whole, is rather unconscious."[72]

The next morning, however, Davis received the long-awaited interpretation of Section 7, signed by Francis Shea as head of the Opinion Section and initialed by Frank and Hiss. In a brief covering memorandum to Davis, Frank said that it "has been approved by Mr. Hiss and me." Its conclusion, no different than that stated by Frank on several earlier occasions, was summarized in these words: "A landlord-producer must keep the same share-tenants and share-croppers for 1934 as were on the farm in 1933, and for 1935 as were on the farm in 1934, provided they were willing to remain, and have not so conducted themselves as to have become a nuisance or a menace to the welfare of the producer."[73]

Davis first reacted to the report by calling Alger Hiss to his office. "He called me in with great perturbation," Hiss recalled, "and he said, 'Alger, this is a dishonest opinion; it isn't true, it can't be.' " Shocked by this reflection on his integrity, Hiss promptly offered his resignation. "Obviously no lawyer can work for a client who doesn't have confidence in him," he told Davis. "If you think this is a dishonest opinion you don't have confidence in me." Davis apologized for his intemperate statement, and Hiss explained that the lawyers who prepared the opinion thought they were following Wallace's policy, although they knew it was opposed by

Cully Cobb and the Cotton Section. "I explained to him the function of a lawyer in giving an opinion. He can often give an opinion either way, depending on what the client wants and depending on the situation. We had not said it *had* to be followed; we had said this was an appropriate reading."[74]

It is unclear whether Davis based his charge that the opinion was dishonest merely on his disagreement with its conclusion or on a close reading of its thirty-two single-spaced pages. Shea made two major arguments: first, he interpreted the wording of Section 7 that the landlord "shall permit all tenants to continue in the occupancy of their houses" during 1934 and 1935 in a literal sense. "Obviously, the only tenant who can 'continue in the occupacy' of his house for the year 1934 is one who resided there prior to, or at the time of, signing the contract." His second argument reflected concern with the situation in Arkansas, and cited the provision in Section 7 that acreage reduction should be effected "in such a manner as to cause the least possible amount of labor, economic and social disturbance." Those conditions "giving rise to dissatisfaction and unrest," Shea wrote, "may interfere with the orderly execution of the cotton adjustment program, perhaps by bringing on strikes or violence among these classes or by leading to the employment of obstructionary tactics." Protecting tenants against eviction was essential to maintain "the social peace necessary to the execution of any planned program."[75] There was, however, one glaring omission in the opinion: Shea's literal reading of Section 7 made no reference to the qualifying phrase "insofar as possible" that Hiss included as a concession to Davis and Peek during the drafting negotiations.

With the help of Solicitor Seth Thomas, Davis hastily drafted a rebuttal to the opinion. All that Section 7 required of landlords, Davis wrote Wallace, was that in order to "prevent the operation of the cotton program from cutting loose from their homes families who would become itinerant dependents on relief," tenants no longer eligible for shares of benefit payments were entitled to remain rent-free in their homes, with access to wood for fuel and garden plots.[76] Davis and Thomas made this argument to Wallace in person later that day. They persuaded the Secretary, after giving their version of the history of Section 7, that their position was based on "commonsense," and Wallace dispatched Thomas from the meeting to prepare a second legal opinion. With the Solicitor gone, Davis got to the real point of his visit. Jerome Frank must be fired.

According to Wallace's diary entry, Davis reported that the situation in the AAA "had reached the breaking point in his mind and that he would have to have a definite showdown with Alger Hiss and Jerome Frank. He feels that Hiss is a splendid fellow of unusual ability and that in this case, he is merely being loyal to Jerome Frank. He feels that he could clean up the situation if he could get rid of Jerome Frank, Lee Pressman, and F. M. Shea and another man whose name I have forgotten. . . ." Wallace had "no doubt that Frank and Hiss were animated by the highest of motives" but agreed with Davis that "from a legal point of view, they had nothing to stand on" and that the opinion simply expressed their "social preconceptions." Taken aback by the sudden turn of events, Wallace asked Davis for some time to consider his demand. But later that afternoon, after another talk with M. L. Wilson, Wallace decided to give in. He instructed Wilson to call Davis and "tell him that he had the green light."[77]

The next day, February 5, Davis began the purge. He first called in Frank and fired him. Having learned the night before from Hiss of what would happen, Frank was not surprised. He rightly suspected that Davis had met with Senator Robinson of Arkansas the previous day while Davis was testifying before the Senate Agriculture Committee after leaving Wallace's office; Frank later recalled that Davis "told me about the farm leaders and how he had to go along with them for the time being. . . . Therefore, I would have to go."[78] With the leading victim dispatched, Davis completed the purge by instructing his press office to issue a statement that Frank, Lee Pressman, Francis Shea, and Victor Rotnem of the Legal Division had been dismissed. The purge extended to the Consumer Counsel's office: Gardner Jackson was fired and Dr. Frederick Howe, its head, was demoted.

The aftermath of the purge illustrates the curious ambivalence of Wallace's position and his second thoughts about his decision. After Frank was fired, he and Hiss went to see Wallace in the afternoon of February 5, not to argue against the dismissals but to urge Wallace not to abandon their position on Section 7. They made a convincing case; Wallace wrote in his diary that he found their argument "entirely reasonable and straightforward and the record sounds just as good as that presented by Chester Davis. Frank said that he didn't think this particular issue was the real issue and that the real issue was a fundamental difference in attitude between him and Davis. I indicated that I believed Frank and Hiss had been completely loyal to me at all times but that it was necessary to clear up an administrative situation and that I agreed with Davis."[79]

Rumors of a possible AAA shake-up had been circulating in Washington for days, and the formal announcement of the purge forced Wallace to face the press on February 6. It was an uncomfortable experience. One observer described Wallace as "grey-faced and haggard" and another said his "face hung sadly" while he parried a barrage of hostile questions. "You can't have the ship listing right and then left," Wallace limply explained; "it must go right straight along, straight down the middle of the road."[80] Considering the magnitude of the purge and its explosive political impact, it is remarkable that President Roosevelt apparently was not consulted or given any forewarning. Rex Tugwell was on a trip to Florida when he learned by telephone of Frank's dismissal. Tugwell promptly wired Roosevelt that "I am being besieged with requests from Department of Agriculture people who want me to tell them what to do. They all want to resign with Jerome Frank."[81] But Roosevelt professed neutrality. In an off-the-record remark to his press conference on February 6, Roosevelt answered a question about the purge with this cryptic comment: "I never knew about it; purely an internal matter of law."[82] Hastening his return from Florida, Tugwell met with Wallace on February 7 to discuss the purge. Tugwell realized that the purge underminded his own position as the most visible Brains Truster in government, and told Wallace that he was "heartsick" about the purge and "felt that it reflected on him." He told Wallace he was meeting with Roosevelt that afternoon and would try to get Frank another job in the government.[83] Wallace, Tugwell recorded in his diary, appeared "red-faced and ashamed" during their meeting.[84]

On February 9, a week after his first crucial talk with Davis, Wallace met with him again. "It seems probable," Wallace recorded in his diary, "that without knowing it, possibly Chester Davis and myself might have committed an injustice to Paul Appleby, Jerome Frank and Rex Tugwell in the recent upset."[85] Nonetheless, after receiving from Seth Thomas an interpretation of Section 7 that landlords were free to evict tenants "whom they knew to be worthless and incompetent,"[86] Wallace authorized on February 12 a telegram to county agents with the last word on the matter: SECTION SEVEN OF COTTON CONTRACT DOES NOT BIND LAND-OWNERS TO KEEP THE SAME TENANTS . . . THAT IS THE OF-FICIAL AND FINAL INTERPRETATION OF THE DEPARTMENT OF AGRICULTURE AND NO OTHER INTERPRETATION WILL BE GIVEN.[87]

The ironic epitaph to this episode was written the next month by the Arkansas Supreme Court, which held that since the contract providing benefit payments was solely between Norcross and the Department of Agriculture, it could not be enforced by tenants since there was "no privity of contract" between them and the government. In legal terminology, tenants were only "incidental beneficiaries" of the contract, with no rights under it. The argument of the tenants that the purpose of the contract was to protect their rights, the court concluded, "is not shared by the Department of Agriculture. . . ."[88] During the same week in which the Arkansas Supreme Court adopted the legal position of Davis and Wallace, a reign of terror began against the Southern Tenant Farmers Union. Bullets riddled the home of the union's 70-year-old black chaplain; the union president moved to Memphis after vigilantes warned him they would "personally see to it that if you don't leave town . . . your brains are blown out''; and Clay East left the South for good after a warning from a mob in Marked Tree that he would be ''shot on sight'' if he remained in Poinsett County.[89]

The AAA purge was considered at the time and has been interpreted since as having been precipitated solely by the conflict over the cotton contract. However, closer examination of the list of its victims raises intriguing questions about the timing and motivation of the purge. Chester Davis claimed to have been surprised by the ''dishonest'' opinion on Section 7, and his actions were certainly affected by pressure from planters, the AAA Cotton Section, and Senator Robinson. But Davis knew that Hiss had supervised preparation of the opinion, and spared him. Francis Shea signed the opinion, but Lee Pressman and Victor Rotnem, a junior member of Frank's staff, had no connection with it. Gardner Jackson and Dr. Howe were not even in the Legal Division. Aside from Shea, most of the lawyers who helped draft the opinion escaped the purge: Telford Taylor, David Kreeger, Robert McConnaughey, and Margaret Bennett were all spared. Taylor, despite his well-known role in drafting the opinion, was promoted by Davis to replace Shea. The list of victims provides evidence for an alternative and perhaps more convincing explanation: Davis ''used the tenants issue to rid the Legal Division of its most outspoken and hard-working advocates'' in retaliation for his embarrassing defeat the previous summer in the conflict over the books and records clauses in marketing agreements.[90]

This analysis helps to explain the dismissal of Pressman and Jackson and the demotion of Fred Howe. All these men, as well as Frank, clashed bitterly with Davis over the books and records issue. Davis later admitted that his break with Frank began in the summer of 1934 and that the ''insistence . . . by Frank and Pressman particularly, on carrying the power of examination of books far beyond the transactions'' regulated by the marketing agreements ''was a cause of difference from the very beginning.''[91] Wallace, however, had sided with the Legal Division and the Consumer Counsel's office on this issue, and Davis lacked the political clout at that time to force a showdown. Davis was far more responsive to the interests of the meat-packers and other processors than to those of cotton growers, and may well have bided his time until a more propitious issue arose. This is not to say that the tenant issue was insubstantial or that the Section 7 opinion merely served as a pretext behind which Davis could mask his real motivation. But the common denominator that links the victims of the purge was not the cotton contract opinion: they had all incurred Davis's wrath during the books and records controversy. Rex Tugwell perhaps best explained the purge when he wrote in his diary that it had little to do with the cotton opinion but was ''part of Davis' studied

179

plan to rid the Department of all liberals and to give the reactionary farm leaders full control of policy and full satisfaction to all the processors. . . ."[92]

None of the purge victims suffered any lasting damage. On Tugwell's intercession with Roosevelt, Frank was quickly appointed special counsel to the Reconstruction Finance Corporation before moving up to head the Securities and Exchange Commission; Hiss resigned shortly after the purge to return to his work on Capitol Hill with the Nye Committee; Lee Pressman became general counsel of the Congress of Industrial Organizations; Gardner Jackson continued his activism on behalf of cotton tenants and other dispossessed groups; and Shea and Rotnem moved to other federal legal offices before returning to private practice. Henry Wallace consoled himself with a statement to a Senate committee a month later, deploring tenant conditions for providing "fertile soil for Communist and Socialist agitators."[93] Roosevelt, whose appointment of Frank to an agency controlled by conservatives set the inevitable conflict in motion, took a detached view of the purge, answering a critical letter from Senator Costigan of Colorado:

"Sometimes situations arise in an administrative organization where two or more people simply do not seem to get on with each other. In most cases neither side is at fault. Nevertheless, when situations like that arise, the first thing to do is to try to smooth out the troubles and if that does not work the next thing to do is to remove one side or other from the picture. . . . All I can tell you is that I am sorry and have the highest respect for all parties concerned."[94]

In retrospect, perhaps the most perceptive assessment of the conflict between the Legal Reformers and the AAA conservatives, and of the anomalous role of lawyers struggling to reconcile social conscience with their limited ability to affect policy in the face of determined institutional and political pressure, emerges from two comments by Alger Hiss. "I'm inclined to think that George Peek was right," he recalled years later, "when he wrote that you cannot change the basic economic structure of a society that doesn't want to change, just by edicts from the center." But realism is a lesson learned by testing idealism: "Unless you have in your mind the picture that we liberals had of what Wallace himself called feudalism and we thought was semi-slavery, you can't understand how seriously we took the issue and our responsibilities."[95]

Chapter Nine

HAMILTON'S GHOST IN THE SUPREME COURT

I. The Legal Trojan Horse

Speaking to an audience of Louisiana farmers in mid-1935, Henry Wallace defended the New Deal's agricultural programs by pointing out the limitations of their deep-rooted Jeffersonian sympathies. Harking back to the historic battle between the states-rights agrarians for whom Jefferson spoke and the nationalist bankers and manufacturers championed by Hamilton, Wallace flayed modern-day Hamiltonians for controlling government in the service of business and finance while forcing farmers to "pay through the nose" by selling goods on an open market while buying in a protected one. "The ghost of Hamilton is abroad in the land," Wallace warned. "He has come back because he sees that his economic victory of a century or more ago is in peril." The programs of the Agricultural Adjustment Administration, he told the farmers, enabled them to fight back against the Hamiltonians with their own weapons. "The processing tax is the farmer's tariff, the marketing agreements and licenses are the farmer's corporation laws." Reminding his listeners that Jefferson was "invariably the practical statesman," Wallace concluded with the admonition that the "only sensible alternative" for farmers in their struggle for economic equality was no longer Jeffersonian populism but their ability through the AAA "to obtain and to use governmental powers comparable with those already used by corporations."[1]

Farmers had long suffered under the Hamiltonian regimen of high industrial tariffs, which blocked their overseas markets, and tax policies that favored business. It was a measure of the New Deal's essential corporatism that AAA lawyers, spiritual and political heirs of the Jeffersonian tradition in their personal views, would appear before the Supreme Court to defend their statute wrapped in Hamilton's mantle. The case testing the constitutionality of the AAA came to the Supreme Court as *United States v. Butler*, and involved a claim by the government against the receivers of a bankrupt Massachusetts cotton mill for the payment of $81,694.28 for overdue processing and floor taxes.[2] The processing tax lay at the heart of the plan to raise farm income to a level of "parity" with that of the 1909-1914 boom period by paying farmers of basic commodities to restrict

181

production in return for benefit payments.[3] These payments would come, not from the general treasury, but from taxes levied on the "first domestic processing of the commodity" and paid by the processor. Congress delegated the task of setting tax levels for each commodity to the Secretary of Agriculture, who was additionally empowered to establish equivalent "floor taxes" on commodities on hand in producers' warehouses and factories but not yet processed on the date the processing tax took effect.[4] It was expected that tax levels would periodically shift to reflect market and price levels.

The remarkable aspect of the *Butler* case is that it arose at all. Since agricultural processors were entitled to recoup their tax losses through higher consumer prices, they actually suffered no out-of-pocket losses.[5] Only the consumer, forced indirectly to subsidize farm income, suffered financially, and the Supreme Court had made it clear in 1923 that an individual taxpayer could not challenge the purposes to which federal appropriations were put.[6] However, the vulnerable feature of the AAA tax scheme, that its proceeds bypassed the Treasury, made it a tempting target for political opponents of the New Deal, who immediately sensed its constitutional weaknesses and saw in it a vehicle for a broader attack on the New Deal's regulatory programs.

That this was the motive behind the attack on the AAA became evident at the beginning of the *Butler* case. In April 1934 Eugene F. Bogan, a lawyer in the AAA's Tax Section, was dispatched to Boston to discuss with lawyers representing the receivers of the bankrupt Hoosac Cotton Mills of North Adams and New Bedford, Massachusetts, collection of the mill's unpaid processing and floor taxes. The New England textile industry, squeezed by declining demand and competition from "runaway" mills in the non-union South, had seen many such marginal mills slide into bankruptcy during the Depression. John W. Lowrance, the lawyer appointed by the federal court in Boston to represent the mill's receivers, was a staunch Republican who told Bogan "he was convinced the tax was unconstitutional." Behind his refusal to authorize payment of the tax assessment was his intention "to make it a test case" of the entire AAA program. Bogan was surprised to learn through discussions with other cotton processors that "no other cotton mills had any sympathy" with the receivers for Hoosac Mills. He reported to his supervisor in Washington, Prew Savoy, that other mill operators "much preferred to see the Government win, as an unfavorable decision would probably ruin their businesses."[7]

Bogan also learned from Lowrance that one of Hoosac's co-receivers was a director of Armour & Company, a giant in the meat processing industry. Although Lowrance did not identify him to Bogan, he was referring to James A. McDonough, a "confidential representative" of Boston financier Frederick Prince, who predicted the stock market crash and survived the Depression with a fortune of $250 million, which he parlayed into control of forty-six railroads. Early in the Depression, Prince wrested control of Armour from its family owners and became chairman of the board, securing a seat for McDonough as well. Armour and other meat processors were then engaged in a bitter struggle with the AAA over the "books and records" clause in the meat marketing agreements; government access to their books, they feared, could provide ammunition for an antitrust action against the highly concentrated industry. It was more inviting, however, to challenge the AAA through the processing tax, and McDonough's role as a receiver of Hoosac Mills gave Prince a chance to use the bankrupt firm as a legal Trojan horse.[8]

In early 1934 the AAA was attempting as much as possible to avoid litigation, and Bogan recommended that "the case should be quietly disposed of with as little publicity as possible," particularly since Lowrance was urging that both sides reach agreement on all the factual issues so that the case could be argued entirely on constitutional issues.[9] But since the initiative in the case rested with the receivers, in asking the federal court to reject the government's tax claim, it was impossible to evade litigation. The case went badly from the beginning, complicated by disagreements between the AAA and the Department of Justice. Through an oversight, the AAA did not learn that the receivers had filed suit until after the case was set for argument in early April and Justice Department lawyers began preparation of a brief answering the constitutional arguments raised by the receivers. When Robert N. Anderson of the Department's Tax Section advised Prew Savoy and Jerome Frank that he was preparing a brief, Frank persuaded the Department to obtain a three-week continuance so that AAA lawyers could cooperate in writing the brief. Anderson then deferred completion of the brief while he waited for word from the AAA lawyers on their suggestions. What he did not realize, until Savoy presented him with a 100-page brief just a week before the postponed argument was set, was that Frank's request for a continuance was a ploy in the AAA's larger battle with the Justice Department over control of the litigation process. Understandably nettled by this attempt to present him with a *fait accompli*, and having learned that Frank was seeking permission from the Attorney General to have an AAA lawyer make the argument, Anderson succeeded in regaining control of the case, but at the cost of strained relations with his AAA counterparts.[10]

As the first challenge to the processing tax, the *Butler* case aroused great anticipation. Even before the district court argument, a leading legal periodical predicted that "the case will eventually reach the Supreme Court of the United States."[11] The lawyers for the receivers threw at the AAA an incredible barrage of constitutional objections. Among their ten points were charges that the Agricultural Adjustment Act set up a "virtual dictatorship" which threatened the constitutional guarantee of a republican form of government; that it violated the due process clause as "class legislation" designed to take property from manufacturers and distribute it to farmers; that the commerce clause was violated; that collection of a tax on agricultural production invaded the rights reserved to the states under the Tenth Amendment; that it was an unlawful price-fixing scheme; that it delegated unchecked power to the executive branch; and that the taxes were neither proportionately levied on the basis of population nor uniform throughout the country.[12] Company lawyers obviously hoped that the district court judge, in weeding out this thicket of claims, would find merit in at least one.

In the first round of litigation, this strategy was frustrated, despite the fact that Elisha Brewster, the federal district judge in Boston, possessed impeccable Republican and country-club credentials. In a lengthy opinion issued in October 1934, almost six months after the case was argued, Judge Brewster pruned the issues down to four and upheld the government's position on each. He first creatively analogized the processing tax to an excise tax, which permitted variable rates on the basis of geography or class of product rather than national uniformity. His treatment of the delegation issue was more cautious and qualified, and retreated to the safe haven of precedent and the principle of *stare decisis*. Acknowledging the "somewhat indefinite" formula for fixing tax rates and the wide discretion given the Secretary, he admitted that the Act "would seem to come near the line" of unlawful delegation. But Congress had extended "ever-increasing power to administrative officers to perform" quasi-legislative functions, and no act of Congress had been held invalid on delegation grounds.

The most difficult issue facing Judge Brewster, which required almost three thousand words to resolve, was the claim that the processing tax was a species of "class legislation" designed to exact from one group tax revenues for the direct benefit of another. The established doctrine was that a limitation on the taxing power of Congress "is that it shall be exercised for public uses as distinguished from private ends." If the act demonstrated that it was calculated to benefit only private interests, "it would be the duty of the court, I take it, to declare the tax unlawful." Only if the purpose of the tax was to raise revenue, and not to purchase compliance with a regulatory scheme, could it pass muster. Straining to find a way around the obvious intent of the production control program, the judge found that since participation was voluntary the tax fell within the power of Congress to appropriate funds under the general welfare clause. Finally, Judge Brewster dismissed the due process challenge to the tax, citing the recently decided *Nebbia* case and holding that Congress had not acted arbitrarily or capriciously and "has seen fit to declare that the means selected have a substantial relation to the object sought to be obtained."

Pervading the opinion were warning signals that Judge Brewster was deferring to precedent and to the exigencies of the "emergency" on which the act was premised, and that he harbored serious reservations about its constitutionality. "One may entertain doubts respecting the right of Congress to exert the powers which it has attempted in the act," he concluded. But he found the historic presumption of constitutionality compelling "when the issue is raised in the District Court in a case involving a statute of great public importance and by virtue of which vast sums have already been expended and equally vast sums have already been levied. . . ."[13] The constitutionality of the AAA, Judge Brewster was saying in an almost plaintive tone, was properly the province of higher courts willing to disregard precedent and make new law.

Between Judge Brewster's opinion and the decision of the First Circuit Court of Appeals in July 1935, some nine months later, several factors intervened to shift the balance decisively against the government. In January 1935 the Supreme Court ruled the "hot oil" provisions of the National Industrial Recovery Act invalid on delegation grounds in the *Panama Refining* case.[14] The next month, Jerome Frank and the Legal Reformers were purged from the AAA and their functions transferred to Agriculture Department Solicitor Seth Thomas. And, at the end of May, the Supreme Court completed its demolition of the NIRA by declaring the entire statute unconstitutional in the *Schechter* case.[15]

The argument before the Court of Appeals in Boston took place less than two weeks after *Schechter* was decided. Although the lawyers for the receivers wisely eliminated some of the more far-fetched and frivolous claims raised before the District Court, they hammered away at their strongest points: unlawful delegation of legislative power; the claim that the processing tax was not a genuine revenue measure but class legislation "masquerading as a tax"; and the charge that regulation of agricultural production was not covered by the commerce clause and invaded the Tenth Amendment rights reserved to the states.[16]

The next month, in a two-to-one decision, the Court of Appeals sustained the receivers on every point. It was "clearly apparent" from the language of the act that Congress intended not to raise revenue "but to control and regulate" agriculture production. Citing the 1918 Supreme Court decision in *Hammer v. Dagenhart* and a dozen other cases narrowly interpreting the commerce clause, the court held that the act "would sanction the invasion by the federal power of the control of a matter purely local in its character," and rested on *Schechter* for the proposition that the attempt "to control or regulate the production of agricultural products . . . is beyond the power of Congress." Rhetorically asking whether Congress provided any "definite standard" for the Secretary to determine tax rates, the court answered that there was "no definite intelligible standard" set out, and cited the *Panama* case in holding against the act on delegation grounds. Having found sufficient reason to invalidate the act, the court concluded that "it is not necessary to consider whether the processing and floor taxes are direct taxes, or, if excise taxes, are not uniformly laid." The court could not resist taking a final swipe, in the language of constitutional fundamentalism, at what it considered the more grandiose claims of the government: "If Congress can take over the control of any intrastate business by a declaration of an economic emergency and a public interest in its regulation, it would be difficult to define the limits of the powers of Congress or to foretell the future limitations of local self-government."[17]

In the wake of the Court of Appeals decision, the government lawyers were immediately confronted with a serious problem. There was little question, in spite of the almost insuperable hurdle created by the *Schechter* decision, that a Supreme Court test of the AAA's powers was necessary. The complicating factor was that on the heels of both *Schechter* and the First Circuit decision came a flood of cases filed by processors seeking injunctions to restrain the AAA from collecting the processing tax, a development the Justice Department had foreseen. Anticipating the *Butler* decision, Assistant Attorney General Frank Wideman wrote Solicitor General Reed in April that it would be "highly desirable" to ask Congress for legislation to prevent recovery of processing taxes. Such a move would prevent the "unjust enrichment" of processors who "have no doubt passed this tax to their consumers" in the form of higher prices, and might "dampen the ardor of processors who are now so active in their attack" on the AAA. "Such legislation," Wideman wrote, "would come with better grace before any adverse court decision."[18]

Wideman's suggestion was not heeded in time. In spite of the seemingly clear language of an 1867 federal law providing that "no suit for the purpose of restraining the assessment or collection of any tax shall be maintained in any court,"[19] processors by the hundreds began filing suit, taking advantage of the Declaratory Judgment Act recently passed by Congress in 1934, which permitted federal judges to block the enforcement of any unconstitutionally applied federal law. Although Congress speedily added an amendment to the act providing that no suit could be brought to restrain the collection of processing taxes or to obtain a declaratory judgment for this purpose, its passage in mid-August came too late to close the barn door on more than twelve hundred injunction suits, almost ninety percent of which were granted by federal judges.[20]

In the face of this gloomy background, the New Deal lawyers began the unenviable task of preparing their defense of the processing tax before the Supreme Court. Two weeks after the Court of Appeals decision, the Agriculture Department formally requested that the Attorney General submit a petition for certiorari. "As you know," Acting Secretary M. L. Wilson wrote, "there have been filed within the past few weeks several hundred suits, each of which attacks the validity of the Act and the taxes levied thereunder."[21] Solicitor General Reed's first move when he assumed responsibility for the *Butler* case was to seek the services of Alger Hiss. After resigning from the AAA in February 1935 in sympathy with his purged colleagues, Hiss had assumed a full-time role as counsel to the Senate committee investigating the munitions industry. Hiss later recalled that "when I decided to leave the Nye Committee for policy reasons, because they were becoming too isolationist, Stanley Reed asked me to come to the Department of Justice to work on the Hoosac Mills case because I knew the background of the whole Triple A approach and had the best contacts with the people in the Triple A we would need to work with."[22] Although charged with the responsibility of representing the government in all cases coming before the Supreme Court, the Solicitor General's office was then a small, clubby operation, with only a handful of lawyers. In addition to Hiss, those working on the *Butler* case included Charles Horsky, W. Marvin Smith, a career Justice Department lawyer, and Paul Freund, a 1931 Harvard Law School graduate and protégé of Felix Frankfurter, who clerked for Justice Brandeis at the Supreme Court before coming to the Solicitor's office from the Reconstruction Finance Corporation with Reed.

Hiss and Freund were assigned primary responsibility for preparing the brief in the *Butler* case. "The whole thing was troublesome," Hiss recalled. "Our first problem was to avoid the appearance of arbitrary, ruthless governmental interference in an area where the government had never attempted to intervene before." Hiss decided to use the tactic of the "Brandeis brief" to demonstrate the government's long-standing concern with the economic health of agriculture. Mordecai Ezekial, Louis Bean, and other Agriculture Department economists and statisticians hurriedly prepared an exhaustive history of congressional attempts to benefit agriculture and the roots of the AAA program which was incorporated as a 60-page segment of the final brief, buttressed with charts illustrating fluctuations in farm prices and parity ratios between agricultural and industrial prices. "This permitted us to refer to economic material which we couldn't have proved otherwise," Hiss said, "and used the concept of taking judicial notice of official documents."[23]

The heart of the government's brief involved a revival of the economic debate of more than a century before, and found the New Deal lawyers in the unusual position of adopting the pro-business economic nationalism of Alexander Hamilton and rejecting the agrarian ideology of Jefferson and his ally, James Madison. Article I, Section 8, of the Constitution empowered Congress to "lay and collect Taxes, Duties, Imposts and Excises, to pay the Debts and provide for the common Defense and general Welfare of the United States. . . ." As an advocate of strictly limited federal powers, Madison viewed the general welfare clause as limiting the taxing power to those enumerated functions given Congress in the subsequent sections of Article I, which did not include agricultural production. Hamilton, the fervent spokesman for business interests seeking federal aid to promote expansion and development, argued that the general welfare clause provided Congress with taxing and spending powers not limited to those enumerated in the Constitution. What forced the New Deal lawyers into adopting the Hamiltonian position was that farmers, as Secretary Wallace admitted, found in the AAA their "only sensible alternative" to the advantage given by New Deal legislation permitting price-fixing and antitrust exemption to their historic enemies, bankers and industrialists. Only through an expansive reading of the general welfare clause could the New Deal lawyers justify the benefit payments provided through the processing tax.

Alger Hiss was frank in attributing adoption of the Hamiltonian position to the exigencies of the situation and a law school training that stressed the necessity of federal regulatory power. "From the beginning of the New Deal we bright lawyers, recently out of law school, tried to make use of the general welfare clause, one way or another, and we stretched it as far as we could."[24] Hiss and his colleagues struggled to overcome the innate constitutional conservatism of Solicitor General Reed, a southerner with ingrained Jeffersonian sympathies. Facing the reality that the AAA could not be sustained under the Madisonian theory, Reed finally capitulated to the arguments of his younger colleagues. He distilled the essence of their position in a memorandum to Hiss written just two weeks before the Supreme Court argument scheduled for early December 1935: "We adopt the Hamiltonian theory. This means we can expend money for the general welfare. This means that the general welfare, insofar as the expenditure of money is concerned, is a grant of power to the Congress. If it is a grant of power, it gets the benefit of the general grant 'to pass all laws that are necessary and proper to carry these powers into execution.' "[25]

Although they wore down Reed's resistance, Hiss and his colleagues had few illusions about the force of the Hamiltonian argument before the Supreme Court. "We had never, in fact, liked the processing tax," Hiss recalled. "We would have been much happier, for legal reasons, if we could have drawn appropriations from the general treasury. Perhaps nobody would have standing in this case. An ordinary taxpayer, we could argue, would not have standing to object if he couldn't show that his taxes went directly to our functions. But there was a direct, stated relationship that obviously was something we knew we'd have trouble with."[26]

Armed with Reed's approval, Hiss went ahead and added to the *Butler* brief a 45-page defense of the AAA's powers under the general welfare clause. He raised the specter of an imminent breakdown of governmental functions. Adoption of the Madisonian theory "would mean the destruction of many of our most familiar and significant governmental policies and activities. The people have long been accustomed to rely on the benefits" provided through governmental expenditures. "These governmental activities have become so interwoven into our commercial, social, and economic life that to strike them down now would result in catastrophic dislocations. An acceptance at this late date of the Madisonian view would mean that the United States . . . would leave this Nation incapable of relieving widespread distress in times of economic disaster." The general welfare section of the brief concluded with an appeal to judicial self-restraint: "It is our position not only that the welfare clause should be construed in the Hamiltonian sense to include anything conducive to the national welfare; it is our position also that the question of what is for the general welfare must have been left primarily to the judgment of Congress, and as to that question, the judicial branch will not substitute its judgment for the judgment of the legislature."[27] However sincere, this was an appeal hardly likely to evoke a sympathetic response from the Supreme Court, which had recently handed down its decision in the *Schechter* case.

II. The General Welfare Clause Gone Mad

As the argument of the *Butler* case before the Supreme Court neared, public anticipation of the outcome increased. In September 1935 the *New York Times* reported that the test of the farm program "is the center of major concern at the Justice Department now. Daily conferences are being held on its legal aspects."[28] A week later, President Roosevelt defended the constitutionality of the AAA before a huge crowd of farmers in Fremont, Nebraska. Arguing that the true function of government was "to promote the general welfare . . . by bringing to the aid of the individual those powers of government which are essential to secure the continuance" of constitutional rights, Roosevelt delivered a defense of the AAA which "might well have been a brief prepared for court presentation," the *Times* concluded.[29]

The brief itself was taking shape in marathon drafting sessions in the Solicitor General's office. Although its preparation did not provoke conflicts over approach as contentious as those which erupted between Justice Department and NRA lawyers over the *Schechter* brief, there were skirmishes between the Agriculture Department and the Solicitor's office, reflecting questions of emphasis more than of substance. Prew Savoy urged Mastin White, who had moved from the Justice Department in late 1935 to replace Seth Thomas as Solicitor of the Agriculture Department, to bring pressure on the Justice Department to pay greater attention to the delegation problem. The draft brief circulated in late October, he felt, shied away from an effective rebuttal of *Panama* and *Schechter*, "but I think we will not remove the question by failing to argue the point and . . . must build on these cases and distinguish them." Savoy also advocated more stress on "our general economic discussion. It seems to me that our economic discussion is far more important to the brief" than the argument based on the general welfare clause.[30]

Hiss admitted his wariness about *Schechter*. "We wanted to dissociate ourselves as much as possible from it. We tried to contend that Congress simply directed the Secretary to institute crop reduction programs. He couldn't exercise discretion; therefore, there was no delegation."[31] The final brief, although devoting more than seventy pages to the delegation question, expressed Hiss's uncompromising view. Determination of the parity price levels on which the processing tax was levied "is a matter of purely mathematical computation involving no exercise of administrative discretion under this Act." In fact, since Congress had authorized the expenditure of the funds raised by the tax, and its implementation "is not a legislative function in any sense, no issue of delegation of legislative power is raised."[32]

In the initial stages of drafting, both groups of lawyers worked independently. Charles F. Sarle, an Agriculture Department economist, analyzed the first effort of each group in a report to Chester Davis. The Justice Department brief, he reported, "is written in the form of an essay and contains no definite points" arguing that the Act "is public in purpose and therefore in the interest of the general welfare. In fact . . . one fails to get the impression that the constitutionality of the Agricultural Adjustment Act is being advocated. It seems more like an apology for the Act."[33] Sarle also criticized Hiss's reliance on Mordecai Ezekial's exhaustive history of the economics of the farm problem. He feared that the Court would disregard it "because of the necessary inclusion of propaganda and the possibility of biased interpretation of facts and figures." Sarle suggested instead that the brief rely on academic and congressional reports to avoid the implication of self-serving economic arguments.[34] Hiss, however, considered the Ezekial report the most authoritative and persuasive basis for the economic argument, and cited it in twelve places in the final brief.

The most difficult problem in drafting a brief, particularly in a major constitutional case raising novel issues, is that of balancing deference to precedent with an aggressive attempt to lead the court to discard encrusted doctrine. In framing their arguments, lawyers seeking to push the Supreme Court to a recognition that the deeper forces of history and social change compel a newer and wider vision of the Constitution face the task of defining the most appropriate strategy through which to apply that push. The initial strategy of the young lawyers in the Solicitor's office was timid and tentative. They recognized that the general welfare clause offered their only real hope of success, but they knew that it had never been construed by the Supreme Court, and were cautious about pressing it to its full limits.

It was Thomas Reed Powell of Harvard Law School, the iconoclastic advocate of constitutional expansionism, who finally persuaded his former students in the Solicitor General's office to take the plunge. Paul Freund had sent Powell a draft that conceded some strength to the Madisonian position that the general welfare clause was limited by the enumerated powers given to Congress in Article I of the Constitution. "I do not see myself," Powell replied, "why you concede that the general welfare phrase in the taxing clause is a limitation on the taxing power. I see that you have later quoted Story in a way that involves some such notion, and this may be the reason for the concession. I had never thought of the clause as a limitation and was shocked when I first heard that position suggested." There was no reason, Powell wrote Freund, "why it would not be well to urge directly that the words 'for the general welfare' were put in for the very purpose of indicating that the restrictions in other clauses were not to apply here."[35] Freund and Hiss bowed to the advice of their mentor. Their final version of the brief, after a lengthy exposition of the debate between the Madisonians and Hamiltonians in the constitutional conventions, concluded with these assertive words: "It seems clear from these discussions that the Constitution was not adopted under any belief that the welfare clause was limited by the enumerated powers which follow it."[36]

Six months before the *Butler* argument, the Supreme Court jerked from under the New Deal its power to regulate business and industry through the commerce clause. Now, in December 1935, New Deal lawyers looked elsewhere in the constitution for sanction to regulate the second pillar of the national economy, agriculture. The young lawyers in the Solicitor General's office and their colleagues in the Agriculture Department presented to the Court a massive brief of 280 pages, citing 284 cases and including a mountain of charts, economic data, and excerpts from century-old debates between partisans of differing views of the general welfare clause. They offered the Court every possible ground on which it could find a way to ignore *Panama, Schechter*, and its own ingrained hostility to expansive federal power.

Butler was the first case involving a major challenge to the New Deal argued in the imposing, newly dedicated Supreme Court building across from the Capitol. Attracted by this novelty as well as the significance of the case, spectators crowded into the huge courtroom. "All day, every day, the courtroom was filled to capacity, even including standing room," Justice Harlan Fiske Stone reported to his sons.[37] Those who anticipated fireworks were not disappointed.

Solicitor General Reed began oral argument for the government, speaking in his deliberate, courtly manner. The conservative justices could hardly conceal their impatience. Reed began with a defense of the Act as a non-coercive program based on voluntary contracts between individual producers and the Secretary "for the purpose of inducing the producer to reduce his production." Without waiting for Reed to explain the method of calculating the processing tax, Justice McReynolds unleashed a barrage of questions. "How is the tax fixed? " he demanded to know. Reed patiently answered that Congress determined the standard for setting tax levels. "The formula is that the tax shall be equal to the difference between the farm value of the commodity and its purchasing power, or fair exchange value." McReynolds could see no way of fixing this parity ratio which did not involve the Secretary's subjective determination. "Farmers buy all sorts of articles, silk stockings, woolen coats, and so on. With which are you going to compare it?" he retorted. He finally extracted from Reed the concession that the Secretary was "at liberty" to decide what goods to include in the parity ratio formula.

Justice Brandeis attempted to rescue Reed by asking him to read the proclamation issued by the Secretary when fixing rates. "Is that not a very definite finding by him?" Brandeis asked rhetorically. Reed hastened to agree, but his damaging concession remained.[38] Eager to move on, if not to safer ground then at least to territory less mined with conservative precedent, Reed sought to end the questioning about discretionary powers. "If the Court should think it proper to go beyond the tax itself, then we contend that the general welfare clause gave Congress power to expend it for rental and benefit payments." But here Reed's innate caution prompted him to back away from the claims of unlimited power made in his brief. "We say that the general welfare clause," he concluded, "is construed not as a general power, but as a special power in Congress to expend this money'' for a public purpose. Completing his retreat, Reed abandoned the attempt made in his brief to distinguish the most troublesome precedent, the 19th-century case of *Loan Association v. Topeka*, in which the Supreme Court held that a state could not appropriate tax revenues to aid a private business, regardless of any ''public purpose'' it would serve.[39] ''We accept the decision . . . where this Court held that a State act was not for a public purpose, where it had authorized the payment to a local manufacturer of funds to operate his business.''[40] Uncomfortable in his reluctant role as a Hamiltonian, he overlooked the vital distinction between appropriation of tax funds to aid a single, favored business and that designed to aid the nation's farmers as a whole. With his concessions on the delegation issue and the reach of the general welfare clause, Reed virtually discarded his brief and the heart of his argument.

Reed's adversary before the Court was an orator of the old school, George Wharton Pepper, a former Republican Senator from Pennsylvania, whose rhetorical histrionics were combined with an enormous ego and an unshakeable constitutional fundamentalism. Pepper had represented several processors in earlier injunction suits and was glad to join the Boston lawyers for the Hoosac Mills receivers. In his autobiography, he immodestly claimed ''the advantage of long study, careful preparation and the experience gained in the argument of the same questions in the lower courts.''[41]

Deferring to his colleague, Edward R. Hale, for the argument on the delegation question, Pepper approached with evident relish the task of rebutting Reed's hesitant defense of the Hamiltonian position on the general welfare clause. His attack cleverly focused not on Reed's oral argument but on the expansive view presented in the government's brief. ''I did not know,'' Pepper said, ''until this statute proposed it, of any interpretation which begins where Hamilton stops, and asserts that because you may appropriate for anything which Congress thinks is consonant with the public welfare, you may, through that appropriation, control the local conduct of the producer in a particular reserved to the States under the Tenth Amendment. That, it seems to me, is the general welfare clause gone mad.''

In spite of the fact that his client was a processor permitted to pass its tax burden on to the unrepresented consumer, Pepper shed the formal attire of the corporate lawyer and appealed to the Court in the overalls of the Jeffersonian farmer, in painting the AAA as an inherently coercive scheme. Pointing the Court back to the certitude of *Hammer v. Dagenhart*, in which the federal government was barred from a back-door attempt to impose child labor laws on the states through a punitive taxing scheme, Pepper argued that the AAA constituted a similar kind of plan. ''It is no more voluntary than it was in the case of the manufacturer of goods made with child labor to continue to pay the tax and still remain in the business of

193

which Congress disapproved. It is not possible for the farmer in any neighborhood who refuses to accept the regime to compete successfully with his next door neighbor who has accepted it.'' In his peroration, Pepper displayed the emotionalism for which he was famous:

"I have tried very hard to argue this case calmly and dispassionately, and without vehement attack upon things which I cannot approve, and I have done it thus because it seems to me that this is the best way in which an advocate can discharge his duty to this Court. But I do not want your Honors to think that my feelings are not involved, and that my emotions are not deeply stirred. Indeed, may it please your Honors, I believe I am standing here today to plead the case of the America I have loved; and I pray Almighty God that not in my time may 'the land of the regimented' be accepted as a worthy substitute for 'the land of the free.' ''[42]

Even Attorney General Cummings was moved by this display of pryotechnics to record in his diary that ''Mr. Pepper presented the other side of the case effectively and the Court listened attentively.''[43]

How attentively the Court listened was evident in the majority opinion written by Pepper's fellow Philadelphia corporation lawyer, Justice Roberts, and handed down less than a month later on January 6, 1936, at the beginning of a presidential election year. The vehemence of Roberts' attack on the Agricultural Adjustment Act shocked all but the most doctrinaire opponents of the New Deal, and its reverberations would explode a year later when the court-packing plan embroiled all three branches of government in a titanic struggle for supremacy. The first intimations of what would follow came even before *Butler* was decided; Attorney General Cummings reported a Cabinet discussion in late December of ''the question of what should be done, and what should be said, if the decisions on pending matters of crucial importance in the Supreme Court should be sweepingly adverse.''[44] Neither Cummings, Hiss, nor the other New Deal lawyers who worked on the case expected to win, but the language of the decision removed all hope that the Roosevelt administration and Congress could frame even the most modest measures to utilize federal powers on behalf of farmers and the agricultural community.

Roberts first declared that the processing tax was not a tax at all, but rather an ''exaction laid upon processors'' with ''an aim foreign to the procurement of revenue for the support of government. . . .'' The term ''taxation,'' he continued, ''has never been thought to connote the expropriation of money from one group for the benefit of another.'' Conceding that such a tax would be constitutional if levied in pursuance of a legitimate congressional power, Roberts cast aside into a footnote the arguments on delegation, due process, and the question of uniformity of the tax rates in his haste to meet this contention, which he acknowledged was "the great and controlling question in the case." Surprisingly, Roberts first embraced the Hamiltonian position advanced by Reed. Hamilton, he wrote, maintained that the general welfare clause conferred on Congress "a power separate and distinct from those later enumerated" in Article I of the Constitution, and "is not restricted in meaning by the grant of them, and Congress subsequently has a substantive power to tax and to appropriate, limited only by the requirement that it shall be exercised to provide for the general welfare of the United States." With a deferential bow to Justice Story and other eminent expositors of the Hamiltonian position, Roberts concluded that "the power of Congress to authorize expenditures of public moneys for public purposes is not limited by the direct grants of legislative power found in the Constitution."

But Roberts then returned to Story for the vital qualification that cut off the limb onto which Reed had retreated. "Story says that if the tax be not proposed for the . . . general welfare, but for other objects wholly extraneous, it would be wholly indefensible upon constitutional principles. And he makes it clear that the powers of taxation and appropriation extend only to matters of national, as distinguished from local, welfare." Herein lay the vice of the statute. "It is a statutory plan to regulate and control agricultural production, a matter beyond the powers delegated to the federal government." In making this argument, however, Roberts exposed himself to the attack of the dissenters, since having embraced the Hamiltonian position he could hardly exclude congressional regulation of agriculture simply because it was not within the enumerated powers of Congress. This logical oversight, however, did not deter him from making the point which underlay his entire opinion, and in the eager pursuit of which he rushed heedless of logic and consistency:

"When an act of Congress is appropriately challenged in the courts as not conforming to the constitutional mandate the judicial branch has only one duty,—to lay the article of the Constitution which is invoked beside the statute which is challenged and to decide whether the latter squares with the former. All the court does, or can do, is to announce its considered judgment upon the question . . . and, having done that, its duty ends."[45]

Roberts' mechanistic reading of the Constitution, relegating the judge to the role of a carpenter with a T-square, provoked the three liberals on the Court into outraged dissent, in what Robert Jackson, Reed's successor as Solicitor General and a future Justice, called an opinion "hardly paralleled in the century and a half of the Court's existence for its scathing rebuke to the majority."[46] Speaking for Brandeis and Cardozo, Harlan Fiske Stone, a former farmer in the rocky New England valleys, excoriated Roberts' opinion as a "tortured construction of the Constitution" resting only on the predilections of the majority. He first exploited Roberts' admission that the Constitution would sanction a voluntary agreement between the government and a farmer. "Of the assertion that the payments to farmers are coercive, it is enough to say that no such contention is pressed by the taxpayers" resisting the tax. One-third of the cotton farmers did not sign crop reduction contracts in 1934, Stone noted, concluding that Roberts' claim that the AAA program was inherently coercive "rests on nothing more substantial than groundless speculation." Here Stone relied on the exhaustive economic data presented in the AAA brief. Stone's most effective response to the majority was his rebuttal of the parade of horribles presented by Roberts, who raised the specter that farmers would be joined by sugar refiners, shoe manufacturers, garment workers, and other "under-privileged" groups to demand income redistribution in the guise of tax relief. This was the underlying fear behind the majority opinion. Stone was by no means an advocate of socialism or egalitarian income redistribution, but he argued that if Congress could move in this direction through direct appropriations to disadvantaged groups, a position he said "is not denied" by the majority, it would lead to "absurd consequences" to deny Congress this power through such an equally effective means as the processing tax.

The final paragraph in the dissenting opinion was the most powerful and resonant, expressing the essentially moderate view of a Supreme Court minority painfully aware of the potential disaster awaiting an institution that substituted "judicial fiat" in imposing its political and economic views on the nation for a realistic awareness of its role in maintaining a delicate balance between coordinate branches of government, each responsible for creating a federal structure responsive to both tradition and change:

"Courts are not the only agency of government that must be assumed to have capacity to govern. Congress and the courts both unhappily may falter or be mistaken in the performance of their constitutional duty. But interpretation of our great charter of government which proceeds on any assumption that the responsibility for the preservation of our institutions is the exclusive concern of any one of the three branches of government, or that it alone can save them from destruction, is far more likely, in the long run, 'to obliterate the constituent members' of 'an indestructible union of indestructible states' than the frank recognition that language, even of a constitution, may mean what it says: that the power to tax and spend includes the power to relieve a nation-wide economic maladjustment by conditional gifts of money."[47]

At least until they are reversed by the Court itself or overridden through constitutional amendment, majority opinions of the Supreme Court have the force of law, and the majority opinion in *United States v. Butler* ended the crop reduction and benefit payment programs of the Agricultural Adjustment Administration. But, in the long run, and occasionally with an immediate impact, dissenting opinions can provide the rallying point behind which political forces coalesce to produce a constitutional crisis. Such an impact resulted from the dissenting opinion in *Dred Scott v. Sandford* in the critical period before the outbreak of the Civil War. Similarly, Stone's dissent in the *Butler* case gave ammunition to those who viewed the Supreme Court in the 1930s as an insuperable barrier to economic and social change. In this regard, the role of *Butler* in the unfolding plan to devise some means of curbing the Court becomes important in placing New Deal litigation in a broader political perspective.

Proposals to limit the powers of the Supreme Court were not new, and in fact had been made in various forms over the decade before Roosevelt took office. More recently, members of Congress and the administration had begun thinking seriously about the question since the blow of the *Schechter* decision. Now the initiative was assumed by Attorney General Cummings, whose political instincts governed his legal decisions. Cummings recorded his reaction to Stone's dissent in his diary immediately: "It may not be the law today, but it will be the law later on by natural developments and realization of the views of the Court. I must say I had expected this result." Later that day, Cummings met at the White House with Roosevelt, Wallace, and congressional leaders to discuss the AAA decision, and then met with Postmaster General Farley and Marvin McIntyre, Roosevelt's chief political advisors, to discuss the Supreme Court situation.[48]

Roosevelt considered the majority opinion the equivalent of a declaration of war by the Supreme Court against the New Deal, but he heeded the advice of Steve Early, his press secretary, that he avoid a repetition of the negative press reaction to his intemperate outburst after the *Schechter* decision. "Please resist all—say nothing," Early beseeched the President.[49] In the face of incessant pressure at his informal press conferences, the President resisted the temptation to denounce the Supreme Court majority.

As an experienced politician, Cummings was well aware that he and Roosevelt needed time to frame a defensible response and choose a propitious occasion for the inevitable counterattack on the Court. The options open to the administration were first laid out to Cummings in a memorandum from Assistant Attorney General John Dickinson, written the day after the Supreme Court decision. Dickinson presented three choices: first, to abandon further efforts to revive the AAA through congressional action; second, to seek a new law that would somehow repair the constitutional infirmities of the AAA; and, third, "to accept the constitutional challenge thrown down by the Supreme Court.'' Acceptance of the second choice, he felt, would be damaging as "an admission of the erroneous character of our agricultural policy to date. . . ." As the most effective political strategy, Dickinson favored a combination of the first and third options. Failure to reenact the AAA in substantially the same form would make the New Deal program a hostage of the Court; if the administration "silently acquiesces in the overthrow of AAA, it will be difficult for it to take any other course with regard to other legislation subsequently held unconstitutional.'' Confronting the Court with this direct challenge would have political advantages, since "it seems inevitable that the constitutional issue will have to be met during the coming campaign. . . . This seems all the more inevitable in view of the practical certainty that the Supreme Court, between now and June, will hold unconstitutional a number of other Administration measures.'' Dickinson urged Cummings to begin exploring the merits of two possible approaches: "On the one hand, the Administration might take a definite position in favor of some form of constitutional amendment. The great difficulty of this course is that of formulating an amendment for which general agreement could be secured.'' The second course was for Roosevelt to adopt "the position taken by Lincoln in regard to the Dred Scott decision, namely, an appeal to the people based on an express purpose of trying to get the court to reverse its position. An election won on the basis of such an appeal might exert a powerful influence on the court'' and even if unsuccessful "would lay the groundwork for a subsequent attempt to procure an amendment.''[50]

Although the *Butler* decision roused a storm of criticism from New Deal supporters, many of whom urged some form of constitutional amendment to restrict the power of the Supreme Court to declare federal laws unconstitutional, it was Dickinson's memorandum that impelled Cummings to seek approval from Roosevelt for the planning of the ultimate challenge to the Court. A week later, after meeting with Cummings, Roosevelt gave his approval. He had not yet decided which of the two alternative strategies to adopt, or even if a third alternative might be preferable, but there was no question that the New Deal could not coexist with the conservative Supreme Court majority.

Before Cummings left the White House, Roosevelt made a final point clear: planning for the assault on the Supreme Court must take place in total secrecy. Until he had weighed the alternative proposals, chosen his course of action, and selected the most propitious time to reveal it, Roosevelt wanted no word to escape from the Justice Department. Cummings agreed, and returned to his office to pass on these instructions to a small group of trusted assistants. By the time the curtain of secrecy was lifted, almost precisely a year later, the *Butler* case would be eclipsed by the magnitude of Roosevelt's reelection victory, and New Deal lawyers would be preparing for Supreme Court argument in the National Labor Relations Board cases.

THE LEGAL CRAFTSMEN OF THE
NATIONAL LABOR RELATIONS
BOARD

Chapter Ten

LABOR UNDER THE BLUE EAGLE

I. LABOR'S BILL OF RIGHTS

Within months of Franklin Roosevelt's inauguration, union organizers plastered thousands of posters on factory gates across the country, emblazoned with a compelling directive: "The President Wants You To Join the Union." Organized labor welcomed the advent of the New Deal as an opportunity to rebuild its shattered strength; from a peak of four million in 1920, membership in unions affiliated with the American Federation of Labor dropped to less than half that number in 1933. The complacent conservatism of labor's leadership contributed to this decline, but more important were the aggressive open-shop movement of employers and the "American Plan" under which company unions displaced AFL unions. When Roosevelt took office, less than ten percent of the industrial work force was unionized, the lowest figure in the century.[1]

What gave labor hope that it could reverse this decline during the New Deal was Section 7(a) of the National Industrial Recovery Act, which provided that "employees shall have the right to organize and bargain collectively through representatives of their own choosing, and shall be free from the interference, restraint, or coercion of employers of labor. . . ."[2] It has become part of popular mythology since the New Deal ended that Roosevelt sponsored this move to protect labor's rights. In fact, Roosevelt had no such intention, and Congress inserted Section 7(a) into the NIRA only as a reluctant concession to labor leaders who initially backed Senator Hugo Black's proposal to increase employment through a thirty-hour work week, an approach Roosevelt opposed on both economic and constitutional grounds.

Faced with Roosevelt's adamant opposition to the Black bill, AFL leaders accepted Section 7(a) as a second-best compromise. Many of those who headed the unions that constituted the AFL, in fact, had no interest in organizing the industrial workers who were the intended beneficiaries of "Labor's Bill of Rights," as Section 7(a) was quickly dubbed. With the exception of John L. Lewis, president of the 300,000-member United Mine Workers, most AFL leaders represented skilled craft workers, the "aristocracy of labor" that already enjoyed collective bargaining rights. Dan Tobin of the Teamsters Union expressed a prevalent attitude when he disparaged industrial workers as "the rubbish at labor's door."[3]

Labor's leverage in the New Deal stemmed less from its political strength, which was negligible in 1933, than from the Roosevelt administration's fear that failure to accept Section 7(a) would unleash a strike wave on the part of militant unorganized workers that might cripple the recovery program. The success of the program depended, as NRA administrator General Hugh Johnson put it, on "the necessary partnership of Labor, Management and Co."[4] AFL leaders in general accepted a junior role in this partnership, in return for expected wage increases and stable employment levels. But if few organizers outside the small but vocal socialist and communist parties based their appeals to workers on rejection of the capitalist system, thousands of workers and local labor officials anticipated aggressive campaigns to organize the unorganized under Section 7(a) and its federal protection. Shortly before passage of the NIRA, a militant labor newspaper in Minnesota expressed this anticipation: "Labor awaits the American industrial revolution, generally wondering under what precise orders it will go to work when the Industrial Recovery bill becomes law."[5]

If labor was awaiting its marching orders from the NRA, it quickly found Johnson to be an unsympathetic commanding officer. Only three days after his appointment as NRA Administrator in May 1933, Johnson shocked the labor movement by declaring that the NRA would not "compel the organization either of industry or labor" and that he would approve provisions of industrial codes dealing with hours, wages, and working conditions even though "such conditions may not have been arrived at by collective bargaining." Even more threatening to labor were Johnson's statements the following month on the legality of "open shop" provisions in NRA codes. At a press conference during negotiations over the iron and steel industry code, Johnson said that "an open shop is a place where any man who is competent and whose services are desired will be employed regardless of whether or not he belongs to a union. That is exactly what the law says. . . . Is anything clearer needed?"[6] The steel industry, with a long history of violent suppression of union organizing efforts, applauded Johnson's statement, although labor protests persuaded Roosevelt to eliminate the open-shop provision from the code he later signed. But Johnson and Roosevelt approved a code provision giving the automobile industry, also a bulwark of anti-unionism, the right to "select, retain, or advance employees on the basis of individual merit," which labor charged would hobble organizing efforts and permit discrimination against union members.[7] Union leaders also protested when Johnson and Richberg underminded the concepts of majority rule and exclusive representation, both crucial to union strength, by stating that employers were free to make "individual bargains with those who choose to act individually."[8]

Many employers viewed Johnson's statements during his first two months in office, and his appointment of subordinates with corporate backgrounds, as a green light for the formation of company unions. By the end of 1933, more than two-thirds of the largest manufacturing companies joined the rush to establish company unions. Unorganized workers responded with the greatest strike wave since the end of World War I. During the first three months of the NRA, the number of man-days lost to strikes quadrupled over the level of the prior six months, from an average of 600,000 per month in the first half of 1933 to 2.4 million in August.[9] During this period, NRA lawyers were preoccupied with the task of drafting hundreds of industrial codes, and lacked any machinery through which to resolve labor disputes or settle strikes. As it became apparent that overburdened NRA lawyers and the agency's small compliance staff were incapable of dealing with the growing strike wave, and as labor complained vociferously that Johnson's statements encouraged employers to violate Section 7(a), Roosevelt soon recognized that defusing labor resentment was a political imperative.

The first effort to separate the code-drafting functions of the NRA from implementation of Section 7(a) began on August 5, 1933, when Roosevelt issued a press release establishing the National Labor Board. In his announcement, Roosevelt stated that the NLB "will consider, adjust, and settle differences and controversies" arising under the labor provisions of the Recovery Act.[10] Roosevelt adopted an interest-group approach to NLB composition. Labor's spokesman in Congress, Senator Robert F. Wagner of New York, was appointed chairman, supposedly representing the public interest. Three members were appointed to represent industry: Walter Teagle of Standard Oil, Gerard Swope of General Electric, and Louis Kerstein of the Filene Company, a Boston-based department store chain. The three labor members were William Green, president of the AFL, John L. Lewis of the United Mine Workers, and Leo Wolman, professor of economics at Columbia University and a former textile union official.

Senator Wagner was committed at this point to a mediation approach to labor disputes. The job of the NLB, he told the press, was "to get rid of the whole idea of war to the limit and to substitute for it the idea of agreements through mediation. . . ."[11] The choice of an experienced labor arbitrator and mediator, William Leiserson, as secretary of the Board reflected this non-adversary approach. Only one of the nine initial staff members of the NLB was a lawyer; Wagner recruited Milton Handler, a 1926 Columbia Law School graduate who began teaching at Columbia the following year and who specialized during his career in antitrust law, to serve as General Counsel. Handler, who later admitted that "my contact with the labor field had been quite limited" before his appointment, acknowledged that the Board "operated initially on a very experimental basis, with virtually no one on the Board having very extensive or comprehensive knowledge of labor law or labor problems."[12] Labor law at the time was in its infancy as a separate field, having recently emerged as a bastard offspring of equity and contracts courses in law school curricula. Few law schools even offered courses in labor law (Harvard became one of the first in 1921), and the few students who took these courses used casebooks that stressed employers' rights to enjoin striking workers and to enforce anti-union "yellow dog" contracts.

The NLB, under Leiserson's day-to-day guidance, gave Handler little legal help. His staff grew to a grand total of two: Philip Levy, a 1933 Columbia Law School graduate, and William G. Rice, on leave from the Wisconsin Law School faculty. The three lawyers confronted serious enforcement problems as the volume of Section 7(a) complaints mounted. Leiserson's mediation approach biased him against litigation; an early directive to the NLB's regional staff made this clear: "Don't consult lawyers; keep them out."[13] NLB subordination to the NRA further complicated enforcement. The NIRA provided no administrative structure or procedure for handling labor disputes, and enforcement of Section 7(a) required action by the NRA's Compliance Division, whose only sanction was the ineffectual removal of the Blue Eagle symbol. Prosecution of violators through injunctive litigation necessitated approval first by the Compliance Division and second by the Justice Department, which Handler soon learned would be granted grudgingly, since Department lawyers viewed the NIRA with ill-concealed distaste.

Despite its lack of enforcement powers, the NLB succeeded during its first few months in settling most of the disputes that came before it, aided by an ebbing of the summer strike wave, a result more of the first flush of NRA success in increasing employment than of employer compliance with Section 7(a). The NLB reported that 88 percent of the cases brought before it during its first three months were settled through mediation, but the Board handled the meager total of 66 cases.[14] In its first formal decision in early September, the NLB held in the *Berkeley Woolen Mills* case that the provision in Section 7(a) giving workers the right to "bargain collectively through representatives of their own choosing" required employers to deal with national unions representing workers. Striking a blow at the company union principle, the Board ruled that the company must negotiate with the United Textile Workers and that workers "have the right to choose anyone they may wish as their representative and are not limited in their choice to fellow employees."[15] The labor press hailed the Board's action as "the most important decision rendered since the adoption of the NIRA."[16] Three weeks later, the Board scored a major victory in averting a strike of more than 10,000 hosiery mill workers in eastern Pennsylvania. Having persuaded both sides to conduct a secret-ballot election under NLB auspices, the Board subsequently ruled, in what became known as the Reading Formula, that operators of the thirty-four mills in which the union won a majority in the elections were required to formally recognize the union and negotiate a written agreement for each plant.[17]

These early victories soon proved illusory, as employer resistance hardened and as the NLB's lack of independent enforcement power became apparent. Most of the companies accepting the Board's mediation efforts and offers to supervise elections were small and vulnerable to strike pressure in the face of competition. During its first three months of operation, the Board conducted only two elections in units covering more than 1,000 employees.[18] Two widely noted cases exposed the Board's weakness. The first involved the Budd Manufacturing Company of Philadelphia, which produced auto bodies and frames. On September 1, 1933, a few days before the NRA automobile industry code took effect, Budd management announced formation of a company union, and a week later conducted an election in which only the company union appeared on the ballot. The company claimed that ninety-two percent of the employees voted, but many workers claimed that they were pressured to vote. Two weeks later, the AFL chartered a "federal local" (one affiliated directly with the AFL and not a national union), and after the company refused to meet with its representatives a majority of Budd workers went on strike on November 14.

The NLB quickly began mediation efforts, which proved fruitless. A recommendation by the Board's regional office in Philadelphia that striking workers be reinstated and that the Board supervise an election giving workers a choice between the AFL and company unions was ignored by the company, which also refused to appear at an NLB hearing in Washington. The Board nonetheless issued a formal decision declaring the first election illegal, holding that the company had interfered with self-organization by the workers: "For an employer to sponsor a particular labor organization, to prepare a plan of organization, and to formulate a constitution whereunder the choice of representatives is limited and the right to vote restricted is hardly compatible with that self-organization which the statute contemplates." Expressing its frustration at company intransigence, the Board added that "where the good offices of a disinterested governmental agency are resisted" the result "can only prolong controversy, increase economic distress, and further industrial unrest."[19] But the decision had no impact; the Board could only refer the case to the NRA, which took no action against Budd.

A more serious challenge to the Board's powers involved the steel industry, the most impregnable bastion of anti-labor sentiment. Ernest

Weir, chairman of the Weirton Steel Company, was "a hard-nosed steel-master who was determined at any cost to keep the union out of his mills" in West Virginia and Ohio.[20] Shortly after the passage of the NIRA, Weir imposed a company union on his employees, but this move did not forestall union organization and in October 1933 some 10,000 Weirton workers struck for recognition of the Amalgamated Association of Iron, Steel and Tin Workers. The impact of the strike initially prompted Weir to accept NLB intervention on the basis of the Reading Formula, and on October 16 he signed an agreement with the Board providing for an election in December under NLB auspices. However, Weir reneged on this pact and conducted an election on December 15 limited to company union candidates. Even Hugh Johnson was moved by this affront to the Board to warn Weir that "you are about to commit a deliberate violation of federal laws," and the NRA Compliance Division authorized the NLB to ask the Justice Department to initiate suit against Weir, as the first test of the government's power to enforce Section 7(a) in court.[21]

With the handicap of a small and inexperienced legal staff, the NLB was dependent in its first suit on Justice Department assistance. Milton Handler frankly admitted that "we never thought in terms of litigation."[22] This aversion to litigation proved costly to the Board, since the Justice Department approached the Weirton case with little enthusiasm. Under the prod of vigorous complaints by Weirton workers that their union organizing efforts were met by company intimidation, the Department dispatched Federal Bureau of Investigation agents to investigate and collect affidavits. Early in January 1934 Assistant Attorney General Harold Stephens summarized the results of the FBI investigation in a report to Attorney General Cummings: the company had "threatened discharges, lay-offs and transfers" and its anti-union tactics also included "calling employees' meetings by company officials and urging . . . support of Company union; . . . occasional physical forcing of employees to polls and marking of ballots; placing pay booths near voting boxes and suggesting voting before pay check offered."

Despite the irrefutable evidence of massive violations documented in 150 affidavits collected by the FBI, Stephens was reluctant to proceed. He laid out for Cummings the arguments on both sides. Conceding that "there seems to exist a prima facie case of Code violations" and that "chances to win are probably a little better than even on the facts and law," Stephens agreed that the NLB "will be weakened by failure to proceed against an apparent Code violation." However, he stressed the difficulty of "proof of a relationship between the violations in question and interstate commerce" and the likelihood that "the fairly good wages and working conditions which have prevailed at the Weirton plant" would expose the government's case to countering testimony by satisfied company union members. Stephens concluded by recommending to Cummings that "the President be requested to consider arranging a conference with . . . Weir and urging him publicly to retire from the position thus far taken and to support a free election." Only if such high-level intervention failed, Stephens said, would "I recommend that legal action be taken. . . ."[23] The Department's balky attitude reflected as much the consensus of its lawyers that the NIRA could not withstand a constitutional test on the interstate commerce issue than any question about the factual issues. Another conservative on the issue, Labor Department Solicitor Charles Wyzanski, agreed with Stephens. "I could hardly imagine a less desirable case upon which to test the NRA labor clauses," Wyzanski wrote his mentor, Felix Frankfurter.[24] Relegated to the sidelines, NLB lawyers could only hope that presidential persuasion would overcome Weir's recalcitrance.

Pressure on Roosevelt to take action grew as Weir gained national publicity, hailed by business and denounced by labor. "From congratulatory wires and letters you might assume that Mr. Weir was the most popular man in the industry," wrote *Business Week*. William Green of the AFL, on the other hand, urged a congressional committee to "pillory Mr. Weir as a public enemy" for destroying labor's faith in the NLB.[25] The issue was clearly more political than legal at this stage, and two days after Stephens submitted his report a White House meeting was called to discuss it, with Cummings, Johnson, Senator Wagner, and Labor Secretary Perkins conferring with Roosevelt. Their conclusion, reported the *New York Times*, was "to press the Weirton Steel case to an early conclusion, and to use it as a test of the labor section of the Recovery Act."[26] Roosevelt did meet with Weir on January 15, but he disregarded Stephens' advice to extract a public commitment from Weir to conduct a fair election and was taken in by the steel magnate. Reporting to Cummings and Johnson, Roosevelt wrote that Weir "reiterated, and I think he really meant, that he is honestly behind the general government program—N.R.A., Labor Board, etc." Roosevelt did not challenge Weir's patently false claim that he had complied with his agreement with the NLB, but "I suggested to him that it is always bad to have an undercurrent of suspicion or of actual charges of an unfair election" and urged Weir to submit to a new election under NLB supervision.[27]

Even this personal plea from the President failed to budge Weir. Faced with a barrage of company objections to election procedures proposed by the NLB, the Board and the Justice Department again began collecting affidavits complaining of company intimidation, and the White House was flooded with letters from union members.[28] Labor pressure mounted to such an extent that Johnson arranged for a delegation of Weirton employees to meet with Roosevelt at the end of January. Confident of an election victory, union leaders agreed to a compromise agreement providing a "preliminary poll" of Weirton workers as a test of union support.[29] This proposal also failed to win company agreement. Its considerable patience finally exhausted, the Justice Department filed suit on March 20, 1934 in federal district court in Delaware, the company's corporate home. Assigned to John Nields, a conservative Republican judge, the case immediately began to unravel. The government filed 234 affidavits in support of its motion for a temporary injunction restraining Weirton from interfering with an NLB-supervised election. As Stephens predicted, management had busily solicited support from company union members, and it filed 826 affidavits opposing the action, 87 of which retracted statements originally made in affidavits for the government.

The argument in the first and only court test of the NLB's power spread over a week. Milton Handler of the NLB and James L. Fly of the Justice Department's Antitrust Division shared the task of presenting the government's affidavits. Handler, who was stricken with appendicitis and hospitalized after three days of argument, recalled that Harold Stephens had made trial preparation difficult: "He drove us crazy by reviewing every word in our pleading, whereas Fly and I wanted to spend our time on perfecting our affidavit proof." Stephens displayed his caution by dispatching a specially appointed lawyer to monitor Fly and Handler in court. Frank K. Nebeker, a 64-year-old former Justice Department lawyer (who had prosecuted "Big Bill" Haywood and other militant leaders of the Industrial Workers of the World in a notorious World War I Espionage Act case) was an old friend of Stephens and a fellow Utah native. Although Handler described his participation in the *Weirton* case as "virtually nil," Nebeker later took charge of the second round of the case.[30]

Judge Nields ensured that the case would require a second round by ruling on May 29, 1934 that he was barred by the Norris-LaGuardia Act from granting a preliminary injunction. Ironically, this 1932 law had been enacted by Congress to protect labor against anti-strike injunctions. However, it required that no injunction could be issued in a labor dispute "except after hearing the testimony of witnesses in open court. . . ." Although Judge Nields left the case open for a subsequent hearing in conformity with the act, he pointedly raised "the question of the constitutionality" of the NIRA.[31] When the *Weirton* case resurfaced months later, after this embarrassing defeat on an elementary point of procedure, it had been inherited by the NLB's successor agency.

Persuading employers to accept an NLB role in conducting union representation elections met widespread resistance, since the Board's authority rested solely on Roosevelt's August 1933 press release, a document hardly calculated to impress judges and company lawyers. As employer opposition hardened in late 1933, the illusory harmony between the Board's labor and industry members eroded. As two close observers noted, the NLB "came close to collapse during the month of January 1934. The machinery of the Board began to creak; members failed to attend meetings; the handling of cases became chaotic, protracted, and indecisive."[32] Two issues in particular split the Board. Union leaders, the Board's labor members, and Handler all insisted on the principles of exclusive representation and majority rule: unless employers were required to recognize the union selected by a majority of their workers as the representative of all the workers, separate agreements with minority unions or individuals workers on more favorable terms would undercut support of the majority union. Labor won its first real victory when Roosevelt issued Executive Order 6580 on February 1, 1934. Drafted largely by Handler, the order signaled abandonment of Leiserson's ineffective mediation approach. Roosevelt authorized the NLB to conduct union representation elections; his order further specified that representatives chosen by a majority of those voting would "represent all the employees . . . for the purpose of collective bargaining. . . ."[33] The NLB remained limited in its enforcement powers, however, empowered only to report to the NRA employers who refused to recognize or deal with majority representatives.

In his Executive Order Roosevelt clearly expressed support of the majority rule principle. Two days later, however, Hugh Johnson and Donald Richberg provoked a political storm by issuing an official NRA "interpretation" of the order which stated that the "selection of majority representatives does not restrict or qualify in any way the rights of minority groups of employees or of individual employees to deal with their employer." The statement directly challenged the majority rule principle by concluding that collective bargaining "can be lawfully carried on by either majority or minority groups, organizing and selecting such representatives in such manner as they see fit."[34] Labor and its supporters reacted angrily to the Johnson-Richberg statement. William Green objected firmly but with characteristically moderate language, but John L. Lewis felt no such inhibition. Richberg, he charged, had "deceived the President" and "betrayed labor"; his statement "has driven a knife to the very heart of labor in this country. . . ."[35] Chairman William Connery of the House Labor Committee claimed that Johnson was administering Section 7(a) in a "ruthless, illegal and high-handed fashion. . . ."[36] Sensitive to this criticism of the NRA, Roosevelt responded three weeks later with an amendment to the Executive Order, authorizing the Board to bypass the NRA in reporting violations directly to the Justice Department, and stripping the NRA Compliance Division of its power to review Board findings.[37]

Heartened by this presidential show of support, the Board quickly moved to implement the majority rule principle. Reaching back in its files to a case initially heard in mid-December 1933 but deferred because of conflict over the issue, the Board ruled on March 1, 1934 that the Denver Tramway Corporation was required to recognize the AFL streetcar workers union as exclusive representative of its employees, even though the AFL group had only narrowly defeated a company union by a vote of 353 to 325. "Any agreement reached in conformity with this decision," the Board wrote, "must apply alike to all employees of the company." The only troubling aspect of the decision was that for the first time the Board's short tradition of unanimity dissolved, as industry member Pierre S. duPont (one of six members added when the Board was expanded from seven to thirteen) dissented, urging that the closely divided AFL and company unions each represent the employees voting for them, and that the company be permitted to bargain individually with workers who voted for neither union.[38] The Board majority, however, assumed that its decision in the *Denver Tramway* case reflected Roosevelt's policy. Less than a month later the NLB was shocked when Roosevelt abruptly abandoned the majority rule principle. Confronted with the power and intransigence of the auto industry, which refused to allow the NLB to conduct a representation election between company unions and striking members of the AFL United Automobile Workers, Roosevelt intervened as a mediator. Without consulting the NLB, he approved a settlement on March 25 allowing management to bargain with "freely chosen representatives of groups" of workers, and providing that "if there be more than one group, each bargaining committee shall have total membership pro rata to the number of men each member represents."[39]

Settlement of the auto strike on the basis of the Johnson-Richberg principle of minority representation sounded the death-knell for the NLB. Limited in staff and totally dependent on the hostile NRA and Justice Department for enforcement, NLB lawyers were virtually impotent. In his last effort to apply the majority rule principle, Milton Handler circulated to Board members in early March 1934 a draft opinion in the *Houde Engineering Company* case, involving a Buffalo auto parts manufacturer organized by the United Automobile Workers, rejecting the company's claim that the union must disclose its members' names before an election. In his draft opinion, Handler wrote that "there is no need for such disclosure" since the Board held in the *Denver Tramway* case that "the collective agreement negotiated by the majority applies to all employees" and no purpose would be served by disclosure of union membership.[40] But industry members of the Board forced Handler to water down this affirmation of the exclusive representation rule in the NLB decision ordering an election; the company was simply obligated to bargain with the majority representatives, and was not barred from reaching a separate agreement with the minority. When the AFL union subsequently won the Board-conducted election and the company refused to bargain with it, Handler again drafted a Board decision based on the exclusive representation rule. By this time, in the wake of Roosevelt's intervention in the auto industry settlement, industry members of the Board frustrated Handler's last-ditch effort to rescue majority rule. Pierre duPont objected to the draft opinion, reminding Handler that "since the decision in the Denver Tramway Corporation case the President has expressed himself as favorable to the recognition of minority representatives in bargaining with the employer."[41]

Even before the auto settlement crippled the Board, Senator Wagner began drafting a bill designed to define more precisely labor's rights and to free the Board's lawyers from dependence on the NRA for enforcement. During January and February 1934, Handler and William Rice worked with Charles Wyzanski of the Labor Department and Leon Keyserling, Wagner's legislative assistant, producing a bill which specified a number of "unfair practices" of employers, including interference with union organizing efforts, refusal to recognize or bargain with representatives elected by workers, domination of company unions, and discrimination against union members. The bill proposed an independent National Labor Board empowered to issue "cease and desist" orders enforceable in the federal district courts, with Justice Department lawyers representing the Board.

Wagner introduced his Labor Disputes Act on March 1, and immediately encountered employer opposition, White House disinterest, and obstruction on the part of the NRA, the Labor Department, and Senate Labor Committee chairman David Walsh, who extracted major concessions from Wagner after the auto industry settlement was announced. Within three months of its introduction, Wagner's bill was virtually unrecognizable. It finally disappeared, supplanted by an alternative bill introduced by Senator Walsh and largely drafted by Wyzanski, who found Walsh more amenable to the Labor Department position on labor relations than Wagner. The Walsh bill proposed creation of a five-member National Industrial Adjustment Board within the Labor Department. Despite the obvious failure of the mediation approach attempted by the NLB, the Walsh bill reflected Labor Secretary Perkins' unshakeable commitment to mediation; the proposed Board would be entitled to conduct hearings and issue orders only after notification by the Secretary that mediation efforts by the Department's Conciliation Service had failed. The bill also permitted employers to initiate company unions, rejected the exclusive representation principle, and eliminated the duty to bargain provision of the Wagner bill.[42]

Although the Roosevelt administration supported the toothless Walsh bill, it was bereft of support outside the government. Labor was disappointed, and business, sensing victory after the auto settlement, denounced it as pro-labor. It is likely that the existing National Labor Board would have limped along, unable to enforce its orders, had not the industrial work force erupted in late April, engulfing the country in virtual class war. Beginning in Toledo among auto parts workers furious at the outcome of the auto industry settlement, the strike wave spread to truck drivers in Minneapolis, longshoremen in San Francisco, and textile workers throughout the South. What Irving Bernstein has called a "social upheaval" built on "the growing conviction of many workers that they must now take matters into their own hands and demonstrate their collective power to recalcitrant employers through the strike" evoked the specter of revolution among conservatives and some New Dealers as well.[43] With labor on the barricades, and with the toll of workers killed and injured in clashes with police, vigilantes, and National Guardsmen mounting, Roosevelt and the Congress were suddenly jolted into action. Faced with the additional threat of a national steel strike in mid-June, Roosevelt instructed Wyzanski and Donald Richberg to draft a new labor relations bill to replace the moribund Walsh bill. On June 12, the day after Wyzanski and Richberg submitted their drafts, Roosevelt called a White House conference attended by congressional leaders as well as by Wagner and Secretary Perkins.

At this meeting, Roosevelt dictated the text of a joint congressional resolution, introduced in both houses the next day as Public Resolution 44. It was a brief document, simply authorizing the President to appoint a board empowered "to order and conduct an election by a secret ballot of any of the employees of any employer" to select representatives for collective bargaining.[44] Intended as a stopgap measure acceptable to all factions in Congress, Resolution 44 had no purpose other than persuading militant workers to end their strikes pending representation elections. Frightened by the prospect of further labor violence, Congress quickly adopted the resolution, which Roosevelt signed on June 19. During the brief debate, a disheartened Wagner called the death of his stronger bill "one of the most embarrassing moments of my whole political life."[45] With the threatened steel strike called off, industry was relieved. The vice-president for industrial relations of U.S. Steel expressed his belief that substitution of the joint resolution for the original Wagner bill "is a mighty good compromise. I have read carefully the joint resolution, and my personal opinion is that it is not going to bother us very much."[46]

II. A Crushing Defeat for Paper Rights

On July 9, 1934, the National Labor Board ceased to exist and the National Labor Relations Board took its place. Its structure and functions were outlined in an Executive Order issued on June 29, providing for a three-member Board "created in connection with the Department of Labor" but authorized to appoint its own staff, including lawyers. Roosevelt empowered the Board to investigate controversies arising under Section 7(a) of the NIRA or otherwise "burdening or obstructing . . . the free flow of interstate commerce" and to "order and conduct elections" for employee representatives. Additionally, the Board was authorized "on its own initiative to take steps to enforce its orders" by petitioning, through the Justice Department, the federal circuit courts of appeals for enforcement. Finally, the Executive Order directed that the Board's findings of fact and orders would "be final and not subject to review by any person or agency in the executive branch of the Government."[47] Still dependent on the Justice Department for enforcement, the new Board had, in fact, no more effective power than its predecessor. But it had at least escaped from the clutches of the NRA; how it would fare in its indefinite relationship with the Labor Department remained to be seen.

From the outset, the Board approached its task with a lawyer's perspective. It was headed by a lawyer, Lloyd Garrison, who took a leave as dean of Wisconsin Law School after informing Roosevelt that he would remain no more than four months. His two colleagues were Harry A. Millis, a labor economist from the University of Chicago, and Edwin Smith, formerly Commissioner of Labor in Massachusetts. All three members, Garrison recalled, were "determined to sit as judges and not to engage in mediation."[48] Garrison established a Legal Division with seven members; Milton Handler returned to Columbia Law School, and William Rice of the NLB legal staff replaced him briefly as general counsel of the new Board. In August, Rice was replaced by Calvert Magruder, a 1916 Harvard Law School graduate who began teaching there in 1920 after serving as the first clerk to Justice Brandeis on the Supreme Court. Like Handler, Magruder had little prior exposure to labor law, having taught torts and acted as vice-dean at Harvard. He had, however, a lively interest in labor relations and a skeptical attitude toward the administration's policies. After the disastrous auto industry settlement, Magruder wrote Felix Frankfurter that Roosevelt's statement announcing the settlement was "illiterate" and "bristling with obscurities." He was equally critical of the industry for seeking a "knock-down" fight with labor and of unions for the "clumsy way" they handled the auto industry negotiations.[49]

The Board and its lawyers began work immediately, having inherited the cases left undecided by the NLB. Two of the hold-over cases, *Houde Engineering* and *Weirton Steel*, quickly tested the Board's powers and once again illustrated the problems of New Deal agencies in dealing with the Justice Department. Two weeks after the Board was established, Paul Herzog, who joined the legal staff after serving as assistant secretary of the NLB, briefed the newly appointed members on the *Houde* case as a test of the Board's intentions and sympathies. As the Buffalo regional office of the NLRB reported in July 1934, the Board's handling of the case "will have a very significant bearing on the future conduct of both employer and employee and the efficacy of our Board."[50] The Board's decision on August 30, 1934 unequivocally reaffirmed both the exclusive representation and duty to bargain principles. The Board found that the company "has violated Section 7(a) by interfering with the self-organization of its employees, impairing their right of collective bargaining and refusing to bargain" with the AFL union. Failure to notify the Board within ten days that it recognized the union and was ready to begin negotiations "when requested by the union" would result in referral of the case to the Justice Department "for appropriate action."[51]

Industry responded to the *Houde* decision with a defiant call to boycott Board hearings. The National Association of Manufacturers urged employers to ignore the decision "until competent judicial authority has passed on the ruling" and praised the statement "made by the President in settling the automobile strike" as well as the minority representation statement of Johnson and Richberg.[52] A general boycott by employers threatened to paralzye the Board. To head off this prospect, Lloyd Garrison quickly urged the Justice Department to file suit against Houde, seeking an injunction requiring the company to bargain with the union. Garrison was initially confident of cooperation, writing the Board's regional staff in September that suit would be filed "very shortly, and this should clear the air."[53] To the dismay of Board lawyers, however, the Justice Department resisted their request. The point of contention was whether there was adequate evidence that the company had refused to bargain with the union. Reviewing the evidence on this issue, a Justice Department lawyer found it "equivocal," adding that although "it is important that the majority rule doctrine be affirmed, it would seem to be highly desirable that a stronger case than this on the facts be selected as the vehicle."[54]

Annoyed by what it considered a dilatory attitude by the Justice Department, the Board took its case to the Attorney General. NLRB lawyer Robert Watts sent a pointed letter to Homer Cummings in early October, insinuating that the Department's reluctance to bring suit reflected a lack of support for the majority rule principle.[55] Annoyed in turn, Cummings responded with the unusual step of taking his case to the press. Assistant

Attorney General Harold Stephens drafted a statement that "scrutiny of the facts disclosed that there had been no refusal by the company to bargain . . . with the majority representatives. There was therefore no foundation for a suit." Stephens added that Garrison "agrees that the matter is at the present time in such a state that it is doubtful whether proceedings should be commenced."[56] Cummings called a press conference on October 11 and released the memorandum from Stephens as a defense of his position.

The issue had now become political, and the NLRB sought relief in the White House. Labor Department Solicitor Charles Wyzanski presented the Board's case to Roosevelt, telling him that morale in the NLRB "is about to break down. Employers everywhere are refusing to bargain with unions and relying on the Attorney General's statement in connection with the Houde case." Hammond Chaffetz of the Justice Department relayed to Stephens Wyzanski's report that Roosevelt "is strongly in favor of maintaining the views of the Labor Relations Board as is the Secretary of Labor. Rather than permit a breakdown in the Labor Board," Chaffetz wrote of Roosevelt's attitude, "it would be better to take a chance on bringing the Houde case if the case is technically sufficient, even though not a strong case."[57] Stephens continued to feel that "it would be a mistake to attempt to present such an important issue with such a poor factual background," but agreed to file suit if the NLRB obtained affidavits from union members establishing the company's refusal to recognize the union and to bargain with it.[58]

Although it considered this proposal a further delaying tactic, the Board secured a number of detailed affidavits from union members and suggested to union leaders that they formally request recognition by the company as the exclusive bargaining agent for Houde workers. The affidavits, establishing beyond doubt that the company had consistently refused to recognize or bargain with the union, were duly filed with the Justice Department.[59] Given the NLRB's satisfaction of its condition and the report of Roosevelt's views, the Justice Department reluctantly filed suit on November 30, 1934. The case immediately ran into a procedural roadblock, as company lawyers countered with a motion for a "further and better statement" of the government's claims, arguing that the Justice Department failed to specify in its complaint just which group of workers the company had failed to bargain with. This tactic succeeded; in a decision on January 25, 1935, Judge John Knight recognized that the case was of "extreme importance" and "will define the rights of employer and employee as respects collective bargaining throughout these United States," but held that the complaint must be redrafted. The government had failed to specify, Judge Knight said, whether the bargaining unit comprised all Houde workers or just those who voted for the AFL union.[60]

Given the earlier NLRB decision in the case ordering exclusive representation, this was a frivolous and hypertechnical objection, but it effectively blocked the Board's first attempt to secure judicial approval of its powers. The Justice Department responded to this setback by casting blame on the NLRB and expressing its lack of sympathy for the majority rule principle. Justice Department lawyer Francis Critchlow reported to Harold Stephens that the NLRB "was given a free hand in drafting the Bill of Complaint. The Department suggested that certain phrasing in the Bill was ambiguous," but the Board "did not wish the phrasing changed." Critchlow also argued against further defense of the majority rule principle. Echoing the earlier position of the National Association of Manufacturers, Critchlow asked Stephens "how many employers who in apparent good faith have adopted Mr. Richberg's interpretation are we justified in putting to the expense of defending these cases? "[61]

The *Houde* case eventually died, a victim first of the Justice Department's reluctance to proceed and then of the Supreme Court decision in the *Schechter* case in May 1935 holding the NIRA unconstitutional. The NLRB did succeed, however, in prodding the Justice Department to revive the *Weirton Steel* case, the second major hold-over case from the NLB, and to bring it to trial. Just four days after taking office in July 1934, NLRB chairman Garrison wrote Donald Richberg that "this is the first case in which the Government on the basis of repeated violations of Section 7(a) has attempted to enjoin further violations. Under these circumstances, our Board is not now prepared to advise that the case should be withdrawn" unless Weir complied with the Board's order to hold an election.[62] Harold Stephens grudgingly bowed to pressure from the Board and approved a second filing of the suit, although he pointed out in a letter to Roosevelt in August the difficulty facing the government: "The rank and file of the employees who joined the Amalgamated have ceased to pay dues therein and appear no longer to be insisting upon recognition of the Amalgamated for collective bargaining. The Government will probably not be able to prove that a substantial number still belong to the Amalgamated."[63] That the union lost strength because of the Justice Department's failure to press its case over the past year was a point Stephens ignored.

Testimony in the *Weirton* case was spread over two months between December 1934 and January 1935; 283 witnesses appeared on both sides and the lawyers consumed four days in presenting final arguments. Frank K. Nebeker returned as special counsel for the government, and Weirton was represented by Earl Reed, the Pittsburgh lawyer who would later organize opposition to the Wagner Act for the American Liberty League and argue for the Jones & Laughlin Steel Company before the Supreme Court. Arguments on the constitutional issues closely paralleled those in prior NIRA cases. Nebeker and his colleagues contended that Congress possessed regulatory power over labor conditions that burdened interstate commerce, citing the line of Supreme Court cases broadly construing the commerce clause.

Reed countered with the restrictive line of cases holding that "manufacture" was not encompassed in the definition of interstate commerce. He additionally attacked Section 7(a) on due process grounds, citing Supreme Court decisions in the "yellow dog" cases holding that Congress lacked power to interfere with contractual relations between employers and workers. In rebuttal, Nebeker played his trump card, the Supreme Court's unanimous 1930 opinion in the *Texas & New Orleans Railroad* case. In this case, Chief Justice Hughes upheld the prohibition in the Railway Labor Act of 1926 against employer coercion and interference with union organizing. Nebeker noted the Court's holding that railway employers "have no constitutional right to interfere with the freedom of the employees in making their selections" of bargaining representatives. At least in industries engaged in interstate commerce, he argued, this doctrine came close to overruling the "yellow dog" cases. Nebeker's problem with this case as precedent was that railroads, indisputably interstate in operation, performed no manufacturing functions.[64]

The constitutional arguments in *Weirton* presented a classic confrontation between antithetical views of federal regulatory power. Judge Nields found the choice easy. In an exhaustive decision of more than 20,000 words issued on February 27, 1935, he came down squarely on the side of the restrictive theory, and ignored the *Texas & New Orleans Railroad* case. "Manufacture is transformation—the fashioning of raw materials into a change of form for use," he quoted from *Kidd v. Pearson*. Weirton Steel was engaged exclusively in manufacturing: "Here the raw materials brought into defendant's plants are never shipped out. No ore, coal, limestone, or scrap iron is shipped out into interstate commerce. What is shipped out are things entirely different from the raw materials shipped in." Judge Nields justified this crabbed view of interstate commerce with the argument that the government's position would result in bringing "practically all of the manufacturing industry" of the country within federal regulation, a result which "has received the unqualified condemnation of the Supreme Court." Concluding that "Section 7(a) . . . is unconstitutional and void," Judge Nields gratuitously added a ringing defense of Weirton's company union plan:

"Manufacture is a co-operative enterprise. . . . A relation acceptable and satisfactory to both workmen and management is an essential feature of the enterprise. If satisfactory, the court will not disturb it. It is said this relation involves the problem of the economic balance of the power of labor against the power of capital. The theory of . . . balancing opposing powers is based upon the assumption of an inevitable and necessary diversity of interest. This is the traditional old world theory. It is not the Twentieth Century American theory of that relation as dependent upon mutual interest, understanding, and good will. This modern theory is embodied in the Weirton plan of employee organization."[65]

A decision more damaging to Section 7(a) could hardly be imagined. In view of the consistent pro-business record of Judge Nields, the outcome of the *Weirton* case was undoubtedly preordained, proving the prophecy made a year earlier by Charles Wyzanski that "it will be hard to find a judge sympathetic with the policy of Section 7(a)."[66] Commentators of all shades recognized, as *U.S. Law Week* wrote, that "labor has suffered its most crushing defeat since the enactment" of the NIRA.[67] Labor's supporters were understandably critical of the decision: "Not a single lawyer with whom I have talked has been able to explain Judge Nields' failure not only to distinguish but even to refer to the *Texas* case," Senator Wagner said.[68] In context, however, the *Weirton* decision was not uniquely reactionary; it simply added one more to the growing number of decisions in early 1935 holding various provisions of the NIRA unconstitutional, as the statute headed for an ultimate test before the Supreme Court.

As it reflected relations between the NLRB and the Justice Department, *Weirton* symbolized the growing acrimony between the two agencies and fueled pressure for legislation providing the Board with independent enforcement powers. The Department's attitude toward Section 7(a) cases had all the elements of a self-fulfilling prophecy: having decided in advance that it would insist on the highest evidentiary standards before filing suit, it tested only two NLRB cases in court, both before judges avowedly hostile to the New Deal. The unfavorable decisions in these cases, attributable at least in part to procedural mistakes by Department lawyers, in turn rationalized its excuse for not bringing additional suits.

During his four months in office, NLRB chairman Lloyd Garrison consistently pressed both the NRA and the Justice Department for more vigorous enforcement. In August 1934 he wrote a critical letter to Hugh Johnson, complaining that prosecution of a violating company was preferable to removal of the Blue Eagle symbol, a punishment that Garrison considered futile. "The public and especially labor," he wrote, "have begun to lose faith not only in the power of the Government to enforce Section 7(a) but in its intention to do so. . . . The increasing use of the strike weapon is due, at least in part, to a feeling that it has become useless to look to the government to enforce the law."[69] By the end of 1934, NRA and Justice Department reluctance to file suit in NLRB cases attracted considerable public comment. In November, the *New York Times* reported growing hostility toward the Department by labor leaders: "The notable lack of vigorous prosecution by the Justice Department of alleged violators . . . is regarded by the union spokesmen that after sixteen months of waiting for action from the government a definite decision has been made to refrain from proceeding" against violators.[70]

The situation reached a crisis point early in 1935. By this time, Lloyd Garrison had returned to his law-school post, replaced in November 1934 by Francis Biddle. A patrician Philadelphia lawyer, Biddle came from a corporate law background and had little experience in labor relations. Felix Frankfurter, who helped Calvert Magruder obtain his position as NLRB general counsel and tried to influence Roosevelt on Board appointments, was skeptical of Biddle. "If I had to put it in a single word," Frankfurter wrote Charles Wyzanski, "I would say that there is a la de da quality to Biddle, which is not merely sartorial but psychic." Frankfurter questioned whether Biddle could deal effectively with John L. Lewis and other militant labor leaders "and the hard-boiled, recalcitrant industrialists, with whom, more and more, if this Labor Board will mean business, it will have some very stiff encounters."[71] Biddle, however, proved the equal of Garrison, not only in dealing even-handedly with labor and industry leaders but in pursuing the Board's complaints against the Justice Department.

By February 1935, three months after his appointment, Biddle felt strongly enough about Justice Department inaction on Board cases to demand a meeting with Harold Stephens to present his grievances. In a letter to Stephens immediately after their meeting on February 12, Biddle summarized the Board's position on each of the twenty-three cases referred by the NLRB to the Department for enforcement. Conceding that "the records are in many cases not as carefully made up as might be" because the Board lacked subpoena power, Biddle argued that court action was nonetheless necessary to assuage complaints by labor, noting that AFL president William Green had told President Roosevelt the day before that labor was disillusioned with the government and that worker resentment "has been deep and bitter and is growing." Biddle concluded with this plea for action:

"Prompt action on the part of the Attorney General will, I believe, prove effective in helping to modify the increasing unrest in labor circles, which has resulted from a belief on the part of labor that the Government is not interested in enforcing the law on their behalf; and a belief on the side of employers that the law cannot be enforced. . . . [E]ven if several of the cases are doubtful and perhaps will not ultimately be won by the Government, the mere fact that action is taken will materially help the situation."[72]

In dealing with Biddle's suggestion, Stephens displayed his sensitivity to political considerations. "I do not accede to Mr. Biddle's suggestions

. . . that four or five cases should be picked out and pressed for trial even if they will be lost, this for the purpose of making a show of activity,'' he wrote to Golden Bell, who handled labor cases for the Department. However, if the NLRB felt strongly enough about the issue that it would risk losing cases just to deflect union criticism, Stephens recommended that ''the question, whether Labor cases likely to be lost should nevertheless be pressed, should be brought to the attention of the President.''[73] Stephens wanted to place responsibility for bringing these cases on the White House, since he doubted that any could be won.

Following his meeting with Biddle on February 12, Stephens arranged a conference three days later to resolve the dispute, inviting Biddle and Calvert Magruder from the NLRB, Richberg and Blackwell Smith from the NRA, and Judge Walter Stacy of the Textile Labor Relations Board, as well as Golden Bell and G. Stanleigh Arnold of the Justice Department. In preparation for this meeting, Stephens asked Francis Critchlow, a Special Assistant to the Attorney General, to prepare a detailed analysis of each case in which Biddle had recommended Justice Department prosecution. Critchlow found flaws in each of the twenty-three cases. Although the facts in each differed, the bases for negative evaluations fell into three categories: the NLRB had conducted an insufficient investigation of the factual record of violations; the Board's record ''contained no information whatever bearing on the question of whether or not the Company's operations were in or had any effect on interstate commerce''; or the Board had failed to accord due process to potential defendants at its hearings.

Critchlow's comments on particular cases stressed factors indicating the Department's political sensitivity. In one case, the NLRB ordered employers in the New York fur trade to recognize and bargain with a left-wing union. An earlier FBI investigation had concluded that the union was associated with ''notorious gangsters and criminals'' and that ''local police officials established that most of the officials of the left wing . . . have long criminal records.'' Consequently, Critchlow warned, the Department should ''look into this whole situation very carefully before filing suit as requested by the Labor Board.'' In another case, a black newspaper owner in Chicago was accused of firing all his white printers, arguing that he was ''forced to do so by the demands of his subscribers that he adopt such a labor policy.'' Filing suit in this case, Critchlow wrote, ''might easily be made to appear that the government was taking sides in a racial dispute. It [looks] like poor policy to file it.''[74]

Critchlow's report placed the onus on the NLRB for overstepping its bounds in conducting hearings and for failing to perform adequate investigations of Section 7(a) violations. The Board, he wrote, ''regards its main function to be that of a *quasi judicial* body charged with the duty of hearing and making findings" and issuing what purported to be judicial opinions. Lacking subpoena power, however, "the record of such hearings contains in reality nothing more than an *ex parte* presentation of one side of the case, composed largely of hearsay testimony, the statement of conclusions, and unproved assertions of fact. It is apparent that such hearings cannot take the place of a full investigation." But the report did raise one issue that went far in explaining the real source of controversy. Discussing several cases in which the Board urged local U.S. attorneys to conduct investigations because it lacked adequate staff, Critchlow wrote that the "investigative failure is to some extent attributable to the failure of the District Attorneys to push these cases. . . . It must be admitted that none of the District Attorneys have any enthusiasm for the cases."[75]

The February 15 conference resolved none of the substantive issues at the heart of the conflict, which is perhaps explained by the fact that both sides knew that Senator Wagner, as he had vowed to the Senate a year before, was preparing a new labor relations bill. Jockeying for position in the emerging political struggle had begun, making it inevitable that attitudes would harden. Calvert Magruder nonetheless felt compelled after the meeting to defend the NLRB and to rebut the charges raised in Critchlow's report, in a long letter to the NRA and Justice Department conferees. First, he argued that despite the Board's inability to compel the attendance of witnesses or the production of documents at hearings, "it is our fixed practice not to make a finding of violation except upon the basis of evidence admissible in a court of law, produced at a hearing of which due notice was given and at which the essentials of due process were observed." Magruder conceded that "we have made some mistakes," but attributed them to "work done at high pressure, not to any lack of appreciation of the requirements of due process." Second, by disposing of 3,500 complaints of Section 7(a) violations, the NLRB had "taken a big load off of the Department of complaints . . . which the Department would otherwise have had to investigate." Of this mass of cases, Magruder noted, the Board had asked the Department for court action in only two dozen.

Magruder repeated Biddle's earlier call for an active litigation policy, even if it posed risks. The NLRB, he wrote, "is the one administrative agency primarily preoccupied with Section 7(a) and undertaking to develop a body of case law giving content to the general language of the section. We feel justified, therefore, in asking the Department to make test cases of our interpretations even though the Department may not be entirely convinced of their validity." It was the Department's responsibility "to make use of the grand jury machinery to complete the case for prosecution" when the NLRB recommended criminal proceedings. Magruder added a swipe at the NRA's reluctance to seek injunctions to remove the Blue

Eagle from violators. "Suppose we lose a couple of these cases; it would at least be preferable to give them a fight. . . . Otherwise the threat of removing the Blue Eagle will become a farce and word will get around that all the employer needs to do is to run to the District [of Columbia] Supreme Court for an injunction, and that will be the end of the case."[76]

Aware that Board lawyers were helping Wagner draft a new bill giving them independent enforcement authority, Attorney General Cummings abandoned diplomacy in his reply to Biddle and Magruder. His lengthy response, written the day after the Department's defeat in the *Weirton* case, repeated almost verbatim the criticisms of the NLRB in Francis Critchlow's report on Board cases. He had "taken pains to acquaint myself as fully as possible with all the cases" in which the NLRB sought prosecution, Cummings wrote. Most of the cases presented evidentiary problems attributable to the Board's lack of investigative thoroughness. "I can only say that it was understood when they were sent out" to local U.S. attorneys "that all of these cases required some further investigation" by the Board staff, which Cummings intimated was inadequate. Urging on Biddle "the necessity of very thorough investigation before cases are filed," Cummings added the sour reminder that "the adverse decision in the *Weirton* case has not decreased our difficulties."

His most pointed barbs were directed at Biddle's plea that only "prompt action" by the Attorney General could quell "unrest in labor circles" and restore labor's confidence in the Justice Department:

"The feeling of dissatisfaction to which you refer, is in no small measure attributable to the form in which the National Labor Relations Board has seen fit to embody the result of its fact finding hearings. Your Board's decisions in these matters have all of the outward appearances of authorized judicial determinations. They embody, in addition to findings of fact, declarations of law and have all of the appearances of authoritative orders. It is, of course, impossible by any legal proceeding to enforce these apparent orders as such. . . . To the employees concerned, however, they are nevertheless orders which have the apparent sanction of Federal authority and when the promise contained in them is not fulfilled, these employees are naturally quite dissatisfied."[77]

As a riposte in the emerging political duel between the two agencies, Cummings' response to the Board was understandable. But as a statement of law it displayed a revealing lack of credibility. In asserting that it was "impossible" to enforce the Board's orders, the Attorney General ignored the fact that the congressional resolution and Roosevelt's executive order establishing the NLRB expressly conferred on the Justice Department the same authority to enforce its orders in the courts as it had to enforce those of the Federal Trade Commission. Cummings obviously viewed the Board solely as a fact-finding agency, responsible only for reporting Section 7(a) violations to the NRA and the Justice Department. Whether this misperception was genuine, or simply a ploy aimed at the congressional committees about to begin hearings on the Wagner bill, it exposed the depth of the chasm separating the Justice Department and the NLRB.

It was obvious, at the time of this acerbic exchange between Biddle and Cummings in early 1935, that the future course of federal labor policy would be decided in the political arena. The consequences of encouraging the hopes of unorganized workers without any prospect of enforcement made inevitable the resulting resentment and strife. Biddle recognized that reality when he told a congressional committee that Section 7(a), "unenforceable as it now is in actual practice, is merely the expression of a paper right, a sort of innocuous moral shibboleth. Such paper rights raise hopes, but when they are shattered the reaction is far worse than if they had never been written in the statute books."[78] But two years of frustration on the part of the first labor boards had at least laid the groundwork for an enforceable labor statute. Milton Handler later summed up this accomplishment: "We had no experience in handling the problems in labor relations administratively, rather than in knock-down, drag-out injunction fights in the courts. The principal accomplishment of the Board was the development of a set of principles which later became the intellectual heritage and the foundation for the National Labor Relations Act."[79] Putting teeth behind these principles, however, promised "an industrial battle to the finish between trade unions and anti-union employers."[80] And during the first two years of the New Deal, Roosevelt had shown no stomach for such a battle.

Chapter Eleven

LEGAL CRAFTSMEN AND THE
WAGNER ACT

I. Shaping the Wagner Act

Senator Robert Wagner conceded defeat in June 1934 when his colleagues rejected the Labor Disputes Act with a defiant vow to resume the fight "when the country will have become sufficiently educated as to the need for it."[1] The lesson the country learned in the next six months was that the labor board created by President Roosevelt under Resolution 44 was as incapable as its predecessor in coping with the thousands of complaints that employers had violated Section 7(a) of the NIRA. Roosevelt, however, proved a stubborn student; he remained committed to the NIRA and showed no inclination to acknowledge the patent inadequacies of the board from which he withheld enforcement powers. But the Democratic sweep in the November congressional elections, which provided the most pro-labor Congress in history, dramatically increased Wagner's chances of success against White House hostility.

The process of drafting an enforceable labor law began in December. Wagner assigned the task to his assertive and self-confident legislative aide, Leon Keyserling. A 1931 Harvard Law School graduate, Keyserling had foregone law practice for the study of economics, which he pursued for the next two years at Columbia (and later applied in the Truman administration as chairman of the Council of Economic Advisors). The young lawyer-economist was already an experienced legislative draftsman, having worked with Rex Tugwell and Jerome Frank on the Agricultural Adjustment Act and then with Wagner on the NIRA and Section 7(a). After he joined Wagner's staff, Keyserling acted as primary draftsman of the first Wagner labor bill. Keyserling was uniquely equipped to put Wagner's concerns into legislative form; he was not only immersed in labor problems but also shared a house with several New Deal lawyers, including Tom Emerson of the existing NLRB. "Keyserling's role was *the* role," Emerson recalled of the drafting process. "We worked over it in great detail and I saw him develop the whole thing."[2] The bill that emerged as the National Labor Relations Act was not, however, solely a one-man product. Keyserling consulted with lawyers on the NLRB staff, among them general counsel Calvert Magruder, William G. Rice, Emerson, and

Philip Levy. Described by an admiring colleague as "easily the lawyer's lawyer among us,"[3] Levy in particular added to Keyserling's stress on the need for an independent agency an emphasis on procedural regularity and exactitude. Levy, whose legal passion was administrative law, was a 1933 Columbia Law School graduate who accompanied his mentor, Milton Handler, to the staff of the first labor board; in 1937 he succeeded Keyserling on Wagner's Senate staff.

Significantly, all of the Wagner Act draftsmen were lawyers. In this regard, the drafting process differed sharply from those which produced the NIRA and AAA, in which lawyers took a back seat to politicians, bureaucrats, and lobbyists. In these earlier hectic and contentious sessions, interest groups with antithetical programs carried their battles from drafting sessions into the White House, and the resulting legislation bore the scars of awkward compromises. And, in these earlier sessions, troubling questions of legal precision and constitutionality were given short shrift. Keyserling and his colleagues were spared from this political cross-fire, and directed their aim at a single target: employer violations of labor's right to organize and bargain collectively. They had, as well, the incomparable advantage of hindsight. The experience of the past eighteen months made it clear that no New Deal statute could survive the judicial gauntlet without the armor of legislative specificity and procedural clarity.

Keyserling had suggested to Wagner in 1933 that Section 7(a) be added to the NIRA as a counterweight to antitrust exemption. In expanding this section into a separate statute, he displayed a keen awareness of the symbolic importance of Section 7(a) to workers' expectations of federal protection, and he deliberately juggled the structure of the new bill to duplicate a Section 7 that defined the basic rights of workers: "Employees shall have the right to self-organization, to form, join, or assist labor organizations, to bargain collectively through representatives of their own choosing, and to engage in concerted activities, for the purpose of collective bargaining or other mutual aid or protection." Drawing on his earlier efforts, Keyserling specified in Section 8 those "unfair labor practices" that would constitute violations of the NLRA. In the final version of the bill, the list included five such proscribed practices:

"It shall be an unfair labor practice for an employer—

"(1) To interfere with, restrain, or coerce employees in the exercise of rights guaranteed in Section 7.

"(2) To dominate or interfere with the formation or administration of any labor organization or contribute financial or other support of it. . . .

"(3) By discrimination in regard to hire or tenure of employment or any term or condition of employment to encourage or discourage membership in any labor organization. . . .

"(4) To discharge or otherwise discriminate against an employee because he has filed charges or given testimony under this Act.

"(5) To refuse to bargain collectively with the representatives of his employees. . . ."

Section 8(2) ended the long debate over employer-dominated company unions, and in Section 9 Keyserling codified the principles of majority rule and exclusive representation, the other bane of lawyers in the first two labor boards.

Philip Levy's major contribution to the Wagner Act came in the procedural provisions through which unfair labor practice charges were handled by the three-member Board established by the NLRA. Levy was attracted to the model of a "full blown, full fledged judicial agency like the Federal Trade Commission" in fashioning these procedures.[4] Section 10 set out the steps in the process: on receiving a charge that "any person" had committed an unfair labor practice specified in Section 8, the Board was authorized to issue a complaint and to set a time and place for a hearing on the charges. Unlike its predecessors, the new NLRB was given subpoena power to compel testimony and production of records at its hearings, at which "the rules of evidence prevailing in courts of law or equity shall not be controlling." If the Board concluded, after considering the record of testimony, that an unfair labor practice had been committed, it would state its findings of fact and issue a cease and desist order, and could further require "such affirmative action" as reinstatement of discharged employees with back pay. The administrative finality of the Board's proceedings was enhanced by a provision that "findings of the Board with respect to questions of fact if supported by evidence shall be conclusive."

The drafters were adamant on the issue that most affected the Board's future litigation. Their provision that NLRB lawyers could "appear for and represent the Board in any case in court" stemmed from the history of conflict with the Justice Department. Tom Emerson summed up this frustration with the charge that Department lawyers "had done nothing except lose a case against Weirton Steel Company." The Justice Department, he added, was "the most political branch of the administration, and . . . its staff was filled with people who were more or less failures as lawyers or else ancient bureaucratic types. They had no particular interest in the New Deal and were just completely out of sympathy with Section 7(a)."[5] Francis Biddle, testifying in support of this provision, reminded members of the Senate Labor Committee that in almost two years the Justice Department had brought suit in only two cases out of the two dozen in which he had sought litigation. "It is hardly necessary to labor the point," Biddle said, "that such delays as this amount to a complete nullification of the law."[6]

Opposed in principle to incursions on its litigation prerogatives, and annoyed in particular at this criticism of its record, the Department vigorously resisted this threat to its institutional power. Before Senate debate on the bill, Department officials prevailed on Majority Leader Joe Robinson to propose an amendment giving the Attorney General authority "to appear for and represent the Board in any judicial proceeding to which the Board is a party." Wagner refused to budge on the issue and warned Robinson that he would lead a fight on the Senate floor should the amendment be formally offered. Faced with this intransigence, Robinson capitulated.[7] The drafters solidified this crucial victory with provisions giving Board lawyers two further litigation advantages. With Judge Nields' recent *Weirton* decision as a galling reminder of the hostility of district court judges, the drafters moved to side-step this initial litigation hurdle by copying the power given the Federal Trade Commission to directly petition the courts of appeals for enforcement of Board orders. Levy's rationale for this provision exhibited an appreciation of the subtleties of strategy. As opposed to district judges, he said, appellate judges "are too busy to read elaborate records and are thus more likely to acquiesce in the findings of fact by the Board." In addition, "decisions by the circuit courts of appeals would in most cases be final, since the Supreme Court will be too busy to grant certiorari in all but a few cases."[8]

One final provision greatly increased the Board's litigation flexibility, giving it the option of filing an enforcement petition either in the judicial circuit in which the unfair labor practice occurred *or* in any circuit in which the violator "resides or transacts business." This latitude allowed the Board to go "forum shopping" for more sympathetic judges in cases involving companies with plants or offices in more than one circuit. Since employers were also accorded a choice of forum in seeking review of a final Board order, this provision gave rise on occasion to undignified races to the court clerks' offices, with the victor's margin often decided by a matter of minutes.

The fine-print precision of the bill's substantive and procedural provisions obscured the constitutional quicksand on which they rested. Like both the NIRA and AAA, the Wagner Act was bottomed on the commerce clause. It was simply a "bet" on the part of the drafters, as one of them put it, that the Supreme Court would ultimately give an expansive reading to the clause. Keyserling hedged this bet by borrowing liberally from the Supreme Court's language in favorable commerce clause cases in the bill's carefully crafted Declaration of Policy. Its basic thrust was that denial of the rights to organize and bargain collectively necessarily led to "strikes and other forms of industrial strife or unrest," which in turn constricted the flow of goods into the "channels of commerce" and adversely affected levels of employment and wages. Keyserling cleverly lit a fuse under the immovable doctrine of substantive due process by finding, on behalf of Congress, that the "inequality of bargaining power" between employers and workers deprived the latter of "actual liberty of contract," and that this deprivation "substantially burdens and affects the flow of commerce. . . . " Given the twin obstacles of restrictive due process and commerce clause precedent that blocked the path of the Wagner Act, Keyserling's chancy strategy was to push one against the other in the hope that both would topple simultaneously.

Wagner introduced the National Labor Relations Act in the Senate on February 21, 1935. Over the next four months, the bill was battered from within and outside the administration. Roosevelt, who shortly proposed to Congress a simple two-year extension of the NIRA, took a hands-off attitude that in reality constituted opposition. Labor Secretary Frances Perkins soon became Wagner's most formidable foe, as she battled doggedly, in her words, "to sell to the trade unions the idea that this whole project, if it was to be a law, should be in the Labor Department, which was their department."[9] Although Wagner and Perkins maintained outwardly cordial relations during this intramural debate, their chief lieutenants were less inhibited. Labor Department Solicitor Charles Wyzanski, cautious on legal questions and institutionally loyal, had helped to torpedo Wagner's Labor Disputes Act in 1934 and drafted Public Resolution 44 to displace it. Keyserling acidly recalled Wyzanski's "look of satisfaction" when the resolution passed "and he thought that the Wagner bill was as dead as a coffin nail." When it turned out that Wyzanski's approach had expired and Wagner revived his bill, "Wyzanski did all he could to ruin the bill," Keyserling charged.[10] Wyzanski's tack was to propose that union organizers be restrained, as was management, from exerting undue pressure or coercion on workers. Keyserling resisted Wyzanski's "preposterous endeavors to treat employers and employees 'equally' under the Wagner Act," arguing that creating "equality of bargaining power where none existed . . . necessarily meant treating some differently from others."[11] Wyzanski's push to impose so-called "correlative responsibilities" on both labor and management reflected the Labor Department's mediation bias rather than anti-labor sentiment. But this proposal surfaced during Senate debate in the form of an industry-sponsored amendment that would add to Section 7 a guarantee that collective bargaining be protected against "coercion or intimidation from any source." Wagner heatedly objected, realizing that the amendment would enable employers to bring unfair labor practice charges against unions, and the Senate rejected the move by a 50–21 vote.[12]

The Wagner Act sailed through the Senate on May 16 by the deceptively lop-sided vote of 63 to 12. House passage of a substantially similar bill, however, was far from assured. Employers had been caught sleeping in the Senate lobbies, and responded with a ferocious propaganda barrage. Even Henry I. Harriman, an early Roosevelt backer and NIRA draftsman, objected on behalf of industry that the Wagner Act portended a "disastrous effect upon the economic life of the country."[13] Frances Perkins prevailed on her friend William Connery, chairman of the House Labor Committee, to amend the bill in his committee to place the Board under Labor Department control. And Donald Richberg of the NRA, well along in his peregrination from labor lawyer to right-wing politician, was privately pushing for a weak bill that would permit company unions and omit the crucial majority rule provision.[14]

Roosevelt was still sitting on the fence after the Wagner Act cleared the Senate. His equilibrium was threatened, however, by a combination of factors that signaled the end of the corporatist First New Deal and the emergence of a populist Second New Deal. Increasing labor militance, the pro-labor cast of Congress, the administrative collapse of the NRA, and the likelihood of its imminent invalidation by the Supreme Court, all tilted the balance in Wagner's favor. With these factors in the background, the immediate annoyance of an acrimonious split within the administration prompted Roosevelt to bring the antagonists together. At a May 24 White House meeting of congressional, administration, and labor leaders, Roosevelt declared his support for the stronger Senate version of the labor bill. He deferred a public statement pending "the ironing out of differences" between Wagner and his opponents.[15]

Three days later the Supreme Court decision in the *Schechter* case eliminated the last of Roosevelt's doubts. The urgent need to salvage a labor policy from its wreckage prompted a White House statement pledging full support for the Senate bill. The House approved its version on June 19 without the formality of a roll-call vote. Several weakening amendments necessitated a Senate-House conference committee, but Wagner succeeded in deleting the most damaging of these. Philip Levy later attributed the survival of the Wagner Act in almost pristine form to the *Schechter* decision, "which persuaded most lawyers and most members of Congress that the law was unconstitutional. The opposition just folded up. There was no reason for them to go on record and to go through a bruising battle on the floor."[16] The last to fold was Attorney General Cummings, who urged Roosevelt in a final plea to veto the bill because of its "rather doubtful constitutionality."[17]

Wagner shared none of Cummings' constitutional doubts. Keyserling had drafted for Wagner a ten-thousand-word speech defending the bill, salted with historical, economic, and legal arguments, which Wagner delivered on May 15. His constitutional points had a poor prognosis, since the *Schechter* decision soon struck down the labor provisions of the NIRA. Wagner's speech, however, clearly anticipated this impending setback and offered an alternate vision of the national economy, one that distinguished the NIRA and Wagner Act at their economic roots. Wagner first traced the historical evolution of American labor law from its origins in the Philadelphia Cordwainer's case in 1806, in which unions were barred as criminal conspiracies. No longer, he argued, did relations between employers and workers affect only a single business or locality. The impact of labor disputes in an economy characterized by "the interpenetration of all industries throughout the country" and the spread of commerce across state lines now "made Nation-wide action essential."

The heart of Wagner's argument was a carefully crafted linkage of the due process and commerce clause issues. Wrapping himself in the mantle of Chief Justice Hughes' 1930 opinion upholding the Railway Labor Act, Wagner noted that the Court had "completely upheld" against due process challenge the power of Congress to prohibit all the unfair labor practices listed in his bill. Since the railroad industry was indisputably interstate in operation, the connecting link to the commerce clause rested on the claim that local strikes "burdened" interstate commerce. It "cannot be denied," Wagner claimed in a highly debatable assertion, that Congress "has the power under the Constitution to prevent any burden whatsoever upon interstate commerce." Congress was not attempting, of course, to deal with strikes *per se*. But the prohibition of unfair labor practices that provoked labor unrest and led to strikes cleared the stream of commerce of these log-jams. Behind this argument lay the assumption that unfair practices, unchecked by regulation, were likely to recur. As authority on this point, Wagner quoted Chief Justice Taft, never accused of sympathy for labor: "If Congress deems certain recurring practices, although not really part of interstate commerce, likely to obstruct, restrain, or burden it, it has the power to subject them to national supervision or restraint."[18]

The commerce clause argument was the stronger link in the constitutional chain by which Wagner hoped to tie a local labor dispute in Virginia to a disruption of commerce with Oregon. The Supreme Court had made it clear in the "yellow dog" cases, *Adair* and *Coppage*, that neither the federal government nor the states, under the due process clause, could interfere with contractual relations between employers and workers, absent a direct burden on interstate commerce. Wagner could only point hopefully to the conjunction between Chief Justice Hughes's dissent in *Coppage* and his opinion in the Railway Labor Act case, which led Wagner to conclude that *Adair* and *Coppage* "have been overruled" by implication.[19] However sound in logic, Wagner's exegesis of constitutional precedent was certainly

speculative as prognostication. His Senate opponents had originally prepared for a full-scale debate on these issues. But with the *Schechter* case
awaiting decision by the Supreme Court, they rested their case on briefs
inserted in the *Congressional Record*.[20]

President Roosevelt signed the National Labor Relations Act at a White
House ceremony on July 5, 1935, presenting symbolic pens to a proud
Senator Wagner and an expectant William Green, eager to enlist the support
of the strengthened NLRB behind labor's renewed organizing drive. The
most pressing task once the Board was established was that of easing the
transition between the old and the new boards. Francis Biddle was anxious
to return to his Philadelphia law practice, and his colleague Harry A.
Millis, after serving on both predecessor boards, wanted to resume his
academic post in the University of Chicago economics department. Edwin
S. Smith, the most pro-labor member, was the only one of the three who
indicated a desire to continue as a Board member.

In a characteristic attempt at conciliation, Roosevelt assigned the task
of finding replacements for Biddle and Millis to Frances Perkins. The jobs
offered no prospect of lengthy tenure in the wake of *Schechter*, and Perkins
ran through an initial list of twenty candidates before she located a willing
candidate in J. Warren Madden, a peripatetic law professor and dean then
teaching at the University of Pittsburgh. Madden, a specialist in tort and
property law, had little experience in labor relations. His only prior exposure to labor problems came through service on a commission appointed
by Governor Gifford Pinchot of Pennsylvania to study the activities of
private police and detectives hired by coal and steel companies to spy on
and disrupt union organizing. Biddle had served with Madden on the
commission, and joined Lloyd Garrison and Charlton Ogburn, counsel for
the AFL, in recommending him to Perkins. His admission that he "just
didn't know anything about labor law" or "anything really about this
board and the statute" delighted Perkins.[21] "Well, that is fine," she replied
at their first meeting. "You will not have any preconceptions about it and
you can just start it from the ground up and learn it as you go."[22]

Madden was designated as chairman, and was joined on the Board by
Edwin S. Smith, the holdover member, and John M. Carmody. Smith, a
Harvard graduate and former newspaper reporter, had gravitated to labor
relations as a researcher for the Russell Sage Foundation, and later became
personnel director of Filene's Department Store in Boston and secretary
to Lincoln Filene, a "progressive" employer. He came to the pre-Wagner
Act NLRB from the post of Commissioner of Labor and Industries in
Massachusetts, and got to know Frances Perkins when she held a similar
post in New York.[23] Smith would become the most consistent union advocate on the Board, and worked closely with the lawyers on the Board's

staff. Although he had no legal training, "he regretted that he wasn't a lawyer, and enjoyed the company of lawyers and talking over legal issues with them," Nat Witt of the Board's legal staff recalled.[24] Smith's political leanings (and those of Witt as well) later provoked partisan attacks on the Board and its decisions. Madden became convinced that Smith "was quite certainly a Communist,"[25] and although congressional Red-hunters never substantiated these charges, his presence on the Board became a political liability.

Carmody, appointed to the Board on Senator Wagner's recommendation, had a varied background as a factory superintendent, industrial engineer, industry magazine editor, and government official, had chaired the National Bituminous Coal Labor Board, and was a member of the National Mediation Board when he assumed his NLRB post. His bias was in favor of a mediation rather than an adversary approach; he "was not particularly sympathetic to what he regarded as a lot of legal rigamarole," Philip Levy felt.[26] Nat Witt found him openminded and gregarious, but called him "impatient" in dealing with legal issues and said Carmody "just wasn't the kind of personality who belonged on the Board."[27] Among the trio of Board members, the ideological spectrum ranged from Smith on the left to Carmody on the right, with Madden as a self-proclaimed moderate and, as chairman and the only lawyer of the three, the dominant figure in working with the Board's legal staff.

II. Fahy's Craftsmen Draft a Master Plan

With the Board finally constituted in August 1935, the personnel search then turned to the crucial post of general counsel. Calvert Magruder, who remained on an interim basis, wanted to return to his professorship at Harvard Law School. Wagner first recommended Leon Keyserling, but Madden was reluctant since "he had never practiced law, and we thought that he was too young and relatively inexperienced. . . ."[28] The Board then took Magruder's advice and approached Charles Fahy, then serving as Assistant Solicitor of the Interior Department and chairman of the Petroleum Administrative Board. The Supreme Court decision in the "hot oil" cases in January 1935 had rendered Fahy's latter post largely superfluous, and Madden discovered him "quite eager to come" to the NLRB, which he joined in August.[29] Fahy remained in the position for the decisive first five years of the Board's history, later moving up to serve as Solicitor General and then as a member of the U.S. Court of Appeals for the District of Columbia.

Born in 1892 in Rome, Georgia, Fahy adopted the religion of his Irish Catholic father, although his mother was Jewish. After one college year at Notre Dame, he entered Georgetown Law School and practiced for a decade in Washington after graduation. Health problems sent him to the drier climate of Santa Fe in 1924, and it was his experience in the Southwest that prepared Fahy for his Interior Department position. Short and slim, with sharp features and a brush mustache, Fahy combined southern courtliness with an iron will and explosive temperament. This first attribute led one observer to describe his public presence in these words: "Fahy's most dominant physical characteristic is a sensationally soft-spoken voice, which has given birth to such sobriquets as that of 'Whispering Charlie.' "[30] His subordinates and opponents, however, on occasion felt the lash of his tongue or pen. Gerhard Van Arkel of the NLRB staff characterized Fahy as "a very hard taskmaster. Usually he was the essence of politeness and cordiality, but, if you got out of line, he could get madder than any human being I've ever seen and express himself in the most scathing terms. . . ."[31] As his earlier handling of the "hot oil" litigation demonstrated, Fahy displayed an extreme sensitivity to criticism.

The stamp Fahy would place on the NLRB reflected the contrasts with his counterparts in the NRA and AAA. Unlike Donald Richberg, Fahy had little interest in politics, either of the partisan or White House variety. Neither did he share Jerome Frank's intellectual breadth and curiosity or reformist view of law. His vision was narrow, legalistic, and singleminded. Both his subsequent approach to NLRB litigation and the recollections of lawyers on his staff illustrate these traits. Tom Emerson called Fahy "quite honest in his opinions and quite sure that he was right. . . ."[32] Stanley Surrey, who came to the Board from the NRA, recalled that he was "liberal in a rugged, fundamentalist sense, a very cautious lawyer, a very careful and methodical type."[33] Nat Witt, a self-described "zealot" in enforcing the law, perceived Fahy from both an admiring and critical perspective. On one hand, he was an able, thorough, painstaking lawyer, "very deliberate, very patient, very careful. . . ." But, on the other, "he was not as devoted to the Act the way I and some of the younger people were. To him it was just another career." Witt summed up the essential difference: "He got there by accident; I got there by design."[34]

If one phrase could capture Fahy's style as a lawyer, it is that he saw his profession fundamentally as a craft. Social policy was the province of politicians, jurisprudential theory that of judges and law professors. His job was to enforce a statute through the presentation of carefully selected cases in the courts, with meticulous attention to detail and the formulation of narrowly drawn issues the keys to success. Almost like an accountant, Fahy had a balance-sheet approach to law (as Solicitor General in the 1940s, he even recorded statistics on the cases he argued before the Supreme Court, and compared his won-lost percentage with those of his predecessors).[35] He also went over, line by line, the briefs prepared by his NLRB lawyers. In short, Fahy was a Legal Craftsman.

Fahy's first major task as general counsel was to recruit additional lawyers to handle the Board's expanded responsibilities. The NLRB had inherited the case docket of its predecessor as well as its personnel, and Fahy was fortunate that most of the fourteen lawyers transferred to the NLRB agreed to continue. It was clear, however, that many more lawyers were required (by 1939, the legal staff of the NLRB mushroomed to 252 lawyers).[36] Unlike Richberg and Frank, Fahy did not have a direct pipeline to Felix Frankfurter's "old boy" network, and he had few contacts in the prestigious corporate firms in Boston, New York and Chicago. Fahy therefore delegated recruitment to two young holdover lawyers, Thomas I. Emerson and Nat Witt. Both were graduates of Ivy League law schools, Emerson from Yale and Witt from Harvard, and they drew both on law-school classmates and the legal staff of the AAA and NRA (having been recently dismantled by the Supreme Court, the latter agency became a major source of NLRB lawyers). A tally made in 1939 showed that Harvard graduates predominated on the NLRB staff, with 36 of 252, followed by Columbia, Georgetown (Fahy's alma mater), and Yale. Between them, these four schools accounted for close to half of the Board's lawyers.[37]

Despite their dissimilar backgrounds, Emerson and Witt shared a common interest in labor and civil liberties law. Emerson, who bore a remarkable physical resemblance to Tommy Corcoran, descended from venerable New England Puritan forebears, and had been first in his class at Yale Law School and editor-in-chief of the *Yale Law Journal*. He studied with Frankfurter one semester when Frankfurter journeyed from Cambridge to New Haven, and turned down offers from prestigious Wall Street firms to work in New York for Walter Pollak, a civil liberties lawyer who first assigned him to the Supreme Court appeal in the infamous Scottsboro Boys case. In 1933, after two years with Pollak, Emerson was recommended by Frankfurter to Donald Richberg, and spent a year with the NRA before moving to the Garrison and Biddle NLRB.[38]

Nat Witt, who graduated from Harvard Law School in 1932, a year after Emerson left Yale, came from an immigrant family in New York's Lower East Side. Motivated to attend Harvard because he admired Frankfurter's unpopular role in defending condemned anarchists Nicola Sacco and Bartolomeo Vanzetti, Witt drove a cab for two years to earn tuition money. He attracted Frankfurter's attention in a third-year administrative law seminar. "He asked me what I was planning to do," Witt recalled, "and I said, 'Well, I'm going to be a labor lawyer, and do civil liberties work.' He said, 'I wouldn't do any of that. I'm going to send you to Wall Street. Before you get to be a labor or civil liberties lawyer, you want to get to be a *good* lawyer, and on Wall Street you get the best possible training; they really mean business down there.' '' So Witt toiled for a year on corporate reorganizations in the prestigious firm headed by William Donovan, and came to enjoy the technicalities of legal drafting. Frankfurter introduced him to Jerome Frank, then practicing in New York, and he went to Washington with Frank to spend a year on the AAA legal staff, after which he was recruited by his friend Charles Wyzanski to work for the first NLRB.[39]

Fahy's staff differed in two significant respects from those of Donald Richberg and Jerome Frank. Unlike his counterparts, and perhaps because of his divided religious heritage, Fahy showed no reluctance to hire Jewish lawyers. Madden later recalled that the NLRB was a haven for "young men who had made excellent records in law school but who, on account of their race, a great many of them being Jewish, did not have good opportunities" for careers in private practice.[40] The NLRB was also the first New Deal agency which made a conscious effort to hire women as lawyers and professional staff members. Barriers in the legal profession were notorious; the Supreme Court in the 19th century had upheld a state law barring women from practice, and Harvard Law School refused to admit women until 1952. Most women lawyers in the 1930s were necessarily graduates of second-rate "female" law schools such as Portia Law School in Boston (as late as 1963, women comprised only 2.7 percent of the legal profession).[41] Although the numbers were relatively small, the NLRB hired women on a basis of equality with men, most of them in the Review Section headed first by Nat Witt and later by Tom Emerson.[42] It is worth remarking, however, that few women served in the male-dominated Litigation Section, a pattern that duplicated the sex bias of most law firms as well.

Shortly after Fahy arrived, he and the Board began organizing its legal work along functional lines. Fahy first appointed Robert Watts to serve as Associate General Counsel. A Yale Law School graduate, he had been chief assistant United States Attorney in New York and practiced there in a private firm before joining the first NLRB in 1934, where he directed litigation efforts. Fahy called him "quite a fine experienced trial lawyer,"[43] although in Nat Witt's view he was "not a crusader of any kind" and was a conservative influence on Fahy and the Board.[44] The Legal Division was set up with two complementary sections. The Litigation Section, directed by Watts, supervised the conduct of hearings before the Board, advised the regional attorneys, and represented the NLRB in court. Under Nat Witt's direction, the Review Section examined the voluminous transcripts of the field hearings, summarized them for presentation to the Board, and assisted lawyers in the Litigation Section in preparing records for enforcement proceedings before the courts of appeals.

In addition, the Board established a Trial Examiners Division outside the Legal Division and under its direct control. Sensitive to Justice Department criticism during the drafting of the Wagner Act that the Board would be both prosecutor and judge, the Board, through its secretary, supervised trial examiners who conducted hearings and made recommendations as to whether the facts warranted issuance of a Board order. At the beginning, the Board accepted Carmody's suggestion that trial examiners be hired on a part-time basis because of the sporadic scheduling of hearings and the difficulty in finding experienced labor lawyers. Many of them had been volunteer members of the public panels utilized by the earlier boards and shared Carmody's mediation bias. Tom Emerson reported a "built-in conflict and tension" between them and the Board's Washington lawyers because of this factor; since the job required extensive travel and paid only $25 per day, "broken-down trial lawyers were the only ones you could get. . . ."[45]

Just as Carmody's mediation background influenced the structure of the Trial Examiners Division, so did Edwin Smith's labor economics interests prompt him to urge creation of a Division of Economic Research. On the recommendation of Harry Millis, David J. Saposs was hired to head this division. Saposs, a Ukrainian immigrant and former socialist, had unique qualifications for the post; his background included academic training and teaching in labor economics, positions in the New York and federal labor departments, and service as education director of the Amalgamated Clothing Workers union.[46] Saposs and his staff had a dual function in the NLRB: they assisted the Board's lawyers in preparing supporting data for individual hearings and litigation, and also provided general studies of labor conditions, wage rates, and the economic structure of industries. Although Tom Emerson and other Board lawyers relied heavily on these studies in preparing briefs and records in the NLRB test cases, Fahy considered Saposs an interloper in the legal realm. Fahy's fear was that a stress on economic data might "downplay the legal part of the problems. . . . It didn't need much in the way of economics to say that a sit-down strike which was caused by an unfair labor practice . . . was not interfering with interstate commerce. . . ."[47] At best, an uneasy truce existed between Fahy and the Board's economists.

Before the NLRB lawyers could deal with the inherited backlog of cases and prepare for the anticipated flood of new cases, Fahy faced the preliminary task of restructuring the Board's regional operations and case-handling procedures. Under the first NLRB, the Board's twenty regional offices operated as virtual fiefdoms, each controlled by a largely autonomous regional director. The directors had absorbed the mediation approach of the prior boards, and were used to settling disputes on an informal basis. Madden and Fahy were determined to eliminate this informality and replace it with a centralized system in which, after receiving an unfair labor practice charge, the director would forward it to Washington for approval before filing a complaint. They also proposed assigning a Board lawyer, called a regional attorney, to the staff of each director to provide legal advice, "draft complaints, interview witnesses, make further investigations, prepare cases for trial, present the board's cases at hearings before trial examiners," and generally control the legal work in each region.[48] Under this scheme the regional attorneys would be ultimately responsible to Fahy. Tom Emerson explained its purpose as giving "the Washington office very substantial control so that it would be able to formulate the litigation strategy."[49]

This move from Washington provoked a brief but intense bureaucratic counterrevolution which came to a head in September 1935 at a conference at Board headquarters. Madden presented the regional directors with a draft of the new case-handling regulations. The draft had already aroused the ire of Carmody, who "threw up his hands and said this was a lot of legalistic nonsense and he just didn't want to be a part of it and threatened to resign," Levy reported.[50] Madden recognized that the directors, who "had been doing the interesting and pleasant work of mediation and persuasion," would object to having "lawyers at their elbows, telling them what not to do and how not to do it."[51] George Pratt, a 1927 Yale Law School graduate and the only lawyer among the directors, felt strongly that the new procedures would "treat each Regional Director as merely a messenger boy. . . ."[52] But the efforts of a rump caucus of directors failed to sway Madden and Fahy, as Board lawyers gained almost complete control over case handling. Fahy's motivation for this move stemmed in part from the embarrassment he suffered at the Petroleum Administrative Board, when the key enforcement provision of the "hot oil" regulations was lost in a bureaucrat's desk drawer. A more important consideration was that Fahy and his staff were determined, from the outset of the NLRB, to begin an aggressive litigation campaign directed toward an early Supreme Court test. "It really wasn't true that the regional directors were just office boys," Tom Emerson explained. "The good ones had an important role to play and nobody ever thought that every case was going to go to trial. But at the beginning we were looking for test cases, and for those few cases we weren't interested in settling, unless the company came in with an offer. Also, there wasn't much chance of settling until the constitutional issues were decided."[53]

Fahy's first move to exercise his greatly enhanced power was to assign sixteen Board lawyers, almost the entire legal staff at that time, to the regional offices. They had little to do in Washington, since the backlog of cases was small. It was obvious that passage of the Wagner Act would spur union organizing efforts, and that employer resistance would soon produce a deluge of unfair labor practice charges. Most of the Board lawyers on temporary assignment to the regional offices would return to Washington after replacement by newly recruited lawyers, but a brief seasoning in the field, Fahy felt, would familiarize them with Board procedures from the ground up, acquaint them with the reality of employer-worker conflict, expose them to combat with company lawyers in hearings, and allow them to impress on the regional directors the Board's determination that the new procedures be followed.

Spread out across the country, the Board lawyers soon found their hands full. During its first nine months of operation, from July 1935 to March 1936, the Board handled 729 cases, about three per day, involving 165,792 workers. Practically all of these cases fell into one of three categories: charges of discrimination against workers for union activities or affiliation; petitions seeking Board-conducted elections or certification following an election; and complaints that an employer refused to bargain in good faith after union certification.[54] Nat Witt, assigned to Cleveland for several months before returning to head the Review Division, recalled that in addition to the hectic work of investigating charges and preparing cases for hearings, "we were under special instructions to look for test cases, since we knew we were headed for the Supreme Court."[55]

Witt and his colleagues were guided in their search by a "master plan" which specified in detail the types of test cases best suited for eventual submission to the Supreme Court. This long-range plan took shape even before the Wagner Act was signed, in the form of a memorandum titled "Selection of Test Cases Under the National Labor Relations Act." Prepared during the transition period by Tom Emerson, Gerhard Van Arkle, Charles Wood, and Garnet Patterson, the strategy memo was submitted to the Board on July 9, 1935 and adopted wholeheartedly by Fahy when he became general counsel a month later. The NLRB lawyers who designed a comprehensive litigation strategy had, of course, the advantages of experience in New Deal agencies and of the body of case law developed by the predecessor boards. But they had also a distinctive approach to litigation. Lawyers in the NRA had fumbled about while they searched for a coherent enforcement policy, and exhibited indecision during debates over the *Belcher* and *Schechter* cases, while AAA lawyers were basically antipathetic to litigation in general. In contrast, even before Fahy arrived NLRB lawyers were eager to press for court enforcement of the Wagner

Act and determined to outline a step-by-step strategy leading from case selection to the Supreme Court.

The NLRB "master plan" recognized that selection of test cases would be dictated by commerce clause issues. There was little question, the memo's authors felt, that "relations between an employer and those of his employees actually engaged 'in interstate commerce' (e.g., engaged in selling or transporting goods across state lines) ordinarily are subject to regulation." It was likely, however, that most NLRB cases would arise not in classic "interstate commerce" industries but in those based on manufacturing, mining, or processing, which required confrontation with the body of Supreme Court precedent holding that manufacturing and commerce were distinct. Two paths around this roadback were possible. It might first be shown that an unfair labor practice in a manufacturing industry "directly and substantially affects interstate commerce." The *Schechter* decision, however, all but blocked this path. The alternative rested on a stronger statement of the impact of labor-management conflict: "Strikes and other forms of industrial unrest obstruct and divert the flow of commerce among the states." Courts were more likely to respond to an argument that Congress possessed power, delegated to the Board, to remove obstructions from the stream of commerce rather than simply to regulate practices affecting it. The first job of the NLRB, then, would be to develop cases in which obstruction, particularly to the flow of goods from one state to another, could be demonstrated conclusively.

With this general objective as a guide, the memo moved on to the practicalities of choosing test cases, and identified four factors: (1) the type of industry; (2) the characteristics of the individual business; (3) the degree of actual or threatened obstruction of interstate commerce; and (4) the type of unfair labor practice charged. Under the first of these factors, the "best industries undoubtedly are those where most of the employees involved are actually engaged 'in' interstate commerce," such as "trucking, bus lines, air lines, pipe lines, shipping, telephone and telegraph companies, etc." Victory in such cases, however, would gain little new ground, even if satisfying to the Board and its lawyers; they would constitute a minor part of the Board's jurisdiction, could easily be distinguished from the manufacturing and mining cases barred by restrictive precedent, and "a favorable decision would leave unsettled many of the most important legal questions."

The "next best" industries identified in the memo were those in which the employees worked on products in the "current" of commerce, which came into and emerged from a state "essentially unchanged in character." This category would include stockyards, meatpackers, and grain elevators; defense of congressional regulatory power would rest on such expansive commerce clause cases as *Stafford v. Wallace* and *Chicago Board of Trade v. Olsen*, which dealt with just these industries. Following these as the "third best" category were those manufacturing industries constituting the bulk of the Board's jurisdiction, those in which "a substantial part of the raw materials flow from other states into the manufacturing plant and a substantial part of the resulting products flow out from the plant to other states." The more important the industry to the national economy, and the more dispersed its collection and distribution of goods, the better; autos, steel, textile, and rubber "are the best of this class," followed by clothing, metal fabrication, chemical, paper, and similar industries.

At this early stage of litigation planning, the Board lawyers were thinking in terms of preparing cases to be presented in sequence to the Supreme Court, with the strongest cases first. Consequently, the memo's authors recommended a two-stage strategy: "Once the authority of the Board has been established by the Supreme Court with respect to these industries, the Board should bring cases to test the extent of its authority with respect to other situations." Included in this second round would be those industries in which goods flowed into but not out of the state of manufacture. Additionally, they saw little hope of success "at least for the indefinite future" in such areas as service trades, amusements, and intrastate transportation. Finally, they recommended that industries "with a long record of industrial unrest are preferable to those in which there have been few strikes or other disturbances." Under this criterion, coal, steel, textiles, and the garment industry were the leading candidates.

Under the factor of selecting individual businesses for test cases, the obvious points were made that candidates should be large in size and important in the industry, have branches in other states, and advertise and have salesmen in more than one state. It was not felt necessary, in selecting cases on the basis of the actual or threatened interruption of commerce, that there be shown a "physical interruption," since the act only required that the unfair labor practice would lead or tend to lead to an obstruction. But a case would be "immeasurably strengthened" both legally and psychologically if a strike was impending or if the company had a history of strikes that interrupted production.

Dominated by the commerce clause question, litigation strategy planning focused on the nature of the industry; but Emerson and his colleagues also paid attention to which category of unfair labor practices would present the best test case. They found it difficult to choose, since from a legal standpoint each had both advantages and disadvantages and "so nearly balance each other" that the most important consideration was whether, in each case, the violation was "flagrant" and easily proved by the facts. The principal weakness of a discriminatory discharge case, under Section

8(1), was that of showing a direct relation to interstate commerce; a "further drawback is that employers have now learned sufficiently subtle methods of eliminating union men" to make proof difficult. Company union cases under Section 8(2) raised great difficulty, since courts were likely to agree with Judge Nields in the *Weirton* case "that cooperation between employer and employee is the 'American' method of handling labor relations," and that the impact on interstate commerce of company unions "is a very remote one." However, the company union issue was serious and it would be "extremely difficult, if not impossible, for the Board to avoid or even to delay this issue." The best test case would be one in which employer support of a company union was combined with discriminatory discharges of legitimate union members. In terms of the commerce clause, cases of refusal to bargain in good faith were preferable, since "strike statistics show a greater proportion of strikes arising from this cause" than from any other unfair labor practice. Finally, election cases, generally involving a refusal to cooperate with the Board, would give the Board the psychological advantage of supporting "the democratic process of the ballot."[56]

It would be hard to overestimate the importance of this initial plan for an overall litigation strategy. Fitting neatly into Fahy's approach to enforcement and litigation, it provided a blueprint for the Board lawyers in the field and in Washington. In one sense, it was merely a logical outgrowth of the structure of the Wagner Act and a perceptive analysis of the limitations and potentialities of the conflicting lines of precedent. But in another, it showed keen insight into the psychological dimension of litigation—which cases would involve the most "flagrant" violators and the most compelling victims; which would most appeal to the sense of fairness of the judges; and which would most easily fit into the certainty of existing law. And, most important, it gave a clear guide to NLRB lawyers in sifting through their massive case loads in search of ideal test cases, charting a clear path from the picket line to the Supreme Court.

III. THE LIBERTY LEAGUE DISRUPTS THE MASTER PLAN

Even before the Board lawyers dispatched to the regions were able to begin the orderly processing of cases, they were hit with a well-coordinated diversionary assault by corporation lawyers. Although the Wagner Act's drafters consciously side-stepped the more conservative federal district courts by placing enforcement power in the circuit courts of appeals, the NLRB soon found itself combatting a barrage of injunction suits brought in the district courts. In the eight months between November 1935 and June 1936, the Board was faced with eighty-three such suits. Most attempted to head off a Board hearing on an unfair labor practice charge by resisting a subpoena requiring company officials to testify or to produce records; company lawyers would seek a temporary restraining order under the district courts' equity powers, arguing that their clients would suffer "irreparable injury" if subjected to an unconstitutional statute. The effect, as Robert Watts complained to a Senate committee in April 1936, was that rather than waiting for a court of appeals forum "in which every opportunity is given for judicial consideration not only of the facts but of all constitutional and other objections which the parties might have," the injunction suits operated to "hamper and delay the administration of the law" and "diverted a large portion of the legal staff to the task of protecting the Board from these attacks."[57]

Behind the injunction assault was the well-heeled American Liberty League, the vociferously anti-New Deal propaganda voice of the duPont family and such allies as Alfred P. Sloan of General Motors and Ernest Weir, both of whom contributed $10,000 to the League in 1935. In June 1935, with the Wagner Act assured of congressional passage, the Liberty League announced the formation of an offshoot, a "Lawyers' Vigilance Committee" headed by Raoul Desvernine, a Wall Street lawyer and president of the Crucible Steel Company. The Vigilance Committee quickly recruited more than two thousand lawyers across the country, and in turn spawned a smaller, elite group of fifty-eight corporation lawyers, known as the National Lawyers Committee, also headed by Desvernine. Joining him were such paladins of the corporate bar as James Beck, former Solicitor General and Republican congressman; Bainbridge Colby, Secretary of State under Woodrow Wilson; Wall Street lawyers Frederic R. Coudert, Jr. and George Wickersham, Attorney General under President Taft; Earl F. Reed and John W. Davis, Democratic presidential candidate in 1924, both of whom would argue against the NLRB in the Supreme Court test cases; and corporate lawyers from twenty states. As the inclusion of Davis and Colby demonstrated, the largely Republican group welcomed anti-Roosevelt Democrats.[58]

Precisely two months after Roosevelt signed the Wagner Act, the National Lawyers Committee issued, with great fanfare, a 132-page brief entitled "Report on the Constitutionality of the National Labor Relations Act," prepared by a subcommittee headed by Earl F. Reed. Broadcast in more than 40,000 copies, the report became the bible of company lawyers fighting the NLRB in injunction suits, and the bane of Board lawyers. There was no subtlety in the report's dissection of the Wagner Act. Although cast in the traditional form of the legal brief and citing seventy-seven cases, it expressed as much outrage at the "arrogant attitude" of union workers toward management prerogatives and paternalistic labor relations, and Roosevelt's deprecation of the "horse and buggy" *Schechter* decision, as it did the act's violation of constitutional fundamentalism. The report raised two predictable objections. First, in its due process argument, it embraced the pristine "freedom of contract" doctrine expressed in *Adair v. United States*. In language reminiscent of Spencerian Social Darwinism, the report said: "Highly competent workmen, who are accustomed to demand and obtain the best price for their labor, may find their wages fixed, to their detriment, by the agreements of the agents of the more numerous, but less capable, employees." The due process objection was reiterated in a dozen citations to *Adair*.

The commerce clause argument in the report rested on an equally emphatic dozen citations to *Schechter* and its lineage in "ancient precedents." Half-heartedly conceding that "liberals" might quarrel with their Lochnerian concept of substantive due process, Reed and his corporate colleagues contended that "they can not, except out of ignorance," attack the conception of commerce set out in *Schechter* and embraced by Justice Cardozo and Judge Learned Hand. Addressing the specific unfair labor practices prohibited by the statute, the report made only two concessions demanded by the *Texas & New Orleans Railroad* case: the bar in Section 8(1) against employer interference with union organizing efforts it called "entirely proper"; and the ban on discrimination against employees giving testimony under the act in Section 8(4) was seen as a "justifiable rule of policy." With these niggling exceptions aside, the jeremiad of the National Lawyers Committee was uncompromising. Viewed in the light of history and of Supreme Court precedent, the report's authors concluded, "we have no hesitation in concluding that [the Wagner Act] is unconstitutional and that it constitutes a complete departure from our constitutional and traditional theories of government."[59]

Armed with this ready-made brief, and with Earl Reed's assurance that "when a lawyer tells a client that a law is unconstitutional it is then a nullity and he need no longer obey that law,"[60] company lawyers set out to create havoc for the NLRB. The Lawyers Committee brief spread across the country like an oil slick; in its first annual report, the NLRB noted that "the growth and fantastic character" of the allegations in injunction suits showed a gradually increasing uniformity. "The allegations in a pleading by an employer in Georgia, for example, would show up in precisely the same wording in a pleading filed in Seattle."[61]

Fahy was apprehensive about the prospect of injunction suits, and clashed with more activist members of his staff over the use of the Board's subpoena powers, which he feared would provoke such suits. At a meeting of the legal staff in September 1935, he cautioned that "if it is at all likely that the District Courts would go into the constitutionality" of the statute, "we want to avoid it if possible." Although several of the lawyers present

245

argued, as one put it, that subpoenas to management witnesses were necessary because "imagination can't take the place of witnesses," Fahy countered that "you have got to wait until you develop your case." He and Nat Witt advocated reliance on union witnesses as the best means of developing facts.[62]

Notwithstanding this advice, Board lawyers found it impossible to stem the tide of injunction suits. Determined to combat this form of harassment, Fahy personally stepped in to argue the first injunction case, brought by lawyers for the Majestic Flour Mills in Missouri. George Pratt, regional director in Kansas City, who issued the complaint and was the target of the suit, briefed Fahy on his arrival in Kansas City on the likely attitude of the district judge assigned to the case, Merrill C. Otis. "I had appeared before him many times," Pratt told Fahy, and "considered him to be an eminently fair, reasonable man."

At the hearing the next day, after the company lawyer argued that the Wagner Act was unconstitutional, Fahy "replied in his quiet voice and even, measured tones, pointing out the decisions" on which Congress in passing the law and the Board in administering it relied.[63] Fahy was unaware, however, that Judge Otis was a member of the American Liberty League. Five days later he handed down a decision, enjoining Pratt from enforcing the statute, in which the Wagner Act was excoriated as officious paternalism: "The individual employee is dealt with by the act as an incompetent. The Government must protect him even from himself. He is the ward of the United States, to be cared for by his guardian even as if he were a member of an uncivilized tribe of Indians or a recently emancipated slave."[64]

Judge John P. Barnes of the federal district court in Chicago subjected the NLRB to the lengthiest denunciation. In March 1936, a month before he declared the AAA unconstitutional, Barnes retreated to *Lochner, Adair*, and *Coppage* to support his finding that the combination of "majority rule" and "compulsory unilateral arbitration" contravened the due process clause. "Take them out of the act, and there is no life left. Accordingly, it is concluded that the whole act is unconstitutional and void." The case before Judge Barnes dealt with an attempt by the NLRB to hold an election at the Bendix automotive and aircraft parts manufacturing plant between a company union and the United Auto Workers, an AFL affiliate. The company claimed that an election would "stir up strife, contention, and ill will" among its employees and subject it to the risk of damage to its property "as a result of acts of violence" likely to accompany an election campaign between the contending unions. Judge Barnes found in this speculative claim the "irreparable injury" needed to justify an injunction, and added that the Board's claim of commerce clause jurisdiction was simply the "familiar, but fallacious" argument rejected by the Supreme Court in its restrictive line of cases.[65] Decisions such as those by judges Otis and Barnes astounded Board lawyers, who found it "appalling to go before the District Courts . . . and get the most amazing revelations as to what the Court thought this Act was. . . ."[66]

Fortunately for the Board lawyers, most district judges agreed with their contention that protesting companies had "an adequate remedy at law" in the courts of appeals, the traditional basis for declining injunctive relief. In the first five months of the injunction litigation, the NLRB was enjoined in only twelve of forty-seven cases, and five of these were heard before one particularly obstructive judge in Wisconsin who, Robert Watts said, not only refused to allow Board lawyers to file briefs in the cases but "has even refused two lawyers for the Board . . . the opportunity to be heard upon oral argument."[67]

Among the decisions upholding the Board in the injunction litigation, the most clearly reasoned was written by Judge Harlan W. Rippey in New York, in the *Precision Castings Co.* case. Setting aside the constitutional objections raised by company lawyers, Judge Rippey first looked at the Board's administrative procedures, finding them "substantially the same" as those of the Federal Trade Commission which had been repeatedly upheld by the Supreme Court. Since the Board provided "all fair and reasonable opportunities to be heard, to present evidence, to review arbitrary administrative action, that is guaranteed by due process of law," the company should be required to exhaust its administrative remedies before seeking judicial review. Displaying his partisan sympathies as a Democrat, Judge Rippey took pains to applaud the Wagner Act's objectives.[68] But most of the judges who upheld the NLRB in the injunction cases were Republicans who swallowed their constitutional objections to the Wagner Act. "Much as it may seem desirable" to decide these questions in the district courts, one of them wrote, "it will prove better in the long run to follow the orderly procedure" of the Act and allow the appellate courts to deal with them.[69]

This series of bouts with the heavily bankrolled Lawyers Committee and the corporate lawyers wielding its brief strained the resources of the NLRB lawyers thinly spread across the country, although they gained experience and confidence in arguing the injunction cases. Fahy and his beleaguered staff received crucial assistance from two unlikely sources. The logistic difficulty in defending dozens of suits simultaneously in widely spread jurisdictions forced Fahy, in late November 1935, to call on the Justice Department for temporary aid. Attorney General Cummings, who had clashed repeatedly with Fahy over the conduct of Petroleum Board litigation and who resented the Department's loss of control over NLRB litigation, nonetheless approved the assignment of several Department lawyers to injunction cases. Even the Supreme Court assisted the Board by refusing to consider appeals from the injunction cases, clearly preferring to wait for cases decided on the merits by the courts of appeals. "They were going to let us have a real chance at them," Fahy remarked approvingly.[70] In the end, the injunction litigation fomented by the Liberty League proved more of a harassment than a roadblock to the NLRB lawyers, although it forced them for six months to divert much of their energy into a defensive effort. The corporate campaign did not derail Fahy's carefully designed litigation strategy; it was merely sidetracked.

IV. Trouble in the Coal Fields

Another development over which the NLRB lawyers had no control, however, threatened to doom the Wagner Act. Under the prodding of John L. Lewis' United Mine Workers and its chief congressional ally, Senator Joseph Guffey of Pennsylvania, Congress in August 1935 passed the Bituminous Coal Conservation Act. Popularly known as the Guffey Act, this law attempted to salvage the main features of the NRA bituminous coal code from the wreckage of the *Schechter* decision. The NRA code had won the support of the union and of most smaller operators for imposing a modicum of price and labor stability on the anarchic, often violent, and highly competitive industry.

The significance of the Guffey Act to the NLRB was that its labor provisions were directly modeled on the Wagner Act, down to the precise wording of the section protecting the rights of miners to organize and bargain collectively. In their trade-off with labor, operators won price-fixing and production control provisions enforced through an ostensible "tax" of 15 percent on the sale price of coal, with 90 percent of the tax refunded to producers who signed the new code. Although Justice Department lawyers were convinced that the Guffey Act was unconstitutional in light of *Schechter*, they swallowed their doubts in the face of Lewis' threats of a crippling nationwide coal strike if the bill was rejected. Roosevelt urged Congress to leave the law's fate to the courts, despite his grave doubts "that the proposed act will withstand constitutional tests. . . ."[71] With this half-hearted endorsement, Congress passed the bill by narrow margins in each house and Roosevelt signed it on August 30, 1935.

The day Roosevelt signed the Guffey Act, three members of the board of the Carter Coal Company, one of the larger producers in Virginia and West Virginia, held an unusual meeting in Washington. James W. Carter, the young president of the company, was a foe of the United Mine Workers and of the smaller, marginal producers who would benefit from the coal code. In a prearranged move calculated to force a court test of the Guffey Act, the other two directors (Carter's father and a company employee) voted to sign the code. The next morning, Frederick Wood, of the Wall Street law firm of Cravath, deGersdorff, Swaine and Wood, who had successfully argued the *Schechter* case a few months earlier before the Supreme Court, appeared in the federal district court in Washington and filed a suit on Carter's behalf, seeking to enjoin his fellow directors from signing the code, and to restrain the National Bituminous Coal Commission from enforcing the code against the Carter Coal Company. A more obviously collusive suit, in which Carter essentially sued himself, could hardly be imagined, but it satisfied legal form and served the purposes of the large producers.[72]

Carter v. Carter Coal Company created consternation among lawyers in the Justice Department and NLRB. Stanley Reed, to whom Wood had given a copy of the petition he was about to file in federal court, promptly informed the White House that Carter's move "will give us plenty of trouble." Reed asked Marvin McIntyre, Roosevelt's secretary, to advise the President that the Justice Department would oppose the suit on the ground that it was premature, since the tax provisions of the Guffey Act would not become effective until November 1. "How successful is doubtful," he added. "Wood is going to shove every way he can to get a prompt decision in the Supreme Court."[73]

It turned out, ironically, that Reed himself pushed the *Carter* case onto the Supreme Court docket, along with three companion cases that joined *Carter* on its peregrination through the district court. By the time Reed decided in late December 1935 to seek Supreme Court review of the Guffey Act, enforcement of the coal code had come to a virtual halt as district judges issued dozens of restraining orders against the Coal Commission and the Internal Revenue Service, which had been delegated responsibility for collecting the tax. The situation was further complicated by divergent rulings in the two sets of Guffey Act cases decided on constitutional grounds. In the first *Carter* case, Judge Jesse Adkins in Washington, a moderate Republican who had earlier upheld the AAA against constitutional challenge, upheld the price-fixing provisions as a valid exercise of Congress's commerce clause powers, but struck down the wage and hour and labor relations provisions on the basis of *Schechter*. In a second suit, however, one brought by Carter Company stockholders against the IRS, Adkins granted an injunction against the Commissioner of Internal Revenue on due process grounds, since company officials had not signed the code which imposed the "tax" on their sales.[74]

The other two cases, identical in their facts, involved the Tway Coal Company of Kentucky. In these suits, Judge Elwood Hamilton, a Democrat and recent Roosevelt appointee, upheld the Guffey Act against all the constitutional objections and denied an injunction against the IRS.[75] On the basis of this split between the district court judges, Solicitor General Reed asked the Supreme Court to hear all four cases without waiting for decisions from the courts of appeals. The Court agreed, and set March 11, 1936 for oral argument. Assistant Attorney General John Dickinson, who had argued both sets of cases in the district courts, agreed to make the Supreme Court arguments and to assist Reed's staff in preparing briefs in the cases. Reed assigned Robert L. Stern the job of working with Dickinson on this task. For additional constitutional expertise, Dickinson and Stern enlisted as consultants Thomas Reed Powell of Harvard Law School and Edward S. Corwin of Princeton.

Because of the NLRB's obvious interest in the labor provisions of the Guffey Act, drafts of the briefs were sent to Charles Fahy. The first draft submitted to Fahy relied primarily on the *Texas & New Orleans Railroad* case for the proposition that government-protected collective bargaining offered a rational alternative to the long history of violent strikes in the coal fields. Although no other case provided the Wagner and Guffey acts alike with more supportive precedent on this point, Fahy was nonetheless upset by the Justice Department's wording of this proposition. "Too much use is made of the word 'strike' all through this part of the draft," Fahy cautioned. Fahy wanted to distract the Court's attention from the localized aspect of labor disputes, and urged that the brief stress instead congressional power to "remove the causes of obstructions to commerce" and emphasize the generalized and national impact of labor strife on the economy.[76] What might seem a trivial semantic quibble was to Fahy part of a long-range strategy, designed to sway any possibly wavering Supreme Court vote.

Argument before the Supreme Court on the Guffey Act cases stretched over two days. The issues seemed so clear-cut and bound by precedent that only two questions from Justice Sutherland interrupted seven hours of oratory. Frederick Wood aimed his fire at the law's labor provisions, resting on *Schechter* for the proposition that employer-worker relations were local in nature and subject only to state regulation. On behalf of the Tway Coal Company, former Kentucky federal judge Charles Dawson, who had recently ruled the NIRA unconstitutional before leaving the bench, hammered away at the commerce clause issue, directing the Court to the solid line of precedent holding that mining was not part of commerce, regardless of the destination of the coal.[77]

Arguing for the government in all four cases, John Dickinson first bowed to the reality of *Butler*, only two months old, and conceded that the "tax" provisions of the act were in fact a penalty designed to coerce acceptance of the coal code. Dickinson's strategy rested on an attempt to rescue the remaining provisions through reliance on the law's separability clause, and on stressing that seven major coal-producing states had filed *amicus* briefs supporting the Guffey Act. The fact that the states welcomed federal regulation of the chaotic coal industry provided the basis of Dickinson's commerce clause argument. Drafted largely by Professor Corwin, this argument raised the specter of a "twilight zone" in which neither the states nor the federal government could regulate important economic activities. "The states," Dickinson said, "are cut off from regulating interstate commerce by the commerce clause. If the federal government cannot regulate interstate commerce and its incidents merely because there are intrastate elements involved, there is no regulation at all. It cannot be said that the federal government has merely a negative power and that an economic doctrine of laissez faire has been written into the Constitution." In discussing the law's labor provisions, Dickinson deferred to Fahy and stressed their role in eliminating "burdens" to interstate commerce.[78]

Justice Sutherland's role as the only questioner at oral argument presaged his authorship of the decision handed down by the Supreme Court on May 18, 1936. The most articulate of the four-man conservative bloc on economic issues, Sutherland produced a majority opinion which, in its uncompromising rigidity, threatened just that twilight zone of governmental impotence feared by Dickinson. Restating the states-rights argument advanced by Wood, Sutherland wrote: "Every journey to a forbidden end begins with the first step; and the danger of such a step by the federal government in the direction of taking over the powers of the states is that the end of the journey may find the states so despoiled of their powers . . . as to reduce them to little more than geographical subdivisions of the national domain." Citing the distinction between commerce and manufacturing in the restrictive commerce clause cases, he disposed of both the price-fixing and labor provisions in the same voice. He found "inescapable" the conclusion that "the labor provisions of the act, including those in respect of minimum wages, wage agreements, collective bargaining, and the [Coal] Labor Board and its powers, primarily falls upon production and not upon commerce; and confirms the further resulting conclusion that production is a purely local activity." Sutherland's answer to the argument that labor strife in the coal industry affected production and thus burdened interstate commerce was that "the evils are all local evils over which the federal government has no legislative control. The relation of employer and employee is a local relation."[79]

In Sutherland's dichotomous mind, the distinction between manufacturing and commerce was one of kind, not degree; since mining fell in the former category, the Guffey Act must fall in its totality, notwithstanding the separability clause which might have rescued the labor provisions.

Chief Justice Hughes was sufficiently offended by the sweep of Sutherland's broadsword to write a concurring opinion. And as they had in *Butler*, the three liberals dissented. Writing for Brandeis and Stone, Justice Cardozo was uncharacteristically direct. The reach of the commerce clause *was* governed by factors of degree; the "direct" and "indirect" distinction applied by Sutherland might better be replaced by the terms "intimate" and "remote." Noting that ninety-seven percent of the coal produced by Carter's company was shipped out of state, Cardozo agreed that mining and manufacture, considered simply as production, did not constitute interstate commerce, "yet their relation to that commerce may be such that for the protection of the one there is need to regulate the other." In discussing the labor provisions, Cardozo was obviously impressed by the voluminous evidence in the government's brief of the bloody history of labor relations in the coalfields. "Commerce had been choked and burdened" by the "violence and bloodshed and misery and bitter feeling" on both sides. And in an ironic inversion of his denunciation of the regulatory scheme in the NRA petroleum code as "delegation run riot," Cardozo now wrote that the rights of coal producers did not include "the right to persist in this anarchic riot."[80]

The impact of the *Carter* decision on the NLRB lawyers was devastating. In a memorandum sent to regional directors just three days later, the Board instructed them that "certain types of cases will have to be completely eliminated for the present and others must be discouraged as much as possible." Cases involving manufacturing concerns in particular were "less desirable."[81] Tom Emerson reported the consensus of his colleagues that *Carter* "was much more disastrous than the Schechter case." Within days of the Supreme Court setback, Emerson appeared before the Fifth Circuit Court of Appeals to argue the most important of the NLRB's test cases, *Jones & Laughlin*, involving a major steel producer threatened with a crippling strike. "I struggled to distinguish the Carter Coal case," he recalled.[82]

Almost alone on the NLRB legal staff, Fahy admitted to discouragement but not defeat. He had never considered *Schechter* an impassable obstacle, since "it was a weak case under the commerce clause." And although *Carter* "loomed with a rather dismal aspect," Fahy was confident that his job in preparing test cases "was immeasurably assisted by the careful draftsmanship of this beautifully drafted statute." In spite of the unwillingness to uphold the Guffey Act labor provisions indicted in Chief Justice Hughes's concurrence, Fahy felt that "he wouldn't be troubled with this much better drafted statute. He'd be with us; I felt fairly confident of that." The only remaining task was to pry Justice Roberts loose from the grip of the four conservatives. Given the careful drafting of the Wagner Act and the detailed findings of Congress in the committee reports, ''how could Roberts resist'' the leadership of Hughes, Fahy reasoned.[83]

It has been said that a good lawyer is one who, confronted with a problem involving two inextricably related factors, can focus on one and ignore the other. In much the same way, Fahy displayed the attitude of the Legal Craftsman by urging his staff to concentrate on developing carefully prepared test cases and to ignore the looming threat of the *Carter* case. There was no need to deviate from the ''master plan'' behind the Board's litigation strategy. As Tom Emerson recalled, ''Fahy consistently refused to concede that the matter was, in terms of legal doctrine, decided.''[84]

Chapter Twelve

THE NLRB IMPLEMENTS ITS
MASTER PLAN

I. Commerce and the Indian Tribes

It took the NLRB almost three months after Roosevelt signed the Wagner Act to clear its administrative decks and begin work on new cases. By late September 1935 the Board had recruited a small but expanding legal and administrative staff, drafted case-handling procedures, and quelled the brief revolt by the regional directors against the Board's centralization of power in Washington. The NLRB lawyers were then ready, as Tom Emerson explained, "to search out good test cases in which to start Board proceedings in accordance with the master plan for testing the constitutionality" of the act outlined by Emerson and his colleagues in early July.[1] The first move in the master plan "was to bring up first a case involving an instrumentality of interstate commerce" as the easiest to sustain under the *Texas & New Orleans Railroad* precedent on which the plan relied.[2] Since the Railway Labor Act covered the most obvious candidate industry, interstate bus and trucking firms provided the most inviting targets.

Only days after the Board's office in Pittsburgh opened under the direction of Clinton Golden, nine mechanics and drivers of the Pennsylvania Greyhound lines brought him a ready-made case. They had been fired in July and August, the men told Golden, for their activities in Local 1063 of the Street, Electric Railway and Motor Coach Employees union, an AFL affiliate. They also charged that the company supported a company union and employed spies to ferret out AFL union members, whom company foremen fired if they refused to give up union activities.

After meeting with the discharged workers, Golden realized that he had a perfect case. In late September he sent his weekly report to Washington, reporting that he was following Board instructions in preparing economic data on the company's interstate activities. The Greyhound company, he wrote, had an "extremely complicated corporate set-up" requiring careful inquiry before deciding on a proper respondent. "A source has been located through which a private study of much of this corporate set-up may be obtained" in addition to publicly available records, Golden added.[3] Within two weeks he had amassed enough material on the company's structure and the events leading up to the firings to support charges that the company interfered with the workers' rights to organize, dominated a company union, and discriminated against union members by firing them. Golden then arranged with Local 1063 to file charges on October 8, and the next day the Board issued an already drafted complaint.

Since the Board envisioned the *Greyhound* case as the first and best test of its powers, all three Board members attended the hearing on the case in Pittsburgh in late October. During the month following the hearing, the Review Section of Fahy's office went over the transcript and prepared the case for submission to the Board. Fahy considered the Review Section's work the most crucial aspect of preparing air-tight cases; the record boiled down from the transcript had to show beyond doubt both the facts linking the company to interstate commerce and proof of the unfair labor practice violations. Nat Witt, who headed the Review Section as Assistant General Counsel, agreed: "We worked hard in being as technically perfect in our cases as possible because we knew that we were going to be gone over with a fine-tooth comb. Not only were we facing some tough customers among members of the bar on Wall Street and other places in the country, the big-shot corporate lawyers, but we were facing, in general, antagonistic judges."[4] Witt's staff of lawyers was largely young and inexperienced, but, as Tom Emerson explained, "you could take students just out of law school, and they would be simply wizards in taking a 10,000-page record and bringing it into manageable shape and telling the Board about it."[5]

Stanley Surrey, a 25-year-old lawyer on Witt's staff who graduated from college at the precocious age of nineteen and from Columbia Law School in 1932, and who came to the Board after a stint in the NRA, was the Review Section "wizard" assigned the job of plowing through the *Greyhound* transcript and drafting the Board's decision and order.[6] Surrey's Findings of Fact on the interstate commerce question shrewdly quoted the company's advertising claim that "Greyhound Bus Lines serve more millions of people, more territory, more cities and national playgrounds than any other travel system in the United States" (drily noting that this was not "an idle boast"), and detailed the company's support of its company union, its espionage activities and hostility to the AFL union, and the events leading to the firing of each of the nine union members.[7] The Board's decision and order was among the first three cases decided on December 7, 1935.

Since company lawyers had indicated in advance their client's unwillingness to abide by the order to end its support for the company union, rehire the dismissed workers, and give them back pay and retroactive seniority, the Board quickly filed an enforcement petition with the Third Circuit Court of Appeals in Philadelphia on December 10. The NLRB lawyers then met the first roadblock in the path of their master plan. Robert

Watts, who directed the Board's litigation, approached the chief judge of the circuit court to seek an expedited hearing on the *Greyhound* case. Judge Joseph Buffington refused his request, explaining that he wished "to avoid deciding the constitutional issues presented by the case until after other appellate courts had acted upon them." Watts then brought his request before the full court, supported by affidavits from Chairman Madden and AFL president William Green, "accentuating the great public policy" issues raised by the case, but the court reiterated its timidity.[8] The Board was forced to wait more than three months before it secured a hearing on April 1, 1936.

Fahy finally discovered the reason behind the circuit court's reluctance when he argued the *Greyhound* case, eager to make the first NLRB argument himself. He confronted three judges of advanced age and diminished ability: Chief Judge Buffington was eighty-one and had been on the federal bench since 1892; his two colleagues, Oliver Dickinson and J. Whitaker Thompson, were comparative youngsters at seventy-nine and seventy-five. Tom Emerson, who accompanied Fahy to Philadelphia for the argument, recalled that the judges "had absolutely no idea of the constitutional issues involved."[9] The normally unflappable Fahy was incredulous when Judge Buffington interrupted him: after sending a clerk for a copy of the Constitution, the judge thumbed through it and asked Fahy, "Does this case involve Indian tribes?" No, the puzzled Fahy answered. "Does it involve trade with foreign nations?" No, again. "Then it must be commerce between the states," Buffington concluded triumphantly.[10] After this inauspicious intervention, the court forced *Greyhound* off the road to the Supreme Court; its stubborn refusal to rule on the case forced Fahy to go shopping for a more responsive forum before which to argue *Jones & Laughlin*, another Pennsylvania case. The court finally decided the *Greyhound* case some fifteen months later, three months after the Supreme Court upheld the Wagner Act.[11] By that time, of course, the decision in what was planned as the first NLRB test case was decidedly anticlimactic. It did show, however, that even the most carefully designed litigation strategy was subject to judicial perversity.

While the search for a substitute transportation case resumed, Board lawyers began working on the "next best" category of test cases outlined in the litigation master plan, manufacturing concerns whose business was largely interstate. On September 24, 1935, the same day that Golden reported the *Greyhound* case to Washington, regional attorney Garnet Patterson in Detroit informed the Board that he had been visited that morning by Roger MacDonald, an organizer for the United Auto Workers, and three union members at the Fruehauf Trailer Company, a leading truck-trailer manufacturer. They charged that company foremen had fired six men for union membership and threatened others with discharge if they did not quit the union: "The result of the threat was that a great number surrendered their membership books and resigned from the Union." MacDonald also told Patterson that a federal grand jury had recently voted a criminal indictment against the company on twenty charges of filing false freight tariffs with the Interstate Commerce Commission. Patterson urged the Board to authorize a complaint against Fruehauf; "proof of a flagrant discrimination is clear," he wrote, since the company "assumed a brazen attitude in the assertion of its reason for discharging the Union men instead of attempting to conceal the reason by some other excuse. For a manufacturing case, it appears that this one has some very favorable possibilities."[12]

Over the next several weeks, as he investigated the pending criminal charges against Fruehauf and interviewed discharged workers, Patterson bombarded the Board with enthusiastic recommendations that the case be given high priority. He was aided by the voluntary confession of J. N. Martin, who appeared in Patterson's office and offered to testify at a hearing that he had been hired to spy on the union.[13] The United States attorney in Detroit confirmed that Fruehauf had offered to plead guilty to the criminal charges, and he was willing to share with the NLRB evidence in the case to buttress the interstate commerce data sought by the Board. "I believe that we are in a particularly good strategic position to 'crack down' on this company," Patterson wrote Fahy. "I am convinced that this case should be one of the first that the Board handles."[14] Fahy was receptive, but cautioned Patterson on the need to compile "a complete statistical picture of the actual business of the company. . . . The interstate commerce question is difficult enough in any event, and unless we are able to show very graphically and clearly" the extent of Fruehauf's interstate transactions, "the case will look weak in the printed record."[15]

A month after Patterson's investigation began, the Board authorized the complaint, which regional director Frank Bowen quickly released to the press, explaining to the Board that the "rank and file of the plant are in a very angry mood concerning the discharges" and that he "had to assure the organizer of the Union of immediate action in order to prevent the Union from striking the plant. . . ."[16] In his press statement, Bowen emphasized that "the case is suited for a test on the constitutionality of the Wagner Act before the United States Supreme Court." The company lawyer, Victor W. Klein, vociferously denied that the discharged workers had been punished for union activities. "We don't care whether they belong to any union. However, we do claim the right to get rid of a worker who does not properly do his work." Besides, Klein told the press, the *Schechter* decision held that "manufacturing is strictly a local affair. On this basis we feel that this Act is entirely unconstitutional."[17]

To underscore the importance of the *Fruehauf* case to the Board, Madden decided to preside at the hearing on the unfair labor practice complaint, as he had in the *Greyhound* case. Before the hearing, scheduled to begin on November 6, Robert Watts instructed Patterson carefully on the presentation of evidence and cross-examination of company witnesses. Since Patterson reported that local federal judges were "inherently antagonistic to New Deal legislation," the Board decided not to use its subpoena power to compel production of company records on its interstate activities, which might provoke delaying injunction litigation, but it had ample evidence on this point from the ICC records in the criminal case.[18] Although J. N. Martin, the repetant company spy, had disappeared (taking the union's modest treasury with him), Watts urged Patterson to question company officials "as to whether or not they used the services of the Railway Audit and Inspection Company or of the Sherman Service. Each of these organizations is a notorious industrial espionage agency." If the official admitted that the company used these spy services, Watts urged Patterson to press them to produce copies of reports submitted by agents, both "to establish knowledge on the part of the company of union activity" and "to afford the Board proof of how far third party agencies are being used to circumvent the law."[19]

The Board lawyers were delighted with the ineptitude of the company lawyer and witnesses at the hearing. Victor Klein first allowed Fruehauf vice-president Earl F. Vosler to testify that the company was the largest truck-trailer manufacturer in the country, that it had 31 branch offices in twelve states, and that it shipped more than 80 percent of its products in interstate commerce. Klein then presented a futile motion to dismiss the complaint on the ground that the Wagner Act was unconstitutional. Patterson reported to Fahy that Madden "very satisfactorily backed Mr. Klein into a corner. The Chairman demonstrated thorough familiarity with the authorities dealing with interstate commerce to such an extent that [Klein] was completely flabbergasted." Klein's brief "appeared to be a series of blank pages to which were pasted clippings. I have a suspicion that said clippings came out of the brief of the National Liberty League."[20]

In his cross-examination of Vosler, Patterson forced an admission that J. N. Martin had been hired from the Pinkerton Detective Agency to spy on the union, and that he reported directly to Vosler two or three times a week. Klein objected so vigorously to this questioning that Madden threatened to expel him and Vosler from the hearing. Patterson was able, however, to fill 25 pages of the record with a full account from Vosler of the company's industrial espionage activities since 1934.[21] John Carmody, who attended the hearing with Madden, professed shock at these revelations. "We heard a good deal yesterday about fundamental Americanism and constitutionalism" from Klein, he told Vosler, "and we heard a good deal about due process. . . . Would you say if a man was discharged because he was mentioned in one of these secret reports, that that could be due process?" Vosler limply disclaimed any opinion, but Klein jumped in: "Yes. An employer is not required to have anyone in the plant that he does not care to have."[22]

Following the hearing and the Board's cease-and-desist order of December 12, which the company refused to obey, both sides filed petitions with the Sixth Circuit Court of Appeals in Cincinnati on December 17, a week after the Board brought the *Greyhound* case before the Third Circuit. At this point, the NLRB lawyers were ambivalent about how best to implement their master plan. The day before filing the *Fruehauf* enforcement petition, Robert Watts asked Patterson to seek approval from both company lawyers and the Sixth Circuit for an expedited appeal, but added that he would prefer not to promise to make an early argument "since I wish the Greyhound case to go through the Circuit Court first in order that we may docket it in the Supreme Court ahead of the Fruehauf case, if possible."[23] Within days, however, the Third Circuit judges denied the Board's application for an expedited hearing on the *Greyhound* case, and Watts changed his mind. In a letter to the Sixth Circuit clerk, he explained that the *Fruehauf* case had been fully tried by the Board and every possible constitutional objection to the Wagner Act had been raised by the company lawyer. "Not only have lawyers' committees and manufacturers' associations made public statements" attacking its constitutionality, Watts added, but districts courts had issued conflicting decisions in injunction cases. "We therefore believe that the most grave reasons of public policy justify us in asking of the Court the very earliest hearing possible. This would permit us to obtain not only a ruling of the Circuit Court on these issues, but would also permit the submission of those constitutional issues by an aggrieved party to the Supreme Court at its Spring session."[24]

A combination of factors soon forced a shift in the plan to secure an early ruling on the *Fruehauf* case. Company lawyers refused to agree on a joint record, and the court indicated its reluctance to advance the case. The major factor, however, was that on January 6, 1936, three days after Watts asked for an early hearing, the Supreme Court decided the *Butler* case and invalidated the Agricultural Adjustment Act. With this additional blow to the New Deal, NLRB lawyers prudently decided to hold off a Supreme Court test of the Wagner Act until the following session of the Court. Without revealing his motivation, Watts then wrote the Sixth Circuit clerk that "it is the wiser thing to do at present not to attempt to set the case down for argument in February, but to let it remain in regular course."[25] The *Fruehauf* case was finally set for argument on June 2.

With arguments before the circuit courts deferred in both *Greyhound* and *Fruehauf* for several months, NLRB lawyers were free to develop additional test cases at a more leisurely pace, and began looking for cases that fit into the master-plan categories. There was no question that *Fruehauf* was a good manufacturing case from the standpoint of both interstate commerce and discrimination against union members. But Fruehauf was not an industrial giant (its yearly gross income was about $3 million), and it had no history of labor violence or strikes that crippled production. The best candidate as a test case would be a corporation that met these criteria, and Clinton Golden of the Pittsburgh regional office was convinced that the Jones & Laughlin Steel Company was ideal for this purpose.

The nation's fourth-largest steel producer and "an antiunion bulwark since 1897,"[26] Jones & Laughlin had assets in 1935 of more than $181 million, and 22,000 employees. It was "a completely integrated steel manufacturer, owning iron ore, coal, and limestone properties in Michigan, Minnesota, Pennsylvania, and West Virginia, and owning railroad and barge subsidiaries. Approximately seventy-five percent of its products were shipped out of the state of Pennsylvania to its subsidiaries scattered across the country."[27] Golden was a holdover from the prior Board as regional director, and even before the Wagner Act was passed he had reported that Jones & Laughlin attempted to forestall a union organizing campaign by holding a company union election on June 19. "Company police were sent to the homes of the workers and there threatened them with discharge unless they did participate in the election," Golden wrote, adding that more than twenty workers were in fact fired. The AFL union, the Amalgamated Association of Iron, Steel and Tin Workers, boycotted the company union election and held a strike vote later in June. "There is a great deal of unrest among the employees of this Company, particularly in the Aliquippa plant, and . . . there is a very real possibility of trouble developing there," Golden concluded.[28]

In his first report to the new Board on September 24, 1935, Golden restated the earlier charges against the company and added that union leaders told him that discharges of pro-union workers had accelerated since the Wagner Act became effective, with union leaders as the primary targets at the Aliquippa plants, scattered in fourteen departments over the grimy Monongahela Valley. "There is an exceedingly vicious history of terrorism in this community," Golden added as a warning of potential violence.[29] Over the next four months, Golden and the young regional attorney, Robert H. Kleeb, interviewed discharged workers and gathered evidence on the company's domination of the company union. In the middle of January,

Kleeb reported that "it can be proven" that nine union leaders had been fired and one demoted for union activities and that "proof of the labor relations history of this Company will definitely establish its hostility towards unions and union activities."[30]

The Board issued a complaint at the end of January, charging violations of workers' rights to organize and discrimination against union members; the charge of dominating the company union was dropped. Since Madden was from Pittsburgh and had earlier served on Governor Pinchot's labor relations commission, he again decided to act as trial examiner. Jones & Laughlin hired as its lawyer Earl Reed, the drafter of the Liberty League attack on the constitutionality of the Wagner Act. Reed was too seasoned and astute to repeat the blunder committed by Victor Klein in the *Fruehauf* hearing in exposing company officials to damaging cross-examination on their use of industrial espionage services, especially because there were reports that the NLRB was pressuring Senator Robert LaFollette to sponsor a Senate investigation of corporate anti-labor practices. When the Jones & Laughlin hearings began in late February, Reed objected to the introduction of any evidence on the unfair labor practice charges before the Board ruled on his challenge to its jurisdiction. His sole witnesses were company officials who testified that only raw materials were shipped into the Aliquippa plants and that only manufacturing operations took place within them.[31]

Reed then moved that the Board dismiss the complaint: "That is all the evidence that the respondent has on the question of the interstate commerce feature of the case, and we move to dismiss, on the ground that . . . the business of the respondent is not interstate commerce, and any labor controversy, therefore, would not be within the jurisdiction of the Board." Madden predictably denied the motion, to which Reed replied that the company "takes the position that it is the sole judge of the right to hire and fire . . . and therefore, declines to offer any testimony on that subject and withdraws from the hearing."[32] Reed knew perfectly well the line of questioning the Board lawyers had prepared for company officials, and put them in the tactical dilemma of either giving up their ambush, which no longer had the advantage of surprise, or provoking a district court injunction suit by pursuing the evidence through subpoena.

Board lawyers then concluded the hearing by calling the discharged workers, who testified about the circumstances of their firings and the history of company hostility to the union. David Saposs of the Economic Research Division then acted on a suggestion made earlier by Tom Emerson, of reopening the hearings in Washington for the submission of more extensive economic data on the company and on the steel industry in general; these hearings, over which Emerson presided, were held between

April 2 and 8. Saposs also proposed summarizing the testimony of the expert witnesses in a pamphlet that could be incorporated in NLRB briefs and circulated "for the information and assistance of the courts and others" concerned with the interstate operations and labor history of the steel industry.[33] The Board's order, issued April 9, ordered the reinstatement with back pay of the ten discharged workers, and took pains to portray Jones & Laughlin as a living organism spread across the country:

"The ramifications of the Jones & Laughlin Steel Corporation are . . . as broadly extended as the nation itself. It is impossible to isolate the operations of the Works in Pittsburgh and Aliquippa or to consider them as detached, separate—'local'—phenomena. These Works might be likened to the heart of a self-contained, highly integrated body. They draw their raw materials from Michigan, Minnesota, West Virginia, and Pennsylvania in part through arteries and by means controlled by respondent; they transform the materials and then pump them out to all parts of the nation through the vast mechanism which the respondent has elaborated."[34]

Even before the *Jones & Laughlin* hearings ended, Board lawyers had begun forum shopping. The case would normally be brought before the Third Circuit Court of Appeals in Philadelphia, but, even though the disastrous argument in the *Greyhound* case had not yet taken place, Watts's earlier experience with the chief judge prompted him to suggest filing an enforcement petition in the Fifth Circuit in New Orleans. A quick investigation revealed that Jones & Laughlin owned a steel fabrication plant in New Orleans, which settled the jurisdictional question. In early April, Watts visited New Orleans and learned from the Fifth Circuit clerk that the court was scheduled to sit for one week in June; if the findings, order, and record in the case were completed by the middle of April, Watts telegraphed Fahy, "we have excellent chance argument June."[35] The enforcement petition was filed on April 9, and a second manufacturing case joined *Fruehauf* on the circuit court dockets.

II. DOTTING THE I'S AND CROSSING THE T'S

With the disappearance of the *Greyhound* case in early April into a judicial rabbit-hole, and with arguments in the two manufacturing cases deferred until June, Fahy decided to flesh out the master plan with a wider range of cases, leaving open for the moment the option of submitting them to the Supreme Court in the fall sequentially or as a package. The Board initially felt it had found a good substitute for *Greyhound* in a case in the Ninth Circuit in California. In February 1936 the Board ordered the Mackay Radio & Telegraph Company to reinstate five members of the American Radio Telegraphists' Association local in San Francisco, whom the Board found had been fired for union activities. The case was argued on April 16, and neatly fit within the master plan's category of "best" cases, since it involved interstate communications. A snag soon developed, however; the court informed the lawyers on both sides that since *Carter v. Carter Coal* was pending before the Supreme Court and might be determinative, the case would be deferred for at least sixty days to await its outcome and permit the filing of supplemental briefs. Although Fahy had predicted before the argument that the court would not "unreasonably delay this decision" and included *Mackay* in his first package of test cases, Board lawyers faced hostile questioning at the argument and quietly abandoned the case after *Carter* was decided.[36]

However, in the months preceding June, three additional cases were developed as potential test cases fitting within the master plan. Fahy had been convinced since the beginning that the Board should test its jurisdiction over small and medium-sized manufacturing companies, "where the volume of interstate inflow and outflow was small in relation to the total in the industry and insignificant in relation to the whole industrial complex of industry and commerce in the United States," as Philip Levy later said. "Mr. Fahy and the Board felt very strongly that the latter type of case should be presented to the Court fully briefed without any reservations, because they felt that the Board in its total operation would stand or fall on the victory or defeat in that type of typical case."[37]

One case that fit this category involved the Friedman-Harry Marks Company of Richmond, Virginia, which manufactured men's clothing and employed about 900 workers. The company was the target of an organizing campaign by the Amalgamated Clothing Workers union, which began in August 1935 to bring pressure on the Board to file charges against the company for harassing union activities and firing union members. In late September, regional attorney Gerhard Van Arkle wrote Fahy that the facts warranted an "immediate investigation" of the case. "Within the last ten days four active union members have been discharged. The plant is a large one and the evidence of discrimination in the case of the four recently discharged seems good."[38] Union organizers told Van Arkle during his investigation that the company president, Morton Marks, and the plant superintendent, Irving November, had been caught spying on a union meeting by peering through a window of the church in which it was held, and that the next day four union members were called in by November and "told they were discharged for attending the union meeting the night before, and were advised to go away for awhile until the trouble cleared up." Marks admitted spying on the meeting, and explained to Van Arkle that the union organizing campaign had led a large customer to withdraw an order because "it was rumored in the trade that a strike was impending within the plant."[39]

The Board issued complaints against Friedman-Harry Marks on October 26 and November 15, alleging the discharge of nineteen workers for union activities. Leonard Weinberg, the company's lawyer, refused to provide the Board any information on its interstate business or to present company witnesses at the hearing, but Board lawyers received cooperation from both the union and unionized garment manufacturers in New York, who had been hurt by competition from low-wage, non-union southern plants. Although the hearing was held on December 5, the Board held up issuance of its decision and order for almost four months, until March 26, 1936. Board lawyers at this time were deliberately holding up decisions in cases involving smaller businesses for two related reasons: first, the overall litigation strategy was still in flux; and, second, they feared that small-company lawyers might force a precipitate test case. The Board's secretary, Benedict Wolf, explained this policy in early March to a regional director who reported increasing pressure from suspicious union leaders. "The delay in issuing decisions is not caused solely by the inability to issue them at a particular time. It was extremely important that the Board be able to control to some extent the test cases which would first get to the Circuit Courts and the Supreme Court." He added that "it is undoubtedly better to put up with some discontent on the part of the unions" than for the Board to "find itself in the Supreme Court with a case which is not particularly strong on interstate commerce and involves a company so small that the courts would be disinclined to believe that the company's business could possibly affect interstate commerce."[40]

Fahy, however, considered *Friedman-Harry Marks* "the kind of case that I thought the Act was intended to apply to" and decided to add it to the package of cases taking shape under the master plan.[41] An initial problem in seeking enforcement of the Board's order was a desire to avoid the conservative Fourth Circuit Court of Appeals, within whose jurisdiction the company was located. Consequently, another forum-shopping expedition began; fortuitously, the company had a sales office in New York City and, as Fahy explained, "we wanted, frankly, to have the opinion of the Second Circuit in a manufacturing case, and we took the case there for review."[42] An enforcement petition was filed in the Second Circuit on March 28, but Leonard Weinberg retaliated three days later by filing a petition to review the Board's order with the Fourth Circuit. The Board paid a price in judicial resentment and public scorn for having barely won the race to the courthouse door. At a hearing in late April before Second Circuit Judge Learned Hand on Weinberg's challenge to the court's jurisdiction, Robert Watts was subjected to excoriation. The *New York Times* reported the exchange:

" 'Why,' Judge Hand asked Mr. Watts, 'should you try to play a trick like that?' 'Under the Act,' Mr. Watts replied, 'we have the right to choose the place for the filing of our petition.' 'The cat's out of the bag,' said Judge Hand. 'You want to keep away from the Fourth Circuit and come here where you think you may get more favorable consideration.' "[43]

The next day, after reading a story in the *Times* headlined "Court Sees 'Trick' By Labor Board," Madden felt compelled to reply with a telegram to Hand issued as a press release: "The Board very greatly deplores the false impression which this report will undoubtedly create." The law clearly allowed the Board to enforce its orders in circuits in which respondents did business, Madden reminded Hand. "We do not think that it is a trick to apply the law as it is written and we think that it is unfair for anyone to so designate it."[44] Despite its public embarrassment, the Board won its point on the jurisdictional issue: the Second Circuit upheld the Board on May 6, and set an argument on the merits in *Friedman-Harry Marks* for June 16.[45]

By the end of April it was clear that another case dealing with interstate transportation or communications was needed to replace the *Greyhound* and *Mackay* cases, both stalled in hostile and dilatory courts. Board lawyers located an acceptable substitute in the *Associated Press* case, which involved a bitter dispute between the AP and the American Newspaper Guild over the restoration of a six-day work week and reassignment of Guild activists to less-desirable night shifts. On October 18, 1935, the AP fired Morris Watson, a national vice-president of the Guild. Watson had been one of the AP's leading political reporters, but was transferred to the night shift and assigned to menial work after he represented the Guild at bargaining with the Brooklyn *Daily Eagle* and was elected to a Guild committee formed to negotiate with the AP management on the six-day-week issue. After Watson's demotion and subsequent firing, the Board's regional director in New York, Elinor Herrick, secured permission from the AP to examine Watson's personnel file. She discovered in the file a memorandum written by J. M. Hendrick, executive news editor of the AP, the day Watson was fired. "He is an agitator and disturbs morale of staff at a time when we need especially their loyalty and best performance," Hendrick wrote in recommending Watson's dismissal.[46]

Elinor Herrick reported to the Board in late November that "Watson was dismissed because of his Guild activities" after the demotion failed to provoke his hoped-for resignation.[47] The Guild filed charges with the NLRB on November 7, and a complaint was issued a month later, with a hearing scheduled for January 8, 1936. The Board's case was soon embroiled in a vociferous debate between two lions of the New York bar, whose aggressive tactics side-tracked it into a district court injunction suit. John W. Davis, a leading anti-Roosevelt Democrat and sponsor of the American Liberty League brief against the Wagner Act, represented the Associated Press. His antagonist as counsel for the Newspaper Guild, permitted to intervene in the case under Board rules, was Morris Ernst, a noted labor and civil liberties lawyer. When Ernst informed Davis that he intended to subpoena key AP officials, Davis quickly brought an injunction suit before federal district judge William Bondy. The Board hearing was postponed while Davis and Ernst clashed at a hearing before Judge Bondy on January 17, with NLRB regional attorney David Moscovitz relegated to a supporting role, arguing the constitutional issues while Ernst blasted the Associated Press for failing to satisfy the "clean hands" injunction criterion by its anti-labor policies. Heywood Broun, the acerbic columnist called by Ernst as Guild president, was denied permission to make a statement to the court following the arguments, but nonetheless shot out to Judge Bondy that "John W. Davis is asking you permission for the Associated Press to run a yellow-dog shop."[48]

Judge Bondy's reluctance to issue a ruling frustrated the lawyers on both sides, who began to inundate him with copies of conflicting decisions by other district courts in injunction suits; Fahy despaired in mid-March that it "begins to look as if his views will remain an unfathomable secret."[49] The irrepressible Broun even breached propriety by writing Bondy that his delay had "presented the Associated Press with an easement, a kind of legal laxative which works while you sleep. . . . We think your Honor should make up your mind."[50] The judge, perhaps weary of this polemical barrage, finally ruled against Davis on March 17, holding on traditional equity grounds that the Associated Press faced no "irreparable damage" if forced to wait for a circuit court decision on the merits of the case. He avoided the constitutional challenge to the Board's jurisdiction, although noting in *dictum* that Davis' argument "seems hardly tenable" in light of the *Texas & New Orleans Railroad* case relied on by Moscovitz.[51]

A Board hearing on the *Associated Press* case was set for April 8, with Dean Charles E. Clark of Yale Law School as trial examiner. Before the case was heard, Fahy cautioned Moscovitz that "care must be taken orderly to present it, and we must prove in fact as well as in law that, as Judge Bondy has decided, our hearings do not wreck anybody's business or unnecessarily expose them to unnamed and horrible injuries. You may find yourself under pressure to make a field day, but remember this is just another case being diligently and vigorously handled by a government agency."[52] At the hearing, John W. Davis followed the precedent set by Earl Reed and Leonard Weinberg and withdrew after Dean Clark denied his motion to dismiss the case on constitutional grounds. Moscovitz, with Davis gone, then presented evidence of the AP's interstate business—since it transmitted news reports to 1,200 daily newspapers across the country, this was not difficult to demonstrate—and Watson testified that his dismissal was based on his Guild activities, corroborated by Elinor Herrick's testimony that Watson's AP personnel file contained evidence of the anti-union motive behind his firing.[53] After Dean Clark supported the Board charge, the NLRB issued an order on May 21 that Watson be reinstated, and filed an enforcement petition with the Second Circuit on May 30. With the *Friedman-Harry Marks* case pending before it, the court scheduled both cases for a hearing on June 16.

The third possible test case was a late addition to the Board's docket as a replacement for the *Greyhound* case. In March 1936 the Washington, Virginia and Maryland Coach Company, which operated a bus line in the Capitol area, discharged eighteen of its employees for union activities. Although the company was small when compared with the giant Greyhound Company, there was no question about its interstate transportation involvement and the anti-union animus behind the discharges; one union member testified at the Board hearings, held between March and early May, that the company owner told him he would not recognize the union "and you can put that in your God damn pipe and smoke it."[54] The Board issued a reinstatement order on May 21. When the bus company refused to obey, Fahy recommended filing an enforcement petition with the Fourth Circuit Court of Appeals, in spite of the Board's earlier avoidance of this court in the *Friedman-Harry Marks* case. But in this case there was no alternative forum, and the petition was filed on June 6. At this time, however, the Board lawyers considered the *Coach Company* case as a back-up alternative to *Greyhound*.

The Board's master plan for selecting Supreme Court test cases had left open two options. It could approach the Court first with the strongest case on the interstate commerce question and later, assuming a favorable decision, submit cases expanding the Board's jurisdiction over smaller companies with less direct interstate commerce involvement. Alternatively, it could present a "package" of cases testing the broadest range of the Board's powers. Each approach had its advocates, but Fahy consistently favored the latter, and by the end of May 1936 the varied factors that led to the scheduling of circuit court arguments in four potential test cases between June 1 and June 16 made the decision almost academic.

The initial package that Fahy presented to the Board in April contained five cases: *Greyhound, Mackay Radio, Fruehauf, Friedman-Harry Marks*, and *Jones & Laughlin*. The first two were scratched from the list during May, with the *Associated Press* case replacing them to fill the essential

267

interstate communications slot. During May, Board lawyers were frantically engaged in preparing for arguments in three circuits, ranging from New York to Cincinnati to New Orleans. Looming ominously over their heads as they prepared briefs and rehearsed arguments was the Supreme Court challenge to the Bituminous Coal Conservation Act in the *Carter* case, which had been argued in early March. Although Fahy encouraged his staff to prepare their arguments on the assumption that an unfavorable decision in *Carter* would not invalidate the Wagner Act, the Supreme Court decision on May 18 made their task immeasurably more difficult, given the close connection of the labor provisions in the two statutes. Tom Emerson, assigned with Robert Watts to argue the *Jones & Laughlin* case in New Orleans, recalled that "we thought you'd almost have to ask the court to overrule the Carter case in order to sustain our arguments."[55] In his "wood-shedding" practice arguments before his Board colleagues, Emerson also recalled that their main suggestion was "to change my pronunciation from 'New Orleans,' which I'd always called it, to 'New Orlins,' which is what the natives apparently called the city."[56]

With the arguments in *Fruehauf* and *Jones & Laughlin* scheduled a day apart in courts separated by seven hundred miles, the Board lawyers divided their assignments. Watts sent Madden a telegram after his argument in *Jones & Laughlin*: "Court appeared friendly but anxious to see way clearly on constitutional issue. Accentuated flow theory. [Company lawyer Earl] Reed argued half hour mainly on Carter thesis."[57] Solicitor General Stanley Reed, whose native Kentucky was within the Sixth Circuit, persuaded Fahy to give him responsibility for the *Fruehauf* argument, an unusual foray by a Solicitor from the familiar precincts of the Supreme Court into the hinterland. Philip Levy, who accompanied Reed and Fahy, recalled the argument:

"I had never before seen a man of reputation and legal skill treated so roughly by judges on any bench, at least in my then limited experience. I was tremendously impressed by the way Reed took it all. He felt that it was mandatory for him as the chief law officer of the government, ultimately responsible for these cases, to try out the arguments as it were, in a court where he felt comfortable and before judges who knew and respected him. It was obvious that the rather harsh treatment and the adverse result had an influence on the Justice Department in its later formulation of the issues."[58]

Two weeks later, the day before Fahy, Madden, and Watts were scheduled to argue the *Friedman-Harry Marks* and *Associated Press* cases before the Second Circuit in New York, Fahy learned that the Fifth Circuit had ruled against the Board in *Jones & Laughlin* on June 15. In a brief *per curiam* opinion, the court held that it was bound by *Carter*. The Board, it wrote, "has no jurisdiction over a labor dispute between employer and employees touching the discharge of laborers in a steel plant, who were engaged only in manufacture."[59] Although Fahy professed to be "keenly disappointed" by this first setback, his realistic assessment was that after *Carter* "we had very little likelihood of sustaining the application of our statute to manufacturing enterprises" in the circuit courts.[60]

While he waited for the decisions in the two Second Circuit cases, Fahy began planning moves designed to leave the Board flexibility in putting together a package of test cases. Since Supreme Court rules required that the losing side in a circuit court case file a petition for certiorari within sixty days, and there was no guarantee that the Second Circuit decisions would be handed down within that time, Fahy asked Watts whether in *Jones & Laughlin* "we should ask for a rehearing from a tactical standpoint in order to keep the case alive in its present status for a longer period of time until our other Circuit Court situation has cleared up and we will have more decisions to consider as a basis for approaching the Supreme Court."[61] On June 30, in an even briefer *per curiam* decision, the Sixth Circuit turned down the Board's enforcement petition in *Fruehauf*, also citing *Carter* in holding that "the control and regulation of the relations between the trailer company and its employees in respect to their activities in the manufacture and production of trailers . . . does not directly affect" interstate commerce.[62] Again, Fahy proposed delaying tactics to keep the case alive, this time instructing the regional attorney to seek a stay of the court's mandate, "although it is not desired that motion state that certiorari will be applied for if it is possible to avoid such commitment at this time. . . ."[63]

These delaying tactics paid off in providing Fahy the time he needed to assemble the final package of test cases. On July 13, less than a month after they were argued, the Second Circuit decided the *Friedman-Harry Marks* and *Associated Press* cases. Predictably, the first was disposed of in another *per curiam* opinion based on *Carter*: "In its manufacturing, respondent was in no way engaged in interstate commerce, nor did its labor practices so directly affect interstate commerce as to come within the federal commerce power."[64] But *Carter* was distinguished in the *Associated Press* case. First, "the federal power to regulate interstate communication which constitutes interstate commerce has been established so far as the instrumentalities of interstate communication are concerned," the court held. Second, the *Texas & New Orleans Railroad* case was cited as authority for the proposition that it was "not an unreasonable method of reducing the danger of strikes, destructive of commerce, to guarantee freedom from interference to employees in those businesses where a strike would have a direct and paralyzing effect on interstate commerce."[65]

Fahy finally received the judicial *imprimatur* he had sought for a case involving the Board's power over businesses in the "best case" category of the master plan, those engaged in interstate transportation or communication. Flushed with success and eager to add a similar case to his package, he promptly sent a copy of the *Associated Press* decision to the Fourth Circuit judges, disarmingly asking them not to "consider it improper thus to address you after the argument" in the *Coach Company* case.[66] Chief Judge John Parker assured Fahy that he saw "no impropriety" in sending the decision, but the court was not hurried by the Board's expression of impatience and held off its decision for almost three months, until October 6.[67]

The only advantage to the Board lawyers in losing the manufacturing cases was that they retained control over whether and when to file petitions for certiorari with the Supreme Court. Their victory in the *Associated Press* case, however, gave this initiative to John W. Davis. Fortunately, Davis was willing to relinquish his power to upset the master plan, and Fahy quickly agreed with his request to ask the circuit court for a forty-day stay of its mandate in order to prepare a certiorari petition.[68] All the elements of the original master plan were now in place, a year after it was first drafted. But Fahy, expressing the caution of the Legal Craftsman, hesitated before committing himself. He had lingering doubts about the strength of the records in the three manufacturing cases. On July 22 he wrote Solicitor General Reed asking "to discuss rather fully with you a rather large question of policy affecting our whole statute, namely, whether it would be wise not to ask the Supreme Court" to review the manufacturing cases and to rely instead on the *Associated Press* case "to be followed, if the Act is upheld, with other cases in which it might be possible to bring before the Court a better record on commerce than the theory" on which the Board decided the manufacturing cases before the *Carter* decision.[69] Fahy's last-minute qualm was that the Board might have a better chance with cases in which strikes attributable to unfair labor practices actually had crippled production and thus "burdened or obstructed" interstate commerce.

But no such cases were available as substitutes, and Reed quieted Fahy's fear and persuaded him to go ahead. After the agreed-upon delay, Davis filed his petition for certiorari in the *Associated Press* case with the Supreme Court on September 14, and Fahy followed suit in the three manufacturing cases on September 30. After a lengthy wait, the Fourth Circuit finally decided the *Washington, Virginia and Maryland Coach Company* case in the Board's favor on October 6, relying largely on the *Texas & New Orleans Railroad* case for authority.[70] The initiative in this case rested with the company as losing party, but Robert Watts, as Madden put it, "persuaded the lawyer for this obscure little bus company that it would be a great feather in their cap to get into the Supreme Court.''[71] Company lawyers filed their petition on October 17. The Supreme Court completed its acceptance of the NLRB package when the last certiorari petition was granted on November 9.

It took little more than a year, in the face of judicial delays and internal shuffling of the deck to sort out the best cases, for the NLRB lawyers to implement their master plan. The work of the Legal Craftsmen on Fahy's staff in preparing for their Supreme Court test, Chairman Madden proudly asserted, "was extremely competently done in a very workmanlike way, with the i's dotted and the t's crossed."[72] With arguments in the five cases set to begin on February 9, the team of lawyers from the NLRB and the Solicitor General's office had exactly three months to prepare their briefs and arguments.

Chapter Thirteen

THE SUPREME COURT OPENS
ITS EYES

I. Court-Packing and Hotel Maids

During the last two months of 1936, the team of young lawyers from the NLRB and the Solicitor General's office assigned to write the briefs in the Wagner Act cases worked without respite on this grueling task. As they shuttled drafts between their offices and met periodically to argue out their differences, events taking place as close as nearby offices in the Justice Department and as far away as Flint and Atlanta were combining to produce a political and legal drama that for the next five months would overshadow their efforts.

On November 3, 1936, six days before the Supreme Court granted review in the last of the five NLRB cases, Franklin Roosevelt fulfilled Jim Farley's astute prediction that he would sweep all but two states in his reelection bid, and carried with him the most overwhelmingly Democratic congressional majority in history. Sensing early in the campaign the magnitude of his victory, Roosevelt had rejected as unnecessary the pleas of some advisors to make the Court's hostility to the New Deal a partisan issue, but within days of the election he met with Attorney General Cummings for a progress report on the secret drafting of the assault on the Court. On December 19 the Court met for its regular Saturday conference to vote on cases argued that week; the most important case on the docket involved a challenge to the state of Washington's minimum wage law for women. And on December 28 auto workers in General Motors' Fisher Body Plant in Cleveland, exasperated by the refusal of management to meet with them for collective bargaining, spontaneously sat down along the assembly line. The sit-down tactic soon spread to plants in Flint, Pontiac, Kansas City, Atlanta, and dozens of other industrial towns, small and large. Before the Wagner Act cases would be decided, almost half a million workers joined the sit-down movement, lustily singing behind their barricades: "When the boss won't talk, don't take a walk, Sit down! Sit down!"[1]

These events—the court-packing plan that emerged from Roosevelt's sessions with Cummings, the Court's review of the minimum wage case, and the wildfire spread of labor militance across the country—obviously affected the climate in which the Wagner Act cases were argued and decided. The reticence of the Court and its members forecloses any attempt to calculate the effect of these factors on the outcome of the cases with any precision. And in the fast-changing flow of events during this period, it becomes futile to untangle them in chronology. Consequently, only narrative structure justifies their separation in the account that follows. Although arguably the least important in direct impact, Roosevelt's proposal to reform the federal judiciary, denounced by its opponents as a "court-packing" plan, incontestably produced the most passion and drama in the most serious conflict between the three branches of government in this century.[2]

Ever since the Supreme Court invalidated the Agricultural Adjustment Act in the *Butler* case, early in 1936, Cummings had compiled studies of ways to end the Court's obstructionism. It was a closely guarded project; aside from Solicitor General Reed, only Cummings' personal assistant, Alexander Holtzoff, was privy to the ultimate purpose of the research. Described by Joseph Alsop and Turner Catledge as "a squat, thickly bespectacled little man with a passion for legal hairsplitting,"[3] Holtzoff was a 50-year-old career government lawyer and a specialist in federal practice and procedure. A 1911 graduate of Columbia Law School, he became Special Assistant to the Attorney General in 1924 and served in this post for twenty years before his appointment to the federal bench in Washington. In their contemporary book *The 168 Days*, Alsop and Catledge described the research process behind the court-packing plan:

"Cummings and Reed and Holtzoff took the most extraordinary precautions to conceal what they were up to. If opinions were desired from the department legal experts they were requested without explanation, and only on the specific point concerned. If data were wanted they were asked for out of the blue, and puzzled Justice Department men found themselves compiling statistics on the ages of federal judges, studying the congestion in the federal courts and collecting figures on the number of petitions of certiorari refused by the high bench without in the least knowing how all the material was to be used."[4]

Proposals to increase the membership of the Supreme Court or to restrict its jurisdiction through legislation or constitutional amendment were hardly new. In fact, the landmark decision in *Marbury v. Madison* in 1803 resulted from the removal of jurisdiction over the Federalist "midnight judges" law repealed by the newly elected Jeffersonian Congress. During the 19th century, Congress juggled the size of the Court from a low of five members to a high of ten. With the exception of its limited original jurisdiction, defined in the Constitution, the scope of the Court's appellate jurisdiction was subject to congressional limitation. As recently as the 1924 presidential election, Robert LaFollette's Progressive Party made an issue of Supreme

273

Court hostility to social and economic legislation. And since the *Schechter* decision in May 1935, New Deal members of Congress had introduced dozens of bills and constitutional amendments designed to restrict the Court's powers, including several proposals to increase its membership.

While the secret drafting went on in the Justice Department, other plans were being discussed by New Deal supporters. One of the busiest was Felix Frankfurter, who favored the constitutional amendment route. He outlined his plan in late November to his old friend Charles C. Burlingham, a patriarch of the New York bar. "I'm sure that if we are to have amending," Frankfurter wrote, "we need (1) *expansion*, through declaratory defining Amendment, of Commerce Clause, (2) *contraction*, through declaratory defining Amendment, of Due Process Clause." Among those Frankfurter suggested enlisting as drafters of the amendments were his Harvard colleague, Thomas Reed Powell, and Charles Wyzanski and Paul Freund, both now working in Reed's office.[5] Burlingham replied that he thought it inappropriate to enlist government lawyers in the project, and added "I am opposed to an amendment but I think one should be drafted all the same."[6]

Wyzanski was fully occupied with drafting the Wagner Act briefs, and Freund was equally busy, but another pair of Frankfurter protégés, Tommy Corcoran and Ben Cohen, did get involved. Perhaps to divert them and Frankfurter from the work going on in Cummings' office, Reed asked Corcoran and Cohen in late November to prepare a memorandum on the problem for him. They took a different tack than did Frankfurter; rather than suggesting the drastic step of revising the commerce and due process clauses, the two young lawyers leaned toward a proposal that had a lengthy history: that Congress be empowered to override the Supreme Court by reenacting legislation held unconstitutional. Earlier proposals differed widely on the mechanics of such a process (some would require reenactment by two successive Congresses; others would permit overriding only of 5-4 or 6-3 decisions), but their proponents agreed that the approach that Frankfurter and others favored raised the frightening prospect of major surgery on the heart of the Constitution and risked upsetting the massive body of precedent behind these central clauses.[7] Frankfurter had no strong commitment to either approach at the time. Cohen visited him in Cambridge in mid-December, after which Frankfurter wrote Reed that "we spent a good part of the day in canvassing the possibilities, and the problems they raise, should there be the need for constitutional reform." They agreed on the amendment approach, Frankfurter reported, without indicating a preference for either version. "We even agreed when and where you should come in—and how," he added.[8] Reed's reply indicated agreement with the second alternative: "The consensus [on] an amendment permitting an unchallengeable reenactment of legislation held unconstitutional . . . has my adherence."[9]

Corcoran and Cohen labored during December producing a memorandum, submitted to Reed early in January, which proposed an amendment permitting Congress to override Supreme Court decisions by a two-thirds majority at once and by a simple majority after an intervening election. Their work was futile, since Cummings had already made up his mind in early December to reject the amendment approach as too slow and cumbersome. As he went over the material prepared by Holtzoff, he recalled that in 1913 then-Attorney General McReynolds recommended to Congress that when any lower-court federal judge failed to retire at age seventy the President should be able to appoint another judge with precedence over the older one. "This will insure at all times," McReynolds wrote, "the presence of a judge sufficiently active to discharge promptly and adequately all the duties of the court."[10] Cummings saw no reason not to apply this argument to the Supreme Court as well. By Christmas, without consulting Reed, he sold the plan to Roosevelt. As finally fleshed out in the bill submitted to Congress, the President would be authorized to appoint up to fifty new federal judges, one for each sitting judge who failed to resign or to retire within six months of his seventieth birthday. No more than six could be added to the Supreme Court, or two in each circuit court.[11]

Roosevelt held his annual White House dinner for the federal judiciary on February 3, with all the members of the Supreme Court in attendance except the reclusive Brandeis and Stone, who was ill. By tradition, judicial matters were not discussed at this social event, and not a hint of the court-packing plan was disclosed. Two days later, Roosevelt sent it to Congress. The presidential message itself did not directly mention the potential increase in Supreme Court membership; this was buried in the accompanying bill prepared by Cummings. Roosevelt's message was clothed in concern for the judicial workload: "The simple fact is that today a new need for legislative action arises because the personnel of the Federal judiciary is insufficient to meet the business before them."

He noted that in the past year the Court had declined to grant petitions for certiorari in 695 of 803 cases presented for review by non-governmental litigants. "Many of the refusals were doubtless warranted. But can it be said that full justice is achieved when a court is forced by the sheer necessity of keeping up with its business to decline, without even an explanation, to hear 87 percent of the cases presented to it by private litigants?" Roosevelt added that more than ten percent of the life-tenured federal judges were over seventy years old, with those on the district and circuit court benches eligible to retire at full pay, and he proposed extending this benefit to Supreme Court justices as well. In what would provide a rallying point for the plan's opponents, Roosevelt expressed his resentment toward reactionary decisions on the basis of age rather than principle:

"The modern tasks of judges call for the use of full energies. Modern complexities call also for a constant infusion of new blood in the courts. . . . A lowered mental or physical vigor leads men to avoid an examination of complicated and changed conditions. Little by little, new facts become blurred through old glasses fitted, as it were, for the needs of another generation; older men, assuming that the scene is the same as it was in the past, cease to explore or inquire into the present or the future."[12]

Roosevelt blundered in basing the rationale for his plan on two demonstrably false premises. First, there was no evidence that the Supreme Court docket was clogged with a backlog of cases. When Chief Justice Hughes finally shed his reluctance to embroil the Court in the controversy, yielding to pressure from Senator Burton Wheeler, he centered his response on this issue. In a letter to the Senate Judiciary Committee, Hughes cited Court statistics to show that the Court "is fully abreast of its work," with "no congestion of cases upon our calendar."[13] Second, Roosevelt's equation of age with incompetence deeply wounded Hughes and Brandeis, at eighty still one of the most productive members of the Court. There were, as Fahy discovered in arguing the *Greyhound* case before the Third Circuit Court of Appeals, elderly judges with a tenuous grasp of constitutional issues. But, given the intellectual and physical vigor of many older judges, it was an issue quickly pounced on as an evasion of the ideological motivation behind the plan.

Within days, as support from all but the most die-hard New Dealers evaporated, Roosevelt realized his miscalculation and countered with a Fireside Chat addressing the real issue: "The Court has been acting not as a judicial body, but as a policy-making body" whose decisions in *Butler* and other New Deal cases "thwart the will of the people."[14] But the damage had been done and was irreparable. The political storm provoked by the court-packing plan has been well documented, and is relevant here only as it formed part of the highly charged background against which the Wagner Act cases were argued and decided within two weeks of its submission. One factor, however, bears mention: Roosevelt's decision to attack the Court on the age issue rather than through the amendment alternative was made in total secrecy, with only Cummings to guide him. Had Frankfurter and lawyers in the Justice Department and other agencies been consulted, the process might have been slower but less politically damaging. On the other hand, the assault on the sacrosanct Court produced exactly the result that Frankfurter intended with his first constitutional amendment proposal: in *West Coast Hotel* (the state minimum wage case) the Supreme Court contracted the reach of the due process clause in economic cases, and in *Jones & Laughlin* it expanded the scope of the commerce clause.

The irony of *West Coast Hotel* is that the New Deal lawyers who struggled during the long winter days (and nights) to distinguish *Schechter* and *Carter* were unaware that only the accident of Justice Stone's illness prevented them from learning that the Supreme Court had already initiated the "constitutional revolution." The barricades of laissez-faire fundamentalism, however, would not topple until Stone recovered and until the Court announced its decision on March 29, 1937, almost two months after the Wagner Act cases were argued. Had the New Deal lawyers known the outcome of the Court's preliminary vote on *West Coast Hotel* in its conference on December 19, they would have been spared many sleepless nights and much anxiety. In that conference, Justice Roberts deserted the conservative bloc he had joined in an almost identical case just six months earlier. When his crucial vote in *West Coast Hotel* was belatedly announced, the timing of the decision—some six weeks after the court-packing plan became public—gave birth to the popular quip that his vote was "the switch in time that saved nine." In reality, the famous "switch" reflected not the prod of the court-packing plan but th' aptness of Mr. Dooley's aphorism that "the Supreme Court reads th' iliction returns."

Since few decisions in the Court's history have been so misinterpreted, the background of *West Coast Hotel* is instructive. On June 1, 1936, two weeks after it struck down the Guffey Act in the *Carter* case, the Court invalidated a New York minimum wage statute for women in *Morehead v. Tipaldo*, with Roberts in the five-man majority. In 1923, an equally narrow majority (with Chief Justice Taft writing the dissent) had held unconstitutional on "liberty of contract" grounds a federal statute setting minimum wages for women in the District of Columbia in *Adkins v. Children's Hospital.*[15] Thirteen years later, with the Depression intervening, Dean Acheson argued on behalf of New York that its statute could be distinguished from the earlier one. In avoiding a direct challenge, Acheson was following Felix Frankfurter's characteristically cautious advice. But it was an impossible task; the two laws were virtually identical. Dismissing Acheson's vain attempt to distinguish them, Justice Butler went on to reassert the "liberty of contract" doctrine in its most arid and pristine laissez-faire form:

"The right to make contracts about one's affairs is a part of the liberty protected by the due process clause. Within this liberty are provisions of contracts between employer and employee fixing the wages to be paid. In making contracts of employment, generally speaking, the parties have equal right to obtain from each other the best terms they can by private bargaining. Legislative abridgement of that freedom can only be justified by the existence of exceptional circumstances. Freedom of contract is the general rule and restraint the exception.''[16]

Butler's intransigent reaffirmation of Social Darwinism provoked two overlapping dissents. Hughes, joined by the three liberals, attempted to thread the needle by distinguishing *Adkins*. Stone, in a separate dissent joined by Brandeis and Cardozo, went further in a frontal attack on *Adkins*:

"There is a grim irony in speaking of the freedom of contract of those who, because of their economic necessities, give their service for less than is needful to keep body and soul together. . . . In the years which have intervened since the Adkins case we have had opportunity to learn that a wage is not always the resultant of free bargaining between employers and employees; that it may be one forced upon employees by their economic necessities and upon employers by the most ruthless of their competitors.''[17]

More than any other decision by the Court during the New Deal period, *Morehead* unleashed a barrage of criticism from conservatives as well as from liberals. In his press conference the next day, Roosevelt said that the combination of *Carter* and *Morehead* made it clear that "the 'no-man's-land' where no government can function is being more clearly defined.'' Between them, he told the press, the two decisions crippled both the state and federal governments.[18] Frankfurter wrote Stone that he placed the blame on Hughes for allowing Roberts to retreat from the pro-regulation stance expressed in the *Nebbia* decision, written two years earlier by Roberts: ". . . the Chief must bear a very considerable part of the responsibility in having encouraged the process of disregard of the judicial function that lies between the Nebbia and the Tipaldo cases.''[19] More unexpected was conservative reaction. Irving Brant, the respected *St. Louis Star-Times* editorialist, caustically wrote that "Because five is a larger number than four, and for no other reason, the law is unconstitutional.''[20] The most important and explicit repudiation came in the 1936 Republican platform, which pledged the party to seek "the adoption of state laws . . . to protect women and children with respect to maximum hours, minimum wages, and working conditions. We believe that this can be done within the Constitution as it now stands.''[21]

In October, on the same day that it denied a petition for rehearing in *Morehead*, the Court agreed to review a Washington state law setting minimum wages for women in *West Coast Hotel v. Parrish*. Since the statute was again virtually indistinguishable from that in *Adkins*, this was a highly unusual move. Roberts, who voted with Hughes and the three liberals to hear the case, later explained his action in a memorandum to Frankfurter: Acheson had not directly asked in *Morehead* that *Adkins* be overruled, but in the *West Coast Hotel* case it "was definitely assailed and the Court was asked to reconsider and overrule it. Thus, for the first time, I was confronted with the necessity of facing the soundness of the *Adkins* case.''[22] This was a disingenuous rationale, since no canon of construction prevented the Court from deciding a case on constitutional grounds not presented by counsel. In any event, on December 19, two days after arguments were concluded, Roberts voted with Cardozo, Brandeis, and Hughes to sustain the Washington statute. Since Stone was ill with a long bout of amoebic dysentery, this created a four-four tie. Although a tie vote would have upheld the statute and Stone's views were known to all the justices, Hughes decided to hold the case over until he returned.[23]

Although accounts differ as to whether Stone added his vote to the majority a day or two before or after Roosevelt announced the court-packing plan on February 5, it is immaterial since Roberts' switch effectively decided the case in mid-December. Hughes delayed issuing the opinion until late March, to avoid suspicion that the Court was immediately capitulating in the face of the court-packing plan, but when he did read it to a packed courtroom there was no doubt that the due process pillar of laissez-faire doctrine had fallen. "We think that the question which was not deemed to be open in the Morehead Case is open and is necessarily presented here," Hughes wrote. In light of "the close division by which the decision in the Adkins Case was reached, and the economic conditions which have supervened," it was "imperative" that it be reconsidered. His first thrust demolished the "freedom of contract" doctrine:

"What is this freedom? The Constitution does not speak of freedom of contract. It speaks of liberty and prohibits the deprivation of liberty without due process of law. . . . But the liberty safeguarded is liberty in a social organization which requires the protection of law against the evils which menace the health, safety, morals and welfare of the people. . . . What can be closer to the public interest than the health of women and their protection from unscrupulous and overreaching employers?"

Citing Roberts' views on due process as stated in *Nebbia*, Hughes added that *Adkins* "was a departure from the true application of the principles governing the regulation by the State of the relation of employer and employed." The impact of the Depression presented an "additional and compelling" reason to overturn *Adkins*, starkly showing the "exploitation of a class of workers who are in an unequal position with respect to bargaining power and are thus relatively defenseless against the denial of a living wage. . . . Our conclusion is that the case of Adkins v. Children's Hospital . . . should be, and it is, overruled.''[24] Finally forced into dissent, the four reactionaries petulantly responded with a veiled but pointed attack on Roberts' integrity. A judge's oath, they wrote, "cannot be consummated justly by an automatic acceptance of the views of others which have neither

279

convinced, nor created a reasonable doubt in, his mind. If upon a question so important he surrender his deliberate judgment, he stands forsworn."[25] Roberts earned this enmity by ending more than fifty years of the reign of substantive due process. His vote in *West Coast Hotel* cleared half of the "no-man's land" of its legal landmines. Now only the half occupied by the commerce clause remained to withstand the final assault.

II. THE TRIUMPH OF MR. ZEITGEIST

Insulated from these outside events, the brief-drafting process in the Wagner Act cases continued at a feverish pace for more than two months. The burden fell largely on five young lawyers: Tom Emerson and Philip Levy of the NLRB; and Charles Wyzanski, Charles Horsky, and Abe Feller of the Solicitor General's office. Wyzanski took the lead in this group of young lawyers who shared ties of age and expertise. They also shared the tie of training at the elite law schools; Emerson at Yale, Levy at Columbia, and the latter three at Harvard. Consequently, they worked closely and harmoniously on a personal level. But their institutional loyalties, and the different emphases stressed by Fahy and Stanley Reed, generated points of conflict, although not nearly to the extent of the dispute that erupted between Reed and Donald Richberg during oral argument of the *Schechter* case before the Supreme Court and embarrassed them both.

The major point of conflict stemmed from the perception by the NLRB lawyers that the Justice Department wanted to concentrate on the "winnable" *Associated Press* and *Coach Company* cases involving interstate communications and transportation, in which the Board was upheld by the circuit courts. Levy felt that his counterparts "saw little hope that we could win in other cases."[26] The approach advocated by Reed was to stress the "stream of commerce" doctrine of the expansive line of commerce clause cases such as *Stafford v. Wallace* and *Chicago Board of Trade v. Olson*. But Fahy disagreed. The Wagner Act, in his opinion, "was intended to apply to any manufacturing concern, whether or not a great stream of commerce was involved, if there was a significant amount."[27] His fear was that an overbalanced stress on the "stream of commerce" theory might encourage the Court to limit the Board's jurisdiction to transportation and communication cases, or at most to those manufacturing industries with a significant inflow of raw materials and outflow of manufactured goods. Fahy urged that the briefs balance the emphasis on the volume of interstate commerce with the disruptive impact of labor strife. This approach would allow the Court to get around the restrictive cases holding that manufacturing was not commerce. "There's nothing quite more local, considered alone, than if you fire a man for union activity," Fahy said.

"But if you fire a man for union activity, that leads to a strike and interstate commerce is obstructed. And in order to prevent that, you protect it from happening."[28]

As Emerson noted, the "stream of commerce" theory "was not really logically consistent with the strike theory." But the Justice Department, he felt, "was rather desperately trying to produce a theory which the Court could rely on without feeling that it had to go all the way to the logical elements of the strike theory."[29] The two positions were not irreconcilable, but the NLRB lawyers were apprehensive that their attempt to "try for the whole shooting match in this set of test cases," could be undercut if the Justice Department's approach dominated the briefs. To resolve these differences, Reed called a conference that included the lawyers working on the briefs as well as Fahy, Madden, and Calvert Magruder and Thomas Reed Powell. Levy recalled that "it was all in good humor and Reed was very amenable" to Fahy's position. Reed said that "he saw no reason why every argument that any one of us felt strongly about should not be included."[30] Fahy was, in fact, a late convert to the "strike theory." He had earlier shied away from the word "strike" itself, urging John Dickinson not to use it in his argument in the *Carter* case; that circumspect approach had failed so miserably that, in light of the sit-down movement raging across the country, it no longer seemed to Fahy so provocative a term.

The outcome of the conference was the adoption of what Levy called "a trifurcated approach to this infinitely difficult argument. . . ."[31] As reflected in the *Jones & Laughlin* brief, it began with an argument focused on the effect of labor strife in a "far-flung, integrated enterprise," which would be "likely to spread to other enterprises for the purpose of stopping shipments out of all plants in order to bring pressure to bear upon the industry as a whole." In these large-scale cases, the NLRB would presume an intent to directly obstruct interstate commerce. The second argument did not depend on the "magnitude" of the industry, but measured a company's size "in relation to the industry as a whole" and "whether it is within a stream or flow of commerce." The impact of labor strife in such cases would depend, not on the intent of strikers to directly obstruct commerce, but on whether the potential curtailment of production would have the "necessary effect of burdening or obstructing interstate commerce. . . ." The third argument expressed Fahy's concern with the limitations of the first two. It would focus attention on "the prevention of certain activities, even though usually only of local concern, which recur with such frequency as to constitute an undue burden on commerce. . . ." The Board would thus be able to deal with unfair labor practices in any industry "where those practices and burdens are reasonably found constantly to recur."[32] What most distinguished this argument from the other two was

281

its stress on the Wagner Act as a preventive rather than a remedial statute. This was an argument "which we advanced vigorously" as the best way to stretch the act to cover smaller industries with only a minimal involvement in interstate commerce, Levy said.[33] As finally written, the briefs somewhat uneasily accommodated the positions of both sides, leaving the Court free to stop at any rung of the ladder.

One further issue complicated relations between the two groups of lawyers. During its first two years, the Board deliberately avoided deciding cases involving the duty to bargain prescribed in Section 8(5) of the Wagner Act. Fahy felt that once the courts sanctioned the negative prohibitions against interference with union organizing it would be easier to impose the positive requirement to bargain in good faith, with the union as the exclusive representative of the employees. The lawyers in the Solicitor General's office, however, were simultaneously writing a brief in the *Virginian Railway Company* case, dealing with a provision of the Railway Labor Act of 1926 requiring management to "treat with" the union elected by its workers. Since the NLRB had no jurisdiction over the railroad industry, the Board lawyers had no role in writing this brief. The Justice Department lawyers, feeling constrained by existing case law and the equivocal legislative history of the Wagner Act on the duty to bargain issue, were willing to concede in the railroad case that employers were free to make individual contracts with workers as long as they recognized the union as the bargaining agent regarding wages, hours, and working conditions. A further concession, however, upset the NLRB lawyers. The railroad case brief said that the statute did not prevent the employer "from refusing to make a collective contract and hiring individuals on whatever terms the carrier may by unilateral action determine."[34] Not only did this threaten to undermine the duty to bargain provision of the Wagner Act, but Justice Department lawyers urged its inclusion in all six briefs. "This did raise the hackles of the Board," Levy recalled. "We felt that it was a very serious limitation—one that would lead to endless difficulties in the development of collective bargaining."[35]

Fahy succeeded in excising this concession from the Wagner Act briefs, but its inclusion in the railroad case brief returned to haunt the Board. The railroad case was decided two weeks before the Wagner Act cases, and Hughes in *Jones & Laughlin* approvingly quoted in it the damaging sentence: "The Act does not compel agreements between employers and employees. . . . It does not prevent the employer from 'refusing to make a collective contract and hiring individuals on whatever terms' " it desired.[36] It took the Court almost a decade to repudiate Hughes' *dictum* inviting employers to resist the majority rule and duty to bargain provisions of the Wagner Act, and the NLRB lawyers resented the overly cautious concession of their counterparts.[37] With the exception of this significant conflict, however, the Wagner Act briefs satisfied both sets of lawyers that the arguments that mattered most to them were presented in their strongest form.

The Supreme Court arguments in the Wagner Act cases began on February 9, 1937, with an eager crowd on hand looking for hints of the Court's reaction to the court-packing plan. Solicitor General Reed first concluded the arguments begun the day before in the *Virginia Railway* case. Eleven lawyers would address the Court over the next three days in the five NLRB cases, seven representing the employers and four arguing for the government. In the first group, John W. Davis for the Associated Press and Earl Reed for Jones & Laughlin were the undisputed stars and bore the brunt of the attack on the Wagner Act. The government lawyers distributed their assignments so that both the NLRB and Justice Department were represented in the two cases that they agreed were most significant; Fahy and Wyzanski shared the *Associated Press* argument, and Stanley Reed and Warren Madden argued the *Jones & Laughlin* case. Reed was "quite taken aback" by Madden's request to join the argument, since Madden had acted in a sense as both prosecutor and judge in the case before the Board, as trial examiner and chairman of the NLRB, but Reed finally acceded to his request.[38] In the other three cases, Fahy and Wyzanski also joined to argue the *Friedman-Harry Marks* case, Fahy argued the *Coach Company* case alone, and Reed argued the *Fruehauf* case.

Before Davis rose to begin the first argument, there was a moment of tension. Morris Ernst, lawyer for the American Newspaper Guild, which had filed a brief in the Associated Press case as *amicus curiae*, took the podium to plead for twenty minutes to speak for the Guild as "the real party at interest" in the case. Ernst had earlier asked the Justice Department for permission to speak, explaining that it would allow the Court to see that "the case is not one of a big bureaucratic United States Government oppressing a single employer" but one of "a large employer oppressing a single employee." The "working people of the country," Ernst added, "will never really understand why they are denied an opportunity to be heard in the Supreme Court."[39] Reed refused this earlier request, and again declined before the Court to give up any of the government's time.

After tolerantly observing this brief disruption, John W. Davis began dissecting the Wagner Act in the florid style of the old-school orator. He would not challenge the merits or wisdom of trade unionism or collective bargaining, he assured the Court; he did challenge "the power of the Federal Government to make collective bargaining compulsory in all the industries of this country." He would not dispute that the Associated Press was engaged in interstate commerce; he argued that "as to its editorial employees their duties are no more interstate commerce than that of a draftsman engaged in drawing plans for a steel mill or the tenders of looms in a textile factory." Finally, he said, the case did not turn on the reason behind the discharge of Morris Watson. "He was an employee at will for no fixed term, and both he and the employer had the right at law to terminate that relationship whenever they saw fit. . . ."

Davis directed his fire particularly at the government's "stream of commerce" theory. "We hear again and again of the 'throat' cases," he said. "There is no throat here. There is no current here. We do not sit like the stockyards, abreast a current of commerce which other men are trying to conduct. . . ." The AP's editorial employees, he argued, were engaged solely in the "production" of news, with its dissemination in interstate commerce the responsibility of management. Davis ended by cloaking himself with the First Amendment: ". . . those who publish and print the news must have the right to choose the people by whom the news is to be written before it is printed." Invoking the specter of Nazi and Communist press restrictions, he asked: "[W]hat more effective engine could dictatorial power take than to name the men who shall furnish the food of facts upon which the public must feed?"[40]

Wyzanski, in response, was restrained and precise. Since Davis acknowledged that the AP was engaged in interstate commerce, the only commerce clause question was whether the Board had the right to prevent industrial strife that burdened it. After canvassing the history of labor strife in the communications and transportation industries and of congressional attempts to limit it, Wyzanski relied on the *Texas & New Orleans Railroad* precedent as the capstone of his argument that Congress had power to prevent discrimination against union activities from disrupting interstate commerce in transportation and communications.[41] Fahy's following argument stressed the nature of the rights that the Board was established to protect. The Wagner Act "requires that the employer be not permitted to use his overwhelming economic power over the individual employee . . . as a weapon to destroy the right of self-organization. . . . Unless that right may be protected by law there is only the recourse to strike in order that it may be protected by combat."

Fahy labeled Davis' First Amendment argument as specious. The AP retained all its rights to gather and publish news, he said; it simply could not "raise the first amendment as a shield behind which it may claim the right to stand protected while it stifles the freedom of the individual employee. . . ." His response to Davis' claim that the Wagner Act would make collective bargaining "compulsory" showed Fahy's aversion to a forthright defense of the "duty to bargain" issue. This provision was not invoked against the AP, he said; it was separable from the other provisions of the Act; and a decision on its validity "would seem clearly unnecessary" until raised by a Board order. Fahy felt compelled to answer Davis' sweeping assertion, but only to defer the issue to a later time.[42]

Government counsel spoke first in *Jones & Laughlin* as the losing side in the court below, and Madden began much like the law professor he was, with a detailed recitation of the facts, stressing the nationally integrated scope of the company's productive process. He emphasized the argument favored by the Board lawyers, that the act was preventive in nature. Forcing the Board to wait until a strike broke out and curtailed production, Madden said, was a "counsel of despair" that would actually make more likely the resort to strikes.[43] It was Stanley Reed's companion argument that most clearly exposed the conceptual gulf between the two sets of government lawyers, tenuously bridged in the briefs. He told the Court that "collective bargaining is not the ultimate end of this act. . . . It is, from our point of view, a regulation of commerce. It deals with labor relations as they directly affect commerce." Reed was seeking to escape from the *Carter* decision, and he disavowed any suggestion that it be overruled. In making this point, he came close to destroying Fahy's argument extending Board jurisdiction to smaller industries engaged in "recurring" practices that obstructed commerce, by stressing that the Wagner Act did not deal with labor relations by themselves but only those practices with the "intent or the necessary effect of interfering with commerce. . . ." Recurring practices, he added, were subject to prohibition only if they were intended to or necessarily obstructed commerce. Having subsumed Fahy's attempt to reach the full limits of the Board's power under the more limited arguments drafted by his staff, Reed was promptly backed into a corner by Justice Sutherland; the curtailment of production brought about by an industrial strike was its primary effect, was it not? When Reed agreed, Sutherland reminded him that it was precisely the distinction between that primary effect and the secondary impact on interstate commerce that doomed the government in *Carter*. Reed quick-wittedly attempted to collapse the two into an "instantaneous" result, but Sutherland continued to insist on the two-step distinction.[44]

Earl Reed, in his *Jones & Laughlin* argument, was too rigidly locked into his laissez-faire ideology to recognize and exploit the subtle but potentially disabling schism in the government's arguments. None of the other company lawyers was any more perspicacious then Reed. His argument was simple and blunt: the Wagner Act was an attempt by Congress "to force national organization in industry." He hammered away at the dangers to "the traditions and precedents of a century," citing *Adair* and *Coppage* as holding "flatly" that "a man had a right to hire whom he wished, and that a statute which forbade the discharge of an employee for

285

union activities was unconstitutional.'' This appeal to the old ''yellow-dog'' cases, for Earl Reed, settled the issue.[45]

The government lawyers were obviously afraid that potentially sympathetic members of the Court were more astute than the seven company lawyers. During the argument in *Friedman-Harry Marks*, the last of the five cases, Wyzanski took pains to repair the breach in their ranks. He returned to the question of ''whether or not this act may be so applied as to cover all industry and labor in the country'' in order to ''develop the lines of possible distinction'' between the three arguments in the briefs. Pointing to their summarization at the beginning of the *Jones & Laughlin* brief, Wyzanski noted that ''there is a distinct difference between the enterprises'' involved in the three manufacturing cases. The vast size and integrated nature of the steel company's operations, in the event of labor strife, ''would be bound to involve intentional interference with interstate commerce'' by striking workers. Thus the first argument in the brief would apply to an industry of this size. In the *Fruehauf* case, the relative importance of the company in the industry would allow the Board to apply the ''necessary effect'' principle, the core of the second argument. But with smaller businesses such as Friedman-Harry Marks, it would be the fact that ''labor disputes recur frequently'' that would constitute the test of the Board's jurisdiction. ''If that doctrine be accepted,'' the cautious Wyzanski later wrote Frankfurter, ''it is admittedly the broadest of the doctrines with which I dealt.''[46] If not mended, the breach was at least patched over to the satisfaction of the NLRB lawyers.

After his Supreme Court arguments, Wyzanski reported to Frankfurter that ''for weeks Abe Feller, Charlie Horsky and I had written or talked six labor briefs to death (or perhaps to life). Any one of the three of us could without a note have told what was in the records, what the difficulties in the cases were, and how we thought they could have been resolved.'' Wyzanski regretted the paucity of questions from the bench; Roberts had been ''rather ominously silent'' and ''his interest clearly flagged in the Government's arguments as they proceeded.'' But Stone's intentness gave Wyzanski hope for a divided Court in *Jones & Laughlin*, and he predicted victory in the *Associated Press* and *Coach Company* cases.[47] It is a measure of the pull of professionalism that Wyzanski, denounced by the Wagner Act's chief draftsman, Leon Keyserling, as a saboteur before its passage, made a ''tour de force'' in its defense, as Tom Emerson judged Wyzanski's performance before the Supreme Court.[48]

Although momentous in their impact both on constitutional doctrine and on labor relations, the decisions handed down on April 12, 1937 in the Wagner Act cases were in a sense anticlimactic. Two weeks earlier, the Supreme Court signaled the beginning of the ''constitutional revolution'' with its decisions in *West Coast Hotel* and the *Virginia Railway* case, in which the Court sustained the collective bargaining provisions of the Railway Labor Act, the Wagner Act's older cousin. Those waiting for the Wagner Act decisions were merely listening for the other shoe to fall. Nonetheless, the drama of the occasion drew more than a thousand spectators on a warm spring day, hoping to find a place among the 220 seats in the red-curtained courtroom.

Tom Emerson sat impatiently through the Court's preliminaries as he waited to see which justice would announce the decision. It was neither a conservative nor a liberal. The Chief Justice himself, without a glance at the audience, sent the second pillar of constitutional fundamentalism crashing into the rubble of the due process clause. "It was an amazing performance," Emerson recalled. "Hughes thundered out the decision with his beard wagging. You would have thought that he was deciding the most run of the mill case, that the law had always been this way, that there had never been any real dispute about it, and that he was just applying hundreds of years of decisions to a slightly new kind of situation, with no recognition whatever that there was any change taking place. And he did it with an air of absolute confidence, as if the Constitution had always been construed this way."[49]

Speaking for the same five-man majority that decided *West Coast Hotel*, Hughes read the opinions in all three manufacturing cases. At this turning-point in constitutional history, Hughes barely looked back at *Schechter* and *Carter Coal*, noting only that the distinction between interstate and intrastate commerce remained "vital to the maintenance of our federal system." His only nod at the "traditions and precedents of a century" evoked by Earl Reed was to acknowledge that the Wagner Act did not "interfere with the normal exercise of the right of the employer to select its employees or to discharge them." But the heart of Hughes' opinion was his recognition of the reality of a national economic system:

"We are asked to shut our eyes to the plainest facts of our national life and to deal with the question of direct and indirect effects in an intellectual vacuum. . . . When industries organize themselves on a national scale, making their relation to interstate commerce the dominant factor in their activities, how can it be maintained that their industrial labor relations constitute a forbidden field into which Congress may not enter when it is necessary to protect interstate commerce from the paralyzing consequences of industrial war?"

To the NLRB lawyers, the greatest significance of the opinion was that Hughes adopted without reservation the position that Fahy persuaded Stanley Reed to add to the briefs. The power of the Board, Hughes said, "is not limited to transactions which can be deemed to be an essential part of a 'flow' of interstate or foreign commerce." Activities which "may be intrastate in character when separately considered" could sufficiently obstruct commerce to warrant regulation. The Board was thus free to impose its jurisdiction on every business substantially engaged in interstate commerce. As noted earlier, Hughes took back some of the Board's power by quoting from the Justice Department's brief in the *Virginia Railway* case the sentence that left the duty to bargain provision in doubt.[50]

Significantly, the opinions in *Fruehauf* and *Friedman-Harry Marks* raised no question of the extent of the Board's jurisdiction; they merely stated the essential facts and cited *Jones & Laughlin*. Justice McReynolds, the most crusty and acerbic member of the conservative bloc, wrote an opinion for the four dissenters covering all three manufacturing cases. He made no attempt to hide his outraged feelings. A news reporter described the scene: "Old McReynolds was sore as hell, . . . poking his pencil angrily at the crowd as he shouted his opinion, without reading it, and his speech was a good deal different from the written one."[51] In his opinion, he rested on *Schechter* and *Carter* on the commerce clause issue, and *Adair* and *Coppage* on the due process question, unwilling to the last to abandon "liberty of contract" doctrine: "The right to contract is fundamental and includes the privilege of selecting those with whom one is willing to assume contractual relations. This right is unduly abridged by the Act now upheld. A private owner is deprived of power to manage his own property by freely selecting those to whom his manufacturing operations are to be entrusted."[52]

Roberts wrote the majority opinion in the *Associated Press* case, and disposed of all but the First Amendment issue on the basis of *Jones & Laughlin*. The Board's order, he added on that issue, did not restrict the right of the AP "to publish the news as it desires it published" and left it free to fire Watson or any other employee for any reason except for union activities. Justice Sutherland wrote for the four dissenters that a publisher should be able to ensure the "fairness and accuracy" of his news accounts by eliminating employees with the "strong prejudice" that union membership might produce.[53] Overlooked by the press in its emphasis on Hughes' opinion in *Jones & Laughlin* was the fact that the Court unanimously sustained the Board's powers in the *Coach Company* case; even the four conservatives were unwilling, as their constitutional edifice crumbled about them, to deny the irreducible minimum of NLRB jurisdiction over interstate transportation.[54]

The Wagner Act decision buoyed the spirits of New Deal lawyers within and outside the NLRB, and helped to erase the gnawing sense of futility that clouded their prior four years of hard but unavailing work. The NLRB lawyers naturally felt vindicated in the success of their master plan. Under

Charles Fahy's exacting supervision, they functioned as Legal Craftsmen; dedicated to the purposes of the Wagner Act and to the rights of labor, they were as much meticulous technicians as partisan advocates. They winnowed and selected cases with care; scrutinized records with a fine-tooth comb; chose courts with a shopper's discriminating eye; and wrote briefs to draw the issues narrowly and precisely. But they were also favored by circumstance in two major ways. They had learned from the errors and overconfidence of their colleagues (and themselves) in earlier, less fortunate New Deal agencies. And, most important, when they came before the Supreme Court they rode on a tide of forces for change which the Court could no longer resist.

Charles Wyzanski, perhaps the most cautious and critical of the New Deal lawyers, best expressed the forces behind their success: "Right along I have said that the cases were won not by Mr. Wyzanski but either by Mr. Roosevelt or, if you prefer it, by Mr. Zeitgeist."[55]

THE LIMITS OF LEGAL LIBERALISM

New Deal lawyers faced their litigation tasks with an entirely different perspective in the years that followed the "constitutional revolution" of 1937. For four years they had entered courtrooms on the defensive, to face opposing lawyers armed with an arsenal of restrictive precedent and a generally hostile federal bench. Between 1937 and 1942 they moved to the offensive, conducting a mopping-up operation designed to stretch to the limits the regulatory powers affirmed by the Supreme Court in *West Coast Hotel* and *Jones & Laughlin*. By the end of this period, a reconstituted Court had upheld not only every New Deal program that it had earlier struck down (with the significant exception of the industrial code scheme of the NIRA) but also every element of the reform package enacted by Congress during the "Second New Deal" that followed Roosevelt's shift in emphasis in 1935 from business self-regulation to direct federal regulation. Only a rear-guard of the original group of New Deal lawyers, joined by a battalion of new recruits, remained behind to argue this second round of cases. The majority of their colleagues left for the rewards of private practice, uniquely qualified by their New Deal experience to guide corporate clients through the regulatory maze they had helped to construct.

A brief review of the second-generation New Deal cases will illustrate the almost illimitable scope given the due process and commerce clauses once the Supreme Court abandoned their restrictive readings. The first of these opinions involved the Social Security Act passed by Congress in August 1935, and came only six weeks after *Jones & Laughlin*. Two cases raising challenges to this statute were on the Court's docket at the time the Wagner Act was upheld. The first challenged Title IX of the Act, designed to prod the states into enacting unemployment compensation laws by imposing a one percent tax on the payrolls of employers with more than eight workers. Employers in states with federally approved programs would receive a federal tax credit of ninety percent of what they paid into the state programs. A small Alabama company sued the federal government to recover $46.14 it had paid into the federal fund under protest. Charles Wyzanski of the Solicitor General's office and Assistant Attorney General Robert H. Jackson argued the case the week before *Jones & Laughlin* was decided. A month later Wyzanski and Jackson argued the second case, which involved a challenge to Title VIII of the Act, a far-reaching program to establish a federal old-age pension program and similarly based on a one percent payroll tax.

Wyzanski's argument in these cases was designed to exploit, in the atmosphere that followed approval of wage and hour legislation in *West Coast Hotel*, the opening provided by the Court the year before in *Butler*, the AAA case, for the Hamiltonian position that Congress could use its taxing power to provide for the "general welfare." The Hamiltonian theory advanced by the New Deal lawyers in *Butler* had been rejected solely because the Court held that regulation of agricultural production was not within the enumerated powers of Congress. On May 24, 1937 the Court decided both social security cases in the government's favor, adopting without reservation the Hamiltonian position on the taxing power. In opinions written by Justice Cardozo, with *West Coast Hotel* as a due process foundation and *Butler* as scaffolding, Cardozo completed the Court's construction of the Hamiltonian position as a constitutional edifice. "It is too late today for the argument to be heard with tolerance that in a crisis so extreme the use of the monies of the nation to relieve the unemployed and their dependents is a use for any purpose narrower than the promotion of the general welfare," he wrote in the unemployment compensation case, *Steward Machine Co. v. Davis*.[1] And, in the old-age pension case, Cardozo added that the Court's new conception of the general welfare clause was not a "static" one: "Needs that were narrow or parochial a century ago may be interwoven in our day with the well-being of the Nation. What is critical or urgent changes with the times."[2]

The first of the social security cases marked the last time the "Four Horsemen of Reaction" voted together as a bloc in a New Deal case. The conservative group on the Court began to disintegrate even before the decision was announced; on May 18, the day the Senate Judiciary Committee nailed shut the coffin of Roosevelt's "court-packing" plan with its formal report of disapproval, Willis Van Devanter submitted his resignation, effective at the end of the term. Roosevelt had been forced to wait more than four years for his first opportunity to name a member of the Court. Within the next four years he would place an indelible stamp on the Court by filling seven of its seats.* Roosevelt also changed the com-

---

* Only Owen Roberts, who resigned two months after Roosevelt's death in April 1945, and Harlan Fiske Stone, who replaced Hughes as Chief Justice in 1941 and who sat until 1946, remained on the Court at the end of the Roosevelt era. Alabama Senator Hugo Black replaced Van Devanter in August 1937; Stanley Reed moved from the Solicitor General's rostrum to the seat vacated by George Sutherland in 1938; Felix Frankfurter joined the Court when Benjamin Cardozo died later that year; William O. Douglas shortly assumed the seat left empty by the resignation of Louis Brandeis; Frank Murphy, the Michigan governor who succeeded Homer Cummings as Attorney General in 1938, moved to the Court a year later after the death of Pierce Butler; South Carolina Senator James Byrnes replaced the last of

position of the lower federal courts; between 1933 and 1945 he appointed 194 judges to the federal courts of appeals and district courts. By 1945 Roosevelt appointees constituted 67 percent of the appellate bench and 59 percent of the district bench.

The Supreme Court contained a New Deal majority in 1940 when government lawyers appeared before it to argue the constitutionality of the Bituminous Coal Act. After the Court struck down the Guffey Act in 1936 in *Carter Coal*, disapproving its labor provisions, Congress had responded by reenacting the statute almost unchanged two weeks after the *Jones & Laughlin* decision. Like its predecessor, this revived attempt to impose order on the chaotic coal industry incorporated price-fixing and production control provisions through an NRA-type code, with non-code producers subject to a prohibitive 19½ percent tax. Robert L. Stern, who had fashioned the government's brief in the earlier coal case, boldly cited Justice Cardozo's dissenting opinion in *Carter Coal* as authority in this second try, *Sunshine Anthracite Coal*. Stern's audacity paid off, as Justice Douglas rested his opinion on the "eloquent testimony" in Cardozo's dissent that the "history of the bituminous coal industry is written in blood as well as in ink." In upholding the statute, Douglas noted its regulatory shift from industry to government initiative: "The commerce clause empowers [Congress] to undertake stabilization of an interstate industry through a process of price-fixing which safeguards the public interest by placing price control in the hands of its administrative representative."[3] Having learned its delegation lesson from *Schechter*, Congress now lived in harmony with the Court.

In two final New Deal cases decided in 1941 and 1942, the Court followed Stern to the end of the road that he had blazed in 1934, in making the commerce clause a congressional freeway. The first of these cases, *United States v. Darby*, involved the Fair Labor Standards Act of 1938, through which Congress set national floors below wages and hours. To put enforcement teeth in the statute, Congress had included a provision forbidding the interstate shipment of goods produced under "substandard labor conditions." In defending this provision, Stern and his Justice Department colleagues directly challenged the Court to overrule *Hammer v. Dagenhart*, which stood squarely in the path of federal wage and hour control. *Darby* was ironically reminiscent of the *Belcher* case, withdrawn by the Justice Department in 1935 just before its scheduled argument. Defendants in both cases were southern sawmill operators charged with

---

the "Four Horsemen" when James McReynolds resigned early in 1941 (and was in turn replaced by law school dean Wiley Rutledge after just one term, when Byrnes tired of the Court and returned to government); and Robert Jackson, Murphy's successor as Attorney General, joined the Court in 1941 after Stone replaced Hughes as Chief Justice.

wage and hour violations; however, the price-fixing provision of the NRA code that the Department feared putting to a test in *Belcher* had now been sanctioned by the Court in the *Sunshine Coal* case. In his opinion in *Darby*, Justice Stone accepted Stern's argument, presented to the Court by Solicitor General Francis Biddle, that congressional power to regulate commerce was limited only by direct constitutional prohibitions. Stone also accepted Stern's challenge to *Hammer*: "The conclusion is inescapable that *Hammer v. Dagenhart* was a departure from the principles which have prevailed in the interpretation of the Commerce Clause both before and since the decision and that such vitality, as a precedent, as it then had has long since been exhausted. It should be and now is overruled."[4]

The opinions in *Sunshine Coal* and *Darby* vindicated the lawyers who had worked in the NRA. The last of the New Deal cases, *Wickard v. Filburn*, similarly vindicated their AAA colleagues. Congress had reenacted the essential features of the Agricultural Adjustment Act in 1938 in a statute with the same name. A similar system of marketing quotas enforced its production control feature, which was challenged by an Ohio farmer who had grown several acres of wheat in excess of his quota. Filburn alleged that this wheat was produced solely to feed his poultry and cattle and that none of the excess production was destined for interstate commerce. Stern directed the briefing and Robert Jackson, who had argued the commerce clause points in *Sunshine Coal* two years earlier, now wrote the Court's opinion, which finally extended Chief Justice Marshall's economic nationalism to its full reach. Filburn's home-consumed wheat, Jackson held, might well have "a substantial influence on price and market conditions" beyond his farm. Even if it was never marketed, "it supplied a need of the man who grew it which would otherwise be reflected by purchases in the open market. Homegrown wheat in this sense competes with wheat in commerce."[5] In adopting the flexible test of "substantial influence" on commerce (first pressed by Justice Stone in his *Carter Coal* dissent), Jackson finally erased the increasingly faint line between "direct" and "indirect" effects on commerce as a standard, planting a precedential seed later harvested in civil rights cases in the 1960s.

The Court's mopping-up in the last round of New Deal cases took place during a period of profound transition in its basic agenda. The discretion given the Court to exercise its powers of review through the grant of certiorari allows virtually unlimited discretion in setting an agenda, as the conflicts of one era are settled and concern shifts to those of the next. During the period from 1937 to 1942, as the issues of economic reform and regulation became settled, the demands of a newly mobilized and insistent group emerged. Black Americans, largely ignored by the New Deal, chafed under Roosevelt's paternalistic policies, which had offered a modicum of economic relief during the Depression but failed to challenge entrenched patterns of racial segregation perpetuated in most New Deal programs. The significant event of this period was the threat by A. Philip Randolph, the black president of the Sleeping Car Porters union, to lead a massive march on Washington in 1941 unless Roosevelt moved to end discrimination in defense employment. This mass mobilization, which won a partial victory, forced the country to confront the segregation issue.[6]

Although its record in cases raising racial issues was mixed, the Hughes Court manifested a concern with the plight of blacks and other minorities, particularly in criminal due process cases; its condemnation of lynch law in the Scottsboro Boys case stood out as a beacon of concern for human rights. The Court first signaled the historic shift in its agenda, from economic regulation to civil rights and liberties, through a footnote to an obscure New Deal case decided in 1938. The *Carolene Products* case involved the Filled Milk Act, passed by Congress in response to dairy industry pleas to outlaw the addition to milk products of such non-nutritive "fillers" as coconut oil. In rebuffing a due process challenge to the statute, Justice Stone adopted a standard of judicial deference in the review of "regulatory legislation affecting ordinary commercial transactions" when the legislative finding of facts behind such laws "rests upon some rational basis within the knowledge and experience of the legislators." But Stone went far beyond this exposition of the standard of "minimal rationality" to outline in *dictum*, in his famous Footnote Four, a standard of "more exacting judicial scrutiny" in the review of legislation in two areas. The first involved "legislation which restricts those political processes which can ordinarily be expected to bring about repeal of undesirable legislation," under which rubric he included laws that restricted the rights of voting, dissemination of information, political organization, and peaceful assembly. Similarly suspect would be legislation directed at particular religious or nationality groups, racial minorities, and other "discrete and insular minorities" who had suffered histories of prejudice or exclusion from the political process.[7]

World War II delayed the full impact of Footnote Four and its implications for blacks. But when civil rights cases reached the Supreme Court in the decade that followed the war (culminating the long-range litigation strategy devised in the early 1930s by such patient but determined NAACP lawyers as Nathan Margold, Charles Houston, and Thurgood Marshall), New Deal cases helped to provide a precedential foundation. Robert L. Stern played a key role in this litigation; one of his last efforts before leaving the Solicitor General's office for private practice in 1954 was to press his reluctant superiors to file a strong *amicus* brief placing the government on the side of the black appellants in *Brown v. Board of Education* and its companion cases.[8] Although the school segregation cases arose under state law and were decided under the Fourteenth Amendment's equal protection clause, later civil rights cases raised the commerce clause issue for which Stern had prepared a modern construction.

In two decades in government practice, Stern preached the gospel according to John Marshall in Supreme Court briefs, with *Gibbons v. Ogden* as his text. In his first exegesis of commerce clause doctrine in 1934, Stern could conceive of only one business too local to fall under federal regulation: barbershops.[9] By the mid-1960s, even barbershops came within the scope of the federal civil rights statutes. And in the first case to reach the Supreme Court after congressional passage of the 1964 Civil Rights Act, the Court adopted Stern's argument that business practices that burdened interstate commerce, no matter how local in nature, were subject to federal regulation. Upholding the prohibition of racial segregation in places of public accommodation in the *Heart of Atlanta Motel* case, the Warren Court began its commerce clause analysis with *Gibbons* and concluded with a New Deal trinity—*Jones & Laughlin, Darby*, and *Wickard*—finding a moral dimension in the economic sphere:

"In framing [the public accommodation section] of this Act Congress was . . . dealing with what it considered a moral problem. But that fact does not detract from the overwhelming evidence of the disruptive effect that racial discrimination has had on commercial intercourse. It was this burden which empowered Congress to enact appropriate legislation, and, given this basis for the exercise of its power, Congress was not restricted by the fact that the particular obstruction to interstate commerce with which it dealt was also deemed a moral and social wrong."[10]

Merged with the demands of the civil rights movement, this aspect of the New Deal legacy served a liberating and progressive purpose. Yet, much like the Progressive era from which it drew inspiration, the New Deal legacy imposed a concomitant restraint on those whose interests it purported to serve. The inchoate ideology of the New Deal lawyers took the form of a uniquely modern brand of legal liberalism, fusing the reformism of the Roosevelt era to the regulatory state that it generated. Legal liberalism, in furthering federal power to ensure a basic standard of living and to counter the erratic swings of the business cycle, depended for its implementation on the administrative-legal process as a system of institutionalized conflict resolution between contending interest groups. Beneficent in purpose and sensitive to the deprivations suffered by "discrete and insular minorities," legal liberalism nonetheless abhorred unstructured and potentially divisive movements that sought to redress grievances and to achieve autonomous power outside the framework of the administrative apparatus of the regulatory state. Its stress on administrative expertise and procedural regularity and finality produced a deep-rooted antipathy toward dissent that overflowed the banks of the administrative canal.

The classic exposition of legal liberalism appeared in 1938 (the year of Footnote Four) in James Landis' book, *The Administrative Process*. Active during his troubled career as a regulator, corporate lawyer, and law school professor and dean at Harvard, Landis despaired of the "sicknesses" that afflicted the economic system in the Depression. His prescription was to place competition under "the fostering guardianship of the state. The mode of exercise of that guardianship [is] the administrative process." In Landis' view, administrative power represented the only feasible response to "the demand that government assume responsibility . . . to provide for the efficient functioning of the economic processes of the state."[11] The functional rationalization of economic relations, justified as the necessary curative to the crisis of the Depression, easily extended its reach under this vision to the management of labor relations, racial conflicts, and other disruptions of the social fabric.

Louis Jaffe, a New Deal lawyer who became Byrne Professor of Administrative Law at Harvard, added a political dimension to legal liberalism in his influential casebook: "The administrative process has, during the last one hundred years, been the characteristic instrument of political and economic reform." By defining "reform" as "the use of new forms to redistribute or to create new centers of social power," Jaffe absorbed political militance and redistributive conflicts into the state-run administrative apparatus. This perspective quite naturally led Jaffe to conclude, in lauding the NLRB for its administrative-judicial form, that American workers have exhibited a "frivolous unconcern for political or organizational method." Legal liberalism thus read out of history the New Deal struggle of unorganized workers to gain autonomous power and to force independent recognition of their unions from employers. As Jaffe put it, creation of the NLRB "was a signal demonstration of the phenomenon of transferring power by the creation of a new jurisdiction."[12] The conclusion, self-evident to Jaffe, was that the power to channel labor militance into the administrative forum best served the interests of the workers.

Legal liberalism is a largely unarticulated ideology, and, like its first cousin, legal realism, encompasses a disputatious family. Landis' certitude in administrative efficacy has been abandoned by his cohorts, as was Jerome Frank's realist stress on judicial psychologizing. Even Jaffe, its most prolific and scholarly expositor, admits to the growing "disillusionment" with the administrative process in practice, in particular the fusion of regulatory and judicial functions in its commission form.[13] There are recent signs that legal liberalism may have reached its limits. The New Deal regulatory structure is in disarray, and deregulation is the current political fever, infecting liberals as well as conservatives.[14] The lawyers now on the offensive work for corporations and corporate-financed groups such as the Mountain States Legal Foundation, dedicated to the dismantling of environmental, consumer protection, and safety and health agencies. Significantly, the litigation strategies of the anti-New Deal lawyers have attempted to revive *Schechter* and the delegation doctrine from decades of disuse. Broad delegations of authority, of course, underlie the administrative apparatus, and New Deal lawyers welcomed the departure from the Supreme Court of those who obstructed it. In his assessment of the Hughes Court, Michael Parrish found it understandable that "New Dealers, flushed with enthusiasm for eliminating the abuses of business and finance, bitterly resented" *Schechter* as a judicial intrusion into the "administrative process which they associated with the triumph of public virtue and disinterested expertise."[15]

As recently as 1974, Justice Thurgood Marshall pronounced the *Schechter* doctrine "as moribund as the substantive due process approach of the same era . . . if not more so."[16] But *Schechter* shows signs of rising from the grave and returning to haunt those who wrote its obituary. It stirred in 1980 in a Supreme Court opinion holding invalid, under authority delegated by the Occupational Safety and Health Act, the Secretary of Labor's action in setting standards for worker exposure to benzene, a widely used carcinogen linked to leukemia. In a suit that pitted the labor movement against industry, Justice Stevens deftly side-stepped the constitutional issue raised by the American Petroleum Institute, although his plurality opinion agreed that the "toxic substance" section of OSHA "might be unconstitutional" under *Schechter*. Such shilly-shallying could not lure Justice Rehnquist into the majority, and his concurring opinion urged the resurrection of the delegation doctrine:

"We ought not to shy away from our judicial duty to invalidate unconstitutional delegations of legislative authority solely out of concern that we should thereby reinvigorate discredited constitutional doctrines of the pre-New Deal era. . . . Indeed, a number of observers have suggested that this Court should once more take up its burden of ensuring that Congress does not unnecessarily delegate important choices of social policy to politically unresponsive administrators."[17]

Rehnquist obviously intended the irony of citing as authority for these comments a passage from the autobiography of a noted New Deal lawyer, William O. Douglas, a *mea culpa* in which Douglas confessed that "freewheeling administrators . . . should be more closely confined to specific ends or goals" by Congress.[18]

The New Deal lawyers left an impact not only on legal thought but on their profession as well. Robert L. Stern was one of the few who remained in government practice at the end of the Roosevelt administration. What of his compatriots, the "boys with their hair ablaze" who flocked to Washington in the 1930s, impelled by idealism and opportunity? The subsequent career patterns of the New Deal lawyers who played a role in this study illustrate, in their considerable diversity, the range of uses to which government practice could be put. As they dispersed from the New Deal agencies they took with them a unique expertise in the regulatory process, a skill of great value to a profession whose clientele deals with state and federal regulatory agencies. Of the eighty-two lawyers whose later careers could be traced, close to two-thirds moved into private practice, most often in large, big-city firms. A substantial number established their own firms in Washington and New York, guiding clients through the maze of federal statutes and regulations they had helped to draft, administer, and interpret.

The regulatory apparatus created by the New Deal and vastly expanded during and after World War II generated a new kind of law firm, the "insider" firm whose partners were adept at statutory drafting, regulatory interpretation, the administrative hearing process, and lobbying. The firm founded by Tommy Corcoran is a prototype of the "insider" firm; Corcoran and his partners all had New Deal experience, generally in the Securities and Exchange Commission whose statute Corcoran helped to draft. Abe Fortas, Paul Porter, and Thurman Arnold, who all worked in the AAA, founded another powerful Washington firm that now employs more than a hundred lawyers. Other New Deal lawyers who set up Washington firms include Norman L. Meyers and J. Howard Marshall of the Petroleum Administrative Board, whose firm concentrates on oil industry clients; Ashley Sellers and James L. Fly, of the Justice Department's Antitrust Division; David A. Morse and Gerhard Van Arkle, of the NLRB. The prestigious firms that antedated the New Deal absorbed other lawyers with regulatory expertise; Charles Horsky and Hugh Cox of the Solicitor General's office, for example, joined Covington & Burling, the powerhouse of Washington firms.

The stock in trade of the "insider" firms is the easy access their partners enjoy to agency administrators and lawyers. "Any Washington lawyer who is worth his salt and who has practiced in Washington for any length of time," Charles Horsky has written, "will have at least a speaking acquaintance with many of the staff in any agency where he may specialize." This access, Horsky added, "will make it easier for him to arrange a conference, or to obtain a hearing for his client, or to discuss and discover the agency's position on particular matters that may come up."[19] Access to the levers of power, of course, can slip over the bounds of aggressive client representation to the shadier practices of influence peddling. Washington lawyers, for example, often participate in congressional "mark-up" sessions at which legislation directly affecting their clients is drafted in supposedly closed committee sessions.

New Deal lawyers also set the pattern of recruiting young associates from lawyers who serve an apprenticeship in regulatory agencies and other government law offices. In 1981, at least half of the partners in most of the Washington "insider" firms had worked for two years or more in federal agencies. In Arnold and Porter, thirteen of the fifty-seven partners came from the Justice Department, most in the Antitrust Division, and twenty of the remaining partners had worked in other agencies. Half of the fourteen partners in Tommy Corcoran's firm had worked in the SEC; close to half of the sixty-six partners at Hogan & Hartson had prior government experience, spread across five cabinet departments and the gamut of regulatory agencies. Federal law practice has become a form of taxpayer-subsidized graduate education, with the benefits reaped by corporate clients.

Of the New Deal lawyers who passed up the rewards of corporate practice, career patterns varied considerably. Twelve of the eighty-two in this group remained in government service as civil service lawyers. Another half dozen, most with NLRB experience, crossed the corporate fence to represent unions. Another dozen followed a scholarly bent and left practice for (or combined it with) law school teaching, generally at the elite schools from which they graduated. Erwin Griswold and James Landis, both New Deal lawyers, served as dean of Harvard Law School, and the Harvard faculty included Paul Freund, Stanley Surrey, Louis Jaffe, Henry Hart, and Milton Katz. Tom Emerson joined the Yale faculty, where he pursued his early civil liberties interests and became a leading First Amendment scholar, and Milton Handler and Telford Taylor joined the Columbia law faculty. The remaining fourteen reached the federal bench at some point in their careers. Stanley Reed, Robert Jackson, and Abe Fortas (along with another New Deal lawyer, William O. Douglas) gained appointment to the Supreme Court. Two of the New Deal general counsel, Jerome Frank and Charles Fahy, sat on the federal appellate bench, Frank after service on the SEC and Fahy after leaving the NLRB to become Solicitor General. They were joined on the appellate bench by Calvert Magruder, Harold Stephens, and Simon Sobeloff. Charles Wyzanski, Alexander Holtzoff, Pierson Hall, and Howard Corcoran left their New Deal posts for the federal district bench. Donald Richberg, the third New Deal general counsel, became the only real apostate; the former labor lawyer established a corporate practice in Washington and turned on the unions he once represented in several polemical attacks on "union monopoly."[20]

The most striking change in Washington since the New Deal era has been the vast expansion of the federal bureaucracy and the concomitant growth of the nation's largest law firm, the federal government. When the New Deal began, the Justice Department's Antitrust Division, then responsible for the bulk of the government's civil litigation, employed 36 lawyers. As antitrust enforcement revived in the late 1930s, the Antitrust Division gained separate status and a Civil Division was formed with a catch-all jurisdiction; by 1980 the two divisions were roughly equivalent in size and between them employed close to 600 lawyers in Washington alone. The NLRB, which began with a legal staff of 14 in 1935, employed 226 lawyers by 1939 and by 1980 its staff included 400 lawyers in its Washington headquarters and another 100 in its regional offices. When Jerome Frank became general counsel of the AAA he had a staff of 10; the Agriculture Department has a current total of 190 lawyers in Washington. Altogether, the number of federal lawyers has grown from some 2,000 in 1933 to more than 20,000 in 1981, a ten-fold expansion in a population that has only doubled in size over the same period. Lawyers have become indispensable in the regulatory state, but whether they function to facilitate its dealings with citizens, or merely reflect its growth and increasing complexity, is a matter of sharp debate.

Five decades have passed since the "plague of young lawyers" settled on Washington. They unsettled administrators, fought among themselves, incurred the wrath of politicians, sparred with judges, and stumbled on their path to the Supreme Court. But as they gained experience and achieved their final victories in the courts, they left an ineradicable mark on the legal profession and in the government. The luster of their idealism is tarnished, exposed to the corrosion of age and success, although it shines brightly in contrast to the cynicism and opportunism of the present era. Law serves politics in any period, but politics is now regulation, and regulation is now the province of the lawyer. Legal Politicians, Legal Reformers, and Legal Craftsmen—each model of the legal style is evident among government lawyers in every succeeding period of our history. But the prototype of each model can be found among the band of New Deal lawyers.

---------------------------- *Notes* ----------------------------

A number of frequently cited sources have been abbreviated in the notes. Those abbreviations are listed below:

CLMOH	Cornell Labor-Management Oral History
COHC	Columbia Oral History Collection
FDRL	Franklin D. Roosevelt Library
—— OF	Official File
—— PSF	President's Secretary's File
HLSL	Harvard Law School Library, Manuscript Division
LC	Library of Congress, Manuscript Division
NA	National Archives
—— RG	Record Group

INTRODUCTION

1. 295 U.S. 495 (1935); 297 U.S. 1 (1936); 301 U.S. 1 (1937).
2. See Barber, *Presidential Character*, and "The Interplay of Presidential Character and Style: A Paradigm and Five Illustrations," in Greenstein and Lerner, eds., *A Source Book for the Study of Personality and Politics*, 386.
3. This group of ninety-five lawyers includes those who were directly involved in the litigation discussed in this book; a good many other lawyers in these agencies, of course, participated in the litigation of other cases. The biographical data scattered through the book has been compiled from a number of sources, which include the *Martindale-Hubbell Directory of Lawyers; Who's Who in America; Who Was Who; Current Biography*; obituaries in the *New York Times*; and personal correspondence.
4. The percentage of lawyers in each agency whose law school graduation date was 1925 or after is as follows: NRA, 67 percent; AAA, 76 percent; NLRB, 68 percent; and Justice Department, 42 percent. The percentage of Harvard, Yale, and Columbia graduates in each agency is as follows (Harvard graduates in parentheses): NRA, 43.8 percent (12.5); AAA, 72 percent (57.7); NLRB, 66.7 percent (38.1); Justice Department, 54.4 percent (43.8). In other words, AAA lawyers were the youngest and Justice Department lawyers the oldest; the AAA was the most Harvard-dominated and the NRA the least.
5. See Purcell, *The Crisis of Democratic Theory*, Chs. 5 ("Legal Realism") and 9 ("Crisis in Jurisprudence").
6. Course data is drawn from Columbia Law School catalogs, 1925-1935.
7. Course data is drawn from Yale Law School catalogs, 1925-1935. For a discussion of legal realism at Yale in the 1920s and 1930s, see Schlegel, "American Legal Realism and Empirical Social Science: From the Yale Experience"; "American Legal Realism and Empirical Social Science: The Singular Case of Underhill Moore."
8. Course data is drawn from Harvard Law School catalogs, 1925-1935. Sutherland, *The Law at Harvard*, provides an authorized history of the law school and some discussion of faculty and curricular issues during this period. There is, so far, no good study of legal education during these crucial decades.
9. See the excellent capsule sketch of Frankfurter's career in Lash, *From the*

Diaries of Felix Frankfurter, 3-98. A recent and highly provocative psycho-biography of Frankfurter, labeling him "a textbook case of a neurotic personality," is Hirsch, *The Enigma of Felix Frankfurter*, which discusses his New Deal role in Ch. 4. Frankfurter's own recollections of this period, in *Felix Frankfurter Reminisces*, are largely unrevealing and occasionally unreliable.

10. On Frankfurter's role in the "Red Scare," see Irons, " 'Fighting Fair': Zechariah Chafee, Jr., the Department of Justice, and the 'Trial at the Harvard Club,' " See also Frankfurter, *The Case of Sacco and Vanzetti*.

11. Lash, *From the Diaries of Felix Frankfurter*, 24.

12. Freedman, ed., *Roosevelt and Frankfurter*, 27.

13. Id., 111-112.

14. Frankfurter, *The Public and Its Government*, 145. Frankfurter's lifelong interest in British law and government flourished through his friendship with Harold Laski, who studied under him at Harvard Law School and later taught at Harvard College.

15. There is a notable paucity of studies of the political context of federal litigation; for brief discussions of the Justice Department, see Horowitz, *The Jurocracy*, and Weaver, *Decision to Prosecute*.

16. Peek, *Why Quit Our Own*, 20.

17. Quoted in "Felix Frankfurter," *Fortune*, January, 1936, 63.

18. In 1940 the House of Representatives established a Special Committee, headed by Howard Smith, a reactionary Virginia Democrat, to investigate the NLRB. For an account of these hearings and Fahy's role in defending his staff, see Gross, *The Making of the National Labor Relations Board*, Vol. II (not published at this writing).

19. Horowitz, *The Jurocracy*, 2.

20. Frankfurter to Stone, July 12, 1933, File 13, Box 171, Frankfurter Papers, HLSL.

21. The demographic data on judges is drawn from Chase, *Biographical Dictionary of the Federal Judiciary*.

22. For biographical sketches of the members of the Hughes Court, see Schlesinger, *The Politics of Upheaval*, 454-467.

CHAPTER 1

1. Stern, "The Commerce Clause and the National Economy," 653.

2. Quoted in Friedel, *FDR: Launching the New Deal*, 12.

3. Schlesinger, *The Coming of the New Deal*, 91-92, 95; Hawley, *The New Deal and the Problem of Monopoly*, 22-23.

4. Kolko, *Main Currents in Modern American History*, 107 (see especially ch. 4, "The Political Economy of Capitalism in Crisis"). For an extended treatment of this topic, see Kolko, *The Triumph of Conservatism*. See also Weinstein, *The Corporate Ideal in the Liberal State*.

5. On the history of antitrust policy and law, see Letwin, *Law and Economic Policy in America*, and Dewey, *Monopoly in Economics and Law*.

6. *Standard Oil Co. of New Jersey v. United States*, 221 U.S. 1 (1911). See also Letwin, *Law and Economic Policy in America*, 253-265; and Dewey, *Monopoly in Economics and Law*, 179-182.

7. See Hawley, *The New Deal and the Problem of Monopoly*, 36-43.

8. See Nash, "Experiments in Industrial Mobilization: WIB and NRA."

9. Rosenman, ed., *The Public Papers and Addresses of Franklin D. Roosevelt*, I, 624-625.

10. Hawley, *The New Deal and the Problem of Monopoly*, 7. Historians have applied different labels to the schools of economic thought during the New Deal. Schlesinger divided them into "planners" and "atomizers" (*Crisis of the Old Order*, 426); Hawley identified three groups: those who believed in a "business commonwealth" based on government sanctioned cartels; advocates of a "collectivist democracy engaged in purposeful national planning"; and those who favored the "competitive model of classical economics" and stressed antitrust enforcement (Hawley, 36-51). The "planners" represented in the New Deal by Rex Tugwell were, in fact, distinct from the corporatists and Brandeisians, but their position had no influence on litigation positions and the opposed constitutional theories.

11. Javits, *Business and the Public Interest*, 19. Several leading New Dealers exhibited an initial corporatist fervor. Sen. Robert Wagner felt that "unbridled competition has led us to ruin," and decried the antitrust tradition as an outmoded "restraint theory of law." Keyserling, "The Wagner Act," 222-224. Attorney General Cummings said in 1933 that the "competitive ideal . . . no longer seems valid as a free working law based on economic stability and social unity," and viewed "cooperation . . . even induced—as the way of least resistance. . . . " Speech to American Bar Association, August 31, 1933, Box 10, RG 9, NA.

12. Himmelberg, *The Origins of the National Recovery Administration*, 75.

13. *Maple Flooring Ass'n v. United States*, 268 U.S. 563, 582-583 (1925).

14. Hawley, *The New Deal and the Problem of Monopoly*, 23-25, 153.

15. Quoted in Schlesinger, *Crisis of the Old Order*, 38.

16. See Mason, *Brandeis*, generally. "Regulation," Brandeis wrote in 1913, "is essential to the preservation of competition and its best development." Quoted in Pollack, *The Brandeis Reader*, 174.

17. See Brandeis to Frankfurter, January 4, 1923 and November 20, 1923, in Urofsky and Levy, eds., *Letters of Louis D. Brandeis*, V, 84-85, 104-105.

18. Brandeis, *The Curse of Bigness*.

19. *Liggett Co. v. Lee*, 288 U.S. 517 (1933) (Brandeis, dissenting in part).

20. Quoted in Fusfeld, *The Economic Thought of Franklin D. Roosevelt*, 219-220.

21. Martin, *Madame Secretary*, 260.

22. Hawley, *The New Deal and the Problem of Monopoly*, 25. For accounts of the NIRA drafting process, see Hawley, 21-25; Schlesinger, *Coming of the New Deal*, 92-93; Moley, *After Seven Years*, 187.

23. National Industrial Recovery Act, 48 Stat. 195 (1933).

24. Moley, *After Seven Years*, 187. Hugh Johnson described the NIRA to a cabinet-level meeting in 1933: "This is a guild-government law." Transcript of meeting of Special Industrial Recovery Board, September 11, 1933, Box 249, Stephens Papers, LC.

25. Wyzanski to Frankfurter, May 21, 1933, File 003043, Box 150, Frankfurter Papers, LC.

26. Wyzanski to Frankfurter, May 24, 1933, NRA file, Box 159, id.

27. Frankfurter memorandum, "The National Industrial Recovery Bill and Wage Standards," May 30, 1933, id.

28. *Congressional Record*, Vol. 77, Part 5 (73rd Cong., 1st Sess.), 5345. Sen. Champ Clark of Missouri added that it was "absolutely foolish to talk about protecting the little fellow when we are turning him over by this very act . . . to the head of the largest concern in each industry." Id., 5239.
29. Id., 5152-5154, 5243-5246.
30. Id., 5154-5156.
31. Id., 5155-5156.
32. Id., 5156; U.S. Cong., Senate Finance Committee, *Hearings on S. 1712 and H.R. 5755* (73rd Cong., 1st Sess.), 6-7.
33. National Industrial Recovery Act, §2(a) and (b), 48 Stat. 195 (1933).
34. No biography of Johnson has yet appeared. Johnson provided the basis for one in his account of his New Deal years, *The Blue Eagle from Egg to Earth*. See also the 1934 *New Yorker* profile by the muckraking journalist, Matthew Josephson: August 18, August 25, September 1.
35. Mussolini reference in Martin, *Madame Secretary*, 269; Moline quote in Johnson, *The Blue Eagle from Egg to Earth*, 115-116.
36. Quoted in Schlesinger, *Coming of the New Deal*, 106.
37. Johnson, *The Blue Eagle from Egg to Earth*, 201.
38. For biographical data on Richberg, see Vadney, *The Wayward Liberal*, 7-15. Also see *Current Biography*, 1949, 520-522.
39. Richberg, *The Rainbow*, 68.
40. Richberg speech to Manufacturers Association of Connecticut, November 16, 1933, Richberg speech file, Box 15, RG 9, NA. Richberg had earlier stated his corporatist views in an article criticizing Brandeis' antitrust views in which he took for granted the "demonstrated incapacity of human beings to administer wisely their superhuman organizations" and envisioned that "redistribution of the control of vast enterprises may be achieved as the result of industrial-social engineering." Richberg, "The Industrial Liberalism of Justice Brandeis," 1102.
41. Richberg, *The Rainbow*, 24, 19; Richberg speech to Sunday Breakfast Club, November 3, 1933, Box 582, RG 9, NA.
42. *Time*, September 10, 1934.
43. Bellush, *The Failure of the NRA*, 158-162.
44. Richberg, *My Hero*, 168-169.
45. Johnson, *The Blue Eagle from Egg to Earth*, 235. The ten industries included textiles, coal, petroleum, iron and steel, automobiles, lumber, garment trades, wholesale trade, retail trade, and construction. The code-drafting push soon centered on the first "Big Six" on this list.
46. On the textile industry and the NRA, see Galambos, *Competition and Cooperation*, Chs. 8-11.
47. Johnson, *The Blue Eagle from Egg to Earth*, 229-233.
48. Id., 248-249.
49. Interview with Milton Katz, November 18, 1977.
50. Lyons, *The National Recovery Administration*, II, 568.
51. Id.
52. Hawley, *The New Deal and the Problem of Monopoly*, 56-61.
53. Johnson, *The Blue Eagle from Egg to Earth*, 251.
54. Quoted in NRA, *Handbook for Speakers*, 5-6.
55. Lyons, *The National Recovery Administration*, II, 900-902.

56. Johnson, *The Blue Eagle from Egg to Earth*, 264; Schlesinger, *Coming of the New Deal*, 114.
57. Johnson, *The Blue Eagle from Egg to Earth*, 267-268.
58. Interview with Blackwell Smith, October 22, 1977.

CHAPTER 2

1. Quoted in Martin, *Madame Secretary*, 269.
2. Minutes of Weekly Meetings of Special Industrial Recovery Board, September 11, 1933, Box 249, Stephens Papers, LC.
3. 1 *U.S. Law Week* 17 (September 12, 1933).
4. 1 *U. S. Law Week* 97 (October 17, 1933).
5. *Purvis v. Bazemore*, 5 F.Supp. 230, 231-232 (S.D.Fla. 1933).
6. NRA Press Release, December 7, 1933, Box 1, RG 9, LC.
7. "Notes for Address by Blackwell Smith," December 13, 1933, Box 581, RG 9, NA. Smith took the occasion to defend the NRA in the most expansive terms, arguing that "today all industry, including the most local types, is part of a single national organism similar to the circulation of blood in the human system."
8. Interview with Blackwell Smith, October 22, 1977.
9. Id.
10. 1 *U.S. Law Week* 845 (May 29, 1934).
11. 1 *U.S. Law Week* 1040 (August 14, 1934).
12. 290 U.S. 398 (1934).
13. 291 U.S. 545 (1934).
14. 1 *U.S. Law Week* 545 (March 6, 1934).
15. Draft of speech, March 27, 1934, Box 20, RG 9, NA.
16. McKnight to Smith, April 17, 1934, Box 45, Richberg Papers, LC.
17. National Recovery Review Board, *First Report to the President*, OF 466, FDRL. On the Darrow Committee report, see Hawley, *The New Deal and the Problem of Monopoly*, 92-97.
18. Blackwell Smith to Averell Harriman, April 9, 1934, Memo file, January-April 1934, Box 45, Richberg Papers, LC.
19. Interview with Blackwell Smith, October 22, 1977.
20. Machiavelli, *The Discourses*, Ch. 37.
21. Cummings to Johnson, April 9, 1934, Box 10, RG 9, NA.
22. Minutes of Special Industrial Recovery Board, June 19, 1933, Folder—NRA, July 1933, Box 1, OF 466, FDRL.
23. U.S. Cong., House Committee on Appropriations, *Hearings on Department of Justice Appropriation Bill for 1936* (74th Cong., 1st Sess.), 122.
24. See reports in Box 247, Stephens Papers, LC.
25. For a brief history of this struggle, see Swisher, "Federal Organization of Legal Functions," 973-979.
26. Arnold to Stephens, December 17, 1934, File 114-3, RG 60, NA.
27. Stephens to Cummings, December 20, 1934, id.
28. 7 F.Supp. 16 (W.D.Ky. 1934).
29. Sparks to A. G. McKnight, April 28, 1934, and Stephens to Sparks, May 1, 1934, File 114-187-15, RG 60, NA.
30. McKnight to Philip Buck, April 13, 1934, Box 571, RG 9, NA.
31. Stephens to Jack Scott, April 13, 1934, id.

32. Philip Murray to Cummings, June 20, 1934, Litigation Division file, Box 581, RG 9, NA.
33. Richberg to Cummings, June 6, 1934, Box 13, RG 9, NA.
34. Stephens to Biggs, June 8, 1934, File 114-187-15, RG 60, NA.
35. Stephens to Cummings, June 12, 1934, id.
36. Cummings to Richberg, June 12, 1934, Box 581, RG 9, NA.
37. Buck to Stephens, July 24, 1934, File 114-187-15, RG 60, NA.
38. *Sparks v. Hart Coal Co.*, 74 F.2d 697, 699 (6th Cir. 1934).
39. Griffin to McKnight, November 26, 1934, Box 506, RG 9, NA.
40. McKnight to Richberg, October 13, 1934, Box 571, RG 9, NA.
41. Smith to McKnight, July 5, 1934, File 114-3, RG 60, NA.
42. Data compiled from Chase, *Biographical Dictionary of the Federal Judiciary.*
43. These cases were selected from those reported in the *Federal Supplement* (Vols. 5-10) in which the decision rested exclusively or largely on constitutional grounds; the dates of decision ranged from December 1933 to May 1935, when the NRA was declared unconstitutional by the Supreme Court.
44. 9 Wheat. 1, 194-195 (1824).
45. 196 U.S. 375 (1905).
46. *Houston, E. & W. Texas Railroad Co. v. United States* (Shreveport case), 234 U.S. 342 (1913).
47. 258 U.S. 495 (1922).
48. 262 U.S. 1 (1923).
49. Stern, "That Commerce Which Concerns More States than One," 1362.
50. 128 U.S. 1, 20 (1888).
51. 156 U.S. 1, 72, 75 (1895).
52. 198 U.S. 45 (1905).
53. 247 U.S. 251, 271-273 (1918). A classic discussion of these restrictive cases and their role in laissez-faire constitutionalism is Twiss, *Lawyers and the Constitution.*
54. Corwin, *The Twilight of the Supreme Court*, 498.
55. 1 S.C.D.C. 58, 62-63, 71-76 (D.D.C. 1933).
56. 7 F.Supp. 547, 558-559 (D.Md. 1934).
57. *United States v. Sutherland*, 9 F.Supp. 204, 207 (W.D.Mo. 1934).
58. 143 U.S. 649, 693 (1892).
59. 192 U.S. 470 (1904).
60. 220 U.S. 506 (1911).
61. 276 U.S. 394, 409 (1928).
62. Address of A. G. McKnight, April 24, 1934, Folder 700/D/1, Central Files of the Legal Division, RG 9, NA.
63. 5 F.Supp. 798, 802 (N.D.Ill. 1934).
64. 10 F.Supp. 1, 8-9 (D.N.J. 1935).
65. "Preparation of Factual Material in Recovery Legislation Cases," undated memorandum, Box 19, RG 9, NA.
66. Address of A. G. McKnight, April 24, 1934, Folder 700/D/1, Central Files of the Legal Division, RG 9, NA.
67. 243 U.S. 332, 348 (1917).
68. 256 U.S. 135 (1921).
69. 290 U.S. 398, 426 (1934).
70. 7 F.Supp. 139, 144 (N.D.Ga. 1934).
71. 7 F.Supp. 694, 697 (D.Neb. 1934).

NOTES

72. *Home Bldg. & Loan Ass'n v. Blaisdell*, 290 U.S. 398 (1934).
73. *United States v. Leito*, 6 F.Supp. 32, 34 (N.D.Tex. 1934).
74. *Purvis v. Bazemore*, 5 F.Supp. 230, 232 (S.D.Fla. 1933).
75. *Ex Parte Milligan*, 4 Wall. 2, 120 (1866).
76. "Fair Trade Practice Provisions of Codes in Light of Compliance Division Experience," July 1935, Box 504, RG 9, NA.
77. "Analysis of NRA Decisions," March 1935, Folder 700/D/1, Central Files of the Legal Division, RG 9, NA.
78. Bellush, *The Failure of the NRA*, 153-157.
79. *United States v. Lieto*, 6 F.Supp. 32, 34-35 (N.D.Tex. 1934).
80. "Notes for Address by Blackwell Smith," December 13, 1933, Box 581, RG 9, NA.
81. Stern, "The Commerce Clause and the National Economy," 652.

CHAPTER 3

1. Friedel, *FDR: Launching the New Deal*, 426. For a survey of New Deal oil policy, see Nordhauser, *The Quest for Stability: Domestic Oil Regulation, 1917-1935*, Chs. 6-9.
2. Hawley, *The New Deal and the Problem of Monopoly*, 213.
3. Friedel, *FDR: Launching the New Deal*, 426. On the governors' meeting, see Nordhauser, *The Quest for Stability*, 101-106.
4. National Industrial Recovery Act, §9(c), 48 Stat. 195 (1933). In providing for "hot oil" regulation through presidential discretion, Congress rejected the Marland-Capper bill that proposed direct production and price controls. Nordhauser, *The Quest for Stability*, 106-110.
5. Executive Order 6199, July 11, 1933.
6. Executive Order 6204, July 14, 1933.
7. See, for example, the comments by Ickes in *Secret Diary*, 87, 209, 219, 245. Also see Ickes, *The Autobiography of a Curmudgeon*.
8. Margold to Frankfurter, April 3, 1933, Microfilm roll 21, Frankfurter Papers, HLSL.
9. Ickes, *Secret Diary*, 85, 87.
10. Id., 94.
11. Richberg to Ickes, September 1, 1933, Reports-Correspondence, September-October 1933, Box 45, Richberg Papers, LC.
12. Snyder to Stephens, September 7, 1933, File 114-04-1, RG 60, NA.
13. Snyder to Stephens, May 16, 1934, File 114-12-9, RG 60, NA.
14. Id.
15. Id.
16. Id.
17. Stephens to L. H. Martineau, March 5, 1934, Box 130, Stephens Papers, LC.
18. *New York Times*, March 9, 1934, 29.
19. Id., March 24, 1934, 1.
20. Id., March 30, 1934, 32.
21. Snyder to Stephens, May 16, 1934, File 114-12-9, RG 60, NA.
22. Stephens to Martineau, March 5, 1934, Box 130, Stephens Papers, LC.
23. Ickes, *Secret Diary*, 243.
24. Fahy to Stephens, August 20, 1934, File 114-57-1, RG 60, NA.

25. The "hot oil" regulations are summarized in *Panama Refining Co. v. Ryan*, 293 U.S. 387, 405-408 (1935).
26. *New York Times*, September 4, 1933, 38.
27. Stern, "The Commerce Clause and the National Economy," 654-655.
28. *Amazon Petroleum Corp. v. Ryan*, 5 F.Supp. 639, 644 (E.D.Tex. 1934).
29. *Amazon Petroleum Corp. v. Railroad Comm'n of Texas*, 5 F.Supp. 633, 637-639 (E.D.Tex. 1934).
30. Swisher, "Federal Organization of Legal Functions," 982.
31. Snyder to Stephens, May 16, 1934, File 114-12-9, RG 60, NA.
32. Swisher, "Federal Organization of Legal Functions," 982.
33. Id., 982-983.
34. Entry for April 20, 1934, Homer Cummings Diary (microfilm), FDRL.
35. Id.
36. Editorial, "Planless Legal Planning," *New Republic*, May 23, 1934, 31-32. This anonymous editorial (surprising in view of Frankfurter's influence on the magazine) constituted a broadside attack on both Justice Department and NRA lawyers, calling the first "old-fashioned trust-busters who look with suspicion upon any scheme of control tainted with 'self-government in industry,' " and lambasting the latter for a "supine policy . . . whose dilatory tactics have earned for them among their associates the heroic title of 'the gutless wonders.' "
37. *Ryan v. Amazon Petroleum Corp.*, 71 F.2d 1, 5, 7-8 (5th Cir. 1934).
38. Surrey to Blackwell Smith, January 5, 1934, Box 516, RG 9, NA.
39. Huberman to Golden Bell, December 13, 1934, File 114-57(1), RG 60, NA.
40. Letter, Fahy to author, August 31, 1978.
41. See Argument for Petitioners, *Panama Refining Co. v. Ryan*, 293 U.S. 388, 394-396 (1935).
42. Quoted in Swisher, "Federal Organization of Legal Functions," 984.
43. Id.
44. Ickes, *Secret Diary*, 247.
45. *Panama Refining Co. v. Ryan*, 293 U.S. 388, 417, 431-432 (1935).
46. 293 U.S. 388, 435-437, 441-443 (Cardozo, dissenting).

CHAPTER 4

1. 294 U.S. 736 (1935).
2. Historians of the New Deal have long debated whether the shift in policies that took place in 1935 constituted a sufficiently sharp contrast to demarcate, in effect, *two* New Deal periods. The most persuasive argument for this position was made in 1944 by Basil Rauch in *The History of the New Deal*. Writing solely from the public record, Rauch provided what still stands as the most perceptive analysis of Roosevelt and his policies. On the outlines of the First and Second New Deals, see Rauch at 205-208.
3. Lyons, *The National Recovery Administration*, 142.
4. Figures from the indictment in *United States v. Belcher*, Records and Briefs of the Supreme Court, 1934 Term, Vol. 29.
5. Lyons, *The National Recovery Administration*, 143.
6. Interview with Bernice Lotwin Bernstein, October 21, 1977.
7. *Belcher* indictment, Records and Briefs of the Supreme Court, 1934 Term, Vol. 29.

8. W. E. Belcher to Lumber Code Authority, October 18, 1933, File 114-160-3 [Belcher case file], RG 60, NA.

9. Letter, Southern Pine Association to Lumber Code Authority, December 6, 1933, id.

10. NRA Press Release, No. 2235, December 12, 1933, id.

11. Memorandum to the Files, Mastin White, December 26, 1933, id.

12. Stephens to Smith, January 13, 1934, id.

13. Memorandum for the Files, Mastin White, January 2, 1934, id.

14. Stephens to Smith, February 7, 1934, id.

15. Stephens to Griffin, February 7, 1934, id.

16. Criminal Appeals Act, 34 Stat. 1246 (1907).

17. *Belcher* indictment, Records and Briefs of the Supreme Court, 1934 Term, Vol. 29.

18. Griffin to Smith, September 22, 1934, Box 506, RG 9, NA.

19. The demurrer and Judge Grubb's order are in *Belcher* case materials, Records and Briefs of the Supreme Court, 1934 Term, Vol. 29.

20. Id.

21. 2 *U.S. Law Week* 157 (November 6, 1934).

22. *New York Times*, January 7, 1935, 16.

23. 2 *U.S. Law Week* 157 (November 6, 1934).

24. Interview with Bernice Lotwin Bernstein, October 21, 1977.

25. Diary entry for February 8, 1935, Homer Cummings Diary (microfilm), FDRL.

26. Blackwell Smith to National Industrial Recovery Board, February 13, 1935, Constitutional Rights File, Box 3, Leon Henderson Papers, FDRL.

27. Leon Marshall to Roosevelt, February 18, 1935, File-NRA January-February 1935, Box 4, OF 466, FDRL.

28. Interview with Blackwell Smith, October 22, 1977.

29. Ickes, *Secret Diary*, 247.

30. Richberg, "The Truth About the Schechter Case," Article file, Box 8, Richberg Papers, LC, 5. I am grateful to Thomas Vadney for providing me with this and the following document.

31. Paula Tully to Frankfurter, March 13, 1935, with attached "Memorandum for the President from—F.F.," n.d., Box 34, Frankfurter Papers, LC.

32. Department of Justice Press Release, March 25, 1935, Box 10, RG 9, NA.

33. *Congressional Record*, Vol. 79, Part 5 (74th Cong., 1st Sess.), 4735 (April 1, 1935); *New York Times*, April 1, 1935, 11.

34. *New York Times*, April 2, 1935, 20.

35. *Southern Lumberman*, April 1, 1935, 18.

36. Samuel E. Ewing, Jr., to Crockett Owen, Case Files of Philip E. Buck, Box 493, RG 9, NA.

37. Robert E. Keebler to Buck, May 3, 1935, id.

38. *New York Times*, March 31, 1935, Sec. IV, 10.

39. Radiogram to the President, April 3, 1935, File—Memorandums, April 1935, Box 45, Richberg Papers, LC.

40. Id.

41. Telegram, Corcoran to Roosevelt, April 4, 1935, Box 11, OF 466, FDRL.

42. Early to Roosevelt, April 4, 1935, OF 200-M-Misc., FDRL.

43. Radiogram, Roosevelt to Cummings (copies to Early and Corcoran), April 4, 1935, OF 10, FDRL.

44. Reed to Roosevelt, April 11, 1935, Box 11, OF 466, FDRL.

45. Interview with Blackwell Smith, October 22, 1977. In a post-mortem of the debates over *Belcher* and *Schechter*, Arthur Krock of the *New York Times* criticized Frankfurter for having given "very bad advice" to Roosevelt: "If Professor Felix Frankfurter's proteges are to be believed, his was the delaying influence, and Congress was supposed meanwhile to reconstitute NRA in modified form, thus strengthening its show of will for Supreme Court consideration. But the dropping of the Belcher case had such a disastrous effect on NRA, and so encouraged its enemies in Congress, that the Schechter case—which had progressed normally through the courts and was not highly thought of as a test—was quickly taken up, and now becomes a cause celebre." *New York Times*, April 16, 1935, 20.

CHAPTER 5

1. Pearson and Allen, *The Nine Old Men*, 263.
2. See the indictment in *Schechter Poultry Corp. v. United States*, Records and Briefs of the Supreme Court, 1934 Term, Vol. 22.
3. Frank Elmore to Thomas Billig, April 23, 1935, Box 523 (*Schechter* case file), RG 9, NA. The code is reproduced in the *Schechter* indictment, Note 2.
4. Pearson and Allen, *The Nine Old Men*, 263-264.
5. See the *Schechter* indictment, Note 2.
6. *Local 167, International Brotherhood of Teamsters v. United States*, 291 U.S. 293 (1934).
7. McKnight to Richberg, Blackwell Smith, and Jack Scott, November 3, 1934, Box 571, RG 9, NA.
8. *United States v. Schechter Poultry Corp.*, 8 F.Supp. 137, 145-148 (E.D.N.Y. 1934).
9. *Schechter Poultry Corp. v. United States*, 76 F.2d 617, 620-623, 624, 624-625 (2nd Cir. 1935).
10. Rice to Harold Stephens, October 24, 1934, File 114-115-2(2), RG 60, NA.
11. Stern, "The Commerce Clause and the National Economy," 660.
12. Smith to Richberg, April 19, 1935, Memos—April 1935, Box 45, Richberg Papers, LC.
13. Smith to Richberg, Reed, and Stanleigh Arnold, April 27, 1935, Box 523, RG 9, NA.
14. Stern, "That Commerce Which Concerns More States than One," 1348, 1337, 1365.
15. Smith to Richberg, July 14, 1935, Box 11, RG 9, NA.
16. *Schechter Poultry Corp. v. United States*, Brief for the United States, Records and Briefs of the Supreme Court, 1934 Term, Vol. 22, 97.
17. Undated and unsigned memorandum (only pp. 26-33 are enclosed in the file), Box 1, RG 9, NA.
18. Id. In a speech to his staff in 1934, NRA Litigation Division chief A. G. McKnight predicted that "the courts will hardly hesitate to sustain the action of Congress" in dealing with the Depression. "The rule of self-preservation justifies every step thus far taken to save the nation from the doom that was so clearly impending" before passage of the NIRA. Speech by A. G. McKnight, April 24, 1934, Folder 700/D/1, Central Files of the Legal Division, RG 9, NA.

19. *Schechter* case, Brief for the United States, 97, Note 16.
20. Frankfurter to Reed, May 4, 1935, File 003031, Box 149, Frankfurter Papers, LC.
21. Richberg, *My Hero*, 193-194.
22. Betty Decatur to Thomas Billig, April 23, 1935, Box 523, RG 9, NA.
23. "Transcripts of Oral Argument," Day 1; 15, 22-26, File—Schechter case 1935, Box 47, Richberg Papers, LC. This transcript, which seems to have been prepared by an NRA stenographer, differs slightly but not in substance from that which appears in the series *Landmark Briefs and Arguments of the Supreme Court*, edited by Philip Kurland and Gerhard Casper. I have relied throughout this chapter on the NRA transcript.
24. Id., Day 2; 15-21, 22-24, 32.
25. 2 *U.S. Law Week* 844 (May 7, 1935).
26. "Transcripts of Oral Arguments," Day 2; 90-96, Note 23.
27. Id., 124-141.
28. Reed to Frankfurter, May 7, 1935, File 003031, Box 149, Frankfurter Papers, LC. Frankfurter later wrote Reed, after a meeting with Richberg: "I had a completely frank talk with him about his performance in the Schechter case, and his attempt to escape responsibility by trying to unload on others. He was very nice about it and confessed error." Frankfurter to Reed, March 25, 1936, Folder 15, Box 170, Frankfurter Papers, HLSL.
29. Pearson and Allen, *The Nine Old Men*, 270.
30. *Humphrey's Executor v. United States*, 295 U.S. 602 (1935); *Louisville Joint Stock Land Bank v. Radford*, 295 U.S. 555 (1935).
31. *Schechter Poultry Corp. v. United States*, 295 U.S. 495, 521 (1935).
32. Interview with Paul Freund, October 3, 1977.
33. 295 U.S. at 528, 529-537.
34. Mason, *Brandeis: A Free Man's Life*, 618.
35. 295 U.S. at 543-549.
36. 295 U.S. at 551-553 (Cardozo, concurring).
37. Richberg speech to Sunday Breakfast Club, "The Objectives, Methods, and Results of the NRA," November 3, 1933, Box 582, RG 9, NA.
38. Quoted in Schlesinger, *The Politics of Upheaval*, 280; interview with Thomas G. Corcoran, June 15, 1978.
39. Reed to Cummings, May 29, 1935, File—March-August 1935, Box 3, OF 10, FDRL.
40. Diary entry for May 29, 1935, Homer Cummings Diary (microfilm), FDRL.
41. Frankfurter to Charles C. Burlingham, June 11, 1935, Folder 13, Box 4, Burlingham Papers, HLSL.
42. These letters and telegrams can be found in OF 466, FDRL.
43. Press conference of May 29, 1935, 310, Presidential Press Conferences (microfilm), FDRL.
44. Id., May 31, 1935, 309-336.
45. *Time*, June 10, 1935, 11.

CHAPTER 6

1. Quoted in Schlesinger, *Coming of the New Deal*, 44.
2. Friedel, *FDR: Launching the New Deal*, 85.

3. Perkins, *Crisis in Agriculture*, 11; Agricultural Adjustment Administration, *Agricultural Adjustment in 1934*, 8.

4. Peek, *Why Quit Our Own*, 14. For accounts of the various incarnations of the McNary-Haugen bills and pre-New Deal agricultural policy, see Moley, *After Seven Years*, 247-248; Tugwell, *The Democratic Roosevelt*, 159-160; Friedel, *FDR: Launching the New Deal*, 87-88; Perkins, *Crisis in Agriculture*, 212-214.

5. Rowley, *M. L. Wilson*, 2-6.

6. See Hawley, *The New Deal and the Problem of Monopoly*, 19-33.

7. Quoted in Moley, *After Seven Years*, 249.

8. Tugwell, *The Brains Trust*, 192, 205-210.

9. Id., 455.

10. Id., 456.

11. Schlesinger, *Coming of the New Deal*, 42-43. Schlesinger recounts the AAA drafting process at 27-84.

12. Accounts of this meeting can be found in Perkins, *Crisis in Agriculture*, 36-38; and Friedel, *FDR: Launching the New Deal*, 308-310.

13. Frank, COHC.

14. Agricultural Adjustment Act, 48 Stat. 31 (1933). The base period for tobacco was set from 1919-1929.

15. *Congressional Record*, Vol. 77, Part 1 (73d Cong., 1st Sess.), 666.

16. Id., 754. In response to Beck's warning that the bill would make Wallace "another Stalin," an Arkansas Democrat answered that the people had demanded that Congress have the "nerve and courage . . . to appoint a man as dictator whose heart and disposition are right in order to obtain results." Id., 759.

17. Id., 1642-1644.

18. Id., 1761.

19. For biographical data on Peek, see Fite, *George N. Peek and the Fight for Farm Parity*, 21-37.

20. Id.

21. Peek, *Why Quit Our Own*, 15.

22. For biographical data on these men, see Perkins, *Crisis in American Agriculture*, 90-94; Peek, *Why Quit Our Own*, 106; *Who Was Who in America*.

23. Frank, *Courts on Trial*, 2. A generally unrevealing biography of Frank is Volkomer, *Passionate Liberal: The Political and Legal Ideas of Jerome Frank*. A more substantial biography is in process, by Robert J. Glennon of Wayne State University Law School.

24. Volkomer, *Passionate Liberal*, 4-6.

25. Frank, *If Men Were Angels*, 165-166.

26. Frank, COHC.

27. Frank, *Law and the Modern Mind*, 18. Frank excoriated the judge who "centers his attention on impersonal so-called rules" and conceals the reality that he is "swayed by human prejudices, passions, and weaknesses." Frank's ideal as a judge was Oliver Wendell Holmes, whom he praised as the "completely adult jurist" who refused to substitute his prejudices for the political and economic choices made by legislators. Frank, "Mr. Justice Holmes and Non-Euclidian Thinking," 580. It is likely, however, that Holmes (who retired from the Court in 1930) would have joined his like-minded colleagues, Brandeis and Stone (and Cardozo, who replaced him) in rejecting the NIRA. Holmes

personally disagreed with much of the legislation that he upheld on the Court, and undoubtedly would have objected to Frank's statement about the Depression that "greater centralization of government was necessary and . . . the New Deal necessarily involved that." Frank, COHC.

28. Frank to Frankfurter, February 26, 1933, Frank Papers, Yale University Library.
29. Frankfurter to Tugwell, March 10, 1933, File 002583, Box 125, Frankfurter Papers, LC.
30. Frank COHC.
31. Peek, *Why Quit Our Own*, 21.
32. Id., 22.
33. Id.
34. Id., 110.
35. Frank, COHC.
36. Frank, "Experimental Jurisprudence and the New Deal," 12413.
37. Frank and Tugwell to Roosevelt, August 3, 1933, File 469, Solicitor's Office records, Department of Agriculture, RG 16, NA.
38. Pressman, COHC.
39. Interview with Alger Hiss, September 20, 1979.
40. [Hiss], "The 'Yellow Dog' Device as a Bar to the Union Organizer," 770.
41. Interview with Alger Hiss, September 20, 1979.
42. Frank memorandum, August 5, 1933, File 469, Solicitor's Office General Files 1933-1937, RG 16, NA.
43. Id.
44. Friant to Frank, October 30, 1933, Folder 84, Box 12, Frank Papers, Yale University Library.
45. Frank to Charles Brand, August 10, 1933, File 469, Solicitor's Office records, RG 16, NA. The pressure on Frank had its source in Postmaster General James Farley, and Frank and Farley sparred for more than six months over the patronage issue. After learning that the appointments of Pressman, Bachrach, and Fortas were being held hostage for seven unwanted patronage appointees, Frank urged Wallace to intervene and make it clear that "the legal staff is not to be a happy hunting ground for politicins." Frank to Wallace, August 1, 1933, id. Farley had convinced the White House that prospective AAA lawyers must secure senatorial endorsements, a move that led Frank to complain to Wallace that the AAA would "break down for lack of an adequate legal staff unless something is done without delay to remove the Farley obstruction. If Mr. Farley wants to play this kind of poker game and ruin our work, he and not I must be held responsible." Frank to Wallace, August 2, 1933, id. The final straw came when Peek's office held up a thirty-day appointment of Yale Law School dean Charles Clark as advisor on constitutional questions; Peek's staff, Frank waspishly commented, "presumably . . . are making up their minds whether or not Dean Clark's legal education is adequate." Frank to Wallace, August 20, 1933, id.
46. Auerbach, *Unequal Justice*, 187-188.
47. This estimate is based on a name analysis of law review editors and is subject to some imprecision. On the role of Jewish lawyers in the New Deal, see Auerbach, *Unequal Justice*, 184-190.
48. Schlesinger, *Coming of the New Deal*, 50-51.

NOTES

49. Frank to Frankfurter, April 18, 1933, quoted in Glennon, "Principles Are What Principles Do," 15.
50. Frank to Wallace, May 17, 1933, File 469, Solicitor's Office files, RG 9, NA.
51. Frank to Wallace, August 20, 1933, id.
52. Frank to Hiss, Francis Shea, and Robert McConnaughey, December 26, 1934, File 469B, id.
53. Johnson, *The Papers of Adlai Stevenson*, Vol. I, 249.
54. Frank to Hopkins, August 19, 1940, quoted in Glennon, "Principles Are What Principles Do," 18.
55. Frank, COHC.
56. Frank to Peek, October 25, 1933, File 469, Solicitor's Office files, RG 9, NA.
57. Wallace to Roosevelt, May 15, 1933, Box 1, OF 1, FDRL.
58. Peek, *Why Quit Our Own*, 119.
59. Id., 146-149. "The meetings between the tobacco representatives and the attorneys from our General Counsel's office grew bitter," Peek reported. "The tobacco men appealed to me," he said, to take their case to the White House to oppose Frank and Wallace's threat to "take over the industry" through the exercise of the Secretary's statutory licensing powers. There is an extensive discusion of the tobacco dispute in Nourse, *Marketing Agreements Under the AAA*, 78-88. Also see Badger, *Prosperity Road: The New Deal, Tobacco, and North Carolina*.
60. Peek, *Why Quit Our Own*, 119.
61. Frank, COHC. Black, *The Dairy Industry and the AAA*, is detailed and definitive on the relation of the industry to the AAA.
62. Frank to King, September 1, 1933, Folder 149, Box 13, Frank Papers, Yale University Library.
63. Quoted in Perkins, *Crisis in Agriculture*, 160.
64. Id., 184.
65. Id.
66. *New York Times*, December 7, 1933, 1.

CHAPTER 7

1. Frankfurter to Stephens, September 18, 1933, Felix Frankfurter file, Box 14, Stephens Papers, LC.
2. Frank memorandum (no addressee), File 469, Solicitor's Office files, RG 16, NA.
3. Johnson, *The Papers of Adlai Stevenson*, Vol. I, 267 and 269.
4. Id., 267 and 249.
5. Agricultural Adjustment Act, §8(3), 48 Stat. 31 (1933).
6. Frank, COHC.
7. Black, *The Dairy Industry and the AAA*, 25-28.
8. Id., 95-96.
9. 1 *U.S. Law Week* 6 (September 5, 1933).
10. 285 U.S. 262 (1932).
11. 1 *U.S. Law Week* 6 (September 5, 1933).
12. Id., 6 and 15.
13. 186 N.E. 694, 697-699 (C.A.N.Y. 1933).

14. *Economy Dairy Co. v. Wallace* and *Beck v. Wallace*, 61 Wash.L.Reporter 633 (S.C.D.C. 1933).
15. 1 *U.S. Law Week* 50 (September 26, 1933).
16. Frank to Stephens, September 13, 1933, File 106-11-8, RG 60, NA.
17. Arnold to Frank, September 21, 1933; H. H. McPike to Attorney General Cummings, October 3, 1933, id.
18. 4 F.Supp. 660, 661-662 (N.D.Cal. 1933).
19. 1 *U.S. Law Week* 82 (October 10, 1933).
20. Id.
21. *Capitol City Milk Producers' Ass'n v. Wallace*, 1 S.C.D.C. (N.S.) 135, 136 (1933).
22. Dawson, *Louis D. Brandeis, Felix Frankfurter, and the New Deal*, 72.
23. Powell to Frankfurter, November 27, 1933, Folder A-5, Box A, Powell Papers, HLSL.
24. Frankfurter to Powell, December 18, 1933, id.
25. *Nebbia v. New York*, 291 U.S. 502, 523, 531-534, 536-537 (1934). In rejecting the due process attack on the statute, Roberts reaffirmed the state's police powers, stating that "there is no closed class or category of business affected with a public interest" and concluding that "upon proper occasion and by appropriate measures the state may regulate a business in any of its aspects, including the prices to be charged for the products or commodities it sells." In a dissent dripping with invective, Jusice McReynolds pointed out that the Court only two years earlier in *New State Ice* had described "the dairyman" as one whose business was "essentially private in nature" and held that the production or sale of food "cannot be subjected to legislative regulation on the basis of a public use." Id. at 554-555.
26. Letter, Fortas to author, July 29, 1981; Sellers to Stephens, February 3, 1934, File 106-18-1, RG 60, NA.
27. *Hillsborough Packing Co. v. Wallace*, oral opinion reported in 1 *U.S. Law Week* 494 (1933).
28. Frank to Stephens, March 15, 1934, File 106-18-1, RG 60, NA.
29. *Yarnell v. Hillsborough Packing Co.*, 70 F.2d 435, 438-439 (5th Cir. 1934).
30. Stephens to Frankfurter, July 26, 1933, Felix Frankfurter file, Box 14, Stephens Papers, LC. Frank was less charitable, fearing that AAA litigation would be "messy because most of the lawyers we encountered in the Department of Justice were not very good in those days." Frank, COHC.
31. Stephens to Attorney General Cummings, August 19, 1933, Box 134, Stephens Papers, LC.
32. Frank to Davis, May 4, 1934, Folder 8, Box 9, Frank Papers, Yale University Library. Frank noted that although "we have not suffered any defeats in court . . . in no case have we been opposed by counsel of outstanding ability. I have the gravest apprehensions, shared by all members of my staff who have considered the problem . . . that when we come before Circuit Courts of Appeals, and particularly if we are then opposed by able lawyers, our licenses . . . will be held defective in vital respects." Id.
33. Stephens to Frank, April 24, 1934, File 469A, Solicitor's Office files, RG 16, NA.
34. Frank to Stephens, May 19, 1934, File 106-33-6, RG 60, NA.
35. Bachrach to Frank, June 14, 1934, File 1165, RG 16, NA.
36. Frank to Bell, June 15, 1934, File 471, RG 16, NA.

37. Cummings to Frank, June 23, 1934, id.
38. Frank to Davis, June 28, 1934, id.
39. Frank, COHC.
40. Moley, "And Now Give Us Good Men," 13.
41. Frank, COHC.
42. Corcoran to Frankfurter, June 18, 1934, File 000906, Frankfurter Papers, LC.
43. Frank, COHC.
44. *United States v. Shissler*, 7 F.Supp. 123, 126-127 (N.D.Ill. 1934).
45. Interview with John Abt, January 24, 1980.
46. 7 F.Supp. 121, 122-123 (N.D.Ill. 1934).
47. "Butter Theory" folder, July 5, 1934, File 751A, Solicitor's Office files, RG 16, NA.
48. Black, *The Dairy Industry and the AAA*, 33.
49. "Butter Theory" folder, Note 47.
50. Victor Christgau (in memorandum prepared by Abt) to Wallace, August 14, 1934, File 471, Solicitor's Office files, RG 16, NA.
51. A. H. Lauterbach to Christgau, August 16, 1934, File 1165, RG 16, NA.
52. Frank to Stephens, August 27, 1934, id.
53. Lewin to Frank, August 25, 1934, File 469B, Solicitor's Office files, RG 16, NA.
54. Frank to Mac Asbill, August 24, 1934, File 1165, RG 16, NA.
55. Frank to Christgau, August 27, 1934, id.
56. Christgau to Frank, August 28, 1934, id.
57. Frank to Stephens, August 30, 1934, File 460, Solicitor's Office files, RG 16, NA.
58. Frank to Stephens, August 31, 1934, id.
59. Frank to Fortas, Lewin, and Bachrach, September 14, 1934, File 469B, Solicitor's Office files, RG 16, NA.
60. In chronological order, the cases were: *Hill v. Darger*, 7 F.Supp. 189 (S.D.Cal. September 7, 1934); *United States v. Greenwood Dairy Farms*, 8 F.Supp. 398 (S.D.Ind. September 27, 1934); *Douglas v. Wallace*, 8 F.Supp. 379 (W.D.Okla. October 17, 1934); *United States v. Neuendorf*, 8 F.Supp. 403 (S.D.Iowa October 19, 1934); *Royal Farms Dairy v. Wallace*, 8 F.Supp. 975 (D.Md. November 16, 1934); *Columbus Milk Producers v. Wallace*, 8 F.Supp. 1014 (N.D.Ill. November 21, 1934).
61. *United States v. Neuendorf*, 8 F.Supp. 403, 406-407 (S.D.Iowa 1934).
62. *Douglas v. Wallace*, 8 F.Supp. 379, 384-385 (W.D.Okla. 1934).
63. Bachrach to Abt, October 20, 1934, File 1165, RG 16, NA.
64. Abt to Frank, November 6, 1934, id.
65. Frank to Davis, January 4, 1935, Folder 4, Box 9, Frank Papers, Yale University Library.
66. Bachrach to Frank, November 6, 1934, File 751A, Solicitor's Office files, RG 16, NA.
67. Stephens to Frank, January 7, 1935, Box 136, Stephens Papers, LC.

CHAPTER 8

1. Johnson, *The Collapse of Cotton Tenancy*, 46-47.
2. Id., 48-49.
3. Gardner Jackson, quoted in Grubbs, *Cry from the Cotton*, 33.

4. Johnson, *The Collapse of Cotton Tenancy*, 47.
5. The 1930 census showed that in the ten major cotton-producing states there were 937,000 white and 671,000 black tenant families. See Venkataramani, "Norman Thomas, Arkansas Sharecroppers, and the Roosevelt Agricultural Policies, 1933-1937," 225 [cited below as "Norman Thomas"].
6. Cobb to Chester Davis, quoted in Oscar Johnston to Davis, January 26, 1935, Box 18, Vol. II, Landlord-Tenant file, RG 145, NA.
7. Department of Agriculture, 1934-1935 Cotton Contract, quoted in Conrad, *The Forgotten Farmers*, 58.
8. Hiss to Frank, January 26, 1935, Box 18, Vol. II, Landlord-Tenant file, RG 145, NA.
9. Richards, *Cotton under the AAA*, 135-136. It is important to note that these categories were somewhat indistinct and subject to variations between regions and even local practice within a state.
10. Hiss memorandum (no addressee), January 13, 1934, File 284, Solicitor's Office files, RG 16, NA.
11. Hiss to Payne, September 5, 1933, id.
12. Hiss to Payne, September 15, 1933, id.
13. Interview with Alger Hiss, July 12, 1978.
14. Wallace to McKinley, no date (1933), File 284, Solicitor's Office files, RG 16, NA.
15. Hiss to Frank, January 4, 1934, id.
16. Frank, COHC.
17. Cobb to Frank, February 27, 1934, File 284, Solicitor's Office files, RG 16, NA.
18. Quoted in Grubbs, *Cry from the Cotton*, 32.
19. Quoted in Johnson, *The Collapse of Cotton Tenancy*, 60.
20. For an account of Thomas' career, see Swanberg, *Norman Thomas: Respectable Rebel*.
21. Quoted in Venkataramani, "Norman Thomas," 229.
22. See Swanberg, *Norman Thomas*, 158-159.
23. Venkataramani, "Norman Thomas," 229.
24. Quoted in Swanberg, *Norman Thomas*, 159.
25. Venkataramani, "Norman Thomas," 230.
26. Wallace to McIntyre, March 3, 1934, Correspondence, October 1933—July 1935, Reel 19, Wallace Papers (microfilm), University of Iowa Libraries.
27. Davis to District Agents, May 5, 1934, Landlord-Tenant file, RG 16, NA (emphasis added).
28. AAA Press Release, May 9, 1934, File 284, Solicitor's Office files, RG 16, NA.
29. Hiss to Frank, June 5, 1934, id.; Frank to Davis, June 29, 1934, id.
30. Kester, *Revolt Among the Sharecroppers*, 55-56.
31. Id., 56-58. In H. L. Mitchell's recently published autobiography, he recalls that he and Clay East attended the first meeting. Mitchell, *Mean Things Happening in This Land*, 47-48. Other accounts have repeated this, but Kester's version seems more likely. At any rate, Mitchell was the key figure in organizing the STFU. See also Auerbach, "Southern Tenant Farmers: Socialist Critics of the New Deal."
32. Hiss, "Memo of Conference Held in Mr. Trent's Office," July 3, 1934, File 284, Solicitor's Office files, RG 16, NA. Hoover, who later became a high-

ranking Commerce Department official, sympathized with the tenants but was also close to Chester Davis, as his later role in the "purge" illustrated.

33. McConnaughey to Margaret Bennett, August 1, 1934, id.
34. "Report of Adjustment Committee," September 1, 1934, File 467, id.
35. Quoted in Grubbs, *Cry from the Cotton*, 37.
36. "Report of Adjustment Committee," Note 34.
37. Petition of 22 tenants to R. L. McGill, Poinsett County Agricultural Agent, December 12, 1934, File 797-105, id.
38. Amberson to Norman Thomas, October 19, 1934, H. L. Mitchell Papers, *New York Times* microfilm edition.
39. Amberson to Thomas, November 12, 1934, id.
40. Norcross to Paul Appleby, January 5, 1935, Box 118, AAA Production Control Program files, RG 145, NA.
41. Victor Anderson to Gardner and Gardner, Hobart, Oklahoma, September 17, 1934, Solicitor's Office files, RG 16, NA.
42. Petition of 22 tenants, Note 37.
43. McGill to Carpenter and Anderson, December 22, 1934, File 467, id.
44. Miller to Cobb, December 26, 1934, id.
45. The Chancery Court order is discussed in *West v. Norcross*, 190 Ark. 667 (1935), the final ruling of the Arkansas Supreme Court in the case.
46. Porter to Frank, January 3, 1935, File 465, Solicitor's Office files, RG 16, NA.
47. Appleby to Cobb, December 27, 1934, quoted in Conrad, *Cry from the Cotton*, 137.
48. Frank to Shea, January 4, 1935, Folder 61, Box 10, Frank Papers, Yale University Library.
49. Cobb to Davis, January 5, 1935, File 467, Solicitor's Office files, RG 16, NA.
50. Bennett, draft memorandum to Wallace, January 9, 1935, id.
51. Memorandum, Committee on Violations, to Wallace, January 10, 1935, id.
52. Frank to Christgau, January 11, 1935, File 797-105, id.
53. Christgau to Cobb, January 11, 1935, id.
54. Frank to Wallace, File 467, id.
55. Mitchell, *Mean Things Happening in This Land*, 56-57.
56. Report of W. J. Green, January 10, 1935, Box 119, Landlord-Tenant file, AAA Production Control Program file, RG 145, NA. Mitchell, in his autobiography, recalled a meeting with Frank the same day (with Hiss and Pressman attending), without discussing its substance. No records of this meeting have been found, and Hiss does not recall it. Letter, Hiss to author, January 5, 1980. There would seem to be no reason for Pressman to attend a meeting on tenant problems. At any rate, if such a meeting was held it seems clear it led to no important decisions; it may simply, as Hiss suggests, have been a brief courtesy call.
57. Richards, *Cotton and the AAA*, 149, no. 9. This account of Rodgers' speech is supposedly based on a stenographic report in the AAA files (which I have not located). For other, slightly different, accounts of the speech and Rodgers' arrest, see Kester, *Revolt Among the Sharecroppers*, 67-69, and Venkataramani, "Norman Thomas," 233.
58. Amberson to Thomas, January 26, 1935, Mitchell Papers, *New York Times* microfilm edition; Conrad, *The Forgotten Farmers*, 138-139.

NOTES

59. Carpenter to Frank, January 11, 1935 and January 15, 1935, File 467, Solicitor's Office files, RG 16, NA.
60. Conrad, *The Forgotten Farmers*, 139.
61. Quoted in Grubbs, *Cry from the Cotton*, 49.
62. Myers to Frank, January 18, 1935, File 467, Solicitor's Office files, RG 16, NA.
63. Amberson to Thomas, January 26, 1935, Mitchell Papers, *New York Times* microfilm edition. Myers's investigation also turned up derogatory information on Norcross, who had moved to Arkansas a few years before from Kansas City. "He is a lawyer and report has it that he was connected with some unlawful performance" in Kansas City, Myers wrote Frank. Myers to Frank, no date (January 1935), Folder 62, Box 11, Frank Papers, Yale University Library.
64. The subsequent history of the Myers report is mystifying and bizarre. Chester Davis ordered that all copies be collected and destroyed, and he apparently went to the extent of rifling desks at the AAA to track down all copies. Shortly after the "purge," Myers wrote that her "connection with this sharecropper situation has been the most humiliating professional experience I have ever had, and I am delighted to see the last of this memorandum." Myers to Solicitor, March 8, 1935, File 467, Solicitor's Office files, RG 16, NA. Word that the report had been suppressed leaked out, and hundreds of protesting letters (most probably instigated by the Socialist Party) flooded the AAA. Paul A. Porter, the AAA press officer, recommended to Chester Davis that he not respond to any inquiries about the Myers report, and that he explain to the press that it might become evidence in future AAA litigation (which was hardly likely). My best efforts have not turned up a copy.
65. American Cotton Cooperative Association to Wallace, January 16, 1935, File 467, Solicitor's Office files, RG 16, NA.
66. Wilding-White to John Abt, January 17, 1935, id.
67. Wilding-White to Abt, January 24, 1935, id.
68. Johnston to Davis, January 26, 1935, Box 118, Vol. II, Landlord-Tenant file, RG 145, NA.
69. Hiss to Frank, January 26, 1935, id.
70. Diary entry for January 30, 1935, Henry Wallace Diary, Microfilming Corporation of America. These diary entries have also been published in Lowitt, "Henry A. Wallace and the 1935 Purge in the Department of Agriculture." Lowitt's article reproduces only the diary excerpts.
71. Diary entry for February 2, 1935, Wallace Diary, MCA.
72. Diary entry for February 3, 1935, id.
73. Shea to McConnaughey, February 4, 1935, Box 118, AAA Production Control Program file, RG 145, NA.
74. Interview with Alger Hiss, July 12, 1978.
75. Shea to McConnaughey, Note 73.
76. Davis to Wallace, February 4, 1935, id.
77. Diary entry for February 4, 1935, Wallace Diary, MCA.
78. Frank, COHC.
79. Diary entry for February 5, 1935, Wallace Diary, MCA.
80. Grubbs, *Cry from the Cotton*, 56-57; *Washington Post*, February 7, 1935, 2.
81. Tugwell to Missy LeHand, February 5, 1935, File-Agriculture Department, 1934-1938, Box 73, PSF, FDRL.

NOTES

82. Roosevelt press conference, February 6, 1935, Presidential Press Conference transcripts, FDRL.
83. Diary entry for February 7, 1935, Wallace Diary, MCA.
84. Diary entry for February 10, 1935, Rexford Tugwell Diary, FDRL.
85. Diary entry for February 9, 1935, Wallace Diary, MCA.
86. Thomas to Wallace, February 6, 1935, File 467, Solicitor's Office files, RG 16, NA.
87. Wallace to Memphis Chamber of Commerce, February 12, 1935, File 466-B, Solicitor's Office files, RG 16, NA.
88. *West v. Norcross*, 190 Ark. 667, 672-673 (Ark. 1935).
89. Kester, *Revolt Among the Sharecroppers*, 82-83.
90. This case is persuasively made in an excellent Yale University senior thesis by Richard H. Lowe, "Fallen Warrior of Reform: Jerome N. Frank as General Counsel of the Agricultural Adjustment Administration." Lowe's conclusions about the motivations for the "purge" are at variance with those of Grubbs and Conrad, who both attribute it to the tenant issue. My own conclusion is that Davis seized on the tenant issue, in response to intense political pressure, as an opportunity to dispose of his critics on the "books and records" issue.
91. Davis, COHC.
92. Diary entry for February 10, 1935, Rexford Tugwell Diary, FDRL.
93. Department of Agriculture Press Release 1680-35, March 5, 1935, Harvard University Library.
94. Quoted in Schlesinger, *Coming of the New Deal*, 80.
95. Interviews with Alger Hiss, July 12, 1978 and September 20, 1979.

CHAPTER 9

1. Wallace speech at Alexandria, Louisiana, "Licking the Ghost of Alexander Hamilton," May 11, 1935, Department of Agriculture Press Release 2124-35, Harvard University Library.
2. The case took its name from William M. Butler, president of the company and the first receiver in alphabetical order. Butler was a pillar of the Republican Party, having managed Calvin Coolidge's presidential campaign in 1924, been national chairman of the party, and represented Massachusetts in the Senate for two years.
3. See Chapter 6 for a discussion of the processing tax plan and its origins.
4. Agricultural Adjustment Act, §§9(a), 9(b), and 16(a), 48 Stat. 31 (1933).
5. In fact, after the Supreme Court decision in *Butler* that the processing tax was unconstitutional, processors attempted to recover more than $1 billion in taxes they had paid to the Treasury, and it took an act of Congress to prevent this.
6. *Massachusetts v. Mellon*, 262 U.S. 467 (1923).
7. Bogan to Prew Savoy, April 16, 1934 and April 20, 1934, File 500-9B (AAA *Butler* case file), RG 16, NA.
8. See *Standard and Poor's Directory of Officers*, 1932-1934, and obituaries of McDonough and Prince in *New York Times*, June 18, 1941, 21, and February 3, 1953, 25. Apparently neither Bogan nor other AAA lawyers knew of McDonough's and Prince's direct connection with the packing company.
9. Bogan to Savoy, April 20, 1934 and April 24, 1934, File 500-9B, RG 16, NA.

320

NOTES

10. Anderson to Assistant Attorney Stanley, April 21, 1934, File 5-36-346 (Justice Department *Butler* case file), RG 60, NA.
11. 1 *U.S. Law Week* 717 (April 24, 1934).
12. Id.
13. *Franklin Process Co. v. Hoosac Mills Corp.*, 8 F.Supp. 552, 556-562 (D.Mass. 1934).
14. *Panama Refining Co. v. Ryan*, 293 U.S. 388 (1935). See Chapter 3 for a discussion of the "hot oil" cases.
15. *Schechter Poultry Corp. v. United States*, 295 U.S. 495 (1935). See Chapter 5 for a discussion of this case.
16. 2 *U.S. Law Week* 970 (June 11, 1935).
17. *Butler v. United States*, 78 F.2d 1, 2, 6-12 (1st Cir. 1935).
18. Wideman to Solicitor General Reed, April 16, 1935, File 5-36-346, RG 60, NA.
19. 26 U.S.C.A. §3653(a) (1935).
20. 2 *U.S. Law Week* 1114 (August 20, 1935).
21. Wilson to Attorney General Cummings, July 27, 1935, File 5-36-346, RG 60, NA.
22. Interview with Alger Hiss, July 12, 1978.
23. Id.
24. Id.
25. Reed to Hiss, November 22, 1935, File 5-36-346, RG 60, NA.
26. Interview with Alger Hiss, July 12, 1978.
27. *United States v. Butler*, 297 U.S. 1 (1936), Brief for the United States, 169-172.
28. *New York Times*, "Map Legal Battle for AAA Program," September 23, 1935, 2.
29. *New York Times*, September 28, 1935, 1.
30. Savoy to Mastin White, October 22, 1935, File 500-9B, Solicitor's Office files, RG 16, NA.
31. Interview with Alger Hiss, July 12, 1978.
32. 297 U.S. 1 (1926), Brief for Petitioners, 71 and 90.
33. Sarle to Davis, October 22, 1935, File 500-9B, Solicitor's Office Files, RG 16, NA.
34. Id.
35. Powell to Freund, November 13, 1935, Folder A5, Box A, Powell Papers, HLSL.
36. 297 U.S. 1 (1936), Brief for Petitioners, 147-148.
37. Quoted in Mason, *Harlan Fiske Stone*, 406.
38. "Transcript of Oral Argument Before Supreme Court," December 9, 1935, File 5-36-346, RG 60, NA.
39. 20 Wall. 655 (1872).
40. 297 U.S. 1, 13 (1936).
41. Pepper, *Philadelphia Lawyer: An Autobiography*, 244.
42. 297 U.S. 1, 39-44 (1936).
43. Diary entry for December 9, 1935, Homer Cummings Diary (microfilm), FDRL.
44. Diary entry for December 27, 1935, id.
45. 297 U.S. 1, 50-68 (1936).
46. Jackson, *The Struggle for Judicial Supremacy*, 134-135.

47. 297 U.S. 1, 78-88 (1936) (Stone, dissenting).
48. Diary entry for January 6, 1936, Homer Cummings Diary, FDRL.
49. Early to Roosevelt, January 9, 1936, Box 15, OF 1-K, FDRL.
50. Dickinson to Cummings, January 7, 1936, File 106-1, RG 60, NA.

CHAPTER 10

1. Lorwin and Wubnig, *Labor Relations Boards*, 20.
2. National Industrial Recovery Act, §7(a), 48 Stat. 195 (1933).
3. Dubofsky and Van Tine, *John L. Lewis*, 203.
4. Johnson, *The Blue Eagle from Egg to Earth*, 349-350.
5. *Minnesota Union Advocate*, May 25, 1933, 1.
6. Quoted in Lorwin and Wubnig, *Labor Relations Boards*, 57 and 63.
7. Id., 67.
8. Id., 74.
9. Bernstein, *The Turbulent Years*, 172-173.
10. *Decisions of the National Labor Relations Board, August 1933-March 1934*, v [cited below as *NLB Decisions*].
11. *New York Times*, November 20, 1933, 3. Wagner also expressed his mediation bias in a letter to a member of the House Labor Committee, writing that industrial disputes "can be amicably settled when the parties have been brought together to discuss their differences in an atmosphere of calmness and disinterestedness with a clearer knowledge of their respective rights and duties." Quoted in Gross, *Making of the National Labor Relations Board*, 16 [cited below as *Making of the NLRB*].
12. Milton Handler, COHC.
13. Quoted in Gross, *Making of the NLRB*, 29.
14. Id., 21.
15. In the Matter of Berkeley Woolen Mills and the United Textile Workers, *NLB Decisions*, 5-6.
16. *Minnesota Union Advocate*, October 14, 1933, 1.
17. *NLB Decisions*, 1-2.
18. Gross, *Making of the NLRB*, 22.
19. *NLB Decisions*, 58-61.
20. Bernstein, *The Turbulent Years*, 177.
21. Lorwin and Wubnig, *Labor Relations Boards*, 104.
22. Milton Handler, COHC.
23. Stephens to Cummings, January 10, 1934, OF 1164 (Weirton Steel Co. file), FDRL.
24. Wyzanski to Frankfurter, December 15, 1933, Wyzanski Papers, HLSL.
25. Quoted in Gross, *Making of the NLRB*, 39.
26. *New York Times*, January 13, 1934, 14.
27. Roosevelt to Cummings and Johnson, January 16, 1934, Box 3, OF 466, FDRL.
28. These letters are collected in OF 1164, FDRL.
29. *New York Times*, January 31, 1934, 5.
30. Handler, letter to author, December 17, 1980. Biographical data on Nebcker from *Who Was Who in America*, Vol. III.
31. *United States v. Weirton Steel Co.*, 7 F.Supp. 255-265 (D.Del. 1934). See Norris-LaGuardia Anti-Injunction Act, 29 U.S.C.A. §107 (1932).

32. Lorwin and Wubnig, *Labor Relations Boards*, 107.
33. Quoted in *NLB Decisions*, vii.
34. Quoted in U.S. Cong., Senate Committee on Education and Labor, *National Labor Relations Board, Hearings on S. 1958* (73rd Cong., 2nd Sess.), 195 [cited below as *Senate Hearings, NLRB*].
35. Id., 119 and 195.
36. Quoted in *Minnesota Union Advocate*, February 15, 1934, 1.
37. *NLB Decisions*, viii (Executive Order 6612-A).
38. Id., 64-65.
39. Quoted in American Liberty League, *National Recovery Acts*, 15. See also Lorwin and Wubnig, *Labor Relations Boards*, 353-359.
40. Draft opinion in Houde Engineering Company case, March 1934, Box 87, National Labor Board records, RG 25, NA.
41. Pierre duPont to Handler, June 19, 1934, id.
42. This account of the Wagner and Walsh bills is largely drawn from Bernstein, *The New Deal Collective Bargaining Policy*, 62-75; and Gross, *Making of the NLRB*, 64-72.
43. Bernstein, *The Turbulent Years*, 218. His account of the 1934 strike wave can be found at 217-317.
44. Quoted in *Decisions of the National Labor Relations Board, January 1, 1934-June 16, 1935*, vii [cited below as *Decisions of the (First) NLRB*].
45. Quoted in Gross, *Making of the NLRB*, 70-71.
46. Quoted in Bernstein, *The New Deal Collective Bargaining Policy*, 81.
47. Quoted in *Decisions of the [First] NLRB*, vii-x.
48. Lloyd Garrison, COHC.
49. Magruder to Frankfurter, May 12, 1934, Folder 1, Box 34, Magruder Papers, HLSL.
50. Buffalo Regional Board to Executive Director, NLRB, July 1934, Box 87, NLB records, RG 25, NA.
51. *Decisions of the [First] NLRB*, Vol. I, 35-40.
52. *New York Times*, September 13, 1934, 1.
53. Quoted in Gross, *Making of the NLRB*, 93.
54. Undated memorandum (September or October 1934), File 114-107, RG 60, NA.
55. Watts to Cummings, October 5, 1934, id.
56. Stephens to Cummings, October 11, 1934, Box 134, Stephens Papers, LC.
57. Chaffetz to Golden Bell, October 30, 1934, File 114-107, RG 60, NA.
58. Stephens to Cummings, October 16, 1934, id.
59. A number of these affidavits can be found in File 114-107, RG 60, NA.
60. *United States v. Houde Engineering Co.*, 9 F.Supp. 833, 834-836 (W.D.N.Y. 1935).
61. Critchlow to Stephens, undated (March 1935), File 114-012-12, RG 60, NA.
62. Garrison to Richberg, July 13, 1934, Box 581, RG 9, NA.
63. Stephens to Roosevelt, August 21, 1934, OF 1164, FDRL.
64. 2 *U.S. Law Week* 455-456 (January 22, 1935).
65. *United States v. Weirton Steel Corp.*, 10 F.Supp. 55, 86-90 (D.Del. 1935).
66. Wyzanski to Frankfurter, December 15, 1933, Folder 9, Box 1, Wyzanski Papers, HLSL.
67. 2 *U.S. Law Week* 589 (March 5, 1935).
68. *Senate Hearings, NLRB*, 55.

69. Garrison to Johnson, August 17, 1934, File—NRA-August-September 1934, Box 3, OF 466, FDRL.
70. *New York Times*, November 1, 1934, 1.
71. Frankfurter to Wyzanski, October 22, 1934, Folder 9, Box 1, Wyzanski Papers, HLSL.
72. Biddle to Stephens, February 12, 1935, File 114-12-12, RG 60, NA.
73. Stephens to Golden Bell, February 13, 1935, id.
74. Critchlow to Stephens, undated (February 1935), id.
75. Id.
76. Magruder to Richberg, February 23, 1935, id.
77. Cummings to Biddle, February 28, 1935, id.
78. Quoted in Gross, *Making of the NLRB*, 130.
79. Handler, letter to author, December 17, 1980.
80. Lyons, *The National Recovery Administration*, 486-487.

CHAPTER 11

1. Quoted in Gross, *Making of the NLRB*, 7071.
2. Interview with Thomas Emerson, July 15, 1980.
3. A. Norman Somers, CLMOH.
4. Philip Levy, CLMOH.
5. Thomas Emerson, CLMOH. Philip Levy also voiced criticism of Justice Department lawyers; they were, he said, "obviously not close to the labor problems—hadn't sweated out the labor issues; weren't familiar with the nuances of labor-management relations." Levy, CLMOH.
6. *Senate Hearings, NLRB*, 95-96. Biddle urged the Senate to give the NLRB its own litigation powers. "The division of responsibility creates chaos," he said of relations with the Justice Department. "The local district attorneys, upon whom falls the responsibility of instituting and conducting litigation, are not familiar with the problems involved, have had no experience in the field, and cannot be expected to give [the NLRB's] administration the same sympathetic support given by the Board."
7. Bernstein, *The New Deal Collective Bargaining Policy*, 114.
8. Quoted in Gross, *Making of the NLRB*, 135.
9. Frances Perkins, COHC, Book IV.
10. Letter, Keyserling to author, April 4, 1981.
11. Id.
12. Berstein, *The New Deal Collective Bargaining Policy*, 115-116.
13. Schlesinger, *Coming of the New Deal*, 404.
14. Bernstein, *The New Deal Collective Bargaining Policy*, 118-119.
15. Id., 118.
16. Philip Levy, CLMOH. In response to *Schechter*, Keyserling and Levy persuaded Wagner to rewrite the Declaration of Policy before House debate. "It was revised," Levy recalled, "to emphasize the effect of labor disputes on interstate commerce and to de-emphasize the mere economic effects which had been rejected by the court." Levy, CLMOH. For example, the bill's definition of the term "affecting commerce" was changed from acts "burdening or affecting commerce" to those "burdening or obstructing commerce." This semantic tinkering aroused scorn from the bill's opponents. "The mere transposition of some of the words in the original bill has brought

about nothing more than the difference between tweedledum and tweedledee,'' Rep. Howard Smith scoffed. *Congressional Record*, Vol. 79, Part 9 (74th Cong., 1st Sess.), 9693.

17. Diary entry for June 20, 1935, Homer Cummings Diary (microfilm), FDRL.
18. *Congressional Record*, Vol 79, Part 7 (74th Cong., 1st Sess.), 7565-7569, 7572.
19. Id., 7571-7572.
20. Id., 7677-7680.
21. J. Warren Madden, CLMOH.
22. Id. Also see Frances Perkins, COHC, Vol, IV.
23. Edwin Smith, CLMOH.
24. Interview with Nathan Witt, November 2, 1979.
25. J. Warren Madden, CLMOH.
26. Quoted in Gross, *Making of the NLRB*, 155.
27. Interview with Nathan Witt, November 2, 1979.
28. J. Warren Madden, CLMOH.
29. Id.
30. *Washington Post* clipping, undated, Charles Fahy file, Box 13, Stephens Papers, LC.
31. Quoted in Gross, *Making of the NLRB*, 171.
32. Thomas Emerson, CLMOH.
33. Stanley Surrey, CLMOH.
34. Nathan Witt, CLMOH; interview with Witt, November 2, 1979.
35. "Cases Tried Before Supreme Court," undated, Box 50, Fahy Papers, FDRL. In comparison, J. Crawford Biggs won 52 percent of his cases; Stanley Reed, 81 percent; and Robert Jackson, 85 percent.
36. Box 25, Smith Committee Investigation files, RG 25, NA.
37. Id.
38. Biographical data from Auerbach, *Unequal Justice*, 183-184, and Emerson, CLMOH.
39. Interview with Nathan Witt, November 2, 1979.
40. J. Warren Madden, CLMOH.
41. Auerbach, *Unequal Justice*, 295.
42. Interview with Nathan Witt, November 2, 1979; interview with Thomas Emerson, July 15, 1980. According to Gross, as of 1939, 12 of the 91 Review Division lawyers were women. *Making of the NLRB*, 169-170.
43. Interview with Charles Fahy, June 22, 1978.
44. Interview with Nathan Witt, November 2, 1979.
45. Thomas Emerson, CLMOH.
46. Gross, *Making of the NLRB*, 175.
47. Charles Fahy, CLMOH.
48. Gross, *Making of the NLRB*, 158.
49. Thomas Emerson, CLMOH.
50. Philip Levy, CLMOH. Carmody did, in fact, resign a year later, and was replaced by Donald W. Smith, a Georgetown Law School graduate who owed his appointment to Senator Guffey of Pennsylvania and who played no discernible role in the Board's work during his term.
51. Quoted in Gross, *Making of the NLRB*, 161.
52. George Pratt, CLMOH. The Regional Directors felt, in Pratt's words, that Board centralization "would result in nothing more than immense backlogs,

traffic jams, and would prevent . . . the preservation of labor peace through the encouragement of strong, responsible labor unions.'' What the Directors sought was ''greater latitude to the regional personnel in the handling of complaints, scheduling of them, determining which complaints were worth expenditures of time and energy, and determining whether efforts should be made to settle disputes rather than proceed with formal charges in the discretion of the Regional Director rather than the Washington office.''

53. Interview with Thomas Emerson, July 15, 1980.
54. U.S. Congress, Senate Education and Labor Committee, *Violations of Free Speech and Assembly and Interference with Rights of Labor*, 75th Cong., 1st Sess., 290 [cited below as *LaFollette Committee Hearings*]. For an excellent account of the LaFollette Committee investigations, see Auerbach, *Labor and Liberty: The LaFollette Committee and the New Deal*.
55. Interview with Nathan Witt, November 2, 1979.
56. Memorandum 410, July 9, 1935, Box 17, Fahy Papers, FDRL.
57. *LaFollette Committee Hearings*, 278-279.
58. See Wolfskill, *Revolt of the Conservatives*, and Auerbach, *Unequal Justice*, 193-199, on the formation of the National Lawyers Committee and biographical data on its leading members.
59. National Lawyers Committee, *Report on the Constitutionality of the National Labor Relations Act*, iii, x-xi, 1, 6-7, 38, 118-119.
60. Quoted in Wolfskill, *Revolt of the Conservatives*, 72.
61. National Labor Relations Board, *First Annual Report*, 47-48. Intervening sentences have been omitted.
62. Transcript of Meeting of Legal Staff, September 14, 1935, File-Working Papers, Box 19, Fahy Papers, FDRL.
63. George Pratt, CLMOH.
64. Quoted in Gross, *Making of the NLRB*, 208-209. This decision was unreported.
65. *Bendix Products Corp. v. Beman*, 14 F.Supp. 58 (N.D.Ill. 1936).
66. Quoted in Gross, *Making of the NLRB*, 208.
67. *LaFollette Committee Hearings*, 278.
68. *Precision Casting Co. v. Boland*, 13 F.Supp. 877, 884 (W.D.N.Y. 1936).
69. *Ohio Custom Garment Co. v. Lind*, 13 F.Supp. 533, 537 (S.D.Ohio 1936).
70. Assistant Attorney General Dickinson to Cummings, November 26, 1935, File 134-76-1, RG 60, NA; interview with Charles Fahy, June 22, 1978. In 1938, the Supreme Court overruled the only Court of Appeals decision upholding a district court injunction against the NLRB. *Myers v. Bethlehem Shipbuilding Corp.*, 303 U.S. 31 (1938).
71. The legislative history of the Guffey Act is detailed in Baker, *The National Bituminous Coal Commission*, 48-51, and Longin, ''Coal, Congress and the Courts,'' 107-111.
72. Longin, ''Coal, Congress and the Courts,'' 111-112.
73. Reed to McIntyre, August 31, 1935, OF 1732-Misc., FDRL.
74. The cases are cited and discussed in Longin, ''Coal, Congress and the Courts,'' 114-115.
75. Id., 116.
76. Fahy memorandum, no date (referring to draft brief dated February 3, 1936), File-Notes and Drafts of Arguments (1), Box 18, Fahy Papers, FDRL.
77. 2 *U.S. Law Week* 638, 663 (March 17, 1936).
78. Id., 663-664.

NOTES

79. *Carter v. Carter Coal Co.*, 298 U.S. 278, 295-308 (1936).
80. 298 U.S. at 317-341 (Brandeis, dissenting).
81. Quoted in Gross, *Making of the NLRB*, 200.
82. Thomas Emerson, CLMOH.
83. Interview with Charles Fahy, June 22, 1978.
84. Thomas Emerson, CLMOH.

CHAPTER 12

1. Thomas Emerson, COHC.
2. Id.
3. Golden to Board, September 24, 1935, Box 335, RG 25 (National Labor Relations Board records), NA.
4. Nathan Witt, CLMOH.
5. Thomas Emerson, CLMOH.
6. Interview with Stanley Surrey, October 12, 1978.
7. Decision and Order in Pennsylvania Greyhound Lines case, 1 *Decisions and Orders of the NLRB*, 1 (December 7, 1935).
8. Watts to Board, no date (late December, 1935), File-Working Papers, Box 19, Fahy papers, FDRL.
9. Thomas Emerson, COHC.
10. Interview with Thomas Emerson, July 15, 1980.
11. *NLRB v. Pennsylvania Greyhound Lines*, 91 F.2d 178 (3rd Cir. 1937). By this time, Judge Thompson had died; Judge Dickinson retired in 1939; and Judge Buffington remained on the bench until 1958, at the age of 103.
12. Patterson to Board, September 24, 1935, Case File C-2, RG 25, NA. Richard C. Cortner, in *The Wagner Act Cases*, provides a detailed account of the background of each of the five test cases, 106-136, based on these case files.
13. Cortner, *The Wagner Act Cases*, 108.
14. Patterson to Fahy, September 27, 1935; October 2, 1935; October 4, 1935, Case File C-2, RG 25, NA.
15. Fahy to Patterson, October 17, 1935, id.
16. Bowen to Benedict Wolf, NLRB Secretary, October 23, 1935, id.
17. Quoted in Cortner, *The Wagner Act Cases*, 108-109.
18. Patterson to Fahy, October 21, 1935, Case File C-2, RG 25, NA.
19. Watts to Patterson, October 30, 1935, id.
20. Patterson to Fahy, November 12, 1935, id.
21. Patterson to Fahy, November 8, 1935, id.
22. Quoted in Cortner, *The Wagner Act Cases*, 11.
23. Watts to Patterson, December 16, 1935, Case File C-2, RG 25, NA.
24. Watts to J. W. Menzies, Clerk, Sixth Circuit Court of Appeals (Cincinnati), January 3, 1936, id.
25. Watts to Menzies, January 16, 1936, id.
26. Brody, *Steelworkers in America: The Nonunion Era*, 200.
27. Cortner, *The Wagner Act Cases*, 116. The Jones & Laughlin case is discussed in Cortner from 114-119.
28. Golden to Board, June 28, 1935, Case File C-57, RG 25, NA.
29. Golden to Board, September 24, 1935, Box 335, RG 25, NA.
30. Kleeb to Board, January 16, 1936, Case File C-57, RG 25, NA.
31. Cortner, *The Wagner Act Cases*, 115-116.

32. Id., 116.
33. NLRB, *Governmental Protection of Labor's Right to Organize*, III.
34. Decision and Order in Jones & Laughlin case, 1 *Decisions and Orders of the NLRB*, 503, 517-518.
35. Watts to Fahy, March 12, 1936; Watts to Fahy, March 13, 1936; Watts to Madden, April 6, 1936, Case File C-57, RG 25, NA.
36. *NLRB v. Mackay Radio and Telegraph Co.*, 82 F.2d 611 (9th Cir. 1937); Fahy to Board, April 9, 1936, Box 24, Legal Division Files, RG 25, NA.
37. Philip Levy, CLMOH.
38. Van Arkle to Fahy, September 19, 1935, Box 19, Regional Labor Board Files, RG 25, NA. Cortner discusses the case at 119-126.
39. Van Arkle to Fahy, October 30, 1935, Box 335, RG 25, NA.
40. Wolf to Elinor Herrick (New York Regional Director), March 12, 1936, Box 16, Regional Labor Board Records, RG 25, NA.
41. Interview with Charles Fahy, June 22, 1978.
42. Charles Fahy, CLMOH.
43. *New York Times*, April 21, 1936.
44. Madden to Hand, April 21, 1936, Folder 18, Box 198, Frankfurter papers, HLSL.
45. *NLRB v. Friedman-Harry Marks Clothing Co.*, 83 F.2d 731 (2nd Cir. 1936).
46. Herrick to Board, November 27, 1935, Case File C-84, RG 25, NA. Cortner discusses the Associated Press case at 126-133.
47. Id.
48. See Cortner, *The Wagner Act Cases*, 127-129.
49. Fahy to Moscovitz, March 11, 1936, Case File C-84, RG 25, NA.
50. Broun to Bondy, February 27, 1936, id.
51. *Associated Press v. Herrick*, 13 F.Supp. 897, 898-899 (S.D.N.Y. 1936).
52. Fahy to Moscovitz, March 18, 1936, Case File C-84, RG 25, NA.
53. See Cortner, *The Wagner Act Cases*, 130-131.
54. Id., 134-136.
55. Thomas Emerson, CLMOH.
56. Thomas Emerson, COHC.
57. Watts to Madden, June 1, 1936, Case File C-57, RG 25, NA.
58. Philip Levy, CLMOH.
59. *NLRB v. Jones & Laughlin Steel Corp.*, 83 F.2d 998 (5th Cir. 1936).
60. Fahy to Watts, June 18, 1936, Case File C-57, RG 25, NA.
62. *Fruehauf Trailer Co. v. NLRB*, 85 F.2d 391, 392 (6th Cir. 1936).
63. Quoted in Cortner, *The Wagner Act Cases*, 137. Cortner dates this telegram from Fahy to Philip G. Phillips as June 25, 1936, which is obviously an error.
64. *NLRB v. Friedman-Harry Marks Clothing Co.*, 85 F.2d 1, 2 (2nd Cir. 1936).
65. *NLRB v. Associated Press*, 85 F.2d 56, 59-60 (2nd Cir. 1936).
66. Fahy to Fourth Circuit Court of Appeals, July 14, 1936, Box 19, Regional Labor Board Files, RG 25, NA.
67. Judge Parker to Fahy, July 20, 1936, id.
68. Fahy to Davis, July 27, 1936; Fahy to Herrick, July 22, 1936, Case File C-84, RG 25, NA.
69. Fahy to Reed, July 22, 1936, File 134-1, RG 60, NA.
70. *NLRB v. Washington, Virginia & Maryland Coach Co.*, 85 F.2d 990 (4th Cir. 1936).

71. J. Warren Madden, COHC.
72. Id.

CHAPTER 13

1. Harris, *American Labor*, 286-288.
2. I have presented here only a brief sketch of the origins and politics of the court-packing plan, which deserves a new recounting. Only two book-length studies exist. Alsop and Catledge, *The 168 Days*, is a contemporary journalistic account of the "insider" variety, reminiscent of the more recent book by Woodward and Armstrong, *The Brethren*. Baker, *Back to Back: The Duel Between FDR and the Supreme Court*, published in 1967, is a popularized account with some documentation from manuscript sources but with little focus on the plan's origins. Leuchtenberg, "The Origins of Franklin D. Roosevelt's 'Court-Packing' Plan," is insightful on this aspect, but none of these studies made use of the diaries of Attorney General Cummings, which detail his meetings and strategy sessions with Roosevelt.
3. Alsop and Catledge, *The 168 Days*, 43.
4. Id.
5. Frankfurter to Burlingham, November 28, 1936, Box 4, Burlingham Papers, HLSL.
6. Burlingham to Frankfurter, December 1, 1936, id.
7. Interview with Thomas Corcoran, June 15, 1978. There were a number of articles on various court reform plans in *U.S. Law Week* from 1935 to 1937.
8. Alsop and Catledge, *The 168 Days*, 36; Frankfurter to Reed, December 14, 1936, Folder 15, Box 170, Frankfurter Papers, HLSL.
9. Reed to Frankfurter, December 17, 1936, id.
10. Alsop and Catledge, *The 168 Days*, 33-37.
11. The text of the bill and the accompanying messages from Roosevelt and Cummings are in *Congressional Record*, Vol. 81, Part 1 (75th Cong., 1st Sess.), 880-881.
12. Id., 877-878.
13. Mason, *Harlan Fiske Stone*, 451.
14. Id., 444.
15. *Adkins v. Childrens Hospital*, 261 U.S. 525 (1923).
16. *Morehead ex rel. New York v. Tipaldo*, 298 U.S. 602, 610-611 (1936).
17. 298 U.S. at 632, 635 (Stone dissenting).
18. Roosevelt press conference, June 2, 1936, Roll 7, 280, Presidential Press conference transcripts, FDRL.
19. Frankfurter to Stone, June 5, 1936, Folder 15, Box 171, Frankfurter Papers, HLSL.
20. *St. Louis Star-Times*, editorial, "Five Bourbons Speak," June 2, 1936.
21. *New York Times*, June 12, 1936, 1.
22. Quoted in Chambers, "The Big Switch: Justice Roberts and the Minimum Wage Cases," 53. See also Parrish, "The Hughes Court, the Great Depression, and the Historians."
23. Chambers, "The Big Switch," 60.
24. *West Coast Hotel v. Parrish*, 300 U.S. 386, 389-399 (1937).
25. 300 U.S. at 401-402.
26. Philip Levy, CLMOH.

27. Interview with Charles Fahy, June 22, 1978.
28. Id.
29. Thomas Emerson, COHC.
30. Philip Levy, CLMOH.
31. Id.
32. *NLRB v. Jones & Laughlin*, 301 U.S. 1 (1937), Brief for Petitioner, 41-43, 50-51, 70, Briefs and Records of the Supreme Court, 1936 Term.
33. Philip Levy, CLMOH.
34. *Virginian Railway Co. v. Southern System Federation*, 300 U.S. 515, 548 (1937).
35. Philip Levy, CLMOH.
36. 301 U.S. 1, 45 (1937).
37. See *J. I.Case Co. v. NLRB*, 321 U.S. 332 (1944).
38. J. Warren Madden, COHC.
39. Ernst to Reed, December 7, 1936, File 134-151-1, RG 60, NA.
40. U.S. Cong., Senate Document No. 52 (75th Cong., 1st Sess.), *Oral Arguments in NLRB Cases*, 58, 66, 70.
41. Id., 72, 82-84.
42. Id., 87, 92, 88.
43. Id., 112-113, 117.
44. Id., 118, 126-128.
45. Id., 170-173.
46. Id., 175-180.
47. Wyzanski to Frankfurter, February 18, 1937, Folder 003033, Box 149, Frankfurter Papers, LC.
48. Interview with Thomas Emerson, July 15, 1980. Fahy was equally cautious after the arguments: "I didn't feel confident. No one could truthfully say we were entitled to feel confident in the manufacturing cases." Interview with Charles Fahy, June 22, 1978.
49. Interview with Thomas Emerson, July 15, 1980.
50. 301 U.S. 1, 30, 45, 41 (1937).
51. Quoted in Leuchtenberg, *Franklin D. Roosevelt and the New Deal*, 236.
52. 301 U.S. 1, 103 (McReynolds, dissenting).
53. *Associated Press v. NLRB*, 301 U.S. 103, 138 (1937) (Sutherland, dissenting).
54. *Washington, Virginia & Maryland Coach Co. v. NLRB*, 301 U.S. 142 (1937).
55. Wyzanski to Frankfurter, April 14, 1937, Folder 003033, Box 149, Frankfurter Papers, LC.

Conclusion

1. 310 U.S. 548, 586-587 (1937).
2. *Helvering v. Davis*, 301 U.S. 619, 641 (1937). Jackson, who argued both Social Security Act cases with Wyzanski, discusses them in *The Struggle for Judicial Supremacy*, 221-234.
3. *Sunshine Anthracite Coal Co. v. Adkins*, 310 U.S. 381, 395-397 (1940).
4. 312 U.S. 100, 116-117 (1941). Stern discusses this case and provides its factual background in "The Commerce Clause and the National Economy," 885-890.
5. 317 U.S. 111, 125-129 (1942). Stern discusses this case in id., 901-907.
6. Anderson, *A. Philip Randolph*, 229-259.

7. *United States v. Carolene Products Co.*, 304 U.S. 144, 152-153, n. 4 (1938).

8. See Kluger, *Simple Justice*, 558, and Navasky, *Kennedy Justice*, 294, for brief and similar accounts of Stern's role in *Brown*.

9. Stern, "That Commerce Which Concerns More States than One," 1365.

10. *Heart of Atlanta Motel v. United States*, 379 U.S. 241, 257 (1964).

11. Landis, *The Administrative Process*, 14-16. On Landis' career, which ended with imprisonment for failure to file federal income tax returns in 1963 and his death the following year, see Ritchie, *James M. Landis: Dean of the Regulators*.

12. Jaffe and Nathanson, *Administrative Law*, 5 and 136-138.

13. Jaffe, "The Illusion of the Ideal Administration," 1183-1189.

14. Evidenced, to cite one example, in Sen. Edward Kennedy's support for deregulation of the trucking and airlines industries.

15. Parrish, "The Hughes Court, the Great Depression, and the Historians," 304.

16. *National Cable Television Ass'n v. United States*, 415 U.S. 336, 378 (1974) (Marshall, dissenting).

17. *Industrial Union Department v. American Petroleum Institute*, 100 S.Ct. 2844, 2866 (Stevens, plurality opinion), 2886 (Rehnquist, concurring) (1980).

18. Douglas, *Go East, Young Man* 217.

19. Horsky, *The Washington Lawyer*, 154.

20. On Richberg's later career, see Vadney, *The Wayward Liberal*.

MANUSCRIPT COLLECTIONS

National Archives, Washington, D.C.

Records of the National Recovery Administration (Record Group 9).
Records of the Department of Agriculture (Record Group 16).
Records of the National Labor Relations Board (Record Group 25).
Records of the Department of Justice (Record Group 60).
Records of the Agricultural Adjustment Administration (Record Group 145).

Library of Congress, Manuscript Division, Washington, D.C.

Papers of Felix Frankfurter
Papers of Donald Richberg
Papers of Harold Stephens

Franklin D. Roosevelt Library, Hyde Park, New York

Department of Agriculture file (OF [Official File] 1).
Court Reform file (OF 10).
National Recovery Administration file (OF 466).
Weirton Steel Co. file (OF 1164).
Carter Coal Co. file (OF 1732-Miscellaneous).
Homer Cummings Diary (on microfilm; original at University of Virginia Library).
Papers of Charles Fahy
Papers of Leon Henderson
Presidential Press Conferences, 1933-1937 (on microfilm).
Department of Agriculture file, President's Secretary's File
Rexford Tugwell Diary

Harvard Law School, Manuscript Division, Cambridge, Massachusetts

Papers of Charles C. Burlingham
Papers of Felix Frankfurter
Papers of Calvert Magruder
Papers of Thomas Reed Powell
Papers of Charles Wyzanski

New York Times Microfilm Editions

Papers of H. L. Mitchell

BIBLIOGRAPHY

University of Iowa Libraries

Papers of Henry A. Wallace (microfilm edition).

Yale University Library, Manuscript Division, New Haven, Connecticut

Papers of Jerome Frank

ORAL HISTORY COLLECTIONS

Columbia Oral History Collection, Columbia University Library, New York

Chester Davis
Thomas Emerson
Jerome Frank
Milton Handler
Frances Perkins
Lee Pressman

Cornell Labor-Management Oral History Collection, School of Industrial and Labor Relations, Cornell University, Ithaca, New York

Thomas Emerson
Charles Fahy
Lloyd Garrison
Leon Keyserling
Philip Levy
J. Warren Madden
George Pratt
Edwin S. Smith
A. Norman Somers
Stanley Surrey
Gerhard Van Arkle
Nathan Witt

INTERVIEWS

John Abt (New York, January 24, 1980)
Bernice Lotwin Bernstein (New York, October 21, 1977)
Thomas Corcoran (Washington, D.C., June 15, 1978)
Thomas Emerson (New Haven, July 15, 1980)
Charles Fahy (Washington, D.C., June 22, 1978)
Paul Freund (Cambridge, Massachusetts, October 3, 1977)
Alger Hiss (New York, July 12, 1978 and September 29, 1979)

Milton Katz (Cambridge, Massachusetts, November 18, 1977)
Blackwell Smith (Princeton, New Jersey, October 22, 1977)
Nathan Witt (New York, November 2, 1979)

Books

American Liberty League. *The National Recovery Act*. New York: American Liberty League, 1935.

Anderson, Jervis. *A. Philip Randolph*. New York: Harcourt, Brace, 1973.

Auerbach, Jerold S. *Labor and Liberty: The LaFollette Committee and the New Deal*. Indianapolis: Bobbs-Merrill, 1966.

——. *Unequal Justice: Lawyers and Social Change in Modern America*. New York: Oxford University Press, 1976.

Badger, Anthony J. *Prosperity Road: The New Deal, Tobacco, and North Carolina*. Chapel Hill: University of North Carolina Press, 1980.

Baker, Leonard. *Back to Back: The Duel Between FDR and the Supreme Court*. New York: Macmillan, 1967.

Baker, Ralph H. *The National Bituminous Coal Commission*. Baltimore: Johns Hopkins University Press, 1941.

Barber, James D. *The Presidential Character: Predicting Performance in the White House*. Englewood Cliffs, N.J.: Prentice-Hall, 1972.

Bellush, Bernard. *The Failure of the NRA*. New York: W. W. Norton, 1975.

Bernstein, Irving. *The New Deal Collective Bargaining Policy*. Berkeley: University of California Press, 1950.

——. *The Turbulent Years: A History of the American Worker, 1933-1941*. Boston: Houghton Mifflin, 1970.

Black, John D. *The Dairy Industry and the AAA*. Washington: Brookings Institution, 1935.

Brandeis, Louis D. *The Curse of Bigness*. New York: Viking Press, 1934.

Brewster, Kingman, et al. *Taxation Under the A.A.A.* New York: Baker, Voorhis & Co., 1934.

Brody, David. *Steelworkers in America: The Nonunion Era*. Cambridge: Harvard University Press, 1960.

Chase, Harold, et al. *Biographical Dictionary of the Federal Judiciary*. Detroit: Gale Research Co., 1976.

Conrad, David. *The Forgotten Farmers: The Story of Sharecroppers in the New Deal*. Urbana: University of Illinois Press, 1965.

Cortner, Richard C. *The Wagner Act Cases*. Knoxville: University of Tennessee Press, 1964.

Corwin, Edward. *The Twilight of the Supreme Court*. New Haven: Yale University Press, 1934.

335

Cummings, Homer, and McFarland, Carl. *Federal Justice: Chapters in the History of Justice and the Federal Executive.* New York: Macmillan, 1937.

Dawson, Nelson L. *Louis D. Brandeis, Felix Frankfurter, and the New Deal.* Hamden, Conn.: Archon Books, 1980.

Dewey, Donald. *Monopoly in Economics and Law.* Chicago: Rand, McNally, 1959.

Dubofsky, Melvyn, and Van Tine, Warren. *John L. Lewis.* New York: Quadrangle-New York Times Books, 1977.

Fite, Gilbert. *George N. Peek and the Fight for Farm Parity.* Norman: Oklahoma University Press, 1954.

Frank, Jerome. *Courts on Trial: Myth and Reality in American Justice.* Princeton: Princeton University Press, 1949.

———. *If Men Were Angels.* New York: Harper, 1942.

———. *Law and the Modern Mind.* New York: Brentano's, 1930.

Frankfurter, Felix. *The Case of Sacco and Vanzetti.* Boston: Little, Brown, 1927.

———. *The Public and Its Government.* New Haven: Yale University Press, 1930.

Freedman, Max, ed. *Roosevelt and Frankfurter: Their Correspondence, 1928-1945.* Boston: Little, Brown, 1967.

Friedel, Frank. *Franklin D. Roosevelt: Launching the New Deal.* Boston: Little, Brown, 1974.

Fusfeld, Daniel. *The Economic Thought of Franklin D. Roosevelt and the Origins of the New Deal.* New York: Columbia University Press, 1956.

Galambos, Louis. *Competition and Cooperation: The Emergence of a National Trade Association.* Baltimore: Johns Hopkins University Press, 1966.

Gross, James A. *The Making of the National Labor Relations Board* (Vol. I). Albany: State University of New York Press, 1974.

Grubbs, Donald H. *Cry from the Cotton: The Southern Tenant Farmers Union and the New Deal.* Chapel Hill: University of North Carolina Press, 1971.

Harris, Hubert. *American Labor.* New Haven: Yale University Press, 1938.

Hawley, Ellis W. *The New Deal and the Problem of Monopoly.* Princeton: Princeton University Press, 1966.

Himmelberg, Robert. *The Origins of the National Recovery Administration: Business, Government and the Antitrust Question.* New York: Fordham University Press, 1975.

Hirsch, H. N. *The Enigma of Felix Frankfurter.* New York: Basic Books, 1981.

Horowitz, Donald. *The Jurocracy: Government Lawyers, Agency Programs, and Judicial Decisions.* Lexington, Mass.: Lexington Books, 1977.

Horsky, Charles. *The Washington Lawyer.* Boston: Little, Brown, 1952.

Ickes, Harold C. *The Autobiography of a Curmudgeon.* New York: Reynal and Hitchcock, 1943.

———. *Secret Diary: The First Thousand Days.* New York: Simon & Shuster, 1953.

Jackson, Robert H. *The Struggle for Judicial Supremacy.* New York: Knopf, 1941.

Jaffe, Louis L., and Nathanson, Nathaniel. *Administrative Law: Cases and Materials.* Boston: Little, Brown, 1976.

Javits, Benjamin A. *Business and the Public Interest: Trade Associations, the Anti-Trust Laws and Industrial Planning.* New York: Macmillan, 1932.

Johnson, Charles S., et al. *The Collapse of Cotton Tenancy.* Chapel Hill: University of North Carolina Press, 1935.

Johnson, Hugh S. *The Blue Eagle from Egg to Earth.* New York: Doubleday, Doran & Co., 1935.

Johnson, Walter, ed. *The Papers of Adlai Stevenson*, Vol. I. Boston: Little, Brown, 1972.

Kester, Howard. *Revolt Among the Sharecroppers.* New York: Covici, Friede, 1936.

Kluger, Richard. *Simple Justice: The History of Brown v. Board of Education and Black America's Struggle for Equality.* New York: Knopf, 1976.

Kolko, Gabriel. *Main Currents in Modern American History.* New York: Harper & Row, 1976.

———. *The Triumph of Conservatism: A Reinterpretation of American History, 1900-1916.* New York: Free Press, 1963.

Landis, James. *The Administrative Process.* New Haven: Yale University Press, 1938.

Lash, Joseph P., ed. *From the Diaries of Felix Frankfurter.* New York: W. W. Norton, 1975.

Letwin, William H. *Law and Economic Policy in America: The Evolution of the Sherman Antitrust Act.* Edinburgh: University Press, 1967.

Leuchtenberg, William E. *Franklin D. Roosevelt and the New Deal.* New York: Harper & Row, 1963.

Lorwin, Lewis L., and Wubnig, Arthur. *Labor Relations Boards: The Regulation of Collective Bargaining Under the National Industrial Recovery Act.* Washington: Brookings Institution, 1935.

Lyons, Leverett, ed. *The National Recovery Administration: An Analysis and Appraisal*. Washington: Brookings Institution, 1935.

Machiavelli, Niccolo. *The Discourses*. Numerous editions available.

Martin, George. *Madame Secretary, Frances Perkins*. Boston: Houghton Mifflin, 1976.

Mason, Alpheus T. *Brandeis: A Free Man's Life*. New York: Viking Press, 1946.

———. *Harlan Fiske Stone, Pillar of the Law*. New York: Viking Press, 1956.

Mitchell, H. L. *Mean Things Happening in This Land*. Montclair, N.J.: Allenheld & Osmond, 1979.

Moley, Raymond. *After Seven Years*. New York: Harper, 1939.

National Lawyers Committee of the American Liberty League. *Report on the Constitutionality of the National Labor Relations Act*. Pittsburgh: Smith Bros., 1935.

Navasky, Victor. *Kennedy Justice*. New York: Atheneum, 1971.

Nordhauser, Norman E. *The Quest for Stability: Domestic Oil Regulation, 1917-1935*. New York: Garland, 1979.

Nourse, Edwin. *Marketing Agreements Under the AAA*. Washington: Brookings Institution, 1935.

Pearson, Drew, and Allen, Robert S. *The Nine Old Men*. New York: Doubleday, Doran, 1936.

Peek, George. *Why Quit Our Own*. New York: Van Nostrand, 1936.

Pepper, George Wharton. *Philadelphia Lawyer: An Autobiography*. Philadelphia: J. B. Lippincott, 1944.

Perkins, Van L. *Crisis in Agriculture: The Agricultural Adjustment Administration and the New Deal, 1933*. Berkeley: University of California Press, 1969.

Purcell, Edward A., Jr. *The Crisis of Democratic Theory: Scientific Naturalism and the Problem of Value*. Lexington: University Press of Kentucky, 1973.

Rauch, Basil. *The History of the New Deal, 1933-1938*. New York: Creative Age Press, 1944.

Richards, Henry I. *Cotton under the Agricultural Adjustment Act: Developments Up to July, 1934*. Washington: Brookings Institution, 1934.

Richberg, Donald. *My Hero: The Indiscreet Memoirs of an Eventful But Unheroic Life*. New York: Putnam, 1954.

———. *The Rainbow*. New York: Doubleday, Doran, 1936.

Ritchie, Donald A. *James M. Landis: Dean of the Regulators*. Cambridge: Harvard University Press, 1980.

Rosenman, Samuel I., ed. *The Public Papers and Addresses of Franklin D. Roosevelt*, Vol. I. New York: Harper, 1938.

Schlesinger, Arthur M., Jr. *The Coming of the New Deal*. Boston: Houghton Mifflin, 1959.

———. *The Politics of Upheaval*. Boston: Houghton Mifflin, 1960.

Swaine, Robert. *The Cravath Firm and Its Predecessors, 1819-1946*. New York: Ad Press, 1946.

Swanberg, W. A. *Norman Thomas: The Last Idealist*. New York: Scribners, 1976.

Swisher, Carl B. *American Constitutional Development*. Boston: Houghton Mifflin, 1943.

———, ed. *Selected Papers of Homer Cummings*. New York: Scribners, 1939.

Tugwell, Rexford. *The Brains Trust*. New York: Viking Press, 1968.

———. *The Democratic Roosevelt*. New York: Doubleday, 1957.

Twiss, Benjamin. *Lawyers and the Constitution*. Princeton: Princeton University Press, 1942.

Urofsky, Melvin I., and Levy, David W., eds. *Letters of Louis D. Brandeis*, Vol. V. Albany: State University of New York Press, 1978.

Vadney, Thomas E. *The Wayward Liberal: A Political Biography of Donald Richberg*. Lexington: University Press of Kentucky, 1970.

Volkomer, Walter E. *Passionate Liberal: The Political and Legal Ideas of Jerome Frank*. The Hague: Nijhoff, 1970.

Weaver, Suzanne. *Decision to Prosecute: Organization and Public Policy in the Antitrust Division*. Cambridge: MIT Press, 1977.

Weinstein, James. *The Corporate Ideal in the Liberal State, 1900-1918*. Boston: Beacon Press, 1968.

Wolfskill, George. *Revolt of the Conservatives*. Boston: Houghton Mifflin, 1962.

ARTICLES AND UNPUBLISHED MATERIAL

Auerbach, Jerold S. "Southern Tenant Farmers: Socialist Critics of the New Deal." 7 *Labor History* 3 (Winter 1966).

Barber, James D. "The Interplay of Presidential Character and Style: A Paradigm and Five Illustrations." Greenstein, Fred I., and Lerner, Michael, eds. *A Sourcebook for the Study of Personality and Politics*. Chicago: Markham, 1976.

Chambers, John W. "The Big Switch: Justice Roberts and the Minimum Wage Cases." 10 *Labor History* 43 (Winter 1969).

"Felix Frankfurter." *Fortune*, January, 1936, 63.

Frank, Jerome. "Experimental Jurisprudence and the New Deal." *Congressional Record*, Vol. 79, Part 11 (73rd Cong., 1st Sess.) 12413.

Frank, Jerome. "Mr. Justice Holmes and Non-Euclidean Thinking." 17 *Cornell Law Quarterly* 568 (1932).

Frankfurter, Felix. "The Young Men Go to Washington." *Fortune*, January, 1936, 63.

Glennon, Robert J., Jr. "Principles Are What Principles Do: Lawyers in the New Deal." Unpublished paper, Wayne State University Law School, 1979.

[Hiss, Alger]. "The 'Yellow Dog' Device as a Bar to the Union Organizer." 41 *Harvard Law Review* 770 (1928).

Irons, Peter H. " 'Fighting Fair': Zechariah Chafee, Jr., the Department of Justice, and the 'Trial at the Harvard Club.' " 94 *Harvard Law Review* 1205 (1981).

Jaffe, Louis L. "The Illusion of the Ideal Administration." 86 *Harvard Law Review* 1183 (1973).

Josephson, Matthew. "Profile of Hugh Johnson." *New Yorker* (August 18, 1934, 21; August 25, 1934, 23; September 1, 1934, 22).

Keyserling, Leon H. "The Wagner Act: Its Origin and Current Significance." 29 *George Washington Law Review* 199 (1960).

Leuchtenberg, William E. "The Origins of Franklin D. Roosevelt's 'Court-Packing' Plan." 1966 *Supreme Court Review* 347.

Lowe, Richard H. "Fallen Warrior of Reform: Jerome N. Frank as General Counsel for the Agricultural Adjustment Administration." Unpublished senior thesis, Yale University, 1979.

Lowitt, Richard. "Henry A. Wallace and the 1935 Purge in the Department of Agriculture." 53 *Agricultural History* 607 (1979).

Moley, Raymond. "And Now Give Us Good Men," *Today*, May 19, 1934, 13.

Nash, Gerald D. "Experiments in Industrial Mobilization: WIB and NRA." 45 *Mid-America* 157 (1963).

Parrish, Michael. "The Hughes Court, the Great Depression, and the Historians." 60 *The Historian* 286 (1978).

Richberg, Donald. "The Industrial Liberalism of Justice Brandeis." 31 *Columbia Law Review* 1094 (1931).

Stern, Robert L. "That Commerce Which Concerns More States Than One." 47 *Harvard Law Review* 1335 (1934).

———. "The Commerce Clause and the National Economy, 1933-1946." 59 *Harvard Law Review* 645 (1946).

Swisher, Carl B. "Federal Organization of Legal Functions." 33 *American Political Science Review* 973 (1939).

Venkataramani, M. S. "Norman Thomas, Arkansas Sharecroppers, and the Roosevelt Agricultural Policies, 1933-1937." 47 *Mississippi Valley Historical Review* 225 (1960).

341

INDEX

issue in hot oil cases, 66, 71; in *Schechter* case, 89-90; in *Schechter* brief, 92-93; in NLRA briefs, 280-282; in *Jones & Laughlin* opinion, 287-288; in later cases, 295
Connery, Cong. William, 211, 231
Coppage v. Kansas, 232, 246, 285, 288
Corcoran, Howard, 125, 299
Corcoran, Thomas, 9, 12, 84, 104-105, 125, 152, 155, 298; conflict with Jerome Frank, 147-149; and court-packing plan, 274-275
Corwin, Edward S., 49; role in *Carter Coal* case, 250-251
cotton industry, role in AAA, 156
Cotton Textile Code, drafting of in NRA, 31
Coudert, Frederic R., Jr., 244
court-packing plan, origins of, 197-199, 272, 275; presented to Congress, 275-276
Criminal Appeals Act, 78, 80
Critchlow, Francis, 218, 222-223
Cummings, Homer S., 105, 144, 150, 195, 247, 291; background of and appointment as Attorney General, 11; and NRA enforcement, 40; and *Hart Coal* case, 43-45; and hot oil cases, 62, 67; and *Belcher* case, 80-81, 84; and AAA litigation, 146-147; and court-packing plan, 197-199; and *Weirton* case, 208-209; and *Houde* case, 216-217; conflict with NLRB, 224-225; doubts on NLRA, 231; and court-packing plan, 272-276
Curse of Bigness, The, 20

dairy industry, conflict within AAA over, 131-132; and AAA litigation, 136-138
Darrow, Clarence, 7, 39
Davis, Chester, 10, 127, 135, 145, 190; appointment to AAA, 119; replaces Peek, 132; role in cotton contract, 158, 161, 163-166, 169-172; and AAA purge, 173-180
Davis, John W., 270; and National Lawyers Committee, 244; and *Associated Press* case, 266-267, 283-284
Dawson, Judge Charles I., and *Hart Coal* case, 42-43; Supreme Court argument in *Tway Coal* case, 250

Declaratory Judgment Act of 1934, 186
delegation doctrine, cases on, 51-52; in *Schechter* case, 90; in *Schechter* brief, 93-94; treatment in *Schechter* opinion, 101-102; in *Butler* case, 190; revival of, 297
Denver Tramway case, 212-213
Desvernine, Raoul, 244
Dickinson, John, appointment as Assistant Attorney General, 12; and court-packing plan, 197-198; argument in Bituminous Coal Conservation Act cases, 250-251
Dickinson, Judge Oliver, and *Greyhound* case, 256
Donohue, Judge James A., decision in *Canfield Lumber Co.* case, 53-54
Douglas, Justice William O., 7, 297, 299
Dred Scott case, 197, 198
Driver, Cong. William, 174
duPont, Pierre S., and NLB, 212-213

Early, Steve, 84, 197
East, Clay, role in STFU, 164-165, 179
Edgewater Dairy Co. v. Wallace, decision in, 150; as AAA test case, 153-154
emergency doctrine, cases on, 52-53; in *Schechter* brief, 93; treatment in *Schechter* decision, 101
Emerson, Thomas I., 226, 228, 235, 238, 239, 252, 253, 254-256, 261, 268, 287, 299; background of, 236; role in NLRB litigation strategy, 240-243; and NLRB briefs, 280-283
Ernst, Morris, and *Associated Press* case, 266, 283
Ezekial, Mordecai, 134, 187, 190-191

Fahy, Charles, 10, 11, 238, 239, 250, 255, 257, 259, 262-264, 266-268, 269-271, 287, 289, 299; and PAB cases, 64-65, 68, 71, 128; background of and appointment to NLRB, 234-235; staffing NLRB, 236-237; and injunction suits, 245-248; reaction to *Carter Coal* decision, 252-253; and NLRB briefs, 280-283; argument in *Associated Press* case, 284-285
Fake, Judge Guy L., decision in *Acme v. Besson*, 52

Farley, James, 197, 272; opposition to Jerome Frank, 122
Federal Trade Commission Act, 18, 23, 96-97, 228, 229, 247; and *Schechter* argument, 101-102
Feller, Abe, 280, 286
Field v. Clark, 51
Fifth Circuit Court of Appeals, and hot oil cases, 69-70; and *Hillsborough* case, 144; and *Jones & Laughlin* case, 262, 268-269
First Circuit Court of Appeals, and *Butler* case, 185-186
Fly, James L., role in AAA litigation, 137-139, 142-144; and *Weirton* case, 210
Ford, Henry, 32
Fortas, Abe, 7, 125, 298, 299; role in AAA litigation, 139, 142-144
Fourth Circuit Court of Appeals, and *Friedman-Harry Marks* case, 264-265; and *Coach Company* case, 267, 270
Francis, Charles I., 67
Frank, Jerome N., 7, 10, 60, 137, 139, 157, 185, 226, 235, 237, 296, 299; role in drafting AAA, 115; background of, and appointment to AAA, 119-122; on role of AAA lawyers, 123-124; conflict over patronage, 125-126; on Jewish lawyers in AAA, 126-128; conflict with Peek, 128-132; attitude toward AAA litigation, 133-134, 135-136, 140-141; conflict with Justice Department, 144-147, 151-155; role in AAA cotton contract, 159, 161, 164-165, 168, 169, 171-173; and AAA purge, 173-180; and *Butler* case, 183
Frankfuter, Felix, 12, 20, 23, 60, 100, 124, 125, 126, 145, 187, 215, 236, 278, 286, 291; background and teaching at Harvard Law School, 7-9; offered post of Solicitor General, 9; role in NIRA, 24; on NRA enforcement, 37; intervention in *Belcher* case, 80-85; views on *Schechter* brief, 94; reaction to *Schechter* decision, 105; role in appointment of Frank, 121-122; on AAA litigation, 133, 140-141; role in Frank-Corcoran rift, 147-149; views on Biddle, 221; and court-packing plan, 274-275

Freund, Paul A., 101, 141, 274, 299; and *Butler* case, 187, 191
Friant, Julian, 125-126
Friedman-Harry Marks case, background of, 263-264; before NLRB, 264; before court of appeals, 265; argument in Supreme Court, 286; Supreme Court opinion in, 288
Fruehauf case, 267, 268, 283; background of, 256-257; before NLRB, 258-259; in court of appeals, 259, 269; argument in Supreme Court, 286; Supreme Court opinion in, 288

Garrison, Lloyd, 233; appointment to NLRB, 215; and *Houde* case, 216-217; and *Weirton* case, 218; conflict with NRA and Justice Department, 220-221
Gautney, Chancellor J.G., and *Norcross* case, 168
general welfare clause, and *Butler* case, 188-189, 195
Gibbons v. Ogden, 47, 92, 137-138, 295
Golden, Clinton, 254-255, 256, 260
Green, William, 205, 209, 211, 221, 233; on 30-hour bill, 22
Greyhound case, 258, 259, 262, 265, 267; background of, 254-255; in court of appeals, 256
Griffin, William H., 44, 78
Grubb, Judge William, and *Belcher* case, 77-79
Guffey, Senator Joseph, and Bituminous Coal Conservation Act, 248
Guffey Act, *see* Bituminous Coal Conservation Act

Hale, Edward R., 193
Hale, R. L., 7
Hall, Pierson, and hot oil cases, 63-64
Hamilton, Judge Elwood, decision in *Tway Coal Co.* case, 249-250
Hamilton, Walton H., 7
Hammer v. Dagenhart, 49, 50, 71, 153, 185, 193; overruled, 292-293
Hampton v. U.S., 51-52
Hand, Judge Learned, 245; concurring opinion in *Schechter* case, 90; and *Friedman-Harry Marks* case, 264-265

INDEX

Handler, Milton, 7, 208, 211, 225, 227, 299; background of, and appointment to NLB, 205-206; and *Weirton* case, 210; and *Houde* case, 212-213; and Labor Disputes Act, 213-214; resigns, 215

Harriman, Henry I., 231; and drafting of NIRA, 18-19

Hart Coal Co. v. Sparks, 42-45

Hawley, Ellis, quoted, 19

Heart of Atlanta Motel case, 295

Heller, Joseph, role in *Schechter* case, 89, 98-99

Herrick, Elinor, 265, 267

Herzog, Paul, 216

Hillsborough Packing Co. v. Wallace, 142-144

Himmelberg, Robert, quoted, 19

Hiss, Alger, 127; background of, and appointment to AAA, 124-125; role in drafting cotton contract, 156-160; administration of cotton contract, 160, 161, 164, 169, 170; and AAA purge, 173, 175-180; and *Butler* case, 187-191, 194

Holly, Judge William, decision in *Shissler* case, 149-150

Holmes, Oliver Wendell, 124

Holtzoff, Alexander, and court-packing plan, 273, 275, 299

Home Building & Loan Association v. Blaisdell, see Blaisdell case

Hoover, Calvin B., role in AAA cotton contract, 161, 165; and AAA purge, 175

Hoosac Mills case, *see Butler* case

Hopkins, Harry, 17, 23, 128

Horowitz, Donald L., quoted, 11

Horsky, Charles, 187, 286, 299; and NLRA briefs, 280-283

Houde Engineering Co. case, 212-213, 216, 218

Howe, Dr. Frederick, as AAA Consumer Counsel, 131; and AAA purge, 177, 179

Huberman, M. S., and hot oil cases, 70-71

Hughes, Chief Justice Charles Evans, 13, 219, 232, 252, 253, 279, 291; opinion in hot oil cases, 72; opinion in *Schechter* case, 101-103; and court-packing plan, 276; dissent in *Morehead* case, 278;

opinion in *Jones & Laughlin* case, 287-288

Hutchins, Robert M., 7

Ickes, Harold, background of, 60; appointment as Interior Secretary and Petroleum Administrator, 60; conflict with Richberg, 61-62; and hot oil cases, 64-68, 71-72

Interstate Commerce Commission, 257

Jackson, Gardner, and AAA cotton contract, 170-171; and AAA purge, 177, 179, 180

Jackson, Robert H., 195, 290-292, 299

Jaffe, Louis, 141, 296, 299

Javits, Benjamin, 19

Johnson, General Hugh, 30, 34, 35, 40, 61, 80, 114, 115, 118, 119, 216, 220; view of New Deal lawyers, 20; drafting of NIRA, 22-23; background of, 27; appointment as NRA Administrator, 27; role in Richberg appointment, 28; and textile code, 31; and PRA, 33; and Section 7(a), 204-205; and NLB, 209; on majority rule, 211, 212; resigns, 55

Johnston, Oscar, joins AAA, 119; and AAA cotton contract, 157-160; and AAA purge, 173

Jones & Laughlin case, 218, 252, 256, 262, 267, 268, 269, 277, 290; background of, 260-261; before NLRB, 261-262; brief in, 281-282; Supreme Court argument in, 285; Supreme Court opinion in, 287-288

Justice Department, and NRA enforcement, 40; control of federal litigation, 41; and *Hart Coal* case, 42-45; and hot oil cases, 61-65; and PAB, 68; and *Belcher* and *Schechter* cases, 86; and AAA litigation, 142-146; and *Butler* case, 183; files *Houde* case, 217; and conflict with NLRB, 220-225

Kahn, Eugen, 7

Katz, Milton, 32, 37, 299

Keyserling, Leon, 125, 234; and Labor Disputes Act, 213-214; and NLRA, 226-231

345

LIBRARY OF CONGRESS CATALOGING IN PUBLICATION DATA

Irons, Peter H., 1940-
  The New Deal lawyers.

  Bibliography: p.
  Includes index.
  1. United States. National Recovery Administration.
2. United States. Agricultural Adjustment Administration.   3. United States. National Labor Relations Board.
4. Government attorneys—United States.   5. United
States—Politics and government—1933-1945. I. Title.
KF6020.I7   342.73'00269   81-47924
ISBN 0-691-04688-3   347.30200269   AACR2